DATE DUE			
Feb 22'72			
Mar 24'73			

In the Name of Life

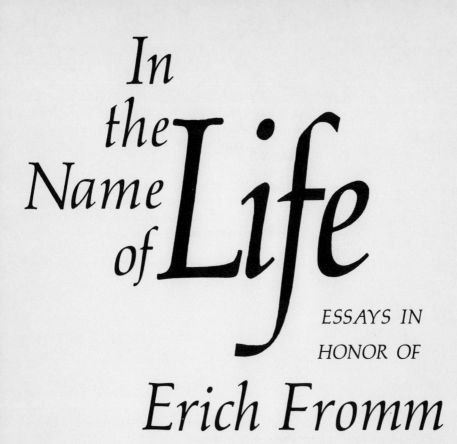

In the Name of Life

ESSAYS IN HONOR OF

Erich Fromm

Edited by
BERNARD LANDIS
AND EDWARD S. TAUBER

with the assistance of *ERICA LANDIS*

Holt, Rinehart and Winston
NEW YORK CHICAGO SAN FRANCISCO

Designer: Ernst Reichl
SBN: 03-086001-6
Printed in the United States of America
The following articles have been previously published:

"Darwin Versus Copernicus" by Theodosius Dobzhansky, which first appeared in *Changing Perspectives on Man,* Ben Rothblatt, ed. Copyright © 1968 by the University of Chicago Press and used with their permission.

"The Uncompleted Man" by Loren Eiseley, which first appeared in *Harper's,* March 1964. Copyright © 1964 by Loren Eiseley.

Frontispiece courtesy of Liss Goldring.

Contents

Preface

The title of this volume, like much of the inspiration that went into it, derives from the man we seek to honor.

The twenty-four contributors are scholars and scientists from different countries representing different disciplines, indicating how broadly Erich Fromm's influence and encouragement are being expressed. We believe that more than any other psychoanalyst, he has utilized the knowledge gained from his clinical experience to study and interpret for a wide audience the decisive concerns of man in society as well as the effects of society on man.

This book, then, is a response to Erich Fromm's lifelong efforts to aid us in putting aside the veils of illusion. Consistent with Dr. Fromm's dedication to independent inquiry, each essayist, while continuing the tradition of the Festschrift, has sought to express out of his personal experience an original formulation of the critical issues of our time. In their diversity and percipience, these essays reflect much of the impact and range of Dr. Fromm's work. Regretfully, limitations of space made it necessary to invite papers from only a few of his many close friends and colleagues.

The three parts of this book pertain to the areas of inquiry most related to Erich Fromm's major contributions. In the first section, on developments in psychoanalysis, two main themes are explored: changing concepts of the patient-therapist relationship, and the nature of growth from symbiosis to individuation. These issues are discussed in the opening essay by Edward S. Tauber and Bernard Landis on Erich Fromm's theory of psychoanalysis. Otto Allen Will depicts the many unique aspects of the patient-analyst relationship. Harry Guntrip views the process of psychoanalytic cure in the light of the analytic encounter, followed by Erwin

Singer's account of how patients' reactions to a catastrophic event in the therapist's life unexpectedly enhanced their growth. Maturation in psychoanalysis is discussed further in essays by Harold F. Searles and by David E. Schecter who investigate the transition from pathological symbiosis to individuation, in the context of the universal struggle between regressive symbiotic yearnings and the drive toward autonomy. Machismo as a social pathological solution to this struggle in Mexico is analyzed by Aniceto Aramoni.

Essays on philosophy, religion, and the humanistic implications of science and technology constitute the second section. George Wald's sermon establishes the theme of the human condition and the particular task required of man "to choose where we are going, for good or evil." From a biological perspective, Francis Otto Schmitt's essay describes the rewarding progress now being made in developing a multilevel, dynamic model of the brain by means of an integrated, interdisciplinary approach. Theodosius Dobzhansky and Loren Eiseley focus on the nature of evolution, and they raise the question of man's role in determining the direction of the evolutionary process. From an evolutionary, as well as existential and religious perspective, Ramon Xirau examines the concepts of freedom, God, and idolatry in Fromm's works. This is followed by Ivan Illich's essay which, through the metaphor of myth, focuses on the achievement of freedom in an out-of-control technology. Relating to man's quest for freedom, James Luther Adams provides a new analysis of Max Weber's study of the Protestant ethic in relation to capitalism and social change.

Section III surveys social, cultural, and educational concerns and the economic and political issues crucial to peace and survival. First, David Riesman analyzes diverse approaches to educational innovation, in connection with the delegitimation of established authority. This is complemented by Edward T. Hall's study of the "hidden rules" of culture—implicit assumptions and values about space, time, and the nature of man—which silently shape man's education and distort character.

The most immediate threats to life—overpopulation, ecological decay, nuclear holocaust, and the erosion of political freedoms—are the fields of inquiry of Jerome D. Frank, Erich Kahler, and Isaac Asimov. From Yugoslavia, essays by Mihailo Marković and Gajo Petrović next take up the achievement of a humane way of life within a humanistic socialist framework. And from Poland, Adam Schaff writes on the achievement of change and the meaning of revisionism in the context of Marxism as an open system. Tom Bottomore concludes with a critical discussion of the

New Left and presents his views on attaining a socialist society without violence.

Each writer shares Erich Fromm's conviction of man's fundamental capacity for love and reason, and his faith that if man knows the truth he will elect to meet constructively the challenges of living.

During the preparation of this volume, we were helped and encouraged by friends and colleagues of the William Alanson White Institute of Psychiatry, Psychoanalysis and Psychology. We would like to thank, in particular, Arthur Rosenthal for his judgment and advice in respect to various editing and publishing issues and David Nachmansohn who served as a consultant in the life sciences. Ruth Nanda Anshen helped in the launching of this project, and we also benefited from the thoughtful reflections of Jerome S. Spivack and Betty Martin. We have a special indebtedness to Andrea Smargon for her valuable suggestions and editorial advice. Finally, we are extremely grateful to Joseph Cunneen for his generous cooperation throughout our working together.

B. L.
E. S. T.

New York, February, 1971

Erich Fromm:
Some Biographical Notes

Erich Fromm comes from an orthodox German Jewish middle-class family with a long rabbinical background on his father's side. An only child, he was born on March 23, 1900, in Frankfurt am Main, Germany, where he received his education through high school. As he describes in a short autobiographical sketch in *Beyond the Chains of Illusion,* a decisive, early influence on his life were the writings of the Old Testament which, he states, "touched me and exhilarated me more than anything else," particularly the prophetic writings of Isaiah, Amos, and Hosea with their vision of universal peace and harmony, and their teachings that there are ethical aspects to history—that nations can do right and wrong, and that history has its moral laws.

But equally important was the spirit of traditional Judaism in which he was brought up. As he has mentioned occasionally in conversation, this mode of life made him somewhat of a stranger in the modern world. The point of view and the principles of the rabbinical world were in sharp contrast to those of contemporary capitalism. Learning and the application of the principles of love and justice in all one's relations, not wealth or power, were the guiding values of this traditional life. That was the way his rabbinical ancestors had lived and that was the style of life which deeply impressed him. To be sure there were men driven by the desire for wealth and luxury; but they were to be pitied for having missed the right way of living. In many respects Fromm grew up in a world closer to the late middle ages than to the twentieth century—but he was also part of the latter—and the experience of the opposition between the two was one of the creative forces in his life.

It was the experience of the First World War that crystalized his concerns with peace and internationalism into passionate, lifelong interests.

During the next four years of living through an hysteria of hate and nationalism, Fromm felt himself grow into a young man filled with protest against war, and obsessed by the question of how war was possible. Having become extremely skeptical of all official ideologies, his focus turned to the desire to understand the irrationality of mass behavior.

During his preadolescence, Fromm was equally stimulated to understand "the strange and mysterious reasons" for individual experiences and actions. A particular event stands out in his mind as one of those incidents that, like a lens, narrows attention on a critical area of interest. When he was twelve, a beautiful young woman, an artist friend of the family, committed suicide following the death of her father, an old and unattractive man, and left a will stating that she wanted to be buried with him. Fromm was struck by the question of how was it possible that a lovely young woman should be so in love with her father as to prefer his company in death to the joy of life and art. This was one of the early experiences that prepared the way for Fromm's subsequent interest in psychoanalysis.

Important influences shaping Fromm's life, since his adolescence, were first of all his talmudic teachers. After Rabbi J. Horowitz, with whom he studied Talmud as an adolescent, the young student became the pupil of S. B. Rabinkov in Heidelberg, N. Nobel, and his mother's uncle, L. Krause, in Frankfurt. Fromm considered the teaching of these masters and the personal contact with them, as the most important influence in his life. While they were all strictly observant Rabbis, they were at the same time humanists of extraordinary tolerance and with a complete absence of authoritarianism. They were also very different among themselves: Rabinkov was a socialist, Nobel a mystic, and Krause, over seventy when Fromm studied with him, liked operatic music; otherwise, he was typical of many other Rabbis who studied the Talmud almost without interruption from morning to evening, with no desire for position and fame—and without the ambition to write. While Fromm in his late twenties gave up religious practices completely, the principles and values of these teachers remained part of him, expressed in his humanist socialist convictions, and in his critique of capitalist society.

These political interests were awakened not only by the First World War, but also by his acquaintance with Karl Marx's work. He saw—and still sees—in Marx's work the key to the understanding of history and the manifestation, in secular terms, of the radical humanism which was expressed in the Messianic vision of the Old Testament prophets. The revolutionary and humanist spirit of Marx, corrupted by both the Stalinist and reformist misinterpretations of his teachings, became for Fromm the second source which deeply shaped his thinking. Only some years later came his encounter with Freud's work. He was as deeply impressed by Freud's point of view as he had been by Marx's. He spent all the years after 1928 in the attempt at a creative synthesis between the two systems.

To finish this sketch of an intellectual biography two more sources must be mentioned, which became an integral part of Fromm's thinking. When he became acquainted with Buddhism in 1926, he felt this as a kind of revelation. For the first time he saw a spiritual system, a way of life, based on pure rationality and without any irrational mystification or appeal to revelation or authority. This initial interest in Buddhism was followed up by his acquaintance with Dr. D. T. Suzuki's work on Zen Buddhism. Fromm and his wife had the opportunity to attend his seminars and they conversed at length.

As to the last major influence on Fromm's intellectual development, one of great importance must be added, the work of J. J. Bachofen on Mother right and on Symbolism. Bachofen, in his study of the concepts of matriarchal and patriarchal principles, had discovered an entirely new aspect of historical as well as of individual development. This opened Fromm's eyes to many phenomena hitherto overlooked, and helped him to recognize the extreme patriarchal bias of Freud's theories as well as to understand the fundamental role of the relationship to the mother figure in the individual life, as well as in an historical context. In short, the writings of the prophets, of the Buddha, of Marx, Bachofen, and Freud, were the most fundamental influences on Fromm, until the age of twenty-six; from then on, the development of his own thinking can be seen as an attempt at a creative synthesis of these ideas, none of which he abandoned, even though he differed in their interpretation, sometimes quite radically, from their respective orthodox followers.

In his academic career, Fromm took up his studies on psychology, philosophy, and sociology at the University of Heidelberg, where he was awarded his Ph.D. at the age of twenty-two, with a thesis on the sociopsychological structure of three Jewish sects (the Karaim, the Chassidim, and the Reform Judaism). In 1925 and 1926, he pursued additional studies in psychiatry and psychology at the University of München. He began his psychoanalytic training with Drs. Landauer and Wittenberg, from 1926 to 1928, and then trained at the famous Berlin Psychoanalytic Institute. Upon graduating in 1931, he became a member of the Berlin Psychoanalytic Institute and practiced psychoanalysis in Berlin. During this period, he founded, together with Dr. Frieda Fromm-Reichmann and others, the Psychoanalytic Institute in Frankfurt and lectured there on fortnightly trips from Berlin. He also taught at, and was a member of, the Institute for Social Research at the University of Frankfurt (and later at Columbia University in New York) from 1928 to 1938.

Fromm came to the United States for the first time in 1933 at the invitation of the Chicago Psychoanalytic Institute to give a series of lectures. In 1934, he moved to New York where he continued his private practice and became active in professional affairs. In 1946, he became one of the founders and trustees of the William Alanson White Institute of Psychiatry, Psychoanalysis and Psychology, and served both as Chairman of the Faculty and Chairman of the Training Committee from 1946 to 1950.

Earl G. Wittenberg, Director of the White Institute, writes that Erich Fromm "participated fully in the first seven years of the Institute as mentor, teacher, and friend, and since 1951, he has continued as trustee, colleague, supervisor, and seminar leader. He introduced a legacy of humanism, an unsurpassed understanding of the socioeconomic situation with its character types and unconscious origins, and a vigor and directness about the analytic situation which have pervaded the Institute since. He is a vital and guiding force. His emphasis on the liveliness, the creativity, and the productive resources of the patient enhances the potential of psychoanalysis as therapy."

For the first ten years of his analytic work, Fromm practiced in the orthodox Freudian vein. What led him to develop his own approach to psychoanalysis was first, a growing awareness that some of his observations were at variance with what he would expect to have found according to Freudian theory and, second, an ever-increasing boredom with a technique that so constricted the analyst-patient relationship. (The nature of Fromm's approach to psychoanalysis is described in the first essay.)

In addition to his practice of psychoanalysis, Erich Fromm was a member of the faculty of Bennington College (1941–1949) and Guest Professor at Yale University (1948–1949) where he gave, together with Professor Ralph Linton, a seminar on social character and anthropology. In 1949, for reasons of his wife's health, he went to Mexico. At that time, he accepted a professorship at the National Autonomous University of Mexico and started the Department of Psychoanalysis at the Graduate Department of the University's Medical School where he taught until he retired in 1965. He is now Honorary Professor at the University. Fromm also founded the Mexican Psychoanalytic Institute and was its director until 1965.

Since the move to Mexico, Fromm has commuted regularly—for his teaching duties at the William Alanson White Institute, at Michigan State University where he was Professor of Psychology (1957–1961) and, since 1962, at New York University where he is Adjunct Professor of Psychology in the Graduate Division of Arts and Sciences. During this time, he has also lectured at Columbia University, the New School for Social Research, and other universities. During these years, and to the present time, Fromm also has been active in the peace movement and in the humanist socialist movement. He has always been a socialist though unaffiliated with any particular party until he joined the Socialist Party, U.S.A. in the fifties. Particularly close were his relations to the Yugoslav humanist socialists, but his orientation has always been an international one, a fact that found its expression in the symposium on *Socialist Humanism,* which he edited and which contains contributions of an international scope. No psychoanalyst has been more outspoken and incisive than Fromm in working for a better society.

Fromm, while under the intellectual influences sketched above, worked as a practicing psychoanalyst for more than forty years—examining in fine detail the experiences, behavior, and dreams of the people whom he has psychoanalyzed; he notes that every one of his theoretical conclusions about man's psychic structure has been based on critical observations of human behavior during the course of his psychoanalytic work.

In recent years, Dr. Fromm has been concentrating on the problem of human aggression. Going beyond the instinctual drive theories of Freud and Lorenz, Fromm has been studying various modes of aggression using data from neurophysiology, ethology, and psychoanalysis, in the context of man's biological nature and development of character. The first volume on the sources of aggression *From Instinct to Character,* will soon be published; a second volume, focussing on findings from the fields of ethology, anthropology, and social psychology, will follow and deal with other empirical evidence against the instinctual, drive-reduction theories of aggression. It will, in its main part, analyze the essential sources of human aggression, manifested in "reactive aggression," "sadism" (absolute control), "necrophilic destructiveness," and trancelike states of hate and blood thirst. His basic principle in this work is to show that the amount of aggression expressed by man is not and cannot be caused by the inheritance from the less aggressive animals, especially from mammals (primates in particular), but must be understood via the conditions of existence specific to man due to his biological situation. His work attempts to show that in man the problem is not that of instincts but one of character, and that human aggression must be understood in terms of social conditions that interact with man's biological needs (by no means only of a physiological nature). The two volumes constitute the beginning of a series of works on humanistic psychoanalysis.

In the Name of Life

On
Erich Fromm

Edward S. Tauber
and Bernard Landis

Erich Fromm is concerned with a transformation of life experience, not simply with adaptive modifications of personality. He challenges conventional standards through fresh and precise inquiry to expose their pretenses and lifelessness. The search for truth, he makes clear, is every man's domain, not restricted to scholars and specialists. His all-absorbing concern is the unfolding of life and, as a consequence, the radical and uncompromising critique of all individual and social factors that impede the development of man and his possibilities "to become what he could be."

It is this spirit that forms Fromm's radical approach to psychoanalysis. Stressing the importance of growth, he sees that the achievement of sanity is not to be found in submission, or power, oriented security operations but through efforts to be authentically oneself. Indeed, to Fromm, the aim of life is the process, fundamental to the nature of human existence, of giving birth to oneself.

Although some comprehensive studies of Fromm's work, past and ongoing, have already been made and others are anticipated, in this celebration volume we would like to sketch an over-view of Fromm's main theoretical ideas. In particular, we would like to refer to certain important themes that are touched on repeatedly throughout Fromm's works and constitute much of the substance of his theoretical position, but have not as yet been put into strong relief.

Of major significance in the history of psychoanalytic theory has been Fromm's development—over a more than forty year span—of a comprehensive dynamic model of man in which his existential disequilibrium and the sociobiological necessity for assimilation and socialization have replaced the physiologizing instinct schema of Freud. Human passions and motives thus arise mainly through the vicissitudes of man's search for relatedness and identity rather than through instinctual thrust.

Perhaps the most insufficiently recognized theme in Fromm's overall writings is his biological frame of reference. This orientation is based on the recognition of the biological conditions of man as he slowly emerged from the animal kingdom. A new configuration evolved with the striking cortical development of man's brain, the diminished importance of instinctive determination in contrast to the rest of the animal kingdom, and the emergence of the unique phenomenon of self-awareness. The convergence of these facts forms the basis for what Fromm calls man's existential dichotomy. Within this framework, Fromm developed a concept of anxiety and the possibilities of coping with it.

Discussing these issues in *The Art of Loving* Fromm writes:

> This awareness of himself as a separate entity, the awareness of his own short life span, of the fact that without his will he is born and against his will he dies, that he will die before those whom he loves, or they before him, the awareness of his aloneness and separateness, of his helplessness before the forces of nature and of society, all this makes his separate, disunited existence an unbearable prison. He would become insane could he not liberate himself from this prison and reach out, unite himself in some form or other with men, with the world outside.
>
> The experience of separateness arouses anxiety; it is, indeed, the source of all anxiety. . . .
>
> The deepest need of man, then, is the need to overcome his separateness, to leave the prison of his aloneness.

Man is inescapably compelled, therefore, to find a solution to the central question posed by life—that is, how to transcend his separateness and relate himself to his world. Fromm delineates two contrasting modes of relatedness: regression to earlier and often archaic forms of relatedness, or to hope-oriented, affirmative responses in the direction of becoming fully human through developing one's creativity, productivity, and ability to love. Each individual has the potential for the most archaic as well as the most progressive solutions. Historically, Fromm sees in the emergence of the great humanist religions and philosophies—prophetic Old Testament religion, Taoism, Confucianism, Buddhism, Greek philosophy—the decisive turn from the regressive to the progressive orientation.

The different solutions man finds to this human condition are the many expressions of human nature. The essence of man's nature is not identical with any of these solutions but consists in the existential contradiction in man's biological constitution. This contradiction, which in itself is not a moral issue, is common to all men, biologically as well as psychologically. It gives rise to certain imperative needs: there is a need for the experience of identity together with a need for a frame of orientation, a picture of his world and of his society in which he can locate himself and which makes sense of his life. Additionally, man needs a substitute for the largely lost instinctive determination.

In Fromm's theory, character structure, in the dynamic sense, serves this purpose. It is not innate as far as its contents are concerned, but is nevertheless determined by man's biological needs (which are by no means only instinctual) and by the conditions of nature under which he has to survive. In *Man for Himself* Fromm has delineated a set of character orientations that go beyond the Freudian theory of libido development by stressing the processes of socialization and the structures of relatedness.

Because of his deep concern and attention to these processes, it has been inferred that Fromm is a culturalist. Fromm, however, is not a culturalist in the common sense of that term whereby man is conceptualized as a *tabula rasa* on which a given culture writes its text. Furthermore, Fromm does not share the current concept of culture or cultural patterns as formulated by Karen Horney, Ruth Benedict, or Margaret Mead. Quite removed from this culturalist position, Fromm deals with the dynamic concept of the socioeconomic process (in Marx's sense) wherein culture essentially forms a superstructure but not the basis. At the same time, for Fromm, the biologically given conditions of human existence remain the psychological basis of personality development. This combination of a biological viewpoint with a sociological one is among Fromm's signal contributions to a theory of man.

In his studies of the ways in which society affects the answers man finds to the questions posed by life, Fromm has described in considerable detail how social patterns may bend man against his real human interests. He observed how significant characteristics and behavior patterns of major importance to a nation or class cluster to form what he called the "social character." Internalized and shared by most of the members of society, the social character—whose positive and negative aspects depend on the particular society—shapes action and thought so that people want to do what they have to do to perpetuate the particular society or class. In addition, character structure not only enables man to make quasi-automatic responses rooted in his character system but also permits him to feel satisfaction through acting in accordance with his particular character structure.

Through the medium of social character, human energy in its general form is transformed into the specific activity patterns that a particular society needs for its functioning. In this way society both furthers and obstructs human development. As Fromm sees it, the social conditions obstructing human development are neither accidental nor the result of the ill will or stupidity of certain individuals. They have their own laws, and major social change is possible only by the combination of two factors: new socioeconomic conditions that permit it, and increased awareness in a large part of the population that makes it possible to undertake the necessary changes.

It may interest some readers to see how Fromm utilizes the construct of social character to integrate dynamic psychoanalytic concepts with Marx's theory. In *Beyond the Chains of Illusion* Fromm observes that: "Marx was capable of connecting a spiritual heritage of the enlightenment humanism and German idealism with the reality of economic and social facts, and thus to lay the foundations for a new science of man and society which is empirical and at the same time filled with the spirit of the Western humanist tradition."

However, Fromm believes that in Marx's theory the relationship between the economic basis of society and the ideology of the society was inadequately explained. Fromm sought to remedy this by developing further the construct of social character as an intermediary between the socioeconomic structure and the ideas and ideals prevalent in a society. That Fromm seeks to relate such apparently contradictory theories as psychoanalysis and Marxism may seem a paradox. Yet the paradox disappears when one considers that both are humanistic disciplines concerned with understanding, via a dynamic and dialectical approach, the reality of man's life—one with the social-economic reality, the other with the intrapsychic and interpersonal reality.

Beyond this, he has called attention to a fact that had been almost completely neglected: Marx, although not in a systematic way, had developed a dynamic psychological theory—which in many ways influenced Fromm's thinking. According to Marx, writes Fromm, "the dynamism of human nature is primarily rooted in this need of man to express his faculties, drives and passions toward the world, rather than to use the world as a means for the satisfaction of his physiological necessities." The concept of self-activity, so crucial in Marx's thinking, appears in Fromm's concept of productivity. This is in contrast to the principle of tension reduction, which has dominated the Freudian theory of motivation and which Fromm sees as having only limited application.

Also intrinsic to Fromm's model of man is his view of the unconscious, which extends the traditional concept of a repository of instinctual drives and repressed memories. Fromm sees unconscious contents as containing all of man's nature: all his potentialities, from being archaic man, a beast of prey, and an idolater, to being fully human with the capacity for reason and love.

In addition to those aspects of Fromm's theory mentioned so far, we would like to touch briefly on certain other significant findings in the fields of clinical psychoanalysis and analytical social psychology. Stimulated by Bachofen's work on matriarchy, with which he became acquainted at the beginning of his psychoanalytic career, Fromm was perhaps the first one to recognize the power and intensity of the affective bond of the child, of both sexes, to the mother; he enriched understanding of the complex nature of this bond, previously viewed within a narrow sexual focus.

In this context, Fromm was the first to use as a psychological metaphor the biological concept of symbiotic relationship. He developed the construct of malignant symbiosis in which the person has hardly separated from the parent figure, usually the mother, the process of individuation being almost completely stunted. In this form, the mother experience represents death, and her womb a tomb. Fromm also delineated less malignant forms of symbiosis in which the interaction between the "partners" is less crippling. In the most favorable circumstances the mother experience represents life, protection, the nourishing earth.

Previously, Fromm had written about the nature of aggression as being either reactive, in the defense of vital interests under attack, or characterological, as a result of "unlived life." Based on his present research, Fromm further distinguishes three different kinds of aggression, each of which has its own genesis: (a) defensive aggression as a reaction to a threat to vital interests, a form of aggression man shares with all animals; (b) sadism, the passion for total control of a living being, including the desire to hurt and torture; (c) necrophilic destructiveness, the hate against life itself and the passion to transcend life by destroying it.

In regard to the last form of aggression, Fromm has, in recent years, made an important formulation, distinguishing between biophilia, the love of life, and necrophilia, the attraction to and desire for all that is unalive, decaying, or purely mechanical. This concept, which seems to throw new

light on the processes of normal and pathological living, is a basic modification of Freud's theory of life and death instincts. It includes the earlier
view that the love for life and the love for death are the most fundamental
strivings in man; however, in contrast to Freud's theory, necrophilia is not
seen as a normal biological tendency but as a pathological one that can
stem from a variety of causes. In *The Heart of Man,* Fromm describes it
as the malignant form of Freud's "anal character." Clinically, Fromm has
demonstrated (in lectures and in a manuscript to be published soon) how
dreams, free associations, and behavior permit recognition of the presence
and intensity of biophilic versus necrophilic strivings. The strength of biophilic tendencies in a person is held to be a decisive factor for the possibility of change.

As part of this brief survey of Fromm's contributions, it should be
mentioned that he advanced the application of psychoanalysis to the historical process, in particular to further the understanding of early Christianity, Protestantism, Fascism, and democratic capitalism. He has also undertaken two large-scale studies in the field of analytic social psychology,
one in the early thirties on authoritarian and democratic character forma-
tions among German blue- and white-collar workers and one, which was
recently published, on the character structure of peasants in a small Mexican village.

Fromm's orientation is not anti-Freudian. He believes that Freud's
major discoveries of unconscious processes, of the dynamic nature of character, of the liberating and curative effect of bringing unconscious contents
into awareness are the essence of psychoanalysis. In his formulations,
Fromm has sought to extend the range of Freud's contributions by freeing
them from the confines of libido theory. It is also characteristic of his
work that he strives to reawaken the early radical spirit of psychoanalysis
that emerged with Freud's first discoveries.

Fromm has also attempted to construct a system of ethical values that
is based not on authority or revelation but on the knowledge of human nature. Independence, truth, and love are the qualities that man acquires
when he liberates himself from symbiosis and fixation, anxiety, and greed;
they are at the same time the supreme values of humanistic ethics. In the
development of these ideas, Fromm has assumed that the most crucial ethi-
cally relevant polarity is that between "having" and "being," which corresponds to his unproductive and productive attitudes. Buddhist thinking,
which is based on an analysis of man's existential condition without mysti-

fication or submission to irrational authority, has, Fromm believes, influenced him in his search for the foundation of ethical norms in the nature of man.

It has always been Fromm's conviction that alienation, lack of integrity, and hence a defective sense of identity, constitute major constrictions in the individual's psyche, and have become everybody's problem in contemporary industrial society. In *Man for Himself* he writes:

> Our moral problem is man's indifference to himself. It lies in the fact that we have lost the sense of the significance and uniqueness of the individual, that we have made ourselves into instruments for purposes outside ourselves, that we experience and treat ourselves as commodities and that our own powers have become alienated from ourselves. We have become things and our neighbors have become things. The result is that we feel powerless and despise ourselves for our impotence.

In arguing against identifying mental health with adaptation, he has spoken of the "pathology of normalcy" and discussed the problem of being sane in an insane society. Early in his work he stated that an alienated person, capable only of relating to the world "objectively" without being able to experience it subjectively, is in some ways no less impaired than the psychotic person who is so immersed in subjective feelings as to be unable to grasp the world objectively.

Fromm's extensive knowledge of philosophy, theological and biblical history, the social sciences, and political issues led him to write several books that are not directly related to psychoanalysis: *May Man Prevail,* a critical analysis of the cold war and of Soviet socialism; *You Shall Be as Gods,* a discussion of the concepts of God, man, and history in the Old Testament and in the Talmudic and Hassidic literature, as well as an analysis of the style of the Psalms; and *Marx's Concept of Man,* an introduction to Marx's humanistic philosophy. Also his active engagement in the cause of peace and socialism has been rare in the psychoanalytic world.

In personal encounters Fromm always seeks the other's independent growth. He asks, implicitly and explicitly, that the other develop his own uniqueness. Emerson once noted that, as a teacher, there was no "wish in me to bring men to me, but to themselves." And so with Fromm.

Even as Fromm depicts society's decisive role in shaping men's character, he makes it explicitly clear that each person must take the responsibility for his own life. That is to say, while Fromm finds society culpable, he insists that man is responsible for his actions. This is not an irreconcilable dichotomy, since he is referring to two different though interacting ways of looking at a situation at any one time—from an individual point of view and from a social perspective.

In his concerned yet unsentimental approach to the analytic process, Fromm has been influenced by Zen teaching. A combination of Eastern spiritual thought with scientific psychoanalysis may seem like another paradox; both systems, however, are concerned with man's nature and his transformation. There are more specific parallels. In both there is a focus on immediate experience—on clearly distinguishing between what is real and what only seems real—rather than relying so much on words and explanations, for words often are used unwittingly to avoid emotions or to provide rationalizations. Fromm's view of the analyst is that he should be capable of absolute concentration—focused on developing skill and competence in illuminating the other person, averse to irrelevant details, and opposed to idolatry and status needs.

Fromm has amplified his sense of the analytic process, delineating those characteristics that an analyst should aim to develop as far as possible:

> The analyst understands the patient only inasmuch as he experiences in himself all that the patient experiences; otherwise he will have only intellectual knowledge about the patient, but will never really know what the patient experiences, nor will he be able to convey to him that he shares and understands his [the patient's] experience. In this productive relatedness between analyst and the patient, in the act of being fully engaged with the patient, in being fully open and responsive to him, in being soaked with him, as it were, in this center-to-center relatedness, lies one of the essential conditions for psychoanalytic understanding and cure. The analyst must become the patient, yet he must be himself; must forget that he is the doctor, yet he must remain aware of it. Only when he accepts this paradox, can he give "interpretations" which carry authority because they are rooted in his own experience. The analyst analyzes the patient, but the patient also analyzes the analyst, because the analyst, by sharing the unconscious of his patient, cannot help clarifying his own unconscious. Hence, the analyst not only cures the patient but is also cured by him.
> [From *Zen Buddhism and Psychoanalysis*]

This concept that the patient and therapist heal each other precludes stereotyped exchanges; it generates new experiences and facilitates true maturity and respect. One must develop the ability to give of himself but there has to be a receiver of the gift; if the exchange is not mutual it is ineffective. Only in a reciprocal and charged encounter can the most dreaded—as well as the richest—parts of the personality become bearable and permissible to experience.

Fromm has written little about psychoanalytic therapy and technique (though he plans to do so during the next four years); but yet in his teaching seminars over the last thirty years he has shared his concepts and methods in the context of detailed case history presentations. In the thirties he began to move away from the Freudian views and methodology of his psychoanalytic training. He opposed that form of the genetic approach that transforms psychoanalysis into artifactual historical research, having observed how often the classic method dwells on past events and "interprets" unconscious experiences by lifeless reconstruction.

His understanding of psychoanalysis led him to develop an active technique. Early in his career he noted the tendency to misuse free association, which is often in the service of resistance. Thus he does not hesitate to bring significant aspects of the patient's life into focus from the very start, thereby helping the patient to move more quickly from the surface to the depth. The overriding goal of his analytic therapy is the patient's experience of, rather than theorizing about, his unconscious reality. This experience is both frightening and exhilarating; the deeper it goes, the greater the liberating effect—but also greater is the chance of transitory disturbances that may be difficult to deal with in the ordinary professional setting.

In Fromm's approach, the analyst aims at constant confrontation of the patient with his dissociated desires and fantasies, mobilizing his healthy strivings for greater integration and productiveness. This process—not soothing words—affords genuine reassurance and hope. The greatest encouragement is to be taken seriously, to be told the truth, and to develop trust in one's efforts to help oneself. Fromm believes that when such confrontation does not lead to mobilization, the psychoanalytic method cannot be helpful.

The nature of Fromm's orientation to psychoanalysis has been further described by one of the editors (E.S.T.) in the *American Handbook of Psychiatry:*

[Fromm considers it essential] that psychoanalysis shall penetrate as deeply and as speedily as possible to the very core of the patient's life, to locate his tenaciously held, unreal, unconscious solution to his separateness, to waste no time on the consequences of his problem and on his adjustments, but to force him to face his resistances and give no quarter. This process is carried out in a setting where the analyst is his full self with the patient. The analyst is not waiting, figuring things out, cautiously weighing what the patient can tolerate because, Fromm regretfully asserts, most delays are in the service of the therapist's anxiety anyway. The therapist should reveal, by his own genuine interest, dedication, openness and true participation, that there is an urgency to grasp life, to live, to search, and to dare uncertainty. Fromm rejects the notion that the analyst must be the passive one. This does not discard the precious ability to listen with all one's powers, but passivity can be exploitive when it merely serves to disguise the analyst's own unaliveness. . . .

He uses, so to speak, his scientific eye to know what is going on, to keep a perspective, but he helps the person to emerge by his own aliveness, by his own daring to know and to feel. He believes it is imperative that the patient be confronted as early as possible with the fact of the patient's decision to live or to die. There should be a feeling of urgency to live. The analyst has to identify carefully the point in his life at which the patient is stuck in a rut, and he must differentiate between the secondary consequences of the basic difficulties so that he does not grapple with the consequences of a problem but rather with the problem itself. He sees the individual as involved in what amounts to a religious dedication to resolve the feeling of separateness or aloneness. The patient himself may not be aware of the intensity and importance of the particular pattern of resolution through which he is living. The analyst must grasp this motif and bring it fully and richly to the patient's attention. These false solutions to the life problem may consist in the desire to be at mother's breast, at mother's hand, on mother's lap, or under mother's protection, or to submit to father's command. These false solutions must be brought into focus because they prevent any real relatedness to the world, to people, to work and to love. All life's energy is centered around nourishing the false solutions —all activity is organized to foster the idolatrous goals. The therapist must himself strive to achieve the very goals that represent the highest potential for himself. Only if the analyst sets himself the task of being fully responsive and aware can he genuinely face the patient's false solutions constructively, unhypocritically and hopefully.

Fromm realizes he is talking about an ideal for himself, and for all of us. He knows that we all fall short, but that does not mean that we become cynics, that we take the easy path. If we have no responsibility to live, we cannot deal with the lives of others.

As some of the contributors to this volume show, we are faced with the danger that within several decades life may end on our planet. Air, water, and soil pollution threaten the integrity of our biosphere; yet the economies of most nations are organized to produce these dangers, as well as the unthinking depletion of other resources. We are menaced by nuclear, chemical, and biological warfare, yet our unyielding commitment to military technology guarantees that the risk curve will go up. The development of the corporate state seems inevitably correlated with declining democracy and increasing alienation and degradation of life experience. The outlook is grim. As Fromm conveys, only a sense of urgency and a radical refocusing on man's authentic concern for himself and his fellow men can provide the basis for real hope.

In this article we have written of Erich Fromm's commitment to life, his work and impact. He is a man whose words are ways and whose ways are reason, love and faith in man's possibilities.

I *Psychoanalysis*

The Patient and the Psychotherapist:

COMMENTS ON THE "UNIQUENESS" OF THEIR RELATIONSHIP

Otto Allen Will, Jr.

> Love is the active concern for the life and
> the growth of that which we love.
> (Erich Fromm, *The Art of Loving*, 1956)

Introduction

My concern here is with certain aspects of the psychotherapeutic relationship that may contribute to what is frequently spoken of as its unique
quality. The intensity and durability of the attachment that is developed
suggest that it contains elements of affection, friendship, and love which
make it "more than" a technical, clinical exercise in the treatment of psychiatric disorder. Speaking to this point William Snyder says: "It is evident that therapy is often a major human experience, one of life's high
spots, especially for the clients, but also many times for the therapists." [1]

I have myself experienced the therapeutic relationship as being marked
by properties uncommon—if not lacking—in other interpersonal contacts.
It is difficult to specify what "works" in therapy—what is therapeutic—

[1] William Snyder, *The Psychotherapeutic Relationship* (New York: Macmillan
Co., 1961), p. 2.

and effectiveness is probably the reflection of a combination of factors, rather than the result simply of gaining insight, and so on. However, our interest at the moment is not so much in what may bring about desired change in a troubled patient, but in some of the elements possibly associated with the participants' sensing of the situation as being extraordinary and curious.

The word love is avoided here, not because I doubt the existence or usefulness of the sentiment, but because the term refers to a wide range of subjects extending beyond my professional competence and my personal knowledge. Some years past I said to a patient that, in my opinion, love was not in itself a curative agent. The reply was—with emphasis: "You are very likely wrong." Perhaps—but I should not speak casually of what I am unable to define or identify with a fair degree of clarity. Thus no attempt is being made to attribute the uniqueness of the therapeutic encounter to a concept—love—which too often is an elusive and ephemeral phenomenon, for the most part private and poorly comprehended. The following remarks by Joseph Conrad seem to me to have some relevance at this juncture:

> Everybody shows a respectful deference to certain sounds that he and his fellows can make. But about feelings people really know nothing. We talk with indignation or enthusiasm; we talk about oppression, cruelty, crime, devotion, self-sacrifice, virtue, and we know nothing real beyond the words. Nobody knows what suffering or sacrifice mean —except, perhaps, the victims of the mysterious purpose of these illusions.[2]

The ideas presented in this report—in no way original—may be applicable in some degree to psychotherapeutic interventions in general, but it may be useful to avoid as far as possible the extension of implications in ways that cannot be firmly supported by theory based on clinical observation. I shall limit my remarks to personal reports of my own work with certain schizophrenic patients, making no claim to true scientific objectivity or the immediate relevance of these views to other persons in differing circumstances.

The Posing of the Question

In considering my own current and past experiences as the therapist of schizophrenic people, I am impressed by the seeming (if not actual) clarity

[2] Joseph Conrad, "An Outpost of Progress," in *Typhoon and Other Tales* (New York: Signet Classic, published by New American Library, 1962), p. 197.

with which I recall them and the details of our- involvements with each other. Although these associations were often stormy, and in a conventional sense unpleasant, they usually persisted and ties developed that were maintained despite the absence of much personal contact after the termination of the work. There was more to these attachments than the therapist's wish to fulfill a professional obligation or the patient's uncertain hope for change. The contacts had been marked by a wide range of shared feeling —tenderness as well as anger, dislike, and the inchoate eruptions in states of panic—and the relationships (in reality and memory) had come to be significant and valued parts of my life. How did this come about? The question has been raised repeatedly—by patients and by myself. There follow some examples.

John was a man in his early twenties when we first met. He had left college in his first year because of an inability to concentrate on his studies, a growing sense of confusion, a conviction that he was worthless, and a persistent fear that he was being followed and spied upon. Awakening from a poorly remembered nightmare that seemed to imply certain implications of incest with a woman vaguely resembling his mother, he leaped from a second-story window without serious injury to himself and thereupon became withdrawn and mute. Although I met with him daily in his hospital room, he was silent for many weeks and seemingly paid no heed to my presence. When he no longer lay quiet on his bed or the floor, he often ordered me out of his presence and attacked me physically if I did not leave. On later occasions he spoke of our relationship: "Somehow we have become important to each other. You often seem very dangerous to me, and I sometimes think that I shall simply do away with you. I don't understand this; why can't I rid myself of you?"

Mary was twenty when I became her therapist in a hospital. She had grown depressed and socially isolated in her third college year, and her thinking became so disorganized that she left school. She went from one psychotherapist to another, finding no one suitable to her, and after a year of moving about made a serious suicidal attempt. During much of the several years that we worked together she directed a hostile vindictive attack at me. She sought out my personal idiosyncrasies and defects with remarkable perceptiveness and precision and often spoke so cruelly and yet realistically that her observations could not be dealt with as "psychotic." At other times she was frightened, hallucinated, self-mutilative, and required almost constant physical care. Frequently she dismissed me, insisting that I

did nothing but harm to her, and accusing me of remaining as her therapist only out of my own evil and destructive intent toward her. After a few
months she said: "You're unique. There is no one like you. You're not my
father or one of my brothers. You're not my mother. You don't seem like
a doctor. You are not anything I can put my finger on. I don't know who
you are, and I don't know what to do with you. What is this I'm getting
into with you?"

Jane also had been in treatment for short periods with several therapists before we met when she was twenty-four. College had been a near
disaster because of her lack of interest in her work despite obvious talent
in painting and her hostility so apparent in situations marked by authority
or increasing intimacy. However, she did graduate and soon married, an
unhappy move made apparently in an effort to shore up a rapidly declining self-esteem. Her marital and social adjustments were marginal, she became withdrawn and moody, and then entered a state of panic in which
she cut herself, attacked her surroundings, and required restraint. The
work with me was stormy and was continued for several years, during
which Jane displayed a variety of behaviors—being recurrently assaultive,
withdrawn, mute, mutilative, dejected, and on occasion apparently free of
anxiety and any discernible evidence of psychosis. With time she improved, and our work drew to a close. My wife, a psychiatric nurse of long
experience and great skill, had worked with me and Jane, and these two
women liked each other.

Some time after the discontinuance of treatment, Jane visited us at our
home, and we had afternoon tea on the lawn in the later hours of a lovely
summer day in Maryland. In the course of the little meal, Jane and I entered upon a discussion—of what I do not remember. Gwen, my wife,
listened with interest and at some juncture said:

"I am fascinated by the way you talk with each other; there's something unusual about it. It isn't quite the way we talk (turning to me). It's as
if you two knew something about each other that I don't know—you've
had some kind of experience that's done something to you, and it's interesting to observe. In some ways I envy you."

Jane looked surprised: "What do you notice? You're married to this
man. You are close to him; you have lived with him a long time, and you
have children by him. As far as I know you get along well together—I expect you love each other. I've just been a patient, and you are a wife and
mother. You two live together and I suppose will continue to do so, while
I'm leaving. What is there to envy?"

Gwen's reply was simple: "Perhaps envy isn't the right word for what I feel because I don't feel unhappy. I have just noticed something that's different. You two don't talk like patient and doctor—and not quite like I talk with him (nodding toward me). Maybe it's a reflection of the experiences that you've had together. Anyhow, there is a difference—something unique."

The therapeutic relationship is at times experienced as being "like" something else, the therapist then dealt with apparently as father, mother, sibling, lover, friend, enemy, nightmare figure, and so on. Other terms may be used to describe its emotional qualities; among these (often borrowed from linear and thermal measurements) are warm, cool, cold, close, distant, or whatever. No terms—or combination of them—can adequately depict the nature of human involvement, and I am not attempting to picture here what can better be done by artist and poet. Our interest now is in what some patients, therapists, and other observers say about certain therapeutic attachments, remarking on such characteristics as durability, intensity, and a quality of "uniqueness" difficult to define.

The Person With Whom We Are Concerned

In the service of avoiding excessive generalization, some comments should be made regarding the kind of person with whom the psychotherapist develops these attachments. Obviously, the therapist himself must be considered as a major component in these transactions—influencing and being influenced by whatever goes on in them. More of the therapist later, it being recognized that other and more detached observers would likely give different—but not necessarily more significant—accounts of these events.

The focus of our attention is a person who has been diagnosed as schizophrenic and saddled with an unwelcome role—patient—which he may deny, resist, or accept with feelings of despair and humiliation. Despite the teachings of the past thirty years or more, the long-standing dread of dementia praecox and schizophrenia persists, the diagnosis continuing to imply hopelessness, irreversible withdrawal if not deterioration, and a "living death." The frequent occurrence of the disorder, the disagreements as to its origins, the multiple and changing modes of treatment, the uncertainty as to outcome, and the expense of attempted relief in terms of effort, money, and time would seem to justify serious concern—but not dread, a word implying something evil, mysterious, and beyond human understanding.

As the word is used here, schizophrenia does not refer to a specific disease entity in the classical medical sense. Psychiatric staff conferences today frequently remind me of those in which I participated years ago, the members attempting—often without clear-cut agreement—to describe and assess the behavior of another human being and to apply a label to him. This is no simple task, as nothing that we say seems to fit, the person and his ways of living being too elusive to be ensnared in the net of our nomenclature. We may refer to him as borderline, schizoid, possessing a schizoid character disorder with obsessional traits, schizophrenic with depressive and hysterical features, and so on. We continue to be unclear regarding the identity of this person and his ailment.

In 1928 Sullivan had the following to say about diagnosis:

> Continued experience with mentally disordered persons weakens the writer's hope of finding clear nosological entities. The more one learns of what is going on in his patient, the less faith he can retain in the alleged types of anomalous and perverted adjustive reactions. The field of mental disorder seems to be a continual gradation, in which little of discrete types is found.[3]

Four decades later, in 1969, Burnham, Gladstone, and Gibson directed their attention to the same topic:

> It may be well . . . to state our belief that as yet we possess no single, comprehensive, and adequate theory of schizophrenia. This is partly because schizophrenia is not a discrete nosological entity. . . . The phenomena which are encompassed by the label schizophrenia are so diverse and far reaching that construction of a unitary explanation is exceedingly difficult. . . . The point we wish to emphasize is that any sense of orderly classification associated with using the label schizophrenia may be partly spurious. Accordingly, when we speak of the "schizophrenic person" we should be aware that our capacity to generalize within a clearly established uniform class of persons is limited.[4]

However much uncertainty there may seem to be, there is evidence to support the following views. Obscure as it often is, schizophrenic behavior

[3] H. S. Sullivan, "Tentative Criteria of Malignancy in Schizophrenia," *American Journal of Psychiatry,* 7 (1928), 760.
[4] D. L. Burnham, A. I. Gladstone, and R. W. Gibson, *Schizophrenia and the Need-Fear Dilemma* (New York: International Universities Press, 1969), p. 15.

is simply human, is not "unpsychological," is to a large extent learned and thus reflective of experience (current, past, and anticipated), and expresses motivation in the sense of a goal being sought. Our attitudes to human relatedness have their origins in infancy and are further molded by social contacts of later years leading to the more permanent consolidations of identity in adolescence. The background of schizophrenic maladjustment can be sought for in the institutions of the past—family, culture, and society; the reasons for its continuance must be looked for in the demands of the present and the expectations of what is to come.

Because of the variety of behaviors encompassed by the word schizophrenia, it is not satisfactory to speak of the unique quality of a therapeutic relationship with a schizophrenic patient. A greater degree of specificity is required—and will be sought.

The people with whom we are concerned in this discussion had, in general, certain characteristics. Their ages ranged from seventeen to thirty-five years, they had passed the puberty change without being identified as a "psychiatric case" (although the early years may have been stormy at times), and they had achieved some recognized social success in adolescence. All had engaged in heterosexual experience with some gratification, although the seeking of bodily contact, physical closeness, and a form of human relationship were more important than the satisfaction of lustful interests. They were of superior intelligence, had completed the twelfth grade or more, and possessed high degrees of verbal skills, usually being able to present themselves in interesting and often picturesque ways. In each instance the appearance of publicly recognized disorder followed upon events experienced as stressful by the individual concerned, although without knowledge of his past life the stress might be looked upon as minimal or not unusual and thus could be overlooked at the time of its occurrence. In the main such stress was related to fear of object loss, separation, and the accompanying threat to self-esteem and personal identity. The time of onset was difficult to specify; as one came to know the person better, it was seen that premonitions of difficulty were present in earlier years (childhood and often infancy), and the disorder seemed to reflect the accumulation of maturational insults and learning defects from the first year of life.

The onset of "clinical signs" in this group is usually acute—an often dramatic separation from the hitherto seemingly normal course of living. Although such a person seems to need and want a close human relationship—and offers promise of giving a great deal to it—he tends to be suspicious and fearful, with the result that contact with him is usually marked by a tantalizing and often seductive quality of approach and withdrawal.

The form of the relationship in respect to its intensity and the way in which it is experienced will depend in part on the sex of patient and therapist, the acceptance of closeness by both in regards to the sex of a partner, and the cultural traditions in this regard—such as closeness between males being looked upon as dangerously "homosexual." However, the features of relatedness to be noted later may be common in any couple designed to be therapeutic.

The Opportunity and Hazard of Adolescence

The people in this group had encountered great difficulties—and had, as a result, exposed personal handicaps—in attempting to deal with the tasks of adolescence. Among the tasks found to be so difficult were these: 1) the development of intimacy with peers of both sexes, permitting self-revelation, and the modification of persistent autistic concepts—most of which should have been corrected in earlier eras of growth (particularly in the juvenile era); 2) the combining of the needs for intimacy, for lustful satisfaction, and for the maintenance of security and self-esteem in such a way that they can all be met to a tolerable extent with another person—usually of the opposite sex; 3) the patterning of sexual behavior in a dependable and gratifying fashion consistent with personal ideals and an acceptable concept of the self; 4) a sense of personal identity that is enduring, pleasing, and to some extent publicly acceptable; 5) a system of values, identifiable, persistent yet modifiable, and harmonious with what one conceives himself to be; 6) separation from the family of origin—emotionally, and frequently physically to some extent; 7) a career choice that fits with—and hopefully may expand—the self-concept; and 8) a social role consistent with personal identity and permissive of further personality growth. The inability to deal with these requirements and their like reveals a social ineptitude reflective of learning deficiencies that have accumulated throughout the years. Attempts to conceal such inadequacies may result in behavior so deviant as to invite public attention and response, leading to the enforced adoption by the youth of the role of patient —if not criminal, or other.

The schizophrenic processes as here dealt with are considered to be largely a resultant of developmental experiences—i.e., personality characteristics formed through failures in the acquisition of interpersonal and social skills, and defects in the matching of biological potential with interpersonal, social, and cultural influences at appropriate times on a sequential scale. We cannot speak of possible genetic differences in this group in contrast to others, but it is noteworthy that these (if present) plus the varied traumata of earlier years have not been sufficient to interfere to such an extent with growth that adjustments (or seemingly adequate compromises) are made to enable living to go on uninterrupted by psychiatric interferences into early or mid adolescence. (These last terms are used here in a developmental rather than a chronological sense, the number of those reaching the latter grouping far exceeding those who attain the former.) It should be noted that adolescence—particularly in its earlier stages—is (like infancy) potentially an era in which there is the opportunity for great change of personality and correction of previously acquired warp or deficit.[5]

Implications Regarding Early Development Derived from the Above

The person described here has great difficulty in relating to people—to a world of "objects"—without the experience of severe anxiety and the resulting development of behavioral complications ("defenses" or "security operations") designed to maintain a sense of personal security and to permit a semblance of intimacy—or at least of human contact. In view of 1) the observation that the troublesome behavior labeled schizophrenic is demonstrated largely in an interpersonal-social field, and 2) that the intrapsychic structure of the personality is a reflection of the transactions involving the developing organism with the "external" environment, attention is drawn inevitably to the earlier life experiences of the individual within the social fields of the mother-child relationship, the family, the immediate society, and the larger culture. In brief, disorder does not come from "out of the blue" but arises from the present dealt with in terms of the past—the biological given and the social influence.

The human infant, lacking a wide range of dependable instinctual re-

[5] See H. S. Sullivan on adolescence, *The Interpersonal Theory of Psychiatry* (New York: W. W. Norton & Co., 1953), chaps. 17 and 18; M. S. Mahler, "On Human Symbiosis and the Vicissitudes of Individuation," vol. 1, *Infantile Psychosis* (New York: International Universities Press, 1968), p. 49.

sponses, must deal with problems of existence in his early months through dependency on a mothering person.

Again, Sullivan:

The human animal is utterly dependent at birth and, diminishingly but still greatly, dependent on the tender cooperation of the human environment for five or six years after birth. . . . The abilities that characterize him are matured serially over a term of no less than ten to twenty years. . . . It is likewise clear that the inborn potentialities which thus mature over a term of years are remarkably labile subject to relatively durable change by experience, and antithetic to the comparatively stable patterns to which the biological concept of *instinct* applies.[6]

And Mahler:

It seems that psychosis is the sad prerogative of the human species. . . . Animals are born with well-developed instincts, which guarantee their independent individual survival long after birth. [A statement too general to be accepted in terms of modern studies in ethology— O. A. W.] In the human young . . . these animal instincts . . . have atrophied and become unreliable. . . . The psychobiological rapport between the nursing mother and the baby complements the infant's undifferentiated ego. This normal empathy on the part of the mother is the human substitute for those instincts on which the animal is able to rely for survival.[7]

Each era of personality development provides an opportunity—in theory, at least—for the matching of action with growth potential resulting in further maturation, and for the correction of earlier developmental deficiencies. The later exposed abnormalities of social facilitations are indications of failures in that which has gone before—the relationship of mother and child, of child with family, of family with society, and so on. The above, however, should not be taken as a recommendation for a continuum of "adjustment" to the compelling mores of any particular culture or society. From this point of view, schizophrenia is not to be explained away as a revolt against the establishment, as a seeking for a "new life," as a superior way of living, or as a philosophy in itself. Schizophrenia—as the word is used here—describes an attempt (overly complicated or simpli-

---

[6] Sullivan, *The Interpersonal Theory of Psychiatry, op. cit.*, pp. 20–21.
[7] Mahler, *op. cit.*, pp. 33–34.

fied) to maintain a relationship with other human beings in the face of severe anxiety. Schizophrenic behavior is in itself not a philosophy but an expensive and complicated attempt to survive as an organism in a troubled interpersonal milieu which is both frightening and necessary.

The early-life interpersonal—or interhuman (a term better suited to infancy before what we call "personality" has advanced in development) —experience of the human being later to become schizophrenic has (by inference) been marked by extreme anxiety prior to the development of speech skills and the clear-cut separation of object and self. The responses of the infant to anxiety are limited; they include somnolence, withdrawal, dissociation, the formation of distorted images of body and self, the perpetuation of autistic processes, and distortions of perceptions. Such malformations are subject to modification—favorable or otherwise—by later events, but the schizophrenic person has benefited but little from such correction.

The human infant is unable to escape physically from a mothering or other social situation upon which his further development depends; for years his inability to care for himself binds him to an environment which may be noxious, as well as beneficial, and which is the major force in forming his personality. In order to keep on living in an atmosphere which may be in many ways (often subtle and dimly perceived) destructive, it may be necessary to develop illusions and misperceptions about the events in which one is involved. Aspects of experience which do not fit in with such illusions and an associated acceptable concept of the self may be "dissociated"—that is, kept out of awareness by the complicated device of carefully noticing what not to notice, and avoiding any elaboration of the implications of those events which might seem to threaten an already flimsy self-esteem.

Under the pressure of various circumstances—such as the demands of adolescence, separation from long-held attachments of great personal importance, acute disruptions of organic integrity (as in disease or injury), prolonged and severe fatigue and fear, and drug intoxication—the "defensive" patterns of behavior (including denial, obsessionalism, hysterical incapacitations, and so on) may prove to be inadequate, with the result that anxiety increases, dissociation "fails," and there enter into awareness symbolic fragments of previous experience hitherto not included in the concept of the person as known to himself. These bits of thought and related emotions have no clearly perceived referents in the past or present; they often embody poorly understood but seemingly fateful cultural prescriptions regarding good and evil, and are so foreign and frightening that the person involved in all of this finds himself in a nightmare that makes no sense but must be resolved rapidly and hopefully understood or else abandoned and somehow forgotten. This is the state of panic—marked by a sense of personality disorganization, of the sudden unreliability of all that one has come to depend upon, and the loss of relationship with those people, things, and ideas that have come to matter in one's life. This is the essential schizophrenic experience, urgently requiring solution, and leaving the victim with a persistent dread of its recurrence.

Mahler speaks of the above as follows:

> I should like to point to the lasting validity of what Freud regarded as the essential criterion for the psychotic break with reality—namely, the slipping away of the libidinal human object world. We can rarely observe, but are often able to reconstruct, the prepsychotic struggle, the desperate efforts to cling, to hold on to the human object world. "Psychotic object relationships," whether with human beings or otherwise, and "psychotic defenses" are therefore no more than restitutive attempts of a rudimentary or fragmented ego which serve the purpose of survival. No organism can live in a vacuum, and no human being can live in an altogether objectless state.[8]

The Patient

When the person under consideration becomes "disturbed"—that is, so incapable of dealing with his predicament in an acceptably conventional manner that his associates no longer want a part of his deviant behavior—he may become a patient, a role for which he usually has no enthusiasm. From his early years has been derived a lack of basic trust and little confidence in himself and others. His low self-esteem leads him to be vulnerable to the opinions of anyone, and his fragile sense of identity is easily shaken when he is made anxious. The tie to human relationships has been formed and is not readily renounced, but the related anxiety leads him to suspect and fear any person whose attention, affection, and regard he needs; he acts as if this person (or "object") might destroy him, be destroyed by him or, despite his (or its) evidences of goodness, finally be revealed as evil—in any case, he will be deserted and alone.

[8] *Ibid.*, p. 64.

In the service of diminishing and controlling anxiety in interpersonal contacts, major systems of ideas and emotions must be kept from awareness through the use of elaborate maneuvers, with the result that any relationship approaching intimacy becomes complicated and tenuous, characterized by suspicion, movements of approach and withdrawal, testing, and the constant threat of separation through flight, psychosis, or suicide.

Although affection and closeness are desired, they bring with them the threat of revealing dissociated experience with the accompanying disturbance of the precarious concept of self and the exposure of the person once again to the horrors of panic. There are "choices" available to the patient —and no one is easily attained or simply desirable; all are unpleasant and each is costly. If the patient withdraws, he foregoes human contact except in a rudimentary and stereotyped form (as in the care given to a chronic "regressed" patient) and in whatever he retains of fantasy. Killing the object is not an adequate solution, as there is the threat of replacement; and suicide, if intended to bring about some magical "rebirth" or change in self and others, is not likely to be successful in any sense. Attempts to distort the world into a more tolerable form through denial, delusion, and hallucination perpetuate estrangement and psychosis and restrict to a large extent further profitable personality change. Psychotherapy that may prove to be useful cannot be in itself persistently pleasurable and is sure to be perceived as recurrently threatening and destructive—as through this relationship the hidden, frightening past, long held to some extent at bay, will come into the open and be made part of the self.

Guntrip's remarks are relevant here:

> The schizoid feels faced with utter loss and the destruction of both ego and object, whether in a relationship or out of it. In a relationship, identification involves loss of the ego, and incorporation involves a hungry devouring and losing of the object. In breaking away to independence, the object is destroyed as you fight a way out to freedom, or lost by separation, and the ego is destroyed or emptied by the loss of the object with whom it is identified. The only real solution is the dissolving of identification and the maturing of the personality, the differentiation of ego and object, and the growth of a capacity for cooperative independence and mutuality; that is, psychic rebirth and development of a real ego.[9]

[9] H. Guntrip, *Schizoid Phenomena, Object Relations, and the Self* (New York: International Universities Press, 1969), p. 48.

The Therapist

In a discussion of the attachment holding our attention here, the therapist as a person must be considered. We refer to someone who has been trained as a therapist, has some familiarity with personality and psychoanalytic theory, and has himself undergone personal analysis. However, personal therapy and knowledge of theory do not—and are not intended to —remove the human qualities of a therapist and make him into some sort of a machine. He continues to be a human being, and will probably discover repeatedly that his objectivity and his therapeutic role (narrowly defined) are encroached upon by his personal needs. It is required of the therapist that he have no major motivational systems outside of his awareness. Should these exist, they will be called into play and will influence his behavior as the integration of the therapeutic relationship develops. Unless he walls himself off through a denial of his own existence, the therapist will be aware of a variety of responses—and is required to deal with these in ways judged to be beneficial to the growing freedom of his patient.

Some of the therapist responses that complicate work with patients (schizophrenic and often otherwise) and that are common in this form of relationship are briefly reviewed as follows:

1 The schizophrenic patient may be looked upon as a "challenge" and his improvement as a way to demonstrate (supposedly) some particular combination of talents in the therapist.

2 The patient may be used as a piece—as in a game of chess—whereby the therapist enters a competition with colleagues to "prove" the alleged superiority of a particular "method" or "school," or seeks to demonstrate that those who taught him were "right"—or perhaps "wrong."

3 The patient may become—unfortunately—an object of fascination revealing (or being led to reveal) behavior actually, or supposedly, confirmatory of some prized theory of personality; such patients, finding an anxiety-reducing and self-perpetuating fitting of personal needs with needs of a therapist, may provide a seemingly unending source of "material" without themselves undergoing significant or beneficial change. They are mines of information, finding strange refuge in the sought-for particularization of their experience; being a patient becomes a career, matching that of "being a therapist."

4 Therapists have, in varying degrees, needs to exercise power—to con-

trol and dominate. Some patients have reciprocal needs—to be controlled and dominated. The matching of such needs may lead to a reduction of discomfort in both participants, in which case each will seek to perpetuate a relationship that is comforting but therapeutically unprofitable in that change is prevented.

5 In his seeking for closeness and security with another person, the schizophrenic patient may display a form of seductiveness and seeming affection that imitate (if there is excessive need for this on the part of the partner) a form of love. The acceptance of such attachment as simple devotion will have—in one sense a useful, and in another a destructive—function. That is, the required therapeutic investigation will be hampered if not destroyed.

6 Over long periods of time with a withdrawn, unresponsive, and perhaps mute patient, there may develop fantastic concepts of patient, therapist's self, and the relationship. In response to personal needs of both participants, the patient (and therapist) may be cast into more or less private roles—such as child, parent, sibling, mother, and so on—without there being understanding or much valid confirmation for any of these.

7 With the passage of time, an analyst may find that his world is—as he sees it—peopled largely with patients, and he may discover (or deny) that he is in some sense isolated and alone—and perhaps lonely. He has become a therapist, teacher, adviser, counselor, and a senior member of an establishment that he may have denied and resisted while it more or less subtly encompassed him. He discovers that there is no longer a place to go or a person to whom he can turn for a revealing of his discontents and personal "weaknesses." Then he may turn—without knowledge, or if with that, then with guilt—to his patient for relief. The patient—who has often known something of what it is to be confidant and parent to a parent—may meet the dependency requirements of his therapist, and in so doing experience a decline of anxiety but fail to separate from his past, having found it in his current present.

8 Therapists properly take pleasure in the betterment of their patients, but the need to heal, to change, and to reform is a handicap in treatment, as it reflects a form of self-involvement—narcissism—that leads to treating the patient impersonally and as an object.

9 The necessity to participate vicariously in the lives of patients—in the reports of their escapades—may lead to a perpetuation of such accounts without benefit. For example, the therapist may respond to an

invitation to play the part of being someone better than an allegedly hurtful parent, or to release (in fantasy at least) his own sadistic feelings now mirrored in his patient's accounts of relatives' cruel behavior.

There are motivations other than the above, operating to continue a therapist in his work but jeopardizing the possibility of its useful outcome. At the very least the therapist must be knowledgeable about these aspects of himself; their persistence or their great strength may disqualify him for his task. However, the therapist is not required to be somehow beyond the frailties and the hazards of his human condition. The existence of his defects, once recognized, can be put to good use as information regarding the course of treatment—signposts of the developing relationship not be to disregarded lightly.

The above is no more than suggestion. We properly can concern ourselves with the "kind of person" who is a therapist and the motives that lead him to form an abiding interest in patients such as these described here. Why does one turn his attention to a line of work that in many ways offers little reward—in terms of money, prestige, professional advancement, or (in the conventional sense) pleasure? The task is in itself not ennobling. Does the therapist simply seek further knowledge of himself through observational involvement with his patient? Does he hope to allay some long-endured guilt because of a suspected—or known—crime against his conception of humanity? Does he repeatedly attempt to correct some failure of his own to be an understanding and loving person by discovering and demonstrating these qualities in the consulting room?

All of the above justifies further consideration—but not here. It is evident, that for better or worse, the therapist as I know him is not an "influencing machine" or a "reflecting mirror" in any simple sense of these descriptions. He is both an observer and a participant—required to know what he is about, to accept with humility the humanity and limitations of his position, to aid another without damage, and to recognize that for whatever he does (or does not do) there will be consequences—often not easily remedied.

Factors Possibly Related to the Quality of "Uniqueness"

There are several factors that may contribute to the special quality of the therapeutic relationship as outlined above. Certain of these influences are operative in any form of psychotherapy, but our concern here is arbitrarily limited to work with the schizophrenic patient. Although the course and the results of treatment will depend to a large extent on the personality characteristics of those involved—irrespective of their designation as therapist or schizophrenic patient—attention at this point is given to the factors themselves without regard to their interplay and to the significance of other possible influences.

The Formation of Relational Bonds

A basic requirement of an organism—such as man and other mammals—is to develop early in life an attachment (commonly to an adult of its own species) that will favor its survival.[10] The human infant will not survive if its behavior is not met by appropriate, tension-relieving responses from the mothering one. If the responses are suitable and well-timed, tensions are reduced and patterns of "needs" are developed through the reciprocal transactions which are the beginnings of interpersonal relatedness. It was suggested earlier that variations in this process of attachment range from disasters marked by the infant's withdrawing from human contact into death (so-called marasmus) to what we sometimes carelessly name "adaptability" and "normalcy." Intermediate reflections of difficulties in the early formation of relational bonds may be found in infantile autism, childhood psychosis, and the schizophrenic phenomena of adolescence described here. (Note that the term adolescence refers more to a developmental stage than to chronological age. Thus a person in his twenties —or older—may continue to struggle with problems supposedly dealt with in the teens.)

The formation of social bonds takes place most readily at certain times of development called "critical periods." This term is defined by Scott and Fuller as "a special time in life when a small amount of experience will produce a great effect on later behavior." [11] In the human being (quoting Scott), "The present evidence indicates that while the period of six weeks to six months is a critical one for the formation and determination of social relationships, the later ages are also critical with regard to psychological damage resulting from breaking off these relationships." [12]

[10] No attempt is made in this paper to review the numerous studies that have been made of the early attachment of the young to a nurturing person.

[11] J. P. Scott and J. L. Fuller, *Genetics and the Social Behavior of the Dog* (Chicago and London: University of Chicago Press, 1965), p. 117.

[12] J. P. Scott, "The Process of Primary Socialization in Canine and Human Infants," *Monographs of the Society for Research in Child Development,* serial no. 85, vol. 28, no. 1 (Yellow Springs, Ohio: Antioch Press, 1963), p. 34.

Although in man the time of primary socialization is from the first six weeks to six months, critical periods are not so clearly delineated or fixed as in other animals, with the result that modifications in the form of relationships can, theoretically, take place at any age. As noted earlier, adolescence is an era of potential rapid learning and alteration of behavior.

The following comment by Scott is relevant to this last:

. . . an individual at the proper period in life will become attached to anything in the surrounding environment, both living and nonliving. . . . In animals like dogs and people, it is likely that the capacity to form these attachments is never actually lost in adult life but simply takes place more slowly, usually because of various interfering patterns of behavior.[13]

In a review of attachment behavior, Cairns notes that research so far "indicates that social attachments can occur in the absence of assorted conditions that have been assumed to be primary." [14] That is, attachment can form despite the absence of the following: lactation (as in the mother), immaturity of the subject (patient), physical contact between subject and object, and nonpunitiveness of the object (mother, for example). In brief, social bonds develop in response to the proximity of one person to another and are not dependent on feeding, touching, age, or even kindness in the ordinary sense, but are facilitated by accompanying emotional arousal. Of particular interest is the observation that unpleasant, noxious components of the situation—elements usually associated with punishment—strengthened the tie between the participants.[15]

Although attachment between adults may be considered to be desirable, it is usually complicated by a variety of ideas regarding its nature and its propriety in terms of the culture. Is the attachment the result of, or evidence of, love, sexual interests, unwanted dependency, regression, or whatever? The schizophrenic patient (and others) may resist contact with the therapist, fearing that he will be "swallowed up," that once dependent he can never be "free," and that to need a relationship is evidence of "weakness" and infantilism.

The following by Bowlby is useful in this regard:

[13] Scott, *ibid.*, p. 38.
[14] R. B. Cairns, "Attachment Behavior of Mammals," *Psychological Review*, 73:5 (1966), 410.
[15] *Ibid.*, p. 414; see also J. P. Scott, "Critical Periods in Behavioral Development," *Science*, 138:3544 (November 30, 1962), 949–958.

That attachment behavior in adult life is a straightforward continuation of attachment behavior in childhood is shown by the circumstances that lead an adult's attachment behavior to become more readily elicited. In sickness and calamity, adults often become demanding of others; in conditions of sudden danger or disaster, a person will almost certainly seek proximity to another known and trusted person. In such circumstances an increase of attachment behavior is recognized by all as natural. It is therefore extremely misleading for the epithet "regressive" to be applied to every manifestation of attachment behavior in adult life, as is so often done in psychoanalytic writing where the term carries the connotation pathological or, at least, undesirable. To dub attachment behavior in adult life regressive is indeed to overlook the vital role that it plays in the life of man from the cradle to the grave.[16]

The basic ingredient of a relationship designed to be therapeutic is the formation of an attachment felt by the participants to be of some moment in their respective lives. Reference here is not made to relationships that develop with rapidity, are of short duration, and yet seem to lead on occasion to enduring change of personality in one or other of those involved. The relationships under discussion were slow to develop, were often threatened by premature dissolution, were repeatedly thought to be unprofitable and unpromising, and endured for two years or more, leaving a lasting impression on both patient and therapist. The elements of these relationships were the following—which is, perhaps, a gross oversimplification of a complex affair.

1   There were repeated meetings of the patient and therapist. These meetings lasted for an hour (sometimes more, if the patient was disturbed near the end of a session) and were held five to six times weekly. During a year there were about two hundred sessions. Although therapy was usually conducted in the therapist's office, there were times when that location was not suitable because of the patient's anxiety, and he might then be seen in his room or on the hospital grounds.

2   In the great majority of these encounters there was a considerable amount of emotional arousal. The patient's anxiety, fear, hostility, despair, negativism, and even muteness stirred up feeling in the therapist. The sessions were usually marked by one's recognizing that he was en-

[16] J. Bowlby, *Attachment and Loss*, vol. 1, *Attachment* (New York: Basic Books, 1969).

gaged in a contest. The patient's need for involvement and his fear of it introduced an approach and withdrawal quality to the encounters that could not be dealt with impassively. The patient often put little trust in the therapist, and there was an almost constant threat to the maintenance of the relationship, which could be destroyed by withdrawal, death, or "outside" events, such as interference of family members. Thus there was often an exciting and almost adventuresome aspect to the work; it seemed to be carried on in an atmosphere of high risk.

3   The developing relationship was not formed in a neutral or friendly setting. The people spoken of here did not voluntarily seek help and expected little good to come from treatment or a human relationship. They were in a sense forced to be in the hospital, not necessarily through legal commitment but by the pressure of relatives and some recognition of their own social failure. As a result the patient frequently complained of being a captive, and the therapist was accused of being—and felt himself to be—unsympathetic, inhuman, and cruel. Therapy was carried on largely in the midst of anxiety and conflict despite the later occurrence with increasing frequency of periods of acknowledged trust and closeness.

The attachment of patient and therapist to each other developed even though the desired results of recognized improvement were not attained. Major ingredients of the tie were the meetings in which proximity was achieved, the stirring up of emotion, and the quality of tension and conflict usually experienced as unpleasant and undesirable.

I find it most satisfactory to meet with a patient five or six times each week and be in each session for at least an hour. However, this is a personal preference, and the formation of relational bonds is not necessarily related to this frequency or duration. Of particular importance, perhaps, is the fact that patient and therapist are caught up in a situation from which neither one can easily escape. The patient may protest that he is a prisoner, and the therapist often feels that he is one also, being bound not only by professional interest and obligation but by the subtly growing relationship, which in a strange way becomes for a time a prison as well as a route to freedom.

There is in this confined struggle something akin to cruelty, which may be a factor in intensifying the attachment. There is also in all of this a symbolic reduplication of earlier life events. The infant is bound to the mothering person by his need for nurturing and by his helplessness. If that situation is marked by anxiety, he cannot escape physically but only by emotional withdrawal (as in somnolence) and later by the manipulation of symbols and perception. In the later therapeutic relationship being considered here, escape is not easy, anxiety levels are often high, and efforts are made to prevent defensive withdrawal, intensifying the sense of frustration and conflict. Both participants usually feel that they have been in a fight, enjoyable at times but unforgettable. (Perhaps this sense of great closeness despite the struggle is not completely different from the emotions experienced by two boxers who embrace each other with appreciation and even tenderness when each has survived a bout entered willingly but not without dread.)

The intensity of the tie between patient and therapist, developed in an atmosphere (at the beginning, at least) of great anxiety and a situation of frustration from which there is no ready escape, may resemble that between infant and anxious mother. This last is suggested by the observation that patients seem to be strongly attached to people and situations that would in the ordinary sense seem to be noxious. Despite the anxiety and destructiveness in such circumstances, patients—and others—return to them and find it difficult, if not impossible, to break the ties which hold them. In brief, the tie that binds most closely has woven into it threads of anxiety and cruelty, and similar components—real or "transference"—may be found in the treatment itself.

The Range of Emotional Response

There are relationships maintained over long periods of time and felt to be of great significance in one's life, despite the fact that the encounters of the participants are brief, formalized, and stereotyped. Thus it was with a man at a filling station which I visited for service once or twice a week for twenty years. Our exchanges were friendly but perfunctory, were concerned with the business of my car, and there was little revealing of self to the other. We have not seen each other for some time now, and I can't say that we "know" each other in any personal sense. I'm not sure that I'd like him if I knew him better, and I have no true desire to meet with him again. Nonetheless, I recall him well, and I think of him as a friend—which is not exactly the case. Let us say that I am "attached" to him; he is significant in my life.

In contrast to the relationship with the garage man, that with the patient is noteworthy for both the intensity and range of emotions brought to awareness during the period of work. On occasions these passions are deeply felt and cannot be dealt with by an attitude of cool detachment. Without a minimum of such feeling, the therapeutic—human—attachment is not likely to be strong.

Let us return now to Jane's remarks at the beginning of this account. She had said that my wife and I seemed close to each other and was surprised at Gwen's idea that Jane and I spoke in a way that seemed strangely personal and different. Where did this "difference" lie? To put it simply, my wife and I care for each other, take pleasure in our children, and share our living willingly and without regret. We have our differences, we can hurt each other, at times we get angry, we know tenderness, and we have no serious illusions about being proper models for others to emulate.

However, the home—with good fortune—is not usually just like the hospital. My wife had expressed confidence and trust in me from our earliest meetings; she anticipated that good rather than evil would come from our being together. She did not again and again call me obscene names; she did not attack me physically and seriously attempt to kill me; she was not found mute, lying on the floor incontinent, wet, and soiled; she did not rapidly swing from one mood to another without obvious cause, and her behavior was not so unpredictable that I could not know what might come next; she did not repeatedly threaten to desert me and to kill herself; she did not ignore me, or deride me to others, or run from me without explanation; she did not picture me as a striking reduplication of some relative or a figure in the phantasmagoria of hallucination; and she did not look upon me as deceiving her and plotting to destroy her.

But all of these—and more—were characteristic of the relationship with Jane. I am glad that such tempests have been spared us in the home, although I know that they can exist there as well as elsewhere. Had my wife dealt with me in this fashion early in our days together, I think that we should soon have gone different ways. With Jane, however, all of this behavior had to be faced and attempts made to comprehend it in terms of the present and what had gone before. Jane often called me cruel and spoke of herself as cruel and destructive. At times I felt cruel and wanted to get out of a situation in which I felt more like a jailor than a physician. But I did not leave, and despite her protests, Jane remained also. Neither one of us could leave; we came to feel bound to each other. But this binding together could not continue—as it does in some families—throughout years of mutual destructiveness, maintained by a subtle fitting of pathological needs and ending or subsiding through exhaustion, death, or discouragement and apathetic withdrawal. Once formed, the bonds had to be understood, loosened, and modified so that separateness could be attained. Early in our work Jane put the matter simply: "I think that we are going to be responsible for each other—maybe forever. Sometimes I think you'll kill me—or I'll kill you. Or maybe I'll get better—and if I do, you'll change also." She did get better—and as is always the case, I think, I also changed through this experience.

I shall not attempt here to state the details of the changes undergone either by myself or the patient. I am attempting rather to describe something of the nature of the relationship which is experienced as unique and which is a factor, I think, in leading to changes in the participants. Although I had been myself in personal analysis for some years at the time of this last experience, I did discover "within myself"—as the saying goes —previously unrecognized qualities of anger, fear, tenderness, and affection. I came to understand more clearly that I often wanted to escape from the impact of another person's anxiety and psychotic behavior, and thus might attempt to deny it or to shut it off to the disadvantage of my patient and her therapeutic needs. I found aspects of myself reflected in her own behavior, and at times such realizations seemed almost intolerable. Sullivan's phrase "We are all more simply human than otherwise" came to have greater meaning to me, and I was more accepting of my own current limitations without the need for denial, fear, or shame. I also learned more about how easily I myself might resist personal change, as did my patient, and how apprehensive I could become about separation from people, from objects, and from characteristics of my own. I trust that these remarks do not appear to be casually sentimental. They are not intended as such. Although the therapist experiences personal change through his work, he is required to be so expert that he can endure this and focus on his primary task—facilitation of his patient's growth. He is not free to wallow in unnecessary preoccupation with himself or a narcissistic concern with his own needs and the intricacies of his personality. I suppose that in some ways this last could be said about a parent who is to a considerable extent responsible for the growth of his child and yet grows himself in his living with that child.

I suggest that the exposure of a wide range of emotions—including anger, fear, repulsion, disgust, tenderness, lust, compassion, and so on—in a situation to which limits are set, frustration endured, and understanding sought—serves to intensify and strengthen the bonds of relationship. Although we speak of these strong emotions as being experienced often as "real" and not assumed, they are brought forth in a particular setting designed to be therapeutic and are not carelessly invited because of some alleged beneficial "cathartic" effect. Despite the terms used, therapeutic contacts are not in themselves amusing or dramatic; they are a form of hard work designed to free a person of the past's nightmare and leading to eventual separation of the participants. This is not the case with one's wife, for example. I am a selfish person. I do trust that my wife and I shall benefit from our relationship, but we seek pleasure in it, as well as growth, and it is not designed to lead to our separation—except through our errors or the end of life itself.

Here again the question can be raised as to what there may be in a therapist's own background that may interest him in—and hold him to—such work. Many people would want no part of all this. I doubt that one would become or continue as a psychotherapist of schizophrenic patients without having been aware of distress in his early family life and without knowing at times intense anxiety in his relationships with others. There often is a need to find in others a further understanding of himself, and the schizophrenic way of life is a startling caricature of man's compounded desire for relationship and his fear of it, his goodness and his evil, his creativity and his destructiveness, his freedom from instinctual control and his subjugation to education and learning, and his power to form and use symbols that could lead to his end as well as his continuance.

Sometimes a therapist may seem to be driven to "cure" his patient, as if his own survival depended upon bringing about change in someone else and in "making sense" of a tumultuous and confusing scene. Such motivations can arise from a child growing up with an anxious and disturbed parent—probably mother—whose distress he felt impelled to reduce in order to guarantee her survival and thus his own. It is the business of the therapist to know about himself, at least to the extent that he does not impose on his patient needs that must be understood and met elsewhere—as in personal treatment and continuing consultation regarding his work.

The Form of Contact

Therapists vary in their practices, but with the patient who is at times grossly disturbed, analytic niceties cannot always be maintained—nor should they be. Often there may be brought into play a wider range of contact than is found in the usual office setting. Some of these will be mentioned here—but briefly.

Sound

The range of sound is wider in this work than in more conventional psychotherapy. If the patient is met with in his hospital room, there will be no soundproofing to keep out the noise of the surrounds, and the patient's world in the institution will become very much a part of the treatment—often with beneficial results. There may be periods of muteness that contrast with the shouting of other times. The therapist himself will not always speak in carefully modulated tones but may find himself attempting to shout down his patient in an effort to disrupt some psychotic outburst.

Touch

Except for the formality of an occasional handshake, there is little, if any, bodily contact between therapist and analytic patient. I am aware of the use of such contact by therapists who advocate massage, holding the patient, bottle-feeding him in states of regression, and so on. A therapist must work in accordance with a theory which makes sense to him and within the limits of what is suitable to him as a person as well as potentially profitable to his patient. It is not suitable to my style to proffer physical contact as being in itself healing. However, I hopefully do not recoil from such contact when its expression is spontaneous and its refusal will be experienced as affront.

For example, a woman patient suddenly stopped her pacing about the room, sat on my lap, and clung to me weeping; all of this after I had commented on her isolation and the great distance that seemed to separate us. I put my arm around her, and we sat in silence for a time until she slid to the floor beside me and spoke of her loneliness. Sometimes I sat beside a mute and catatonic patient and rubbed her back until the rigidity of her muscles relaxed and she could be more at ease. Frequently, I have been impressed by the seeking for bodily touching being disguised as assault. Thus a patient would hit at me and then briefly cling to me before withdrawing his hands. The use of wet sheet packs, continuous tubs, massage, and showers are useful ways of providing stimulation to the skin that is greatly needed by many who have had little of such comfort since infancy —if then.[17]

[17] On this subject see, for example, the following: L. K. Frank, "Tactile Communication," *Genetic Psychology Monographs,* 56 (November, 1957), 211–255; H. F. Harlow, "The Nature of Love," *The American Psychologist,* 13 (1958), 673–685.

Sight

The anxious schizophrenic patient fears not only the relationship into which he is invited but also its loss. Although such a person may turn his head away and hide his face, he needs to be able to look at the therapist at times to reassure himself that the "object" is not leaving him. Frequent visual contact with the therapist and the contents of the office is required for orientation and for the building up of a reassuring and persistent gestalt or picture in which the patient can find a place for himself. To look at the ceiling or one wall from the vantage point of the couch is not enough, and the sharing and exploring with the therapist of a broad range of visual and other patterns may become a useful symbolic reduplication of experiences in earlier developmental eras.

Motion

There is more movement in these treatment procedures than in those that are more formal. The patient may be too restless to sit and may move about the room; at times patient and therapist may walk together. With such activity an additional dimension is added to the therapeutic experience—kinesthetic sensation. The person who has become estranged from himself may gain an increasing awareness of the unity of his existence as he feels the movement of his body in activity shared with another.

Odor

There is little variety in the usual smells of a therapist's office, and we soon grow accustomed to what little there is. The range of odor may be greatly increased in working with a disturbed patient who may bring feces, urine, and food into the situation in ways that may be disconcerting yet revealing.

The forms of contact briefly mentioned here are more common in infancy and childhood than in later adult life. We tend to "outgrow" and restrain these expressions, but we should not forget their communicative aspects or our often poorly concealed need for renewed contact with them. They can be powerful reminders of our past—as both child and parent— and their sharing can greatly intensify the bond of relationship.

In more conventional office therapy these contacts are restricted or muted in the service of social requirements and the facilitation of introspection and revery. Such limitations may not be possible—or desirable

—with some patients, and ways must be found to make use of the behaviors that are available. Although I have no great sympathy for a careless disregard for convention—social and professional—I think it necessary for the therapist to be fully aware of any personal, anxious withdrawing from expressions of human relatedness as so briefly noted above. Such aversions may close off or leave undiscovered the only remaining ways to the fading hopes of another person.

Transference

It is characteristic of the schizophrenic person to invest his associates with attitudes derived from his own past without correcting these through a careful observation of what is occurring in the reality of the present. Such perceptual distortions—transference phenomena—often have a protective quality in that current figures are seen in terms of past and known dangers and thus avoided as potential sources of harm. The accompanying difficulty, of course, is that the person who has become so sensitive to the faintest warnings of danger may attack or flee so rapidly that he never notices that the threat is minimal or nonexistent.

The therapist may be seen in many guises—usually more fearful than benign. He is dealt with as a violent man, a seductive rake, an embodiment of evil, or occasionally as a good person endowed with more than his actual virtues. The transference distortions may be presented with such intensity and conviction as to seem real, and under persistent assault the therapist may feel pulled out of himself and find it difficult to distinguish clearly between who he is and what he is alleged to be.

The patient, suspicious of all who come near him and anticipating harm, must search carefully for any sign of deceit, hypocrisy, evasion, cruelty, or whatever in the therapist. In the more conventional task of therapy the patient's "ego strength" is judged sufficient to distinguish between distortions of the present governed by his past and the truth of the moment. With the schizophrenic person, active assistance must be given in this task of sorting out the private component of perception from that which can be validated with others.

The therapist himself becomes an object of this sorting process. That is, he is searched to find that which rings true and that which does not. Thus it is that he is exposed more thoroughly and ruthlessly than in other therapeutic encounters, finding that his "real" as well as his "transference" self will be revealed. The therapist's consistency over a long span of time is not to be found in "being the same" from one session to another, but in being "whole" in each session; that is, he is one in his action, feeling, thought, and speech, giving out none of the "mixed messages" that confuse the recipient to such an extent that what is felt as hate is labeled love, distance closeness, and the command to be free leaves the listener faced by the necessity to resolve a "double-bind."

Often the perfection of these therapeutic tasks is not achieved. The therapist does not always ring true, he will on occasion give out mixed messages, and he may catch a patient in a net of double-binding, as he himself is often caught. Over the long stretches of time required in some instances, the therapist will vary in the exhibition of his skills, being more competent at some times than at others. In all of this he will be revealed, not only as a professional therapist, but with increasing clarity as the person he is.

In "real life" there may be no great quarrel with the maintenance of some illusions. Love, which has been said in frivolous (or even serious) moments to make the world go round, has usually been supported and maintained by illusion. In therapy, however, illusion is to be revealed, given its due of respect, and put aside. This attempt to forego illusion and to discover what "is" (even with the recognition that reality itself is not readily defined) is with time shared by patient and therapist. The effort to find and know "truth" is the basis of a mutual respect even though the proposed goal is never reached.

The relational bond is formed and strengthened in this search. The therapist is not simply divested of transference adornments and finally revealed as being nonexistent. Rather does he emerge as a person, with his strengths and weaknesses recognized and accepted for what they are. Early in their relationship the participants may view each other as "objects" rather than persons, this tendency being reinforced by the presence of anxiety. One may be depersonalized as "a schizophrenic" and the other as a "shrink." As the therapist looks for the person in the patient, he is himself explored, attacked, manipulated, searched, and seemingly torn apart in a hunt for inconsistencies, incongruities, and imperfections. Such seeking— if endured—should lead to the transformation of object into person and the development of trust and confidence that will permit the final separation without undue distress. In this process of transmutation the bond between the participants is further toughened.

In Conclusion

The therapeutic relationship is sometimes described as having a quality of friendship. A friend can listen, sympathize, advise, reassure, understand, comfort, tolerate, and to an extent reveal himself. However, he wants for himself sympathy, reassurance, and so on, and the seeking of such satisfactions will require him to ignore some aspects of the relationship or imagine others that do not exist. The goal of friendship and love —for the most part, at least—is not change, growth, and separation. Friend and lover often wish to keep the other one "just as he is," perhaps hoping that in so doing the passage of time itself can be defeated.

In contrast the therapist (and also the parent and teacher) seeks in part the fulfillment of his needs through the facilitation of another's growth, the achievement of which leads to change and separation. The therapist acquires a range of tolerances not easily maintained; involved, he is detached; alone, he is close; expert and experienced, he accepts the limitations of these terms; with change he is constant; and seeking to mold another, he is to an extent molded. His experience, training, and technique become a part of himself, there then being no gross separation of the personal from the professional. It is this combination of self, experience, and indoctrination that is presented to the patient for his investigation, manipulation, and contemplation—the transactions through which his own self-knowledge and growth can be furthered.

The therapist is not an "object," a friend, a lover, a transference figure, a teacher, or whatever—nor even a combination of these, although representations of each may recurrently seem to find transient support in his being. He is not like something else; he is a therapist, and the relationship with him reflects many aspects of living but is itself unique.

The
Promise
of
Psychoanalysis   *Harry Guntrip*

What is life about? Any response is difficult to formulate because we are so inextricably bound up in the bundle of life that we cannot achieve the answer by our separate selves. It is easier to state what life is not about. Certainly life should not be living as a secretly lonely millionaire, a hate-filled nationalist, or a power-hungry racist. Nor being a never-satisfied, avant-garde searcher after change for change's sake, or a tense executive on his way to a coronary thrombosis. And life is not about ignoring social evils and unmet community and world needs while safeguarding the luxury of private oases.

What life *is* about is the urge to develop our creative potentials for love and work, with and for each other. This arises in human response to the genuine security and valuation others have provided for us and permits and encourages us to pass on to others these priceless conditions of enjoyable and meaningful living. A psychoanalyst should be someone who can use his training, experience, and humanity to do this for those in dire need; his real reward is to grow with his patients. This is what life is about, in various ways, for all of us.

Surprisingly, within the field of psychotherapy, this idea is by no means generally accepted, a factor that contributes substantially to the contemporary doubts and questions that currently limit the status and influence of psychoanalysis.

A recent letter from America said: "Psychoanalysis is on the decline with fewer analysts and patients dedicated to the task." This is a representative obituary on the demise of psychoanalysis which is usually attributed to its lack of relevance, its costly and time-consuming demands, and its alleged frequent lack of success. In this essay I would like to examine the pessimism that informs this position and also to contrast the following point of view: a psychoanalysis which is closely related to the realities of everyday living, that penetrates to the depths of suffering human beings, has nothing to fear for the future and will flourish.

Such a therapy, in fact, has become indispensable not only for individuals in personal need of it, but also for the contribution it makes to those professions concerned with the fate of human beings in their struggles to maintain themselves as viable persons in stressful situations. However, psychoanalysis will hold the attention of the public only insofar as it speaks truly to the human condition, and insofar as people realize that the psychoanalyst should not be just a professional man with a theory—a psychotechnician—but a human being with a developing experience of understanding, able to help others with their struggles to be real persons living meaningful lives with their fellowmen.

This kind of psychoanalysis has been in the making but it still requires a certain evolution in theory and practice, an evolution that was actually implicit in Freud's own development. For beginning as a physician seeking to cure an illness, he started a process that is now carrying psychoanalysis far beyond the narrow medical model of a doctor treating a patient toward a relationship in which both participants explore together the meaning and value of living. (Freud's almost compulsive interest in religion and culture was not a sign of a simply speculative bent but was the inevitable development of his inquiry into human living, its mysteries and ultimate implications.)

These issues were central in my own development as an analyst. I began with a very thorough philosophical and theological education, which I would not have missed, but then decided to lay these subjects aside until I had a more adequate knowledge of "human nature," of what it means to be a "person" possessing intellectual curiosity, moral values, and the spiritual aspiration that life should be meaningful. Accordingly I studied with Professor J. C. Flugel, one of Britain's finest psychoanalysts, and Professor J. Macmurray, a penetrating "personal relations" philosopher. I had sensed the tension between these two points of view throughout the 1930s. Psychoanalysis was exploring the right approach to the study of personality but it was burdened by the weight of a physicalistic (instinctual) bias; Macmurray was unburdened by an instinctively based theory but lacked the dynamic grasp that psychoanalysis could supply.

I had sought to unite these two streams of thought, for the more I delved into psychotherapy the more I felt that classical Freudian theory was insufficient to understand aspects of human suffering that went far deeper than the vicissitudes of instinctual drives and straightforward Oedipal phenomena. In the immediate postwar years I became familiar with the works of Sullivan, Horney, and Fromm, which greatly broadened my vista. A little later the work of Fairbairn further widened my scope of psychoanalysis and I saw it could continue, not as a mechanistic late-nineteenth- and early-twentieth-century psychobiology dealing with the two mighty, turbulent drives of sex and aggression, but as a fully psychological study of the profound intrapsychic and interpersonal problems of human beings living together.

Freud himself prepared the groundwork for this evolution when he defined psychoanalysis mainly in terms of transference and resistance when he wrote that "Any line of investigation, no matter what its direction, which recognizes transference and resistance, and takes them as the starting point of its work may call itself psychoanalysis, though it arrives at results other than my own" (*On the History of the Psycho-Analytic Movement,* 1914); thus his model of man changed in time from a biological machine toward that of a person engaged in relating with others and with himself. However, the intellectual outlook and the philosophy of science in Freud's era did not make possible the formulation of a thoroughly psychodynamic science; Jones, Kris, and Erikson to the contrary, I do not think that Freud ever resolved the conflict between physicalistic and psychological constructs in his thinking. In fact it still persists in the thinking of many of his followers and is implicit in Anna Freud's recent description of psychoanalysis as relating to man's struggle against himself (i.e., biological Id versus mental Ego).

This concept, however, is already changing in contemporary psychoanalysis, with emphasis being placed on man's struggle to *be* himself. The argument is now likely to be raised that this is not the business of science. Why not? Science is knowledge, all knowledge, and the real question is not "Is psychoanalysis a science?" but "What kind of science is it?"

The views of many scientists have changed since Freud's time when Brucke's dictum, that "there are no other energies in the organism than physical and chemical ones" gave Freud no standing ground for the creation of what his own genius led him to: a fully psychodynamic science which could take man's physiological substrata for granted and devote its energies to the study of interpersonal relationships. Such a science would focus on our experiences of ourselves as persons emerging out of a social field, beginning with the crucial mother-infant relationship. Even today Freudian theory implies too limited and too pessimistic a view of human nature, like those views expressed so clearly by St. Paul and Plato (views that are still important because they affect how we treat sex, aggression, and social violence). Freud's concepts of Ego and Id parallel St. Paul's concepts of the "Law of the Mind" and "Law of the Members," the lusts of the flesh which "are not subject to the law . . . neither indeed can they be." Thus Freud believed that men are hostile to culture because it demands the renunciation of instinctual drives. But the hypothesis that a relaxation of sexual morality in society would diminish modern man's nervousness has been manifestly disproved.

Freud's prognostic statement that the outcome of psychoanalysis is limited where the quantitative factor of instinctual strength overpowers the efforts of the ego also parallels Plato's concept of human nature. Employing the metaphor of a chariot to describe personality, Plato viewed a charioteer of reason who used a courageous, spirited (aggressive) horse to hold back another horse, the beast of the passions. In *The Republic,* Glaucon and Adeimantus anticipate Freud in holding that men are violent and nonmoral by nature, arguing that men submit to social control for convenience; Socrates responds with a social analysis of the Just State ruled by philosophers who forego personal gain (i.e., sublimate their instincts) and who have at their command the Soldiers (aggression) to ascertain that the Workers (their instincts unsublimated) are kept in a state of obedience: a blueprint for the totalitarian state.

What led men of the intellectual and personal stature of Plato, St. Paul, and Freud to take this hopeless view of human nature? In good measure it was a powerful theoretical assumption—one that appeared to be true on the surface—that human nature was dualistic, an imposition of an intellectual-spiritual mind on an impersonal, animal, passionate body; for Freud this translated into an ego with scientific reason struggling, and mostly failing, to master the turmoil of the biological id. Erikson's citing of the analogy of the Centaur with a human top and equestrian underpinnings is in the same spirit; but this is as impossible a view of the human evolutionary process as the traditional religious schema of man as born in sin and shaped in iniquity, doomed by biological inheritance to be lustful and destructive. So many educated people still hold roughly to this view that it is necessary to say that the natural sciences have outgrown such crude materialism and that contemporary psychoanalysis is also outgrowing the pessimistic Ego-Id dualism.

However, this does not mean that one may not look at certain phenomena from different points of view. In this spirit Bronowski holds that because man is at once an organic machine and a self there are qualitatively different kinds of knowledge, knowledge of the machine, which constitutes physical science, and knowledge of the self, which constitutes psychodynamic science. Going back, then, to the question of what kind of science is psychoanalysis, we can benefit from Medawar's account of the scientific method and the hierarchical structure of knowledge. He likens knowledge to a building with a ground floor and a series of floors or tiers rising above it. The ground floor is physics and chemistry, the successive tiers rising above it are physiology, neurology and biology, then sociology. Medawar fails to add psychology as the topmost tier, but we must remedy his omission of the study of "personal mind" as the highest phenomenon of which we know—that without which the whole of science and culture, and Medawar himself, would not exist.

He writes (in *Induction and Intuition in Scientific Thought*) that, "In each plane or tier of the hierarchy new notions or ideas seem to emerge that are inexplicable in the language or with the conceptual resources of the tier below. We cannot 'interpret' sociology in terms of biology, or biology in terms of physics"—nor, we must add, psychology in terms of any lower-tier science. Were this view of scientific theory available to Freud, say in the 1920s, it might have allowed him to develop his approach to an ego psychology as a study not of drive control apparatuses, but of whole persons in intensely personal relationships. Thus sex would have been viewed not as an engine threatening to run out of control, but as one of the bodily "appetites" or needs, along with hunger, thirst, excretion, breathing, and sleep, all in the primary service of biological survival. And aggression would have been seen, not as an innate volcano that needs to be capped, but as a reaction to threat, above all the psychic threat to the integrity of our personality. (Naturally the *capacity* to respond to threat in an aggressive way is innate but this is quite different from holding that a storehouse of violence, per se, is built-in.) Man's antisocial hostility would then be seen as a secondary product of intense fears and frustrations, allowing for a more affirmative view of man than the pessimistic one of classical Freudian theory.

As it was, it fell to Erich Fromm, a social psychologist trained in classical psychoanalysis, to make, in the 1930s and 1940s, the most trenchant criticisms of instinct theory in order to widen the purview of psychoanalysis. For example, he reinterpreted the Oedipus complex within a much broader framework. Recognizing Freud's discovery of the central importance of the child's relationships with his parents as a primary determinant of personality development, Fromm went beyond a focus on the individual's sexual bonds with his parents as the main issue of living. Although sexual attraction does arise between parents and children and may result in neurotic conflicts, Fromm observed that this is not the essential aspect of child-parent relationships. Rather it is when the parents inhibit the child's development and thwart his growth so that the child is unable to stand on his own feet that the more basic issue arises—the conflict between remaining passively dependent on parents or other authorities versus the quest for independence and authenticity. Not sexual attachments, but the tension between wanting safety-through-submission on the one hand, and braving anxiety to achieve autonomy on the other, was seen by Fromm as the core struggle to keep oneself in being as an intact person, especially when no genuine or affirming relationships were experienced in the course of growing up.

As a consequence of such broader views, psychoanalysis today has a far clearer picture of how profoundly the day-in, day-out atmosphere of family life shapes the child's stability and approach to life. This has serious consequences for the goals of psychoanalysis. Of course, those who desire only a control of symptoms or a restoration to a prebreakdown level of functioning may well benefit from such psychiatric treatments as electric shock or drugs which have made mental distress more manageable. But this does not lead to a creative maturing of the personality. (Following electric shock, one patient was relieved that his depression lifted but complained that his personality took on an "automatic" quality.) However, when psychoanalysis sets as a broader task the liberation of the person from the emotional traumata of the past and the development of his creative potentials, then the analytic work and the analytic relationship must set about to repair the damage done by past faulty relationships day by day, often from the very beginning.

To illustrate, a patient of mine began a lengthy psychoanalysis as a junior in his profession, then out of work, ill, exhausted, and suffering from poor sleep, waking up intermittently and screaming. He had had a psychotic mother who had literally terrorized his childhood. Though dead, she lived with him in his nightmares. As the analysis proceeded, he felt better and steadily rose to the top of his profession. He continued with analysis, however, because he still experienced a quite unrealistic apprehensiveness before any interview or meeting. But this problem, too, was fading away when, in one session, he shut his eyes and fell silent for half an hour. Silence has so often been interpreted as resistance, and at times is; but I knew that this was not such an occasion. Finally he opened his eyes and said, "I felt I needed to relax. For a time there was a tight knot of tension behind my forehead. Gradually it died down and for some time I've forgotten all about you. Something new has happened. I feel free of something, and I know what it is. The old atmosphere of apprehension has gone and I feel safe at last."

I observed that he had slowly come to feel sufficiently sure of my positive feelings for him that he felt safe enough to be with me and yet forget all about me, something he had never dared to risk with his domineering and threatening mother. The internal atmosphere of apprehension of living with his mother had at last been dissipated; for the first time he felt safe and free to experience himself directly as a real person, achieving a new kind of self-discovery that no pill could have given. His newly won capacity to be alone without anxiety was the hallmark of his maturity. This experience my patient had of feeling real to himself, in a new way, goes deeper than an account of Oedipal dynamics would allow for.

At this point, a brief excursion into an object relations theory of psychoanalysis may serve to contrast the therapeutic approach I am referring to with the traditional; and, additionally, since object relations theory has become increasingly important in Great Britain as well as in South America and elsewhere, it seems timely to acquaint American readers with it. The central difference with Freudian theory is that the latter has regarded man primarily as a pleasure-seeker whose instincts need to be tamed, while the object relations view as developed by Fairbairn regards man as primarily in search of relatedness. As Fromm wrote in *The Art of Loving,*

> The deepest need of man, then, is the need to overcome his separateness, to leave the prison of his aloneness.

The formation of relationships, not the reduction of pain, is the primary struggle of man. On this basis there is no theoretical requirement for the concept of an Id; impulse tensions arising in the course of searching for relatedness account for motivational forces. Another difference is that object relations theory regards development as determined not by stages in instinct maturation (from oral to anal to genital), but by the changing quality of the growing child's relationship with others. Neuroses are seen as arising out of the difficulty of moving from infantile to adult modes of relating.

Object relations theory has its beginnings in Freud's concept of the superego which is based on an internal, psychic representation of the parents. Melanie Klein developed this approach into a broader phenomenology of intrapsychic life, regarding the psyche as an inner world where the ego was deeply involved in enduring and patterned relationships with internal "objects" or representations. This internal stage—as distinct from the outer world—became central to her thinking, and was the point of departure for Fairbairn.

He never regarded the ego as developing out of discrete nuclei, but as a global whole at the outset, which then became increasingly differentiated as a result of interpersonal experiences. For him psychoanalysis was predicated on the idea that the ego cannot develop, in fact becomes "lost" in schizoid withdrawal, without sufficient experiencing of good relationships. When the child experiences the mother as frustrating, his helpless, weak ego splits the object into two parts and internalizes them as a way of mastering them. The experience of the parent has been divided into an Exciting Object—that part of the parent that has aroused feelings and needs in the infant—and into a Rejecting Object—the unsatisfactory and hated aspects of the parent. The ego splits to relate to these internalized objects. Specifically, these are now a thwarted, hungry Libidinal Ego that continues to struggle for life, and an Antilibidinal Ego that gives up and fails to grow. The Antilibidinal Ego is also called the Internal Saboteur because it is related to the Rejecting Object through identifying with it; this unholy alliance jointly attacks or condemns the Libidinal Ego (which is similarly allied to the Exciting Object through hope of sustenance). All of this occurs out of range of awareness. However, on the conscious level, a Central Ego emerges as that portion of the personality that carries on the daily life of the person in the outer world, while unconsciously the person is radically divided against himself.

Thus, in the analysis of the intrapsychic world in terms of object relations, self-hatred is understood as the Antilibidinal Ego and Rejecting Object constantly attacking the Libidinal Ego which grips on to life at the expense of suffering. Here is the hard core of neurosis, the unconscious sadomasochistic dynamic from which numerous symptoms arise. In the course of therapy the Antilibidinal Ego shifts from an allegiance to the Rejecting Object to an alliance with the accepting analyst, allowing the split ego to move toward a healing integration and wholeness. This is why psychoanalysis should not be so strongly focused on repressed drives and hidden memories; the crucial issue is to develop the immature ego which is fighting to preserve its psychic existence. Certainly the control of antisocial impulses is socially necessary, but this is a secondary matter compared to the fundamental growth of the ego.

It can now be seen why analysis is of necessity a slow process. The relationship must gradually develop so that it is secure enough to permit the patient to live through the traumatic early disturbances again, so as to resolve them within the new relationship, which affords the needed mothering and fathering that foster growth. Analysis is also difficult because, through his Antilibidinal Ego, the child identifies with a powerful albeit persecutory figure and—in the closed system of his neurotic unconscious —is unwilling to give up this protection. Additionally, the person may suffer at the hands of his bad objects, but he at least has a relationship; better a persecutory relationship than none at all. No wonder that the resistance to change is usually intense.

Many diverse dramas are enacted on the inner stage, with front row seats provided by dreams which I believe are usually not wish fulfillments but direct views and insights into the endopsychic situation. For example, one patient dreamed of looking on helplessly while a male horse slashed with a knife at a female horse who just endured it. A primal scene interpretation had little effect. The important point was that his Central Ego, the observer, was helpless to halt a cruel inner conflict. After the patient had shown much progress, he dreamed of an angry man shouting harshly at a terrified boy. Then the man was friendly and said, "I know you're nervous but you hold my hand," and the boy lost his fear. As the patient said, "The harsh chap is the attitude I've always had to myself and the friendly man is your attitude to me which I'm slowly adopting."

To summarize, the first ego split leaves a Central Ego to cope with the outer world while a Libidinal Ego retreats to an inner world, out of consciousness, where it deals with its internalized objects. This inner ego has been divided by conflicts between its needs and fears into an oral, needy Libidinal Ego relating to an Exciting Object to keep it going, and an Antilibidinal Ego which is identified with, and relates to, a persecutory Rejecting Object. In addition, I have found that the Libidinal Ego may be so assailed by anxiety that it makes a further withdrawal, this time from bad internal object relations, and a third and final ego split occurs. I refer to this last split-off portion as the Regressed Libidinal Ego which seeks a passive security in a womblike state.

No psychoanalysis can be complete unless this regressed part of the personality is reached so as to turn regression into regrowth. This requires that the patient face his ultimate fears and flight from life. However, the patient also hates his Regressed Ego for its weakness and he is, at times, going to hate the analyst who seeks to help it. Equally important, the patient is deadly afraid that his Regressed Ego, if given any acceptance in the context of the analytic relationship, will lure and betray him into abject infantile dependence. The only solution is to endure and outgrow these fears of a good object relationship with the analyst.

As Fromm wrote, the goal of psychoanalysis should include "freedom from" emotional conflicts but go beyond it to achieve "freedom to" develop our potentialities to their maximum. He talked about the discovery of the "true self." Today, Winnicott writes of the "true self put into cold storage" when a baby is born into a family environment that fails to nourish it. The child, then, must grow "a false self on a conformity basis" or on "a rebellion basis." Getting a start at all in the growth of a real self depends initially on the warmth, interest, and constancy flowing to the baby in the mother relationship. Thus Winnicott holds that the experience of relationship is earlier and far stronger than the experience of the satisfaction of bodily needs, so that the true model for psychotherapy is the mother-child relationship, not a tension-reduction model. In a related vein, Fairbairn held that the origin of all personality problems lies in the inability of "the parents to get it across to the child that he is loved for his own sake, as a person in his own right"; therapy, perforce, involves the patient's working through unrealistic transference relations to the analyst, to arrive at a mature, realistic relationship in which he finds his authentic self. In this context, Balint distinguished two different levels of psychoanalysis—the level of the "Basic Fault" and the Oedipal level—ascribing to the former the necessity to deal with the patient's earliest failures to attain the foundations of a secure personality within the pre-Oedipal, mother-infant matrix. The patient must reexperience this level in order to make "a new beginning"; but if he merely regresses to seek endless satisfactions for unmet early needs, then the regression becomes malignant and may not lead to cure. Benign regression, on the other hand, is essentially a search for recognition as a person by the analyst; this is what leads to a cure.

The work of Fromm, Winnicott, Fairbairn, and Balint illustrates the way psychoanalysis is now in process of transformation from a theory and analysis of "instinctual frustration and control" into a theory and therapy that encourage the rebirth and growth of an authentic self within an authentic relationship. Here the demands of the patient are understood less as a craving for immediate gratification and more as a need for a real person to begin to relate to, and to be real with—a need that is basically psychological not physiological. Clearly, this is not to deny the fact that man's total biological and psychological nature inherently provides the conditions for the experience of relatedness to occur.

It is true that things can go wrong even after a good start with reliable mothering, but not so seriously wrong. The growing child is certainly helped or hindered by the extent to which he finds good or bad relationships in the community, but if a sound foundation has been laid, it is astonishing what stresses can be taken in adult life. What compelled me to focus increasingly on these issues was the fact that many analyses that had moved along on a conventional Oedipal level eventually betrayed signs that Oedipal dynamics concealed far deeper problems which involved the patient feeling himself to be insignificant, a nonperson as it were, whom no one could like or respect. These more basic issues—intractable to analyses of ego inhibition and superego tyranny—clearly required reparative experiences to offset the person's inability to get off to a proper start in self-formation within a destructive family atmosphere: not the patient's "reparation" for his destructive impulses (see Melanie Klein), but the analyst's "repairing" the mother's failure to give basic ego support.

This discussion brings us back to the opening theme. Freud began as a physician seeking to cure an illness but he initiated a thrust that is now carrying psychoanalysis from a medical treatment model to a relationship in which both participants explore living. The way in which analysis is developing into a deepening study of how we succeed or fail in emerging as persons in the media of good or bad personal relations again raises the issue of goals and the ultimate questions of life. Certainly the traditional notion of "cure" becomes increasingly irrelevant in comparison with such concepts as self-discovery and self-realization, with the person no longer bound by unrealistic anxieties but affirmed in rewarding relationships. We all know implicitly that every human being needs and seeks to be validated by others. Thus a tough young psychopath in group therapy shouted, "Look at me when you speak to me! I don't want to be treated as if I wasn't here!" He absolutely needed someone's recognition of his presence; otherwise he had to act out violently to escape a fall into a vacuum of schizoid isolation.

As I stated at the outset, a psychoanalysis that comes to grip with these concerns, that is not parochial, that addresses itself to the human condition, is here to stay. It is of no importance whether it waxes or wanes in popularity in any given period. Psychoanalysis will decline only if it becomes a closed society of the initiated defending an older, undeveloping theory as dogma. Nor is it crucial that there can never be enough psychoanalysts to meet the needs for individual analysis; for our ultimate aim must be one of prevention, through the acquisition of a body of knowledge and experience that helps us to understand how to live and be truly human.

The Patient Aids the Analyst:

SOME CLINICAL AND THEORETICAL OBSERVATIONS

Erwin Singer

From their very beginnings most publications on psychoanalytic technique have stressed at least implicitly a dominant theme: that the analyst derive little personal satisfaction from his work other than the gratification the healer inevitably derives from the sense of a job well done and, of course, from the financial rewards attending his efforts. All other satisfactions arising in his working day have been suspect of countertransference tendencies rooted in the analyst's unresolved conflicts.

Structuring the psychoanalytic relationship in these terms molded the process into a one-way street: the helping relationship was to be one in which the analyst aided the patient, in which he could not and should not expect any comparable aid from his client. As is well known, at least two important factors were responsible for the development of this posture: First, the basic medical model and the medical tradition under whose aegis psychoanalysis unfolded imply that the doctor's superior knowledge and skills actively applied to a relatively passive patient would bring about cure; and second, any genuine and realistic help which the patient might offer the therapist would involve the former's familiarity with the therapist's personality and with his difficulties and problems in living. Yet such knowledge, it was said, would interfere with the development and the purity of the desired transference and would therefore militate against the therapeutic process.

It is the purpose of this paper to explore the potential shortcomings of this austere stance without detracting from its merits; to outline and to illustrate with clinical material the potential therapeutic power of the analyst's revealing his own life situation, thereby making it possible for the patient to be realistically helpful; and finally, as its main contribution, to support implications for a theory of personality development derived from these observations, implications at variance with those traditionally advanced in the psychoanalytic literature.

An analyst's willingness to be aided by his patient when it was he who was asked to be the helper may easily reflect conscious or unconscious exploitive efforts. Little could be more crippling to a presumably already badly damaged person than to be exploited. In addition, an analyst's making reference to events or issues in his own life while inquiring about the patient's existence or while reacting to the latter's utterances may well indicate self-indulgence and an attempt to ingratiate himself through flattery, since he is now treating the patient as a confidant. A host of other contratherapeutic attitudes potentially lurking behind the therapist's self-revealing comments will readily come to mind. Therefore the admonitions Freud and others offered to the analyst are well taken: to keep in mind that the central considerations in analytic therapy are the patient's emotional growth, his development of insight, his being helped to know himself, and to avoid most strenuously all extraneous material.

Without questioning these basic and admirable objectives of analytic psychotherapy, some (relatively few) authors have seriously questioned the belief that such goals are actually advanced by the analyst's maintaining strict anonymity. Among those who have expressed doubts are Jourard, Searles, and most prominently Tauber, and Tauber and Green in their book *Prelogical Experience*. The latter have cogently demonstrated how the analyst's discussion of his dreams and fleeting thoughts about his patient—clearly an expression of his willingness to reveal himself to his analysand—may, in the ensuing exchange, lead to an important understanding of the patient-therapist relationship and the psychodynamics of both patient and therapist. By pointing to the potentially constructive, creative, and communicative use of countertransference phenomena, they make it clear that the analyst's insistence on anonymity may prove deleterious to the aims of the analytic process.

There is an additional dangerous shortcoming implicit in the analyst's anonymity and the following pages examine this danger. If the analyst maintains a one-way-street position and is simply the person who holds up the mirror in which Dorian Gray may see his image, then the analytic situation will not likely lend itself to the spontaneous sharing of the patient's authentically positive reactions and to the revelation of that which is most constructive in his makeup. A rather one-sided and caricatured picture of the patient is likely to emerge. Certainly the anonymity of the analyst lends itself exquisitely to the development of all kinds of transference reactions. But, unbending anonymity, while furthering the denouement of hidden destructive and other primitive tendencies, does not promote and activate reality-oriented and constructive qualities. Of course, the patient may reveal his strengths in examining constructive reactions that occur outside the consultation room. But just as we are able to see the patient's pathology and its roots most pointedly in his transference reactions to the analyst, it is reasonable to suggest that we are equally likely to best see his strengths—his constructive reactions to life's realities—in comparably immediate and intimate terms. Only then is the analytic situation a naturalistic microcosm of the patient's life. But such expressions of health would demand, as pointed out earlier, the patient's familiarity with at least some aspects of the analyst's life.

I will now sketch a very painful event in my life, the considerations which moved me to reveal it to my patients, and their reactions to my sharing my pain with them.

Some time ago my wife became seriously ill. Upon learning the tentative diagnosis, knowing full well that I would be unwilling and unable to concentrate on my work and in my eagerness to be at her side while further diagnostic procedures were in progress, I canceled all appointments till further notice. My patients, although they knew that I took frequent and at times suddenly announced vacations, sensed from my voice that this cancellation did not reflect a frivolous impulse and spontaneously inquired, "What's up?" Too troubled to engage in lengthy conversations and hesitant about how much I wanted to say, I merely replied that I would explain when I saw them again.

I was of course preoccupied during this period. Yet I had to give the question of what to tell my patients upon my return some thought. My immediate inclination was to tell them candidly what had happened. After all, it seemed only fair that an analyst who investigated the reasons for his patient's breaking appointments be equally frank when he absented himself.

But then doubts about this course arose. Was it all that simple? Were my motives really as pure as they appeared to me? Was I perhaps looking for sympathy and a chance to talk about my pain when the patient's trials should be my legitimate concern? Was I trying to stop some of the more difficult among them from sniping at me—surely they would be less demanding if they knew the painful reality of my life? Was I trying to induce guilt or show some patients how trivial many of their complaints were by presenting to them real troubles? And was I not about to burden unduly human beings already distressed enough? These and similar ruminations occupied my thoughts while the days passed.

Clearly one or more of such countertransference motives could lurk behind the impulse to reveal to the patients this development in my life. And now looking back I believe that these deliberations with myself were essential.

With some trepidation I decided to tell them the truth. But the uncertainty about my motivations, about the possibility of my exploiting the patients, made me, when I faced them, less sure of myself than I had hoped to be. It led me to the occasional expression of an embarrassing preamble: a statement to the effect that I regretted burdening the person with my problems. But in any case I informed all patients about the reason for my absence.

Their responses seemed to me astonishing, and that I was astonished reflected poorly on me. Concern, genuine sympathy, eagerness to be helpful with problems likely to arise, and above all efforts to be supportive and comforting—these reactions were eye openers. As I listened, deeply moved and profoundly grateful, to the patients' efforts, it became apparent that each person expressed his desire to be helpful in his particular style, a manner which often, when occurring under different circumstances, had been identified as reflecting a pathological character orientation. I will give a few illustrations.

Mrs. N., a woman torn between her desires to be an effective domineering manager of other people's affairs (as was her socially successful mother) and her simultaneous longings for magical gratification of dependent needs for nurturance, immediately responded in terms of both facets. She eagerly informed me about the outstanding authorities on my wife's illness and intimated that she might be able to get us an entree to one of them, a man indeed quite prominent but, since he was semiretired, difficult to reach. At the same time she insisted with great self-confidence that my wife was going to be "all right," that she knew this as a fact. Her eager-

ness to be comforting and encouraging, while at times expressed in childish fashion and at other times couched in unrealistic but seemingly author-
itative pronouncements, was very moving.

Dr. S., a fiercely competitive physician—though he managed to obscure this tendency very well—was constantly suspicious and fearful of
being exploited professionally and personally. Hearing my story immediately made him feel that he wanted to withdraw, with a sense of "Oh, my
God, now I will have to take care of him, too!" Yet secretly he had always
longed for the savior's role, to be the last of the just, to shoulder the burdens of the world, fearful only that he would be exploited by being denied
the proper recognition. And therefore he always played the martyr. But it
also became apparent that he was genuinely eager to press his considerable
knowledge into the service of being helpful to me. Although he actually
expressed resentment about feeling obligated to inquire about details of the
findings, he also persisted in asking about my wife's condition and encouraged me by keeping me abreast of little-known and promising research
findings. By putting the many facets of the illness into proper perspective
for me, he offered me genuine aid and comfort. Thus it was by no means
surprising that one day, after once again ruminating about his resentment,
he suddenly sat up and exclaimed: "For pity's sake, I really would like to
help you and yet I always insist on feeling put upon, resentful, and suspicious. If I cannot learn here how to enjoy being helpful, what the hell am I
here for?"

Mr. D. was a successful businessman in his early forties. Despite his
accomplishments, his lifelong meekness and submissiveness knew no bounds,
and were always accompanied by a preoccupation with finding shortcomings in others, with detecting the weak spots in precisely those whom
he claimed to admire, in those whom he tended to approach in almost
groveling deference. It frequently turned out that they were actually rather
pathetic people, individuals whose pathos he had sensed, acquaintances
whom he could flatter with his "adoration" of them, people who therefore
could fall hard and easily from the heights of his esteem. In his transference reactions he had been on a constant lookout for my "hang-ups" and
shortcomings and indeed he discovered quite a few of them. In any case,
his approach to others, made up of a strange mixture of self-debasement
and contempt, pointedly expressed itself in troublesome symptoms which
caused him and those around him a good deal of grief.

One of his preferred ways of detecting the character flaws of his
friends and associates was to "buy" them, to shower them with gifts and

entertainment, only to look down on them if they fell for his bribes and accepted his largesse. Then, with a little deprecatory gesture of the hand, he would do away with them, feeling delighted about having found them out as tarts of sorts, yet simultaneously feeling depressed by his conviction that he was cared for only because he had money.

Hearing about my wife's and my plight caused him deep consternation and he cried silently for a while. Then his constructive and supportive impulses came to the fore and characteristically expressed themselves in, to him, familiar terms: He inquired about my financial situation, whether I was going to be hard pressed by enormous medical expenses, and made assurances of his readiness to lend me money. In spite of his frequent use of affluence for manipulative purposes, this offer sounded genuine. I thanked him with sincerity and explained that I could manage. When he insisted, "Please don't forget if you should need it," I promised him that I would certainly remember his offer and that I would not hesitate to call on him if need should arise. He looked at me as if startled and once again began to weep.

One final illustration. Dr. L., an embittered and tight-lipped young scientist, had just gone through painful divorce proceedings. His marital difficulties arose partly from his persistently detached manner. He had always prized this detachment as the reflection of a calm and reasonable disposition, of the importance he had placed on "objectivity," and of his belief that keeping reserved, dignified, and unmindful of any turmoil would help reason prevail. No matter what his wife did or did not do, "She could not ruffle my cool"; and this, he thought, was all to his credit. It was not apparent to him that his very equanimity had markedly cruel overtones.

After I had told him what calamity had occasioned my absence, he remained stiff and silent for quite a while. Then calmly and in contrast to my depressed mood he inquired about the prognosis; and when I told him that the physicians were quite confident, he nodded his head in "objective" concurrence and told me about his familiarity with similar cases and their "objectively" satisfactory outcomes. Strangely enough, his seeming unconcern and calmness, though uncongenial to my temperament, had a reassuring effect on me. It was only several sessions later that he remarked with a good deal of sadness—and I believe this was the first time I had seen him genuinely sad—how distressed he had been during that session. Not that he had pretended feeling calm, but that he had also felt like hugging me and putting his arm around my shoulder. This he could not do, he remarked with distress. Every fiber had fought against it, and he regretted having remained once again outwardly detached when inwardly he had been eager to be more involved.

I hope that these vignettes illustrate what I have learned: that the capacity to rise to the occasion when compassion and helpfulness are called for is part and parcel of the makeup of all human beings. Importantly, in no single instance did my disclosures have any ill effects; on the contrary, the insights, memories, and heightened awareness which followed my self-exposure proved remarkable, and I have the deep conviction that my frankness accelerated the therapeutic process in several instances.

These observations confirm in a personal way the doubts others have expressed previously as to the validity of the position that the analyst's anonymity has universal therapeutic value. Strict psychoanalytic anonymity would have reduced my patients' opportunities to see their own strengths; and certainly it would have limited my knowledge of their caring and compassionate capacities.

In addition, my observations lend support to one of Erich Fromm's hypotheses when he outlined the dialectic relationship between productive and nonproductive character facets. He suggests that in every personality we observe traits capable of being expressed in either positive or negative terms. For instance, he points out that the human trait which may express itself constructively in generosity perversely comes to the fore as wastefulness in the nonproductive marketing character. Similarly, he observes that the potentiality for man's following productively the directions of others can express itself in the nonproductive pathology of submission; or that the capacity to guide constructively can make itself felt pathologically in tendencies to dominate. In the reactions of the people I have discussed we observe the positive manifestations of potentials and attitudes usually and unfortunately expressed by them in nonproductive and pathological terms. Thus Mrs. N.'s manipulative and domineering efforts may be seen as a perverted expression of her capacity to take charge and to be helpful. Or Mr. D.'s penchant for depriving others of genuine satisfactions can be viewed as a perverse and pathological manifestation of his capacity to preserve and eventually muster his resources for moments of real need.

It is not the aim of this paper to definitively outline those of life's circumstances which make human beings "decide" to overcome life's difficulties through destructiveness rather than through constructiveness, to use Fromm's terminology. Suffice it to say—as will be seen—my disclosures and the patients' reactions to them became excellent points of departure for emotionally meaningful instead of intellectually sterile inquiries into the origins of these decisions.

My patients' efforts to search themselves, much more seriously after my disclosures than ever before, brought to light certain themes which up to now had never emerged or had at best been mentioned only fleetingly.

Mrs. N., for instance, now genuinely attempted to grasp the truth of critical childhood experiences and of the affect associated with certain of her present-day reactions to them. She had grown up in an atmosphere dominated by a mother not only immensely resourceful and socially successful, but also vain and attractive. Her father had been equally towering in his professional, financial, and social successes, though he was severely depressed and withdrawn. With great pain Mrs. N. now began to reexperience instances of feeling totally unable to make any meaningful contributions to these all-knowing, all-successful, and seemingly "need-less" people. These feelings became particularly obvious in relation to her mother. On the other hand, she had somehow sensed the father's essential loneliness and on occasions she had caught his need for her, a tendency vigorously repressed, yet at moments betrayed by him to the girl. While his repressed needs contributed to her symptoms, they left her at least with some dim sense of being potentially useful. But in relation to mother all she could do was to sit in awe, and to hope that some day she would be able secretly to approach her mother's successes. Of course, any such success should never be attained openly, lest it represent in her eyes too much of a challenge to mother's superiority—a superiority that my patient was unwittingly substantiating through her own submissive behavior. Growth and maturity would therefore have to descend upon her magically, i.e., in ways for which she could not be held responsible, and her actual capabilities would have to be expressed in negative terms. Concern with the welfare of others was to be shown primarily through often abrasive manipulations, persistence through petulant power operations, and intimacy through pathetic helplessness.

Pointed recall of childhood events associated with the crystallization of this character orientation, together with penetrating examinations of her present behavior and affect, were now in evidence; there is little doubt in my mind that these developments and my frankness about my situation were causally related, that the admission of my pain made the vision of genuine usefulness a realistic possibility for her. In sincere bewilderment she remarked a few days after my return to work: "I feel so strange, as if it were really possible to be truly useful to you, not just being busy trying to accumulate points . . ."

Dr. S. also felt impelled by my report to search his life more thoughtfully than before. While eminently successful at a relatively early age, he often felt like a fraud, and indeed in certain ways he was just that. He frequently published manuscripts less in the hope of making a contribution than with the desire to show off and develop an impressive list of publication credits.

Several times he had discussed with some puzzlement little incidents in the hospital and his reactions to them. For instance, he was quite embarrassed when a patient praised his medical ability to others, or when he was thanked with profound gratitude for having restored health. He was honest enough not to ascribe this embarrassment to the modesty of the humanitarian physician for whom running his errands of mercy successfully is its own reward. But he did notice within himself a desire to experience the superiority "of the white man who willingly accepts his burden." Fortunately his search for such haughty exultation seemed embarrassing to him when faced with heartfelt gratitude.

My gratitude for his genuine helpfulness forced him into further self-examination. This in turn led him to pay more careful attention to daily events, his reactions to them, and memories they evoked. Thus he reported one day with great agitation that his father, feeling ill, had made an appointment to see a physician practicing the son's specialty. But he had not called the patient to inquire about the doctor—actually a prominent physician at the hospital where the patient worked—until he had made all the arrangements. The patient did feel deeply hurt about not having been consulted earlier, and about having been treated as if his training were of little consequence.

Reflection on this and similar incidents led to important insight. With shock he grasped his lifelong sense of having been incapable of making any authentic contributions to his family, that all he had ever been asked to do was to *appear* competent. The real substance of his knowledge and skills had never mattered. What was even more painful and saddening to him was his growing recognition that he had allied himself with this orientation, that he had grown up to cherish the grandstand play and had come to value form over substance. This realization became more poignant through his gradual recall of how, in quest for status within the family, he had forged silent alliances with one parent against the other. They had usually been expressed in the exchange of knowing looks and supercilious smiles. Because of this, demands for genuine relatedness now loomed as threats, as if they would interfere with old alliances and his concentration on form and style. Thus he resented them and met them with suspiciousness and complaining self-pity about being exploited. That in the process he would also invite actual exploitation by others, making his self-righteous accusations and whining appear justified, became obvious.

The point that I am clearly eager to make is this: much of the neurotic distress experienced by my patients seemed associated with their profound sense of personal uselessness and their sense of having failed as human beings because they knew that the only contributions they had made were embodied in nonconstructive reactions and behavior responding to equally nonconstructive demands. And so destructive interaction with others became a virtuous, alas pernicious life-style governed by the motto: I will contribute by sham and by lack of authenticity—I will contribute by destructiveness. The genuineness of my distress and of my needs had disturbed the smooth operation of this style.

The sample presented is small. Nevertheless I believe that the findings point in a direction proposed occasionally during the past few years in the psychological and psychoanalytic literature. This direction suggests that those concerned with the origins of psychopathology and with efforts to rekindle emotional growth must give serious attention to the possibility that the most devastating of human experiences is the sense of uselessness. This meshes with Fromm's idea that destructiveness is an alternative in living when constructive strivings have been thwarted; with Binswanger's discussion of Ellen West's sacrifice; with Searles' view that the origins of schizophrenia can often be found in the child's pathetic effort to be useful to a pathetic parent; and with Feiner and Levenson's discussion of what they call the "compassionate sacrifice" observed by them in their young patients.

Implied is the thought that anxiety does not emanate from the *fear* of castration but from the terror of the recognition that one *is already* castrated; or that one need not look for the causes of anxiety in a man's *fear* of disapproval but in his horrifying realization that he *is already* disapproved since he is deemed unnecessary. That is, the roots of anxiety and of emotional derangement can often be found in a person's sense of futility in living, as expressed in his feelings of isolation and uselessness culminating in his dread of loneliness. But since human beings cannot endure this nightmare of being irrelevant, they must find themselves a pseudo "usefulness" in neurotic or psychotic living.

This is not an effort to absolve the person from his real-enough guilt. For in accepting his role assignment of insignificance he becomes a collaborator with his casting director, causing discomfort to himself and spreading it to the world around him. If this conception of neurotic and psychotic processes has merit, then the therapeutic experience must afford the patient an opportunity to grasp not only his failure to be useful but also his potential for achieving human worth and fulfillment in constructive contributions. Therefore the therapeutic encounter demands an attempt to help the patient see his difficulties in living, at least in part, as the inevitable outcome of his attempt to deny justified feelings of personal insignificance.

The effort to deny this sense of personal insignificance may also be partly responsible for the enormous increase of pathology among middle- and upper-class youngsters. These strata have practiced child rearing procedures that protect their offspring from the rough winds of emotional pain no matter how real the tragedies and the sadness in life around them were. The child-centered home becomes all too readily perverted into a home in which the child is shielded from psychological reality. Caring for the child became perverted into making too few significant human demands on him. Of course this assignment to the status of uselessness and inability to shoulder human burdens is easily obscured by procedures giving the impression that demands were really made. "Clean your room," "take out the garbage," "wash the dishes," "do your school work"—these are poor substitutes for "hold my hand," "dance with me in joy," and "dry my tears." The former are empty and ritualistic steps, the latter are genuine human calls and demands upon the emotional depths of others. The former are inauthentic and usually irrelevant demands because they do not offer an opportunity for giving of oneself in humanly supportive, caring, empathic, and compassionate terms. When the environment fails to make demands for the expression of these human potentialities, when in fact their very expression is precluded by sterile arrangements, then individuals cannot help but feel useless. In making these comments I am not joining the chorus of those who rail against permissiveness; on the contrary, I suggest that true permissiveness has been lacking when the child has not been permitted to experience the full range of human reactions and when he has been kept from making meaningful contributions to others. The permissiveness of Dewey and Spock was accepted by many in its form, while the substance of their thoughts has all too often been neglected.

This lack of authenticity in parent-child relations, the child's inadequate opportunities to express constructive relatedness, finds an analogue in the traditional analytic relationship. The great promise of psychoanalysis to provide a situation in which the totality of one's inner life can be heard is at least in part negated by stultifying arrangements that prevent the patient's directly experiencing and expressing his constructive tendencies. For here, too, no authentic demands are made on the person. And so, based on the experiences I have described, I believe that a marked reduction of the analyst's anonymity is essential to therapeutic progress. This requires the analyst's willingness to share with his patient his own moods and feelings, not as a therapeutic "technique" but as a genuine expression of his concern. Fortunately this does not mean exclusively the sharing of catastrophic news. In the analyst's working day there arise inevitably innumerable "extra-therapeutic" reactions, be they fatigue or verve, joys or sorrows, excitement or irritation. To share these at least occasionally so that one's patient can be a helpful companion without intruding on the patient's life and without precluding his opportunities to express all his other reactions—this, I believe, is the road the therapist must travel.

I am aware of the possibility that my own concerns during this period in my life forced me to selectively attend to and interpret the data provided by my patients. And it is certainly conceivable that my own sense of helplessness in the face of grave illness and my eagerness to be useful by being reassuring to my wife were sensed by the people with whom I worked, causing them to respond to me in the manner I described. Worse, it is possible that I was eager to think that I was offered that for which I longed even though it was not really forthcoming.

However, I am inclined to dismiss these possibilities at this time. The patients' growth and their reflections on my and their experiences during this time support the formulations I have advanced. For some patients the events described here accelerated a process of growth well underway. But others were reached emotionally for the first time in therapy by my disclosures and willingness to accept their help. Overall some patients seemed more moved than others; to some my frankness and willingness to accept help were more meaningful than to others; and consequently their therapeutic impact varied from individual to individual. I have some hunches about these individual variations. First, I told of my situation with varying degrees of comfort and I suspect that the therapeutic impact of my disclosures was less in those instances where I was most hesitant. Second, the younger the patient, and therefore the less likely to have been personally acquainted with realistic tragedies, the less likely was he to be able to empathize with me, and therefore the less profound was his personal reaction to my situation. And finally, the longer and the more intensively we had worked together, the stronger was the positive therapeutic reaction evoked by my self-exposure.

These formulations are presented with caution. Only further investigations and reports from colleagues who had similar personal and analytical experiences will provide more definitive knowledge about the issues raised here. What I have tried to do is to point to a, to my mind, profitable direction of inquiry into the developmental aspects of a person's sense of uselessness and to the analytic issues that derive from it.

Pathologic Symbiosis and Autism
Harold F. Searles

In my experience, I have found the concepts of *autism, symbiosis,* and *individuation* to be reliably helpful in understanding not only the bewildering and awesome phenomena of schizophrenia, but also the psychodynamics of therapeutic change in one's analytic work with any patient, whether neurotic or psychotic.

This paper will be the first of a series reporting what I have learned of these processes in recent years. It flows mainly from the following sources: 1) psychoanalytic work with nonpsychotic patients for twenty-two years, 2) intensive psychotherapy with eighteen chronically schizophrenic patients at Chestnut Lodge and subsequently, in some instances for nearly eighteen years, and 3) single consultation-and-teaching interviews at a variety of institutions with some thirteen hundred patients, the vast majority of them suffering from schizophrenia of widely varying acuteness, type, and severity (interviews held mainly during the six years since my departure from the staff of Chestnut Lodge).

These papers are not intended to replace my earlier ones, most of which were written from a vantage point of my immersion in work with relatively few chronically schizophrenic patients, among colleagues similarly engaged, at Chestnut Lodge. That is a vantage point I cannot recapture, and I feel a kind of respect for what I then found valid, such that I wish here to put these more recent findings alongside those earlier ones, rather than suggesting that my present views invalidate my earlier ones. Since 1958 I have been a supervising and training analyst in the Washington Psychoanalytic Institute, and for the past six years I have been mainly that, but meanwhile continuing to work with two long-term, chronically schizophrenic patients and accumulating, through my consultation-and-teaching interviews, far greater experience with a multitude of schizophrenic individuals, including many acute cases, than I ever had occasion to encounter at Chestnut Lodge.

The categories that I will describe of pathologic symbiosis, autism, therapeutic symbiosis, and individuation depict what I regard as successive phases of ego development in therapy. Whether any one patient needs to run that whole course will depend upon the level of ego development he has already attained at the beginning. He may already have achieved, for example, a strong capacity for a therapeutically symbiotic relatedness, in which case the first two phases of ego development would be relatively little in evidence in one's work with him.

In writing this paper I have had, more often than not, great difficulty in deciding what particular phase of the evolving process of illness resolution is being manifested in any one of the clinical vignettes presented here. For example, it is often difficult to evaluate whether some striking and indubitably significant incident of patient-therapist interaction signifies a transition, on the part of the patient, from autistic relatedness toward symbiotic relatedness, or whether it is giving a glimpse, instead, of his transition from a predominantly therapeutically symbiotic type of relatedness, toward individuation, which would imply that the work is much nearer to completion. Even what one experiences with the most chronic, slowly changing patient does not lend itself to an effortless conceptualizing of the work in terms of the stages of ego formation; but it is particularly the relatively well patient, the borderline schizophrenic patient, or the neurotic patient, who is much involved in the therapy, whose ego-functioning is so flexible, so elusive, so subtle, quite simply so alive, as powerfully to resist one's efforts to characterize his development through such theoretic crystallizations as are depicted here.

Despite the high degree of felt artificiality in this effort to categorize these part aspects of living processes, the effort is, nonetheless, surely worth making. I have more than once felt, when assaulted by a psychotic patient's ways of responding to me, that both to protect one's own sanity and to help the patient regain his, one must develop a weapon and an instrument exceeding in power his psychotic thought processes, namely that represented by a strong, accurate, and well-thought-out armamentarium of theory concerning these psychotic processes.

Pathologic Symbiosis

The individual who, at the beginning of therapy, gives us to understand that his characteristic mode of relating to other persons is dominated by the ego defense of pathologically symbiotic relatedness, forms with us a relationship in which he is a part of a whole person, and we (the therapist) are the other, complementary, part. This is in contrast to the autistic patient, who functions as though he himself, or contrariwise the therapist, were the whole—the single conceivable and perceivable and palpable—world. Pathologically symbiotic relatedness is in contrast, also, to therapeutically symbiotic relatedness, in many regards; whereas in pathologic symbiosis the patient and therapist form two relatively fixed, complementary parts of a whole system, in therapeutic symbiosis both persons function in thoroughgoing and rapidly changing flux and interchangeability, with all parts of potentially whole and separate persons and, far beyond that, whole and separate worlds, flowing from and into and between, and encompassing, both of them. Also, the affective tone of therapeutic symbiosis is one of liveliness or contentment or fulfillment, while that of pathologic symbiosis is one of constriction, incompleteness, unfulfillment, or inner disturbance to the point of threatened insanity.

Typically, the pathologically symbiotic patient either coercively puts parts of himself into the therapist, or coercively evokes the therapist's attempt to complete his (the patient's) self, manifested as poignantly needful and incomplete.

On numerous occasions, for example at The Sheppard and Enoch Pratt Hospital in Baltimore, I have had teaching interviews during the course of a day with two or three schizophrenic patients, each of whom tended powerfully to deny unconsciously the presence of the crazy, sadistic introjects within him, to attribute these instead to me—to, quite literally, experience them as residing within me—and to leave at the end of the interview with its having been formidably established, in not only his mind but in the minds of the onlooking staff and in my own mind, that he is the human being deserving of compassionate rescue from the inhuman, unfeeling monster of schizophrenia personified by myself. Then, at the end of the day, during the hour and a half of high speed and hazardous rush-hour beltway driving to my office in Washington to see training analysands in the evening. I would feel one or more of those patients as disturbingly present within myself.

These are the patients who, barred from access to an initial human identification in infancy and early childhood with a healthy mother, but presented instead with a chronically depressed or schizoidally remote mother or an openly psychotic mother who disturbingly and unpredictably invaded them with her own inner contents, now in a sense identify with the therapist; but they do so coercively, vengefully, and invasively in the manner described by Bion.[1]

These are the patients who have little healthy ego of their own but are, instead, a constellation of vengeful identifications with other persons, present and past. These identifications, because of the hatred and guilt and unworked-through grief which have attended their installation in the patient's personality, are indigestible by his ego; hence his unconscious effort to rid himself of them, to expel them into the therapist. Consequently, the therapist may find his sleep troubled by the patient who has invaded, and now disturbingly pervades, his whole life.

To the extent that the analyst-in-training manifests such ego defenses as do these schizophrenic patients, and to the degree that the training analyst's own ego-functioning relies much upon introjecting the experiences of others, the training analyst may feel that the collective problems—the uncured components—of all the patients of his training analysands are being attributed to or funneled into him as, variously, a satanic source from whom all malevolence radiates, an omniscient oracle and healer, or, more mundanely, an omnipotently responsible grandparent. Similarly, the schizophrenic person whose ego-functioning depends (as is true for all these pathologically symbiotic patients) upon complementing the ego incompleteness of those about him will come to one's office from his daily life on a ward surrounded by schizophrenic patients, and in a palpable sense bring with him all the most urgently disturbed among his fellow patients —his own patients, in a sense—in the ambivalent and secret hope that this rival therapist will convey the cure for all of them, in what happens between the two participants here in the office.

A patient's therapeutic striving is no less valid and real than one's own. The differences are mainly that (1) the patient's ego identity is *predominantly* as a therapist whose own hope for ego wholeness resides in his effort to complement the incompleteness of the other person's ego; (2) his effort is largely unformulated as such by himself, and is unshared in col-

[1] W. R. Bion, "Attacks on Linking," *International Journal of Psycho-Analysis*, 40 (1959), 308–315.

laboration with acknowledged colleagues; and (3) his effort goes largely unsung by those about him, including his therapist, a hated rival who enjoys the distinction of being acknowledged as a therapist in title if not, so the patient is largely determined, in actual functional effectiveness.

The pathologically symbiotic patient whose poignant incompleteness tends to evoke our functioning so as to complete his wholeness—or who, instead, reacts to us as being poignantly incomplete and needing him to make us whole—differs much in his style of relating from the more clearly sadistically attacking patient who rapes us with his introjects. But these so-different styles of relating bespeak, so far as I can discern, a similar level of incomplete ego development, and surely any one patient may manifest, at one time or another, either style of relating (as, of course, at one time or another, may the therapist himself).

The sense of threat that often pervades one's sessions with these patients has basically to do, I believe, with the patient's paranoid sense (however unformulated it may be) that if this effort of patient and therapist to complement one another and achieve a single wholeness is successful, his only known identity, as a part of a person, will be lost.

The most dangerously paranoid patients, in my experience, are those most formidably able to involve one in intensely ambivalent conflict over this issue: namely, that the patient and oneself can exist psychologically only by achieving and maintaining complementarity to one another; but just as failure to complement the other will mean the loss of existence through nonengagement, so a too-successful complementing of him will mean a loss, beyond recapture, of one's individuality as a part person.

As to the kinds of part person which I have found various pathologically symbiotic patients to be toward me, I want to mention, as examples, the silent and immobile patient who is my own subjective deadness—safely externalized and apart from, and yet complementing, the parts of me more readily acceptable to my own sense of ego identity; the easily labeled crazy patient who personifies my own subjective, repressed craziness; the patient who has the quality of an eternal child, who personifies my lost-child self or, more probably, the child I never was but never gave up hoping to be; the patient who personifies the unconsciously fantasied ideal woman I could have been, had I been born female, or even—in one recent instance, so the evidence went—the child of my fantasied woman-self; the patient who holds within herself, if only I can "cure" her, the key to the realization of my omnipotent strivings; the patient who represents one or another of the nonhuman ingredients of my past, whether a pet dog, or beloved trees, or diabolically frightening things, or whatever; the patient whose changelessness is my immortality; and so on.

In both my own analytic (i.e., therapeutic) work and in doing supervision, I have encountered many instances of the patient's functioning as though he were the only link between the analyst and a real world where there are real people who are living, who are involved in doing things and experiencing feelings. In short, the patient functions as though he were the analyst's aliveness, as though the analyst could gain access to living only vicariously, through the patient's own living outside the office.

To some degree this is a realistic reaction on the part of the patient to the sedentary aspects, the recluse aspects, of the analyst's living as the patient can only limitedly know it. But it is more significantly a transference reaction to the analyst as personifying the more schizoid, detached, preoccupied components of one or another figure from the patient's early life, and as personifying, by the same token, the patient's own detachment from living. That is, the schizoid part of the patient himself, the part which participates little in his own daily living, he projects upon the analyst.

Thus the patient, in his recounting of various daily-life incidents, communicates these in a fashion which tends to make the analyst feel a recluse in this garret, secretly jealous of all the living the patient is doing; or secretly guilty because he cannot be filled, as he feels he should be filled, with altruistic joy on behalf of the actually narcissistic patient immersed in this recounting; or secretly grateful to the patient for speaking in a fashion which enables him to share the "reliving" of the incident. Neither the subtly schizoid patient nor the analyst may realize that the former was not at all fully living the original incident now being "relived"—that he is only now really living it for the first time, in this setting of "reliving" it in connection with the analyst who symbiotically personifies his own unconscious and projected schizoid self.

In one session with a deeply oral-dependent man, I felt considerably under pressure from him to share his radiant happiness about his imminent vacation, until the thought struck me, "Why should *I* be so happy?—It is *his* vacation, not *mine*." He in his narcissism had been giving me to feel that his happiness should be the center of my happiness, too, and of course at the same time he had been leaving it to me to feel the separation-anxiety-born inertness he was having to repress and project upon me. In a supervisory session, the supervisee reported a recent session in which his schizoid patient had been describing, so vividly and amusingly and absorbingly, a recent evening of bowling, that the supervisee had felt himself to be there at the very bowling alley, sharing the experience with fully as much pleasure as the patient purportedly had enjoyed in the original experience. In supervision, it is oftentimes the supervisor who, finding himself left wooden by a supervisee's delighted recounting of such data (as I felt left in this instance), senses the warded-off schizoid aspect of the patient's psychopathology.

Much more often, the analyst wonders what is wrong with himself if he fails unambivalently to rejoice in the patient's reporting of an incident, since the previous session, which indicates newly achieved growth on the patient's part. The analyst uneasily wonders, for the millionth time, if deep down he is basically opposed to health; the possibility does not occur to him that the patient's transference to him is symbiotic in nature, a transference in which the analyst personifies the patient's "older"—more accustomed—self which tends to feel left behind by, and jealous of, the new growth in the patient.

Autism

The patient who functions autistically in the transference functions, as I mentioned before, as though he himself were the whole world or, contrastingly, as though the therapist were the whole world. At other times, patient and therapist function as separate and unrelated worlds.

Parenthetically, it seems to me that the pathologically symbiotic patient needs to come, gradually and slowly, to have the experience, in analysis, of what one might call "healthy autism," an experience fostered by the analyst's functioning in a fashion impervious to the patient's efforts to coerce him into dovetailing with the patient's customary pathologically symbiotic relatedness. Now, confronted by this wall, the patient is thrown back into himself; and out of the consequent changes within him, a capacity emerges for healthy symbiotic relatedness with the analyst.

But here I wish to discuss those patients who come to us either with autism manifestly permeating their whole daily-life functioning, as is true of the most severely and chronically ill among schizophrenic patients,[2] or

---

[2] In a paper in 1961, I described such patients in discussing what I then preferred to call the "out-of-contact" phase in the course of psychotherapy with the schizophrenic patient. H. F. Searles, "Phases of Patient-Therapist Interaction in the Psychotherapy of Chronic Schizophrenia," *British Journal of Medical Psychology,* 34 (1961), 169–193. (Reprinted on pp. 521–559 of *Collected Papers on Schizophrenia and Re-*

with autism present far more subtly at the core of the ego-functioning of
the much less ill, schizoid, or pseudoneurotically schizophrenic patient.
The "as-if" patient described by Helene Deutsch,[3] Greenson,[4] and others
should be placed, for the purposes of this discussion, with the latter patients, whose ego-functioning is flawed at its foundation by autism which,
masked in their relatively capable daily living, emerges with clarity in the
evolution of their transference.

Many patients who seem to be leading lives filled with relatively active
and well-differentiated interpersonal relationships prove, on closer scrutiny, to be living predominantly autistically. What seem to be genuinely interpersonal relationships in their lives are not so but are, instead, unconsciously fostered reenactments of early-life relationships, with the aim of
achieving a solid sense of identification with a parent from long ago. This
earliest human identification was never sufficiently achieved for the patient
to be said, yet, to have a basically human identity and be capable of genuinely interpersonal relationships. (These are patients to whom we give one
or another of various diagnostic labels, including schizoid personality, borderline schizophrenia, "as-if" character structure, and hysteria.)

Some twenty years ago I began seeing evidence that the child identifies,
unconsciously and pathogenically, not merely with the aggressor in the
parent but with, in particular, the detached, out-of-touch aspects of the
parent. It is as if the forming of this primitive identification is the child's
unconscious way of grasping the parent in circumstances when the parent
is being especially remote and inaccessible.

I first observed this in a borderline psychotic young woman who evidently had copied unconsciously, in detail, the behavior of her father at
those times when he was being at his most psychologically remote, having
secluded himself in the fortress of his library. He provided her at other
times with her earliest human model for identification, for her more schizoid mother was much less utilizable for this purpose; hence it was desper-
ately important to her to maintain an internal image of him, as the foundation for her own developing self.

Incidentally, I believe that much "as-if" behavior, which strikes us as

lated Subjects [New York: International Universities Press, and London: Hogarth
Press, 1965].)

[3] H. Deutsch, "Some Forms of Emotional Disturbance and Their Relationship to
Schizophrenia," *Psychoanalytic Quarterly,* 11 (1942), 301–321.

[4] R. R. Greenson, "On Screen Defenses, Screen Hunger and Screen Identity," *Journal of the American Psychoanalytic Association,* 6 (1958), 242–262.

repellently and contemptibly "phony," relates to an early-life impoverishment as regards any living, human models for the behavior which the patient presently feels called upon to evidence; in his need for adequate models, he has to resort to what he has seen in others with whom he was barred from genuinely identifying, or fall back on characters he has seen only in movies, or read of in books. Viewing these patients in such a light yields a sense of compassion which one badly needs in one's work with these exasperating persons.

Since that incident of some twenty years ago, I have found many times that instances of what one might call masochistic suffering in the patient actually stem from an unconscious effort to consolidate previously unachieved bits of the necessary mother-infant symbiosis, in order to become free of a basically early-infantile-autism mode of ego-functioning. I am convinced that many instances of what appears to be masochistic love of suffering are unconsciously motivated, in part, by what is basically a healthy striving for identification. For example, a man, in describing a particularly bleak and despair-filled experience of the day before, said, in a tone of notable pleasure and fulfillment, "I felt like my father yesterday . . . I was thinking to myself, 'This must be how he always felt!' . . ." A woman, describing a recent experience of much inner conflict in relation to her marital family, said, in a similarly memorable tone of pleasurable discovery and fulfillment, "I thought, 'My God, *this* must've been what my mother was up against!' " Another man, saying that his sons at times reproach him that he does not love them, added, "This is what I did to my parents, and I'm feeling how it feels to have your child tell you you don't love them."

This man, like some but by no means all the patients I am discussing, was often told by his father, "Just wait and see when *you're* a father, then *you'll* know how it feels to have your children tell you you don't love them!" I am not trying to do justice, here, to all the complex psychodynamics of such a despairful and vindictive curse from a father to a child. Surely one resultant motive in the child is the unconscious effort to prove that the vindictive but supposedly omniscient father was, indeed, right; the child, now chronologically adult, still has a deep need to maintain an image of the father as omnipotent as regards, for example, this supposed omniscience concerning the child's future destiny. Such an unconscious striving on the patient's part is a milder form of the schizophrenic patient's unconscious determination to live out his life in such a fashion as to give reality to what were in actuality delusions on the part of an ambulatorily schizophrenic mother, whose craziness the patient cannot yet see as having been there.

The point I wish to focus on is the basically healthy unconscious striving to gain a greater sense of immediately felt reality as to what was going on inside the emotionally inaccessible parent many years ago, by unconsciously contriving present-day "interpersonal" situations (no matter how grievous) to yield that discovery.

It is awesome to see to what tenacious lengths some patients will go in this effort. One hebephrenic woman, for example, with whom I worked for seven years, would say at the end of each session some variation of, "Is that all, Doctor?" To this exasperatingly repetitious question I would reply variously, in a more or less guilty and attemptedly gentle, or annoyed, or disgusted, or curt fashion, "There's plenty more; but that's all the time we have for today," or, "Of course that isn't all; but I have to go now," and so on. Surely I made dozens of different brief replies to this question of hers upon my leaving her room where our sessions had to be held by reason of the severity of her schizophrenic symptoms. It was only after several years that I learned that she had been trying, each time, to maneuver me into saying, "That settles it," an expression frequently used by a sister of hers who had been the most healthy and therefore most available-for-identification among the other members of her parental family. I now understood a little better why, as I left the building where she lived, I could so often hear her raging furiously in her room: she never succeeded, in all those hundreds of hours, in impelling me to say, "That settles it," and so to foster the identification she was struggling to attain. This is only one example of the extent to which this woman's life was given over to such game-playing. She had been married for some ten years to a man who did not at all share her love of art, and she once gave me to understand what a memorable triumph it had been to her, evidently quite unbeknownst to him, when she had once succeeded in maneuvering him into bringing up something, interestedly and so far as he knew spontaneously, about art.

The child who in later years is striving unconsciously to experience, at first hand, what mother (or father) used to feel in such and such a situation is trying not only to build more firmly an own self, but is trying also to complement the mother's incomplete self. The father who had said, "Just wait . . . *you'll* know how it feels . . ." does not himself know, at a full feeling level, what it—this immediate situation—feels to him, and is in a sense asking the child to some day discover what his—the father's—inaccessible feelings are. Such a father is being toward his child as a schizophrenic woman used to be toward me. This woman, a hebephrenic woman with whom I worked nearly fifteen years, clearly had enormous difficulty in experiencing feelings and being able to differentiate among them. For years she had unconsciously to deny that she had this problem. Finally, one day, in describing some daily-life situation on the ward, she said, vehemently and in a tone of protest, "How do you think *I* feel?" That cliché seemed intended to make me think she was quite aware of anger; but I felt that she was trying to gloss over, as usual, how unknown to her were her own feelings. I replied, "I guess it *is* hard for you to know how you feel, isn't it, Margaret?" to which she replied thoughtfully and, so I felt, very usefully, "Yes, I guess it is hard for me to know how I feel."

Invariably, when the patient says, "Now I know just how my mother (or father) used to feel!" this is said in such a tone of fulfillment as to make clear that this expressed discovery is so long-sought, so cherished, as to make worthwhile all the years of struggle—in treatment and before— toward it.

Now I shall give a number of examples of patients' autistic modes of experience. One young woman consciously hungered for emotional responses from me, and repeatedly expressed feelings of hurt, anger, dissatisfaction, disappointment, and discouragement at my silence. Yet the nature of the material she presented, despite its being in many regards analytically rich, did not enable me to make transference interpretations. What gradually became apparent to me was that the more the analysis proceeded in a spirit as though she were the only person in it, the more she throve, and that the consciously desired responses from me were unconsciously warded off by her as intrusions upon an experience of herself as an oceanic world-self. A male patient gave a glimpse of this same unconscious wish for the absence of any interpersonal relationship by saying, ". . . the feelings that exist between you and me." It was the tone in which he said this seemingly unremarkable phrase which was so striking: it made clear that he was unconsciously saying, ". . . the unwanted barriers that exist between you and me."

The patient immersed in autism is having so complex an experience that the analyst can be sensed only as an encompassing matrix which must not become separate and add to the already overwhelming complexity. For example, a patient who is experiencing himself as a shifting flux of unrelated somatic sensations, thoughts, mental images, memories, and so on, is in no condition to hear and utilize a verbal interpretation from the analyst. But such a patient may, at the same time, be highly attuned to any sound, any physical movement, from the analyst as a hoped-for beacon in his mystifying world. In this regard, he functions as if the analyst were omnipotent, were the only reality, and comprised the whole world. The patient may experience himself only as an appendage or a reflection of that world, a world from which all initiating of thoughts and feelings must flow. He experiences no feelings or thoughts of his own and mystifiedly scans that analyst-world, in the spirit that if he can discern what it is calling for, *then* he will know how to feel and what to think. All his responsibility for being is attributed to it. One chronically schizophrenic woman, seeing the huge trees outside on the sanitarium grounds waving in the wind, wondered whether my air-conditioner were causing them to move; and whenever she heard a sound from any other part of the building where my office was located, or from far away outside, would immediately ask, "What's that, Dr. Searles?" as if I of course knew instantly—as though I were omniscient, as though my eyes and ears extended everywhere.

A long-hebephrenic woman said, "If people think I'm a prostitute, I'll act like a prostitute," as indeed she did. There was much more than mere spite in this; she was helpless to be anything other than what she felt the world outside her called upon her to be. At another time she said, "People think I'm crazy; so I act crazy."

This same woman once said, of a colleague of mine on the sanitarium staff, to whom she was tenaciously and mindlessly attached for years, "Dr. Edwards sees the world through me." During her upbringing she had seen the world through the eyes of her father until, in her teens, her disillusionment with him had caused her world, and her fragile ego which had been founded and structured upon that world, to fall into pieces.

In the fifth month of my work with another hebephrenic woman she said, in the midst of much of her usual scattered talk, "I feel like a china doll in pieces." She said this with a demeanor and in a tone of helplessness and despair. Then, after approximately three years of therapy, there occurred a session immediately after a visit from her long-idealized father, who visited her every few months, and toward whom she had begun to experience some of the scorn and anger which had underlain her idealization of him. She began saying something of how he had looked and behaved during the visit, then exclaimed, in a tone of amazed discovery, "Why, he is really like a little boy!" and a few minutes later she suddenly seized her forehead, saying in a tone of terror and anguish, "My whole forehead is shattered!" I felt shocked, but understood her communication to spring from a tangibly somatic experiencing, on her part, of the shattering of her idealized picture of her father—of the shattering, that is, of an introjected, idealized image of him, an image which had formed part of her own body-image. In retrospect it seemed quite possible that her having experienced herself as a "china doll in pieces" had been a product, similarly, of her struggle to cope with feelings of disillusionment with some person outside herself, by introjecting that now-shattered image into her own body-image.

Another hebephrenic woman, whose husband failed to fulfill her hopes that he would rescue her from her long hospitalization, but who instead after several years divorced her, came to experience tiny fragments of him as being scattered all over the grounds of the sanitarium. She made relatively casual mention of this experience of hers, which—like all her experiences—she apparently assumed to be obvious to her supposedly omniscient therapist. I found much evidence that this perception was based in part upon her still-unconscious murderousness toward him. But the predominant feeling-tone in her casual remark was memorably poignant: it gave me a momentary glimpse into how deeply unable she felt to cope with her devastating feelings of disillusionment with him and her loss of him. She had to perceive him as vast in extent, something like an invisible covering of snowflakes over everything, and here, rather than—as he actually was—a person far away and in her past.

Autistic patients tend to assume that they have essentially no effect upon the analyst and that any effect they might conceivably have would be a shattering impact upon this world-matrix-analyst. Data from the parental-family relationships show how far from fanciful are such convictions. One schizophrenic woman had lived, as the social worker described it, only as the dim shadow of her mother. For months in my work with her, of the life she had had she could only say, "I went to the corner grocery store." Almost everything she said during her sessions was expressed highly tentatively, in the form of a question directed to me. It seemed clear that any functioning on her own was equivalent to terrifying craziness. Her rigidly controlled and controlling father refused, for a long time, to let her see her mother; he was convinced that were her mother to see her "changed," this would "crush" the mother. Years later, after she had improved very markedly, he confided to me his persisting apprehension lest word of her hospitalization at Chestnut Lodge reach the midwestern university where the patient's brother held a prestigious post. "It would be shattering to Leonard," he said.

A woman in her twenties with a borderline psychotic character structure manifested an almost rocklike resistance to analysis until, after several years, we were able gradually to explore the identification with her schizoid mother which had formed the core of her own subtly autistic mode of functioning in the analysis and elsewhere. She reported now, in exasperation and with desperate intensity, "I have the sudden conviction that for me to grow, I must abolish my mother; but my mother is a thing permeating everything. . . . damnable part of myself; it's like a boulder . . ." During the following day's session she reported in a similar tone, "Whenever I think of my mother I think of just tiny fragments—she's someone I must enclose somehow—she's explosive—she's menacing . . ." For years she had reacted to me in the transference as being such a mother—a dangerous force which she had to control so tightly and unwaveringly that she could scarcely afford the luxury of any emotional spontaneity on her own part, lest I explode. Her so-conflictual views of her mother as being essentially nonhuman, whether in the form of something ineradicably all-permeating, or of a maddeningly unyielding boulder, or of dangerously explosive fragments, are strikingly similar to data conveyed to me by other patients with illnesses of markedly varied degrees of severity.

In my monograph in 1960 I included much data relevant to this present topic, concerning patients' transferences to the analyst as being something nonhuman.[5] Rosenfeld [6] and Little [7] are among the other writers who have reported related clinical phenomena.

As the months and years of the analyst's work with the autistic patient wear on, the analyst is given to feel unneeded, incompetent, useless, callous, and essentially *nonhuman* in relation to his so troubled and beseeching and reproachful, but so persistently autistic, patient. It is essential that the analyst be able to endure this long period—a period in which, despite perhaps abundant data from the patient, transference interpretations are rarely feasible—in order that the patient's transference regression can reach the early level of ego development at which, in the patient's infancy or very early childhood, his potentialities for a healthy mother-infant symbiosis became distorted into a defensively autistic mode of ego-functioning. At that level of ego development, the infant or young child had not yet come to achieve a perceptual and experiential differentiation between him-

[5] H. F. Searles, *The Nonhuman Environment in Normal Development and in Schizophrenia* (New York: International Universities Press, 1960).

[6] H. A. Rosenfeld, *Psychotic States—A Psycho-Analytical Approach* (New York: International Universities Press, 1965).

[7] M. Little, "Transference in Borderline States," *International Journal of Psychoanalysis,* 47 (1966), 476–485.

self and his mother, *nor between his mother and the surrounding nonhu-man world.* When in the evolution of the transference that early level of ego-functioning becomes accessible, then it is possible for therapeutically symbiotic processes to occur between patient and therapist, and be inter-pretable as such. In due course, this phase of therapeutic symbiosis will subsequently usher in the phase of individuation.

Of
Human Bonds
and
Bondage   *David E. Schecter*

One of the core problems faced by humans is the polar tension between the striving toward individuation and the yearning for symbiotic unity with some person, group, or power "outside" of one's self. The universality of this human dilemma is derived, in part, from the biological helplessness of the infant who requires prolonged protection, nourishment, and stimulation for his very survival and development. The particular shape of the symbiotic unit and the qualities of the individuation process are, of course, very much a function of the particular culture and family in which the child develops. The child in India or in some Mediterranean countries experiences a much more prolonged dependency upon and unity with his mother in comparison with the middle-class American child of whom weaning, toilet training, and psychic individuation are expected at a much earlier age. Nevertheless, in all cultures—even those with extended families or clans—varying degrees of psychic individuation are experienced, deriving from maturational forces unfolding within the organism as well as through cultural molding. One way of looking at individual and family development would be as a struggle or conflict to achieve a certain equilibrium between the polar tendencies of individuation and symbiotic fusion.

In 1941, in *Escape from Freedom,*[1] Erich Fromm distinguished two kinds of human bonds: 1) "primary ties," which are "organic in the sense that they are part of normal development" and "exist before the process of individuation";[2] and 2) "secondary bonds," as a "substitute for the pri-

[1] Erich Fromm, *Escape from Freedom* (New York: Rinehart & Co., 1941).
[2] *Ibid.*, p. 25.

mary bonds which have been lost." [3] Fromm described the secondary bonds as mechanisms of escape from the terrible sense of separateness, aloneness, powerlessness, and inferiority stemming from faulty individuation and inadequate forms of subsequent relatedness. He introduced the concept of *symbiosis,* which "means the union of one individual self with another self (or any other power outside the own self) in such a way as to make each lose the integrity of its own self and to make them completely dependent on each other." [4] A new depth of understanding of authoritarianism, sadomasochism, and symbiotic relatedness was brought into focus when these latter three concepts were viewed as being thoroughly interwoven one with the other. The sadistic person was seen to need his object as much as the masochistic one needed his. Both character types—sadistic and masochistic—were seen as essentially authoritarian and failing to stand the "aloneness of one's individual self that leads to the drive to enter into the symbiotic relationship with someone else . . . there is a constant oscillation between the active and passive side of the symbiotic complex . . ." [5] In *The Heart of Man* Fromm takes a more developmental view of symbiosis when he states that it would be misleading to use the concept of "dependency" in speaking of symbiotic attachment since the "dependency" presupposes "the clear distinction of two persons one of whom is dependent on the other." [6]

It is of historic psychoanalytic interest that in 1941 when the Oedipus and castration complex held sway as principal motivational sources of behavior, Fromm had observed that man's fear of separateness was an even more primary source of motivation in his interpersonal behavior. In the ensuing thirty years the research work connected with psychoanalysis and early child development was to go exactly in a similar direction. The work of Spitz,[7] Bowlby,[8] and Mahler,[9] for example, have all emphasized *by direct observation of infants* what Fromm had hypothesized in connection with his psychoanalytic and social-psychological work. In this paper our

[3] *Ibid.,* p. 141.
[4] *Ibid.,* p. 158.
[5] *Ibid.,* p. 158.
[6] Erich Fromm, *The Heart of Man* (New York: Harper & Row, 1964), p. 104.
[7] Rene Spitz, *The First Year of Life: A Psychoanalytic Study of Normal and Deviant Development of Object Relations* (New York: International Universities Press, 1965).
[8] John Bowlby, *Attachment and Loss:* Vol. I, *Attachment* (New York: Basic Books, 1969).
[9] Margaret Mahler in collaboration with Manuel Furer, *On Human Symbiosis and the Vicissitudes of Individuation* (New York: International Universities Press, 1968).

goal is to point to some of the individual developmental precursors to Fromm's concepts concerning man's ultimate dilemma—the fear and the wish to be free—as well as some early observations connected with the "answers" to this dilemma. Three classes of developmental responses or tendency systems—corresponding only roughly to the "mechanisms of escape" and "productive orientation" that Fromm has described as man's means of coping with his ultimate sense of separateness and finitude— could be grouped as follows:

I Attachment, Symbiosis, Relatedness
II Individuation, Detachment, Isolation
III Integration, Reconciliation, Creation

Of these, only the first two groups will be dealt with in this paper. Each class of responses will be seen to have a healthy or pathologic potential, depending upon the developmental context in which they were born and upon the defensive function which they may have to serve in relation to anxiety and stress. Class III refers to the integrations and reconciliations that arise, in part, out of conflicts and tensions engendered by the child's yearnings toward fusion, dependency, and his strivings for personal autonomy—representing his own developmental progression from the relatively global symbiotic stages to the more differentiated stages of individuation which will be considered in this paper. Some of these higher-level integrations include: the increasing working through of ambivalence (the reconciliation of good and bad dissociated personifications); the movement from exclusivity, possessiveness, and control to mutuality in relationships; the development and elaboration of imagination, play, creativity, and a set of ideals—which all function as the means by which new-level integrations can take place. For example, in the movement from simple use of transitional objects to structured dramatic play, the child increasingly can achieve the sense of creating his world, as he is producer, director, and actor in his drama all at the same time.

I   Attachment, Symbiosis, Relatedness

This group of behaviors and attitudes refers to tendencies in which one person finds or puts himself in proximity or in relationship to another person or persons. In his recent theoretical reformulation, Bowlby dispenses with his former theory of "instinctual drives" and replaces this with a more sophisticated ethological model wherein certain behavioral systems become activated *in interaction with the environment* in such a way that proximity to mother becomes a "set-goal." [10] Nevertheless, Bowlby tends to remain behaviorally oriented—underplaying the psychoanalytic aspects of attachment behavior—namely, the *mental representations* or *personifications* of mother by infant and infant by mother, and how these mutually influence one another.

Mahler has most specifically focused on both the pathological and, in her later work, the normal developmental phases of symbiosis and separation-individuation. The mother is seen to function as the "executive ego" for the relatively undifferentiated and helpless ego of the infant within a "dual unity." [11] As the infant's ego and its functions develop in their capacity to differentiate self from other, to reach and later locomote toward a goal and attain the relative autonomy and mastery in a number of other ego functions, the infant is said to "hatch" from the symbiotic membrane and achieve a beginning individuated selfhood. [12]

It is useful in conceptualizing the first human relationship (mother-child) to attempt to go beyond the descriptive behavioral attachment model of Bowlby and the symbiotic model of Mahler to a model of *reciprocal relatedness* that is more fully developmentally interactional. In such a model not only is the infant seen to be going through maturational and developmental changes but mother, and indeed the *whole family* and *cultural* matrix, is seen to have a transactional feedback effect upon the developing infant as well as vice versa. [13] From our own observations of mother-child couples, the *mother* can also be seen as part of the symbiotic unit from which *she* gradually "individuates," partly in reciprocal relation to various developments on the infant's part. For instance, in the third to fourth

[10] Bowlby, *op. cit.,* pp. 179–180.

[11] As with Fromm's and Sullivan's shift from libidinal drive theory to interpersonal relatedness, Mahler's concept of symbiosis is cast largely in social terms, e.g., "The intra-uterine parasite-host relationship . . . must be replaced in the post-natal period by the infant's being enveloped, as it were, in the extra-uterine matrix of the mother's nursing care, a kind of *social symbiosis*" (Margaret Mahler, "On Child Psychosis and Schizophrenia: Autistic and Symbiotic Infantile Psychoses," *The Psychoanalytic Study of the Child,* 7 [1952], 286–305).

[12] Mahler, *On Human Symbiosis and the Vicissitudes of Individuation, op. cit.,* pp. 16–17.

[13] I have elsewhere (David E. Schecter and H. Corman, "Some Developments in Early Parent-Child Interaction" [unpublished paper, 1970]) reported in detail on the very early development of two mother-child couples using this frame of reference, which we can refer to as *family development.* See also the concept of "dialogue" in Rene Spitz, "Life and the Dialogue," in *Counterpoint: Libidinal Object and Subject,* Herbert S. Gaskill (ed.) (New York: International Universities Press, 1963).

months of life, when the infant can grasp and mouth certain objects and thereby entertain himself, mother feels more ready to provide some life space and time between herself and her child. If the mother needs to cling to the symbiotic unit at any stage of early development and is threatened by the infant's newfound capacities to function more independently, she will find ways to obstruct—or at least not facilitate—individuation on the part of the infant. On the other hand, we have also become sensitized to developmental lags and deviations in the infant that necessitate a more prolonged or altered phase of symbiotic relatedness between mother and child. Whereas not too long ago the parent was simplistically seen as the sole culprit in the obstruction of healthy individuation—the primeval prototype being the "schizophrenogenic" mother—we now look for the mutual influences of parental *and* child development on a given outcome of the individuation process. We are also aware of the tremendous burden carried by the parents of the average nuclear family alienated from a meaningful communal matrix. As extended families and their value systems disintegrate, young parents are attempting—with difficulty—to form new extended family surrogates through groups of friends with common ideals—including experimental communes—in which they take care of and teach each others' children. Parents unsupported by traditional frames of orientation connected with child rearing find it an awesome and anxiety-ridden task to bring up their children, and often do so in a spirit of quiet and alienated desperation. The adolescent and young adult uses a variety of "secondary ties" to achieve new levels of symbioticlike forms of relatedness, partly in preparation for the task of parenting a new generation.

In a recent paper, "The Emergence of Human Relatedness," [14] I have attempted to review the literature on the theories of the origins of human attachment and to indicate the many dimensions of experience that contribute to the formation of such attachment. In order to examine the subtle relationship between the concepts of human *bonds* and human *bondage* it will be necessary to summarize in some detail the experiential roots of the first human relationships. The sources of our data derive from the literature of infant research as well as from our own research.[15] In the above-

[14] David E. Schecter, "The Emergence of Human Relatedness." A chapter in a collection of papers commemorating the twenty-fifth anniversary of the William Alanson White Institute (New York: Basic Books, in press).

[15] This project ("Studies in Ego Development") still in progress at the Albert Einstein College of Medicine (New York) was made possible by Grant#HD 01155-01 provided by the National Institute of Child Health and Human Development.

mentioned paper we stated that the roots of the primary social bond could not be reduced to oral drive, to need for contact comfort, tension reduction, nor to the five primary "instinctual responses" (sucking, clinging, following, crying, and smiling) postulated by Bowlby in 1958. Though all of these factors obviously play a significant role, we turned our attention to the experience associated with sensory and social stimulation and *reciprocal interaction*—often playful and not necessarily drive-connected or tension-reducing—as constituting a basis for the development of specific social attachment. The human face when presented in the form of a social approach—with nodding, smiling, and musical vocalizations—is a most potent evocator of the infant's smiling response. Within the facial gestalt the eyes, as well as the mouth, are crucial elements in determining the affective response in the infant.[16] After a certain age a forbidding frown evokes an affect of displeasure in the infant in contrast to his pleasurable response to the adult's smile. This kind of more or less predictable sequence lays the groundwork for certain basic forms of behavior patterns which, in interaction with the infant's constitutionally given temperamental equipment, lead to relatively stable structures of character and personality. We have seen how, through reciprocal playful experience, the infant comes to anticipate and learn that *he can evoke* a social response even when he is not in an uncomfortable need state such as hunger or pain. Correspondingly, as the child develops a sense of *social potency*—that is, a confidence in making an impact on others—he learns that he can effectuate not only relief of tension but positively stimulating and even playful patterns of response in relation to a human partner as well as with objects of various kinds. These two classes of experience—1) effecting a social response that leads to reduction in physiological need tension as against 2) a response associated with reciprocal social stimulation, including play—are important to distinguish from one another, even though they may overlap in actual life experience. Later in life we see character structures and relationships that may correspond in large degree to each class of experience. Examples of the first type of relatedness (tension reduction) would include partnerships that achieve an equilibrium based on the mutual reduction of tensions associated with sex, hunger, psychosomatic suffering, and anxiety. A second class of relatedness would be predominantly associated with the evocation of social response and playfulness and the complex cultural elaborations thereof. We know that *any* class of pleasurable experience, includ-

[16] Spitz, *op. cit.*

ing the primarily social and reciprocal, *can come to be psychologically represented as a need tension.* This is illustrated clearly in the language of children: "I need you to play with me." Hence, the human attachment that is based primarily on social interaction can develop a *quality of habituation* just as the attachment which had been predominantly associated with tension reduction in the original physiological sense. This addictivelike need for a response and the lengths to which the individual will go to bring about a response represent one dimension of the quality of *bondage* in the human bond.[17]

If we take seriously the idea of *habituation* to a social response, we can see how this form of social hunger can constitute the soil of *socialization* and the structuring of various forms of relatedness—including the authoritarian, sadomasochistic, conformist types described by Fromm.[18] Observations of human infants indicate that once a specific preferential attachment is formed to mother—usually between four to seven months— the mother in the ensuing months will become the increasingly preferred and sought-after figure despite the frustrations and punishments the infant may have to undergo in the interim.[19] Out of this selfsame developing achievement during the second year of life—which is psychoanalytically

[17] The dictionary's (*Oxford Universal,* 1955) definitions of the words "bond" and "bondage" overlap to a surprising degree. We refer to a "bond" in the sense of a social and emotional tie or attachment. In the concept of bondage we wish to emphasize the quality of being "tied up," "tied down," or "subjected to some binding power, influence or obligation." Psychologically, bondage is recognized largely by the qualities of compulsion, obligation, subjugation, and ego passivity. When we speak of "a bond" (without bondage), there is still a potential for relative freedom, ego activity, and developmental change within the association.

[18] Bowlby (*op. cit.,* pp. 212–213) reports how isolated puppies who, on social contact with a human experimenter, were physically punished soon ceased to run away from the human—after punishment was stopped—and actually spent more time with him than did control puppies whose approaches after isolation had been rewarded with "petting and kindness." Similar results indicated that lambs, like puppies, will develop attachments in spite of receiving punishing treatment from a companion. Analogously, we know that isolation of men in "reindoctrination centers" produces strong craving for contact, and that men under such stress will become submissive and psychologically malleable in the phenomenon that has been described as "brainwashing."

[19] It is of interest that according to the work of R. Schaffer and P. Emerson ("The Development of Social Attachments in Infancy," *Monograph of Society for Research in Child Development* 29:3 [1964], 1–77) the variables associated with the figures to whom the children become attached were 1) the speed with which a person responded to the infant, and 2) the intensity of the interaction in which the infant was engaged—rather than the maternal caretaking function in the narrow sense of feeding, diapering, etc.

referred to as object constancy—the child becomes capable of experiencing care and concern for another human being which will eventuate in what Fromm has described as mature love.[20] The point we would like to stress is that out of the development of the original forms of symbiotic relatedness can come the most distorted psychotic warps (e.g., symbiotic psychosis), the commonly found varieties and degrees of symbiotic relatedness,[21] or the most mature form of love. The fate of the symbiotic developmental phase depends in large part on the vicissitudes of the individuation process, which we will now consider.

II Individuation, Detachment, Isolation

This class of processes is hardly homogeneous; yet there is in common —unlike the tendency to symbiotic fusion—increasing differentiation and structuralization in the direction of a more delineated sense of self. We include here processes that can lead to a healthy integration as well as those that lead to warps of individuation. There are signs of a dawning sense of self in the first year of life as the infant remembers and anticipates events, and comes to discriminate his mother, himself, and others. As maturation together with environmental facilitation make this possible, the child begins to do for himself what had been done for him: he feeds himself, manipulates objects and toys to produce a certain result, he transports himself —finally in the upright posture—he decides on a course of action, even if this means *negating* or *opposing* those who are closest to him. He even learns a gesture and a word—"No"—to semantically express his autonomous strivings. As Spitz [22] has pointed out, the "No" is, in a basic sense, a first sign of affirmation of the ego as decision maker. And it is through *decision-making, goal-setting,* and *goal mastery* that the sense of self is experienced in its most heightened intensity.

With these exciting achievements (of the latter part of the first year and of the second year of life) come some potentially grievous complications. The very achievement of the sense of self exposes the young child to an awareness of being *observed* and *evaluated,* giving rise to self-consciousness and the potential for *shame* and *doubt.*[23] Fromm's biblical reference to the Fall of Man illustrates some of the problems of this developmental

[20] Erich Fromm, *The Art of Loving* (New York: Harper and Bros., 1956), pp. 108–129.
[21] These are described in some detail in Fromm's *Heart of Man, op. cit.,* in the chapter on incestuous ties, pp. 95–113.
[22] Rene Spitz, *No and Yes* (New York: International Universities Press, 1957), p. 129.
[23] Eric Erikson, "Identity and the Life Cycle," *Psychological Issues* 1:1 (1959), 65–68.

stage. As man eats from the Tree of Knowledge (self-awareness), he finds himself separated from Nature (including mother) and is *ashamed*. At this point the child—as well as God's first children—begins to *cover up* in self-awareness and manipulate his *social presentation*.[24] He gradually becomes all too conscious that a socially disapproved act will bring a disapproving frown—or more subtly, but not less potently—a withdrawal of maternal behaviors which reduce anxiety or induce security. A striking example of the myriad of ways in which a mother can reduce her child's anxiety is the way she will mediate his fear of a strange person, stimulus, or strange environment. Her "magic blessing"—for example, her vocalization or touch in relation to the strange object—will render it "detoxified" for the child and he will feel free to relate to it and explore it.

Mother, or her surrogate, is also a *home base* from which sanctuary the child can make forays into the novel and strange and return when he needs reassurance or what Mahler and Furer[25] have referred to as "emotional re-fuelling." This model of the toddler using mother as home base from which to explore on his own is analogous, and no doubt related, to intrapsychic processes that occur at the same time. There is a parallel oscillation from psychic states of symbiotic fusion to states of increased boundedness of self. Children show these variations from states of fatigue, illness, or fright to states in which they are autonomously goal-directed, for instance, when involved in some challenging task. As adults we also experience a spectrum in the degree of self-boundedness: The "oceanic feeling," the orgiastic state, the mystical, communal, or drug experience for some individuals represent a relative blurring or loss of self-boundary while other states including intense concentration, loneliness, fears of separation or death may be associated with a sense of a relatively impermeable boundary of self.

We know how important it is for the nursery school child to periodically "rest" from his most individuated level of functioning required of him at school. This "rest" may include the use of a transitional object,[26] and play or fantasy during which he may experience a symbolic fusion or closeness with mother for short periods. *The relative freedom to oscillate*

[24] See later developments of these trends in E. Goffman's *The Presentation of Self in Everyday Life* (Garden City, N.Y.: Doubleday Anchor Books, 1959), in Jung's concept of "persona," and Winnicott's "false self."

[25] Mahler, *On Human Symbiosis and the Vicissitudes of Individuation, op. cit.*

[26] D. W. Winnicott, "Transitional Objects and Transitional Phenomena," *International Journal of Psycho-Analysis*, 34 (1953), 1–9. Reprinted in *Collected Papers* by D. W. Winnicott (London: Tavistock Publications, 1958).

between symbiotic and individuated forms of relatedness cannot be over-stressed in importance at any stage of development.[27] It is easier to enunciate this statement as a principle than it is to offer as a developmental prescription, since the issues involved are so complex. A sensitive parent and educator intuitively grasp the need for such flux in ego states. The freedom of oscillation—within realistic bounds—affords the possibility of a natural rather than a forced equilibrium to be reached by the ego in the polarity of its strivings toward fusion on the one hand and individuation and separateness on the other.

In all psychological theoretical developments a danger is to make out of the latest discovery an ultimate value or ideal. This, I believe, had happened some years ago with the concept of ego autonomy with which the height of individual human development came to be associated.[28] In recent years a counterreaction set in, with increased interest in various social groups in the mystical and quasi-mystical, in boundary-melting drugs, and in beguiling writings of such authors as Norman O. Brown for whom the true corporeal body is seen as humanity, whereas the individual ego is devalued as a culturally induced persona.[29] The question for us in human development is always one of balance, of equilibrium rather than of achieving idealized end points. Only after a self has an *individuated center* can it voluntarily give up its boundaries (as in the orgiastic love or mystical experience) without loss of integrity.[30] Hence the danger of drugs in the

[27] This fluidity overlaps but is by no means identical with the mental processes described by Freud as "primary" (wish) and "secondary" (reality-bound, logical).

[28] Rapaport has developed the notion of ego autonomy (David Rapaport, "The Theory of Ego Autonomy: A Generalization," in *The Collected Papers of David Rapaport*, Merton M. Gill [ed.], [New York: Basic Books, 1967], pp. 722–745) and the concepts of ego activity vs. passivity (David Rapaport, "Some Metapsychological Considerations Concerning Activity and Passivity," in *The Collected Papers of David Rapaport*, Merton M. Gill [ed.], [New York: Basic Books, 1967], pp. 530–569) in a most clarifying way. It is of interest to the history of psychoanalytic theory that Rappaport—an outstanding scholar in metapsychology—enthusiastically acknowledged Fromm's contributions to the understanding of individuation and of ego activity and passivity as "growing points" in psychoanalytic developments (Rapaport's lectures on "The Points of View of Metapsychology," given at the William Alanson White Institute of Psychiatry and Psychoanalysis, May 22–23, 1959). Nevertheless, except for passing superficial reference (e.g., *The Collected Papers of David Rapaport, op. cit.*, p. 921), nowhere in Rapaport's voluminous written works is Fromm's contribution to the above-mentioned issues properly acknowledged. For Fromm's specific written references to this subject see Addendum at the end of this paper.

[29] Norman O. Brown, *Love's Body* (New York: Random House, 1966).

[30] D. T. Suzuki has stressed that the Zen Satori experience—in which the individual experiences himself at one with Nature—comes after a gradual developmental

still developing adolescent whose sense of identity and its boundedn ss is already tenuous enough.

In the psychoanalytic experience with a particular individual, one of our tasks is to discover the imbalances or conflict-ridden forces of the fusion-individuation polarity. We can learn about these personality conflicts by coming back to early development. When a child is secure in feeling that he has a "home-base mother" to whom he may return, he will actively initiate ventures into strange territory without evidence of anxiety when he returns.[31] However, when he is *passively left* by mother, especially after seven months of age, he experiences anxiety, will protest actively and try to follow mother. This intense attachment only gradually abates in the third year through the rest of childhood and is loosened significantly during adolescence in many cultures, although the attachment to mother persists in some form throughout life.[32]

The child's vigilance in avoiding or undoing potential separation is another instance in which the originally "innocent" tie to another human (the mother) will come to be internalized as a feeling of entrapment or of being "possessed."

In this regard we wish to deal principally with one set of reactions, namely with the development of *defenses against* these *feelings of bondage* that are associated with the fear of abandonment. Bowlby [33] has described "normal" children (ages one to three) who when left in the hospital, without mother, went through reactions which could be described in three stages:

1   Protest—loud crying, rejection of alternative figures, with apparent expectation that mother would return.

2   Despair—with behavior suggesting increasing hopelessness and deep mourning (for instance withdrawal, inactivity, lack of demands).

3   Detachment—a recovery of interest in surroundings, acceptance of surrogates' care and food, but when mother visits there is a "striking absence of the behavior characteristic of the strong attachment normal at this age." The child will in time *"commit himself less and less to succeeding*

---

achievement, including ego-boundedness. Moreover, he stressed that Satori was a peak experience which one could not expect to maintain, living as we must for the most part in the plateaus of life. (Personal communication, 1957.)

[31] See Rheingold's interesting experiments in this regard. (Harriet L. Rheingold and Carol O. Eckerman, "The Infant Separates Himself from His Mother," *Science* 168:3927 [1970], 78–83.)

[32] Bowlby, *op. cit.*

[33] *Ibid.*, pp. 26–28.

figures," [34] become increasingly self-centered, more "preoccupied with material things such as sweets, toys, food."

Aside from the different variables involved in these situations, it would seem that the separation from mother was the crucial one in the above sequence of reactions.

Tennes and Lampl [35] have recently reported significant findings—largely confirmatory of naturalistic observations—in "normal" infants who were experimentally separated from their mothers for brief periods at bimonthly intervals between six and thirty-six months. The authors describe a number of classes of reactions which they consider to be defenses against separation anxiety—*reactions which may indeed represent prototypic precursors for major human defensive systems throughout life.*

1   After mother left the experimental room and the infants cried they would be held by the caretaker. The infants for the most part *visually avoided* the strange caretaker but on a number of occasions completely relaxed in a regressivelike posture which the authors interpreted as an *attempt at kinesthetic restitution* of the missing object.

Whatever interpretation we give this behavior, it is similar to that in which the infant is found in a highly relaxed or feeding state in the presence of his actual mother. When the baby looks at the strange researcher, discovering that she is "not-mother," he bursts into tears again.

2   A second category of response to the missing mother is one we commonly see—the *active attempt at mastery* through locomotor following in order to regain the missing mother. Thus, once the infant could walk he tried to find his mother, and if he was not thwarted from reunion with her the regressive reactions described above were not seen.[36]

3   When the infants' attempts to pursue mother were blocked by a closed door, some reacted with rage, stamping their feet, hitting, or screaming. After these outbursts some reactions were marked by *inhibition of activity,* including the bowed sad postures seen in Kaufman and Rosenblum's [37] infant monkeys who had been separated from their mothers.

[34] Italics mine.
[35] Katherine H. Tennes and E. Esther Lampl, "Defensive Reactions to Infantile Separation Anxiety," *Journal of the American Psychoanalytic Association,* 17:4 (1969), 1142–1162.
[36] Much of the psychopathology we clinically see later represents the psychological detours that have been patterned by a self that has come to feel anxious, weak, or obstructed in the achievement of its goals.
[37] L. Rosenblum and I. Kaufman, "The Reaction to Separation in Infant Monkeys: Anaclitic Depression and Conservation-Withdrawal," *Psychosomatic Medicine,* 29 (1967), 648–675.

Both Tennes and Lampl's and Kaufman's interpretations of these inhibitory responses concern aggression: in the former case the inhibition was seen as a reaction to the infant's own aggressive impulses; in the latter instance as a means of reducing provocation of aggression from the remaining adults and as a way of eliciting comforting responses. Although these explanations at some point in development are no doubt quite relevant, the experience of *futility* (loss of hope) and helplessness postulated by Tennes and Lampl seems more fundamental to the infants' observable expressions of sadness and sobbing—as well as the *inhibition* of activity—all of which affects appear quite distinct phenomenologically from anxiety and distress or from anger and rage. Thus, with the thwarting of the infant's central goal and purpose we find infantile aggression and the precursors of a depressive type of reaction—a hypothesis Fromm and others have put forth in contrast to the theory of a primary aggressive drive as the major source of man's destructive or depressive behavior.[38]

Bowlby's, and Tennes and Lampl's work is reviewed in some detail because of the enormous implication their observations may have for *character development*. Both groups of observations derive essentially from *physical separation* of the normal child from his mother. In the latter part of the first year of life—and increasingly so as the child grows older—he begins to *anticipate* that mother can leave him, that he potentially can be abandoned, especially if he is *bad* or has a *bad-mother,* as he comes to represent, in part, himself and his mother. Now physical separations are no longer necessary to bring on the dread of abandonment; "symbolic separations" will be sufficient. Such separations—as with physical separation —are part of life, but are heightened when the child has failed to properly internalize a *good relatedness* between himself and his significant figures. This memory bank of good experience can be drawn upon when he is actually alone or feels cut off for various reasons, as when mother is anxiously disapproving, forbidding, or *psychologically turning away* from him —acting "dead"—by becoming unresponsive or, in various ways, not the "familiar-mother-that-makes-me-feel-good." Under these conditions we see there are a variety of coping mechanisms that the child may turn to, including regression and *detachment with an implicit loss of hope of good*

[38] *The development of futility as a chronic underlying life affect* has obvious importance in our times when depressive and violent modes of expression seem to be the principal challenge our society faces. For a penetrating analysis of hope and hopelessness see Fromm's *The Revolution of Hope* (New York: Harper & Row, 1968) and, from a different point of view, E. Stotland's *The Psychology of Hope* (San Francisco: Jossey-Bass, 1969).

reunion. It is through the mode of detachment that the child protects himself, so to speak, by sealing off his boundaries and preventing interpersonal affective exchange. He may give appearances of independence, of *actual precocious individuation* and self-reliance, but all this is at the price of his hope for the return to real commitment to human relatedness, as described by Bowlby in his stages of Despair and Detachment. There now develops a greater interest in what objects people may bring than in the persons themselves. The children become, so to speak, "consumer-minded" and learn to market their charm for particular rewards. (In some families such behavior is not the result only of deprivation of reciprocal relatedness but is actually taught and fostered as a dominant mode of interpersonal relatedness.) The character outcome described here involves repression, isolation, and splitting off of warm joyful affects connected with reciprocal relatedness. In the extreme of pathology we see autisticlike defenses in persons who are diagnosed as autistic or schizoid isolates. More frequently, as Fromm has described, the relatively "detached character" is considered "normal" and fits rather well with Fromm's description of "automaton conformity," seen, for example, in what used to be referred to as the "organization man."

There are also potentially *healthy* aspects to defenses involving detachment. With the traumata of necessary separations detachment may be a useful adaptive mechanism, if it does not become chronic and part of the core character structure. Moreover, with certain types of parents and teachers children need defenses against symbioticlike or intrusive emotional encroachments. A detached attitude would seem to be a necessary defense at various points in development to maintain one's individual and creative integrity.[39]

[39] Maurice Sendak, in his delightful little book for children—*Pierre* (New York: Harper & Row, 1962) "who didn't care"—graphically reveals how a child's defensive detachment can develop into an attitude toward life in general—as a fear to invest care or interest in anyone or anything, in part as a protection against its potential loss. Many children and adults fully recognize Pierre's poignant dilemma when he is caught in his own defiant disdain for care or attachment. *The child and adult can thus be as much bound down by their defenses against attachment as by the various forms of symbiotic attachment.*

It is interesting that H. S. Sullivan described the very young infant's reaction of *somnolent detachment* and *apathy* when he is overstimulated by excessive anxiety or tensions from other sources. There would thus seem to be a red-thread of continuity —albeit on different levels of complexity—between reactions of detachment from infancy through childhood to adulthood. During adolescence, keeping "cool"—or even isolated—can have a usefully temporary adaptive significance in the search for identity, or, on the other hand, represent a premature closure of development in the

A brief comment on the resolution of separation anxiety: Most inter-estingly, in the Book of Genesis there is an injunction which states, "Thou shalt leave thy father and mother and cleave [40] unto thy wife." This com-mandment comes from God (the "parental" creator of man) and signifies the permission, encouragement, and necessity of separating from the sym-biotic matrix. At the same time, man is not cast into loneliness; he is given a direction of reaffiliation with someone outside his own family. In-deed this biblical reference parallels what we see in child and adolescent development.

As the child develops positive identifications with various loving, pro-tective, and facilitating parental functions he becomes more equipped to stand on his own and able to take care of himself and others (interdepend-ency). In fortunate developmental circumstances there occurs an ever-wid-ening spread of trustworthy persons from mother, father, siblings to one's group of peers and hopefully to increasing varieties of human brothers and sisters, including those who are at first defined as "strangers." [41] These de-velopments become closely intertwined with the resolution of Oedipal tri-angular jealousies one of whose root problems is the failure in overcoming the exclusive symbiotic and postsymbiotic attachments through adequate individuation and capacity for sharing. There is more likelihood of achiev-ing a capacity to share the less we are reared on the economic and psycho-logic principles of scarcity (K. Marx).

Whatever we find out about the needs and nutrients for healthy human growth and development—and for prevention of emotional and mental suffering and constriction—becomes potentially a force for social change. True, matters are much more complex than delivering psychic vitamin drops in the proper dosage at the proper time. [42]

The writings and teachings of Erich Fromm have made a lasting im-

---

form of a detached identity. Among adults I believe it is this class of entrenched character defenses that accounts for Fromm's observation that most of our citizens are "half-asleep" (somnolent) and alienated from their potential feeling life. How-ever, even adults need to protect their integrity at times by mechanisms of detach-ment and isolation.

[40] The word "cleave," interestingly enough, has a double lexical meaning, expressing the two polar tendencies with which we have been concerned: (1) "to stick fast, ad-here"; (2) "to separate, split, or cut asunder."

[41] Fromm's emphasis on the love of the stranger as a condition for the achievement of mature love is most relevant in this developmental sequence (Fromm, *The Art of Loving, op. cit.,* p. 129).

[42] On the other hand, on a more modest level, the work of pioneers such as Spitz and Bowlby on institutionalized and hospitalized children has already made a signif-icant impact on the structure of the institutions involved with crucial phases of the child's development.

pact on and inspired at least two generations of thinking people of various professions, revealing, in a radical way, the underpinnings of our social and psychic functioning, and offering new directions and hope for their healthy development.

ADDENDUM

There is in Fromm's writings a red thread of concern with the concepts of *activity* and *passivity* in the sense that ego psychology has recently referred to as ego activity and passivity. Thus, Fromm points out in *Man for Himself* (p. 85), that activity or "productiveness" is best defined *in relation to* "the underlying psychic conditions governing the activities." Fromm's polarity of activity-passivity is variously defined as:

1   Nonproductive or submissive activity in the *interpersonal* sense of man's submission to an *external* authority, as in the hypnotic state.

2   Submission to *internal* authority, as with an overbearing sense of duty.

3   "Automaton activity" in which the activity depends on the submission by *conformity* to an "anonymous authority" related to the broader patterns of culture such as public opinion, convention, etc.

In these three examples we see, in effect, definitions of what corresponds structurally to *ego passivity*.

Fromm sees the passions as the most powerful source of activity (*Man for Himself,* p. 87), but in several instances he clearly relates "productive activity" to:

1   Active independent *control* as against compulsive effort (*Escape from Freedom,* p. 92).

2   *Transcendence* (*Escape from Freedom,* p. 33), which implies an organization of activity into "higher" levels of integrative functioning. Man "changes his role toward nature from that of purely passive adaptation to an active one: he produces."

Both (1) and (2) would be examples in which ego functions would be exercised in an "active" sense. Fromm is constantly alert to the temptation to equate submission with adaptation—a temptation which is not infrequently indulged in in the field of psychology.

In a recent book, *Revolution of Hope* (p. 12), Fromm makes clear by his adoption of the word "activeness"—as against overt activity—that he is referring to what we may call an ego "quality" rather than to a mere display of active motion in the lexical sense of the term.

The
Machismo
Solution   *Aniceto Aramoni*

Machismo—from the word "macho" (male)—is a way of being, a particular cultural solution to the existential problems of living, that can be considered positive or negative depending on one's viewpoint. It refers to exaggerated masculine characteristics ranging from male genital prowess and a particular type of valor, to a special way of resolving human controversies through demonstrating towering pride and fearlessness; it also expresses a specific counterphobic attitude toward women, and the anxieties of life and death.

From the outsider's perspective, machismo represents an essentially pointless and destructive struggle on the part of the man to overcome the humiliating feeling of being like an ineffectual little boy, especially in his mother's eyes. It is an ill-fated drama wherein the man, painfully attached to mother, sisters, and the Virgin, seeks their exclusive admiration and worship.

Overcompensating for his acute inner feelings of inadequacy and guilt, the machista struts through life giving and seeking challenges answerable in blood. Yet there is a positive striving in this absurd struggle which, in its own special way, epitomizes the fundamental problem of any person who is trying to emerge from a profound symbiosis; that is, the machista is impelled to deny his own weakness, extreme dependency, and a regressive undertow, and he attempts this through dominating others.

In other words, machismo is a uniquely Mexican answer—albeit a disturbed one—to the universal quest for individuation, dignity, and relatedness. There are many different ways for a person to come to terms with an entrenched sense of fear and inadequacy. The machismo response is not to yield to it, not to surrender to depression and apathy, but to go to the opposite extreme: to transcend the universally unbearable fear of aloneness and weakness through acting bigger, stronger, more gloriously.

As Erich Fromm described so well in *Escape from Freedom,* the need to dominate another person (the essence of sadism) is a false solution that arises in the absence of active relatedness and mutual affirmation. Thus, overwhelmed by doubts as to the meaning of his life, the nature of his identity, and his effectiveness as a man, the machista—in Fromm's terms —seeks security in the overpowering and enslavement of others.

In this paper I want to show how this state of affairs shapes character in certain parts of Mexico, where and when the machista is facing another man. As I shall discuss below, this is based partly on an attitude of submission by the machista toward his own mother.

It is said that during some of the early battles in the Mexican Revolution, certain peasants attempted to muffle the sound of the cannon by covering the mouths of the cannon with their hats. Those who survived stopped doing it.

Analogously, some Mexicans have tried to mitigate problems stemming from male-female relationships, by means of violent and absurd behavior—by means of "machismo," but with the difference that they still continue to do so.

It is an intelligent principle not to place a person in the position of being unable to find any way out during a dispute. It generates hate and resentment in the other, and the wish to take revenge.

One day God told Davan, a peasant who lived across the river from Yavan, whom he cordially hated and who hated him in return, "Ask of me anything you wish, I am willing to grant you any request, whatever it may be, with only one condition: remember that I shall give Yavan double of whatever I give you. Tell me, what do you ask of me?"

Davan removed his hat, slowly scratched his head, turned toward God and said: "Tear out one of my eyes!"

Something similar happens between man and woman in machista behavior. She wreaks vengeance by taking half the suffering on herself, in order to leave a double amount to her lord and master. As she annuls herself, she becomes an absolutely passive being, whom the great man must then drag along, while she clings to his shoulder and lets her feet hang.

He on his part is so focused on revenge, unconsciously or consciously, that he makes impossible the alternatives of understanding and happiness.

Treating the woman like a thing, the machista man tries to make her feel inferior and good for nothing unless it is related to serving the master, in bed and out. And, like the feudal lord, he obtains: a docile woman but resentful; submissive but passively resistant, or actively negativistic. She will react by taking possession of the children and exerting a powerful influence over them. She will also have her lord defend her, and perhaps meet his death in his struggle against other men in order to keep face in front of her.

It would be interesting to consider a continuum: At one end is the extreme machista attitude; at the other, the society of "Amazons" whose customs resemble those of machistas, except in reverse, with the man being dominated. Unfortunately, the "Amazons" are either a legend, or stemmed from an historical cultural condition that was transcended thousands of years ago, while machismo currently exists and even receives praise within a certain social stratum, even though it produces destructiveness and a high rate of homicide.

Of course machismo is not a typical trait of the Mexican. But within a certain social class with specific economic characteristics and a certain family constellation, the machista reaction is not rare. Actually, many factors make up a symptomatic complex like machismo and all these variables must be understood to account for something so confused and apparently so irrational.

In saying this I am including the intervention of all sorts of factors, from climate to food, as well as atavism, tradition, and destitution. One must consider subtle psychological aspects related to education, the structure of the family, and the hierarchies within the social group—not to mention frustration, violence, exhibitionism, a promiscuous environment, and vital scarcities in every area. Also involved are the lack of respect for human life, the type of religion as applied to the concept of life and death; the forms of government and political action; feelings of manipulation, impotence and despair; laxity, and the monstrous socioeconomic problems that seem insurmountable; destructiveness in word and action, accompanied by the high rate of homicide, criminality, and alcoholism. To understand machismo one must also know the common amusements, the games and interests of children, the stories listened to during childhood, and the type of father and mother within the family nucleus.

Clearly it is very difficult to find the main effective causes. Perhaps one might proceed by way of establishing certain reliable statements related to the individual personality and social character of those who suffer from machismo.

Perhaps the most expressive media for transmitting the characteristics of machismo are rural Mexican songs. These contain qualities that are unique, and unlike songs from other parts. Therefore, it seems useful to quote some representative passages:

I am a Mexican and proud of it
from birth I have scorned life and death
and if I utter bravados, so do I uphold them.
I am Mexican, and it is my good fortune
that life has so willed that in every place
I am recognized for my bravery.

It matters nothing to find death
by the window of a thankless woman
or to carry in your conscience
one more burden due to killing.
In search of their kisses go their men
without fear of the fight
between bloody scrapes
and gashes of a dagger.

I was one of the
"golden ones" of Villa
of those who have
no love for life
of those who going to war
carry with us our women
loving and singing
I'm a member of that band.

I come in search of an ingrate
a conceited young girl
she ran away with my love,
I desire now to find her
to teach her that a man
cannot be scoffed by a woman.

She left me suddenly
giving reason to the people
idly to gossip
but let's see now when I find her
and we meet face to face
what she will then say to me.

It is not difficult to formulate some conclusions from these texts; certain refrains occur persistently to constitute the leitmotiv of machismo.

The machista wants a woman for his personal use, in a wholly disrespectful way. He makes the choice; she must guard against mistakes, and certainly not decide between two men. Even if she likes someone who cares for her and desires her, *she* must not choose; neither may she reject or scorn, because the consequences may be terrible. For the mere rejection of a dance, the macho is fully justified in shooting the woman. For a man to show interest in a woman whom another has noticed first is to gamble with his life.

The woman, like a toy in a shop window, can be selected and relinquished without any participation on her part. But tragically, as soon as she is possessed she loses all, or almost all, the interest she held for the wild and petulant macho, who regarded her mainly as an object of conquest. Nevertheless, he is capable of fighting to the death with another man over her! Both men act as though the woman were an element that produces a form of hyperesthesia, thus constituting a reason for machismo.

In actual fact the woman is a trophy in an arena disputed by men. It is reminiscent of knighthood, with its tournaments, except that the woman then was courted as a lady, and winning her was a supreme joy. Among machos things are different: The woman is a prize in a competitive struggle; but as a person, she matters little.

Significantly, three types of women are spared this depreciating and humiliating attitude: the sister, the mother, and the Virgin. Two of them are close, kindred beings; the third is close for another reason. All three are above contempt, not to be subjugated. It is not permitted to insult them under any condition. With women linked to them by blood ties, the machistas adopt a different attitude—one which they also demand from strangers who must beware of provoking their women.

It is paradoxical and absurd that the same individuals who demand respect for their sisters and mothers show none for the sisters and mothers of others whom they insult, seduce, and abandon. All agree, however, about the Virgin; she is idolized, the quintessence of a sublimated and all-powerful mother.

As I have described, machismo is an attitude toward existence; it reflects the way a special type of man responds to conditions of life which cast major doubts on his security. The response is usually stereotyped; it tends to be automatic and predictable because what matters most to the machista individual is achieving a compensatory narcissism based on a sense of manliness in terms of genital functioning.

Although the machismo attitude functions among men, the justification for it, one might say, is the woman; it is a matter, therefore, of a closely linked triangle. Machismo represents a kind of a solution to life which occurs in an underdeveloped country of Latin America, one that is "so far from God and so close to the United States," rather nationalistic, and with a homicide rate that occupied first place in the world for many years and still remains among the highest five. It is the country where man-woman difficulties have been resolved in the most efficient form, with absolute domination by the masculine sex.

Maintaining a situation of slavery and surveillance that does not permit the least expression of hostility or rebellion, he has so defeated her in the tournament of sex that she accepts his "use" of her during the sexual act. In this environment of domination and patriarchal unbalance the best portion is for the man and he demands of the woman chastity and virginity.

In this war the man apparently defeats all women, in front of whom he exhibits an extraordinary ferocity; all banners and booty are used by him as an offering to be placed on two different dates at the feet of the same person attired in different garments: on the Day of the Virgin of Guadalupe, December 12, and on Mother's Day, May 10, thus making her a participant in his overwhelming triumph.

Paradoxically, he has defeated the woman in bed and perhaps in the home itself, but when proceeding to enjoy his triumph it is the general of the opposing army, in her two manifestations, who takes possession of the spoils: the *Virgin* and the *Mother,* who in their turn defeat the God-man-father and son.

As if it were a make-believe war, he wins all the battles, and in the end surrenders to the opposing leader. Such behavior offers a solution, but one full of absurdities. Ostensibly the opponent to be defeated is the woman, but on looking closely, only occasionally is the woman destroyed; more frequently, one man attacks another who should be considered a member of one's own army.

This alienated behavior mixed with a treacherous attitude has no simple explanation. If a warrior, during a battle, were to hurl himself against the soldiers of his own army he might be examined by a psychiatrist, or be considered a traitor.

No such thing happens with the machista.

This situation would be paradoxical, unless one knows that what matters is to acquit oneself well before the hidden commanding general: Virgin-Mother. Once this is understood, the attitude becomes plausible: It is a war in appearance only, dominion in appearance only; the war is really an operetta with traces of a melodrama, although unfortunately it frequently ends in tragedy and death.

In other words, this tragic comedy of errors makes sense if we assume that it is the goal of life to prove to the mother that one is a man. To achieve this, it has become necessary to dominate the woman and conquer another man in taking her away from him, destroying the rival. This shows one's mother—before whom one feels like an impotent child—that one is a man who can go to bed with many women; that is, one informs the mother about them, like a notorious seducer. The hope is that one's mother will acknowledge the fact, and finally bestow the accolade of manhood.

It is with a primitive and archaic attitude that the male relates manliness to the domination of woman, to hypersexuality, to enormous genitals, and to the defeat of another man equal or similar to himself. It is, then, a war *sui generis:* one man against another man, over a booty neither cares about deeply. This war, as though it were the "flowery war" of the Aztecs, is performed in a ritualistic and stereotyped way.

Furthermore, there is reason to assume that the woman who is apparently loved is unconsciously hated and feared. This is why she must be disarmed and subdued, until she is made impotent and harmless. But then the woman, subjugated and regarded as an object, resorts to her children to justify her existence, reflecting in her relationships to them all her hopes and frustrations, her hatred and vindictiveness.

By means of overt seduction, or even without it, she manages to become the most important woman in her son's life; all the others, outsiders, will appear as usurpers. Frequently, the son, encouraged by her, will adopt the position of surrogate husband and savior, showing loyalty and devotion. He will try to fulfill the hopes that the inadequate father was unable to achieve, sometimes remaining a bachelor as long as his mother is alive.

The son, then, belongs to the faction of the mother and women, to the feminine world; his role is to betray the father, the masculine faction and, it goes without saying, himself as a person.

One might imagine that the son would leave his mother, and try to become an adult. He is held back, however, by powerful guilt feelings and by a sense of inferiority, as well as by the anxiety evolved by these reactions. He is also undermined by guilt over the abandonment of his father and the surrender of his own masculinity. Other barriers are a religion which demands reverence for parents, and cultural elements that reward loyalty to parents and also punish its absence with ostracism. Hence the cycle is perpetuated.

In summary, machismo is a reaction and a paradoxical behavior in which the attempt is being made not only to show manliness, but hypertrophied manliness to prove oneself "very much a man," or "very macho." Grammatically, though, the word "man" cannot be qualified in a comparative and superlative manner: man, more man, most man. The optimum quality has to do here with the attributes of man which must mature until they reach, simply, the category "man," which is sufficient, even though, if the truth be said, not often achieved.

II *Philosophy and Science*

On the
Human
Condition *

George Wald

Genesis 3:22–23: "And the Lord God said, Behold the man has become as one of us, to know good and evil: and now, lest he put forth his hand and take also of the Tree of Life and eat, and live forever: therefore the Lord God sent him forth from the Garden of Eden, to till the ground from whence he was taken."

What most distinguishes man from other living creatures is the capacity to know, that is the basis of his science, and to create, that is the foundation of his art. In all other things he is an animal like any other—if you like, a social animal like any other. In these things he is unique: he is the knowing and creating animal—*Homo sapiens* and *faciens*.

These noble proclivities rest in part upon a substrate of mere anatomy. The great Canadian neurosurgeon Wilder Penfield, exploring the areas of the human brain concerned with sensations from various parts of the body and bodily motions, found an altogether exaggerated representation in the cerebral cortex of two organs: the hands and the mouth. The image of man that is projected upon his brain is distorted in this way: it has huge hands and a huge mouth. For man is also the handling and the talking animal; and these uniquely human attributes have much to do with his knowing and creating.

The human hand with its five fingers is a very general vertebrate character; but in man one of those fingers, the thumb, is joined so as to meet the others; and that opposable thumb, that permits precise manipulation, is one of the ultimate sources of his technology and his art.

* Every weekday morning a fifteen-minute service that includes a six-minute sermon is held in the Harvard Chapel. In the past few years I have given several such sermons, and have written this paper in that format. I have nothing to do with the rest of the service, but I like to do the sermon, since it lets me say things for which there is no place in my teaching, and makes me say them in six minutes—an almost biblical degree of constraint.

Also that human mouth can form words. Those words, spoken from man to man and eventually written down, introduced a new mode of inheritance into the evolution of living things—cultural inheritance; so that each generation of men need not begin anew, but might go on from where earlier generations had left off.

In *Murder in the Cathedral,* T. S. Eliot has Thomas Becket speak of "the greatest treason: To do the right deed for the wrong reason."

Animals for the most part do the right deeds, because they must to have survived, because they are made that way. They act ceaselessly, but in silence. They offer us no reasons.

It is only man who accompanies every action with an explanation. He is forever talking, telling all who will listen just why he is doing whatever he does. It is plain enough that frequently the reasons he gives are improvisations, altogether suspect; but real or illusory, there are always his reasons.

Once I heard Niels Bohr put the matter supremely well. He was speaking of the eel migrations. All the eels off the shores of the Atlantic, European and American, migrate at sexual maturity to the depths of the Sargasso Sea, there to spawn and die. The little larval eels make their way back alone. It takes them a long time, but eventually they arrive. The American larvae come back to the American shores, whereas the European larvae, which are of another species, go on eventually to reach Europe. So far as we know, they never get mixed up. Bohr said these for me unforgettable words: "It is just because they do not know where they are going that they always do it perfectly."

It is only we, who to a degree know and decide where we are going, who have lost thereby the assurance that we will do it perfectly. We have it in us, not only to do the right deed for the wrong reason, but the wrong deed for whatever reason. We have ceased to be the automatic creatures of nonhuman nature, and nature has to this degree ceased to take care of us. We have lost the safeguards of instinctual life—have been expelled from the Garden—and must fend for ourselves. We have our destiny somewhat within our own hands; and as God says in the story, that makes us one with the gods. It is the measure of our freedom: to choose where we are going, for good or evil.

Dynamism in Neuroscience*

Francis Otto Schmitt

The brain and its properties are perhaps best characterized as *dynamic,* but only in recent years have we been shown how ceaselessly active the brain really is. From their diagnostic and clinical studies, psychologists and psychiatrists have long been aware of this ongoing dynamic aspect of behavior and its conscious and unconscious substrates, but the biophysical and biochemical dynamism of brain cells and of the brain as a whole is an exciting discovery in neuroscience. Stimulus-response, reflexological research strategies and concepts—i.e., that the brain reacts only when acted on—missed essential aspects of brain dynamics. New approaches in neuroscience, based on principles of dynamic integration of brain activity at all levels—from molecules and cells, through brain circuits and behavior —have given us invaluable new insights into brain and behavior.

For this essay, I have chosen a few illustrations, at each level of organization, to depict some of the dynamic aspects of the functions concerned. Quite possibly, discoveries to be made in the near future make even the present description seem almost static.

Neuroscience may be thought of as the most central of all the sciences in its interest to man. This is because, if he were able to understand learning, memory, thinking, and emotion, to mention but a few mental processes, we should be in a position not only to improve our methods of alleviating functional and organic ills, but even to revolutionize science itself and thereby to improve man's interaction with his fellowman and with his environment. Such an advance may be able to help man gain insight into the biological substrates of those aspects of his own nature that are now comprehended only in terms of psychological data and concepts or in the metaphors of art, philosophy, and religion.

* The Neurosciences Research Program is supported in part by National Institutes of Health Grant No. GM10211, National Aeronautics and Space Administration Grant No. Nsg 462, Office of Naval Research, The Rogosin Foundation, and Neurosciences Research Foundation.

The fearsome complexity of the brain with its billions of cells and connections has been the chief deterrent keeping gifted scientists in other disciplines from entering the field, but the complexity is beginning to show promise of unraveling, as more and more investigators from other fields are attracted to neuroscience.

A major difficulty in unifying the neurosciences and attempting novel theoretical approaches is that of meaningful communication between neuroscientists working at different levels of organization; each level has its own sophisticated vocabulary and conceptual framework. If it were possible for individual scientists to comprehend the major theories and tenets of *all* levels from molecular to behavioral, advance might well be spectacular. This is patently impossible, because it takes a lifetime to master portions of neuroscience even at the same organizational level.

To attempt a substantial step in solving this problem, a new experiment in interpersonal communication was undertaken by the writer in 1962. A group of Associates, who are eminent scientists from all disciplines relevant to neuroscience and with a high commitment to making original contributions in this field, were brought together, under the sponsorship of the Massachusetts Institute of Technology, to form the Neurosciences Research Program (NRP). NRP surveys, evaluates, and innovates in the various phases of neuroscience; holds meetings, such as "Work Sessions," of the most gifted experts in each particular subject; and publishes a series of monographs [1] (and anthologies) [2] conveying the upshot of Work Sessions and also large volumes [3] resulting from triennial Intensive Study Programs held at Boulder, Colorado. In addition to these activities, and believing with Michael Polanyi that people know more than they can say, the NRP manages to achieve a kind of intellectual allosterism,[4] resulting from the group

[1] *Neurosciences Research Program Bulletin.*
[2] *Neurosciences Research Symposium Summaries* (Cambridge: M.I.T. Press), vols. 1 (1966)–4 (1970).
[3] *The Neurosciences: A Study Program,* 1967, G. C. Quarton, T. Melnechuk, and F. O. Schmitt (eds.), 962 pp.; *The Neurosciences: Second Study Program,* 1970, F. O. Schmitt (ed.), 1,068 pp. (New York: Rockefeller University Press.)
[4] Enzymes, in addition to their active site which binds and acts on the substrate, have another site which, by reaction with appropriate metabolite, can be caused to stimulate the enzyme to greater—or lesser—activity (J. Monod, J.-P. Changeux, and F. Jacob, "Allosteric proteins and cellular control systems," *Journal of Molecular Biology,* 6 [1963], 306–329). The model (J. Monod, J. Wyman, and J.-P. Changeux, "On the nature of allosteric transitions: a plausible model," *Journal of Molecular Biology,* 12 (1965), 88–118) views subunits of enzyme proteins as "molecular amplifiers" of highly specific, organized, metabolic interactions. Participants, like protein subunits, can be "turned on" by discussional "metabolites" and their discussional interactions amplified.

dynamics engendered in its various meetings. The psychodynamics of this new form of group creativity, in itself, would constitute an interesting study.

The task of NRP at its founding in 1962 was to identify and define the several sciences relevant to brain and behavior and to help nucleate a coherent neuroscience field by building bridges between conceptually and methodologically disparate disciplines and subdisciplines. NRP planning and evolution was timely, occurring only a few years before the worldwide trend toward developing neuroscience gained momentum. Indications of the rapid expansion of the field are the recent appearance of a number of journals and book series with the terms "brain" and "neuroscience" in their titles and the formation of new multidisciplinary societies concerned with neuroscience, in addition to the International Brain Research Organization (IBRO), organized a decade ago as a participating member of UNESCO. New professional associations have been formed more recently, e.g., the Brain Research Association of the United Kingdom, the Society for Neuroscience of the United States, the European Brain and Behaviour Organization, and specialty groups like the International Neurochemical Society and the American Society for Neurochemistry. NRP, while continuing its major ongoing programs, seeks to provide theoretical formulations essential for the ordering of new data, methods, and concepts in a form catalytic for progress.

Illustrations of the dynamic processes of the brain described herein were taken, in the main, from meetings and publications of NRP during the past few years.

Molecular Neurobiology

Half a century ago biologists would not have been willing to attribute the enormously complex processes of heredity, development, and biosynthesis to a particular category of macromolecules. Nevertheless, through discovery of the way that DNA, RNA, and protein interact, science has illuminated at least the basic processes in genetic dynamics.

Perhaps in the next half-century (or half-decade) historians may comment similarly on the reluctance of scientists of our day to attribute to macromolecular parameters—not necessarily coding as such—learning, memory, awareness, and consciousness emerging from human central-nervous-system states. Molecular coding, as the basic principle of genetics, may provide a conceptual model for related possibilities regarding the role of molecular processes in brain functions. For example, it is possible that new dimensions of understanding of the nervous system and behavior will arise from the discovery of the functional significance of specific aggregations of macromolecules of various types in, or on, the neural membranes. The neuron may indeed wear important computational equipment on its skin!

The examples of molecular neurobiology to be cited exemplify the dynamic nature of brain processes; these citations, it is hoped, predict directions of future progress.

Molecular biology is a term that is frequently used synonymously with molecular genetics. The former is of course the broader, because it includes molecular genetics as well as molecular neurobiology, which deals with fundamental brain mechanisms at the molecular level whether or not they have to do with genetics or biosynthesis, and which is beginning to loom large on the horizon of neuroscience.

Enzymes and Brain Function

Some enzymes can act upon substrate more than a hundred thousand times per second; to achieve such high rates requires still faster intramolecular gyrations. An "induced fit" of enzyme upon substrate is accomplished by a portion of the polypeptide chain of the molecular whipping around, by fast configurational change, until a close fit is made. In the case of the proteolytic enzyme carboxypeptidase, for example, one particular group moves nearly half the diameter of the protein molecule, about 12 Ångström units, and does so exceedingly rapidly. Recently the discovery by Storm and Koshland [5] of a second dynamic property further illuminates the process by which the reacting molecules align in precisely the best position for reacting, thus accelerating the reaction by some ten thousandfold and achieving greater molecular cooperativity: they utilize electron orbitals, i.e., the enzyme molecules "steer" their orbitals along a path that takes advantage of the strong directional preference. Storm and Koshland suggest that this "orbital steering" factor may bridge the gap that existed in our knowledge of enzyme catalysis.

It has long been known that, to accomplish a cyclic process involving several individual enzyme-catalyzed steps (e.g., the Krebs cycle of oxidative phosphorylation and the electron transfer chain of cytochromes on mitochondrial membranes), the enzymes are clustered in a precise three-dimensional array permitting allosteric interactions made possible through

[5] D. R. Storm and D. E. Koshland, Jr., "A source for the special catalytic power of enzymes: orbital steering," *Proceedings of the National Academy of Sciences, U.S.*, 66 (1970), 445–452.

supermolecular, quaternary bonding which allows control of the reactions by their products and by other factors in the environment. Aggregation of energy-transducing enzymes with additional molecular machines, such as transferases, on the neuronal membrane may well prove vital to brain cell function.

Like cells of other tissues, brain cells command a large repertoire of enzymes that can be induced, i.e., the gene necessary for making a particular enzyme can be "turned on" by various agents acting as derepressors. What makes this induction so important for neuroscience is that such enzyme synthesis can be triggered bioelectrically or by appropriate synaptic stimulation or action of transmitter. Axelrod, et al.[6] demonstrated that excitation of the neuronal input to an autonomically innervated tissue, e.g., the adrenal gland, accelerates synthesis of enzymes producing the transmitter noradrenaline. Similar processes have been demonstrated in other synaptic situations.

McIlwain [7] (1970) points out that this ability to induce, by bioelectric and metabolic effectors of adaptation, a multiplicity of *enzymes* may be as significant for brain processes (such as ontogenetic specification, adaptation, and plasticity) as is the ability of the central nervous system to form a multiplicity of *synaptic connections* commonly considered the basis of physiological plasticity.

Brain enzymes are needed not only for the tasks common to tissue cells generally, but also for the special tasks related to high speed excitatory and inhibitory processes, and especially for the storage, delocalization, and fast retrieval of experiential information—a kind of temporal microminiaturization of the evolutionary process for which the enzymes were equally vital.

Coupling Between
Excitable Neuronal Membranes and Biosynthesis

The experiments of Axelrod, et al.[8] well exemplify coupling between excitable postsynaptic membranes and the biosynthetic centers of the cell. Incidentally, elevation of noradrenaline as Axelrod found for direct nerve stimulation was also produced indirectly by excessive crowding in a colony

[6] J. Axelrod, R. A. Mueller, J. P. Henry, and P. M. Stephens, "Changes in enzymes involved in the biosynthesis and metabolism of noradrenaline and adrenaline after psychosocial stimulation," *Nature*, 225 (1970), 1059–1060.
[7] H. McIlwain, "Metabolic adaptation in the brain," *Nature*, 226 (1970), 803–806.
[8] Axelrod, *op. cit.*

of mice. One wonders to what extent similar factors in the human environment, as in the overpopulous teeming ghettos, may also lead to elevated production of noradrenaline, known to incite various kinds of affective and emotional behavior.

Another striking case of induction by presynaptic stimulation of postsynaptic synthesis, this time of RNA, was shown by Peterson and Kernell [9] and Kernell and Peterson [10] in isolated *Aplysia* abdominal ganglia. If RNA synthesized under these conditions generates specific proteins, a "permanent" response might result from synaptic excitation. If dicarboxylic acid transmitters (glutamate), which have inhibitory action on the cortex, are added to slices of cortex, a stimulation of protein synthesis is observed.[11]

FIGURE 1 portrays another coupling possibility; materials synthesized in the neuronal cell center, when deposited in or upon the membrane of the initial segment (axon hillock), may modulate the excitability of this membrane zone, hence the triggering of propagated action waves in the axon.

Highly suggestive is the situation in certain bacteria in which DNA and enzymes for protein synthesis and oxidative phosphorylation are all associated with the cell membrane. Because of this association, a single colicine particle, on impact with the bacterial membrane, can interact directly with the vital coding and synthesizing equipment and kill the cell.[12] One wonders whether in certain circumstances, DNA (and/or RNA) could be associated with neuronal membranes that are sensitive to electrical or transmitter stimulation. If this were the case, the coupling between stimulus and synthesis would be direct and require no diffusion or translocation of messengers or metabolites between membrane and cell center. Only recently has DNA been shown to exist in mitochondria and certain other "self-reproducing" organelles.[13] The DNA, present in low concentrations, is demonstrated chemically after extraction with phenol. This DNA

[9] R. P. Peterson and D. Kernell, "Effects of nerve stimulation on the metabolism of ribonucleic acid in a molluscan giant neurone," *Journal of Neurochemistry,* 17 (1970), 1075–1085.

[10] D. Kernell and R. P. Peterson, "The effect of spike activity versus synaptic activation on the metabolism of ribonucleic acid in a molluscan giant neurone," *Journal of Neurochemistry,* 17 (1970), 1087–1094.

[11] F. Orrego and F. Lipmann, "Protein synthesis in brain slices," *Journal of Biological Chemistry,* 242 (1967), 665–671.

[12] M. Nomura, "Mechanism of action of colicines," *Proceedings of the National Academy of Sciences, U.S.,* 52 (1964), 1514–1521.

[13] See J. L. Jinks, *Extrachromosomal Inheritance* (Englewood Cliffs, N.J.: Prentice-Hall, 1964).

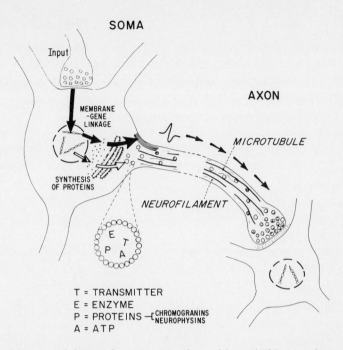

SOMA

Input

AXON

MEMBRANE
-GENE
LINKAGE

MICROTUBULE

SYNTHESIS
OF PROTEINS

NEUROFILAMENT

E T
P A

T = TRANSMITTER
E = ENZYME
P = PROTEINS —[CHROMOGRANINS
                NEUROPHYSINS
A = ATP

FIGURE 1   Linkage of gene expression with excitable membranes
and with translocation of vesicle-bound transmitters and proteins.

might not have been detected in mitochondria and localized by electron
microscopic and histochemical means. The fact that DNA has not thus far
been demonstrated electron microscopically or histochemically in excitable
neuronal membranes is not definitive proof of its absence there. Quite possibly, after techniques are developed for fractionation and isolation of neuronal membranes, application of chemical tests for nucleic acids (and perhaps other metabolic systems) may prove them to be associated with or
bonded to neuronal membranes. Such membrane-borne ensembles of nucleic acids and enzymes could conceivably provide a unique mechanism by
which bioelectric factors might mediate gene expression *directly,* rather
than through the transmitters, receptors, adenyl cyclase, prostaglandins,
etc., as intermediates. If no such mechanism exists, we shall have to seek
slower processes by which substances may be transported between the active neuronal membrane and the biosynthetic center—perhaps mediated
by microtubules appropriately arrayed in initial segments or in dendrites.

Neuroplasmic Dynamics

It is now generally believed that neuroplasm is constantly synthesized
in the cell body and moves as a gel down the axon (and probably also

along the dendrites) at a rate of about 1 mm per day.[14] Particular substances, e.g., neurosecretions, transmitter-synthesizing enzymes, and organelles such as vesicles, are translocated differentially and at much higher velocities (100–2000 mm per day).[15] The mechanisms actuating the two types of translocation differ. Weiss thinks the slow flow is due to peristaltic contractions in regions not closely specified in membranous investments of the axon. The fast, specific translocation characteristically occurs in the presence of microtubules and of vesicles (as in the case of sympathetic fibers only 0.5 to 1.0 micron in thickness).[16]

Translocation has been pictured as a saltatory, i.e., jumpwise, interaction between enzyme-containing vesicles and microtubules.[17] The translocating mechanism, apparently universally present in cells, is primitive and conservative evolutionarily. Its investigation poses one of the most exciting problems of present-day neurobiology. Chemomechanical coupling of energy is pictured as underlying neuroplasmic translocation in a manner similar to the coupling that underlies contractility in muscle, in microtubular structures, cilia, flagella, and perhaps also in the apparatus for the injection of nucleic acid into micro-organisms by viruses. In some instances, as in the unmyelinated neurons of lamprey, Smith, et al.[18] have observed vesicles closely applied upon and between microtubules in the synaptic region, supporting the view that such association may be functionally meaningful.

Another exciting line of investigation that may benefit from methods developed to demonstrate neuroplasmic flow and fast translocation is that dealing with the trophic relationship between neurons and the tissue they innervate, as, for example, in the neural regulation of gene expression in

[14] P. A. Weiss, "Neuronal dynamics and neuroplasmic ('axonal') flow," in *Symposium of the International Society of Cell Biology*, vol. 8 (1969), S. H. Barondes (ed.), pp. 3–34 (New York: Academic Press).

[15] S. H. Barondes, *Axoplasmic Transport*, in: *Neurosciences Research Symposium Summaries*, vol. 3 (1969), F. O. Schmitt, et al. (eds.), pp. 191–299 (Cambridge: M.I.T. Press).

[16] A. Dahlström, "The transport of noradrenaline between two simultaneously performed ligations of the sciatic nerves of rat and cat," *Acta Physiologica Scandinavica*, 69 (1967), 158–166.

[17] F. O. Schmitt, "Fibrous proteins—neuronal organelles," *Proceedings of the National Academy of Sciences, U.S.*, 60 (1968), 1092–1101; F. O. Schmitt, "The molecular biology of neuronal fibrous proteins," in *Neurosciences Research Symposium Summaries*, vol. 3 (1969), F. O. Schmitt, et al. (eds.), pp. 307–332 (Cambridge: M.I.T. Press).

[18] D. S. Smith, U. Järlfors, and R. Beránek, "The organization of synaptic axoplasm in the lamprey (*Petromyzon marinus*) central nervous system," *Journal of Cell Biology*, 46 (1970), 199–219.

muscle,[19] i.e., materials still poorly characterized presumably pass from the axon across the synapse into postsynaptic tissue and are required metabolically for that tissue. This is strikingly shown in the changes that ensue when fast nerves are sutured to slow muscles and vice versa. Recently, hypersensitivity to transmitter following denervation was demonstrated in relation to trophic processes by Fambrough.[20]

Membrane Dynamics

Because of the crucial bioelectric role played by membranes, the dynamic, fast processes that occur on and in membrane are of primary concern in neuroscience. Consideration of only the lipid-protein matrix of the membrane is likely to lead to impressions of static structural properties of a device meant to be primarily a semipermeable barrier between cytoplasm and exterior; such a view misses the dynamic operation of the molecular machines that are mounted on the membrane "floor space."

It is commonly believed that the action potential's influx of Na + and efflux of K + is mediated by fast conformational changes in membrane macromolecules; fast and sensitive physical methods, such as polarization optics, light scattering, and fluorescent probes, are being applied in an effort to characterize these configurational changes.

Model systems of lipid biomolecular layers containing specific ion carriers suggest a solution to the problem that has eluded physiologists for generations, i.e., how the cell distinguishes ions so similar physically and chemically as Na + and K +.[21] The ion carrier is pictured as an ion-specific peptide-cage molecule that engulfs the cation, desolvates it as it enters the opened cage, and closes by fast conformational change; then, facilitated by outwardly directed lipophilic side-chains, the ion-bearing cage-peptide traverses the membrane under the potential gradient and discharges the resolvated ion on the cytoplasmic side of the membrane.[22]

[19] L. Guth, *"Trophic" Effects of Vertebrate Neurons,* in *Neurosciences Research Symposium Summaries,* vol. 4 (1970), F. O. Schmitt, et al. (eds.), pp. 327–396 (Cambridge: M.I.T. Press).

[20] D. M. Fambrough, "Acetylcholine sensitivity of muscle fiber membranes: mechanism of regulation by motoneurons," *Science,* 168 (1970), 372–373.

[21] D. C. Tosteson (ed.), *The Molecular Basis of Membrane Function* (1969), Symposium of the Society of General Physiologists, Durham, N.C., August 20–23, 1968 (Englewood Cliffs, N.J.: Prentice-Hall); M. Eigen and L. C. M. DeMaeyer, *Carriers and Specificity in Membranes, Neurosciences Research Program Bulletin,* 9:3 (in press, 1971).

[22] M. Eigen and R. Winkler, "Alkali-ion carriers: dynamics and selectivity," in *The Neurosciences: Second Study Program,* F. O. Schmitt (ed.) (New York: Rockefeller University Press, 1970), pp. 685–696.

Isolation and characterization of the actual membrane carriers are difficult because of their low concentration in the neuronal membrane.

Dynamic Interactions at Synaptic Junctions

Arising from application of new electron microscope techniques, discoveries about the microstructure of the synapse [23] indicate that conventional notions are greatly oversimplified. Proteinaceous material constitutes a kind of "synaptic apparatus" that extends from presynaptic to postsynaptic regions across the cleft; this apparatus develops when the synapse becomes physiologically operable and may prove an important part of dynamic synaptic processes.

The forming of ontogenetically and physiologically appropriate synaptic connections during development has been explained on the basis of molecular recognition by acidic glycoproteins through terminal groups of their carbohydrate moieties.[24] The same groups, by changing synaptic connectivity, may achieve the plasticity required for the consolidation of experiential information as learning. The transferase enzymes, which bring about changes in terminal glycosyl or fucosyl groups, act with ample rapidity, but it has been questioned whether such enzymes are present on the extracellular surfaces of the presynaptic and postsynaptic members.

The interesting possibility has recently been examined that macromolecules, which can be much richer informationwise than transmitters, may modulate transmission and synaptic function.[25] If this were the case, some type of plasticity might result. Actually, an acidic protein, *chromogranin A,* is present in the vesicles of adrenergic neurons along with noradrenaline, enzymes, and ATP; this protein is thought to be released from vesicles at varicosities and endings of sympathetic neurons. The function of the protein is unknown.

[23] F. E. Bloom and G. A. Aghajanian, "Fine structural and cytochemical analysis of the staining of synaptic junctions with phosphotungstic acid," *Journal of Ultrastructure Research,* 22 (1968), 361–375; K. Akert and K. Pfenninger, "Synaptic fine structure and neural dynamics," in *Symposium of International Society of Cell Biology,* vol. 8 (1969), S. H. Barondes, ed., pp. 245–260 (New York: Academic Press); F. E. Bloom, "Correlating structure and function of synaptic ultrastructure," in *The Neurosciences: Second Study Program,* F. O. Schmitt, ed. (New York: Rockefeller University Press, 1970), pp. 729–746.

[24] S. Bogoch, *The Biochemistry of Memory,* London and New York: Oxford University Press (1968); S. H. Barondes, "Two sites of synthesis of macromolecules in neurons," in *Symposium of International Society of Cell Biology,* vol. 8 (1969), S. H. Barondes (ed.) (New York: Academic Press), pp. 351–364.

[25] F. E. Bloom, L. L. Iversen, and F. O. Schmitt, *Macromolecules in Synaptic Function, Neurosciences Research Program Bulletin,* 8:4 (1970), 325–425.

Another exciting and dynamic biochemical process occurring at the synapse is the liberation of a substance called cyclic AMP (adenosine 3', 5'-phosphate), generated by action on ATP of the enzyme adenyl cyclase. This enzyme, located in the membrane, is thought to be in close interaction with receptor molecules, the crucial transducing molecules specifically binding biodynamic substances, such as hormones and transmitters, which, in extremely low concentrations (10^{-6} to 10^{-12} M), produce the appropriate response in the tissue. As the hormone (or transmitter) may be called the first messenger, the cyclic AMP is the second messenger,[26] triggering a number of vital intracellular reactions catalyzed chiefly by kinase enzymes. The mode of action is diagrammatically illustrated in FIGURE 2.

Brain cortex contains the highest concentration of adenyl cyclase of

ROLE OF CYCLASE AND CYCLIC AMP

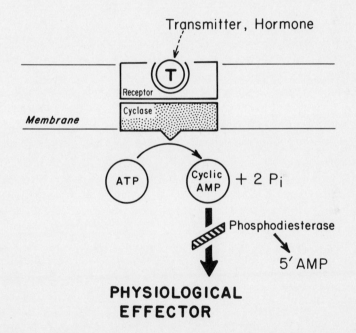

FIGURE 2 Diagrammatic representation of the role of membrane-bound adenyl cyclase in the postulated linkage between transmitter and intracellular effector (cyclic AMP).

[26] E. W. Sutherland and T. W. Rall, "The relation of adenosine-3',5'-phosphate and phosphorylase to the actions of catecholamines and other hormones," *Pharmacological Reviews*, 12 (1960), 265–299.

any tissue.[27] Synaptic transmission in the cerebellum is believed to activate adenyl cyclase, a finding that links transmitter action with the cyclic AMP system.[28] The concentration of cyclic AMP in the brain can be increased fortyfold by electrical or neurohumoral stimulation.[29] The adenyl cyclase-cyclic AMP system provides a dynamic dimension in neurobiology, discovered only a few years ago, but doubtless destined to prove even more significant as more information is obtained.

More than one hundred thousand synaptic terminals impinge on the dendritic trees of some neurons. It is hard to picture these as simple stimulus-response systems, even on the assumption of simple electrotonic additivity of multiple excitatory and inhibitory inputs, but the system seems rather to imply a computation by the postsynaptic cell to determine, on the background of its own ongoing activity and from the complex input pattern, what moment-to-moment output response is appropriate. The dendritic or somatic spatial positioning of each input could conceivably be fairly precise and is genetically determined. Temporal spacing of each input would be an additional factor in the computation, together with optimal adjustment in relation to diffusional, electrotonic, and other variables—a spectacular and dynamic process.

Neural Dynamics in Brain Systems and Subsystems

Action potentials and reflex arcs have figured prominently in the development of neurophysiology, because they are easier to observe and interpret than is the bioelectric traffic in the reticular formation, limbic system, and most of the cortex. Nevertheless, it is becoming increasingly clear that consolidation of experience in long-term storage and plastic learning processes are not readily assessible from classical neurophysiological techniques. Adey [30] suggests that although many transient phenomena, e.g., electrophysiological responses, pulse-coded firing, and slower, wavelike events (EEG, evoked potential), may provide indices of brain cell state,

---

[27] T. W. Rall and A. G. Gilman, *The Role of Cyclic AMP in the Nervous System,* in *Neurosciences Research Program Bulletin,* 8:3 (1970), 221–323.

[28] G. R. Siggins, B. J. Hoffer, and F. E. Bloom, "Cyclic adenosine monophosphate: stimulation of melatonin and serotonin synthesis in cultured rat pineals," *Science,* 165 (1969), 1018–1020.

[29] S. Kakiuchi, T. W. Rall, and H. McIlwain, "The effect of electrical stimulation upon the accumulation of adenosine 3′,5′-phosphate in isolated cerebral tissue," *Journal of Neurochemistry,* 16 (1969), 485–491.

[30] W. R. Adey, *Slow Electrical Phenomena in the Central Nervous System,* Neurosciences Research Program Bulletin, 7:2 (1969), 75–180.

[40] E. R. Kandel, "Nerve cells and behavior," *Scientific American,* 223 (1970), 57–70.

they probably reflect transactional rather than storage processes. However, "slow electrical phenomena"—dc shifts across bulk tissue as well as across neuronal and glial membranes—reflect subtle but important plastic changes in long-term states that occur during learning. Gavalas, et al.[31] found that very small electric fields across the head produce measurable behavioral effects at levels of energy or gradients below that needed to stimulate synapses. Slow-wave phenomena have dynamic qualities, although they may seem less impressive than the major fast-wave grist of neurophysiology. Technical developments such as the remote monitoring of localized fields in brain regions [32] may help realize the promising potentialities of this aspect of neuroscience.

Steady potential gradients [33] may importantly affect memory storage processes; surface-positive transcortical polarization can induce the formation of cellular short-term memory by influencing neuronal responses to normal and established synaptic inputs. Anodal current fires cells otherwise below threshold to auditory stimulation. Pairing polarization with stimulation produces effects outlasting the stimulus by 20 minutes. Cathodal polarization tends to prevent or inhibit storage of training experience during flow of the polarizing current.

The obverse of these results was shown by Rowland: [34] small dc shifts measured in various parts of the brain are a neurophysiological criterion of psychological reinforcement for food, sex, and rewarding or aversive stimulation of the hypothalamus.

Another experiment of Morrell [35] deserves inclusion in our showcase

[31] R. J. Gavalas, D. O. Walter, J. Hamer, and W. R. Adey, "Effect of low-level, low-frequency electric fields on EEG and behavior in *Macaca nemestrina*," *Brain Research*, 18 (1970), 491–501.

[32] O. H. Schmitt, personal communication.

[33] V. S. Rusinov, "An electrophysiological analysis of the connecting function in the cerebral cortex in the presence of a dominant area," Communications at the XIX International Physiological Congress, Montreal, 1953; F. Morrell, "Effect of anodal polarization on the firing pattern of single cortical cells," *Annals of the New York Academy of Sciences*, 92 (1961), 860–876; F. Morrell and P. Naitoh, "Effect of cortical polarization on a conditioned avoidance response," *Experimental Neurology*, 6 (1962), 507–523.

[34] V. Rowland, "Steady potential phenomena of cortex," in *The Neurosciences: A Study Program*, G. C. Quarton, et al. (eds.) (New York, Rockefeller University Press, 1967), pp. 482–495.

[35] F. Morrell, "Information storage in nerve cells," in *Information Storage and Neural Control*, W. S. Fields and W. Abbott (eds.) (Springfield, Ill.: C. C Thomas, 1963), pp. 189–229; F. Morrell, "Electrical signs of sensory coding," in *The Neurosciences: A Study Program*, G. C. Quarton, et al. (eds.) (New York: Rockefeller University Press, 1967), pp. 452–469.

of examples of dynamic brain processes underlying psychological processes. Poststimulus histograms of unit cell recordings from the cat cortex demonstrate that the pattern of the unit's response changes with "experience"; in visual cortical neurons the simultaneous presentation of visual and auditory or visual and somato-sensory stimuli result in a pronounced alteration of subsequent responses to the visual stimulus alone. More recent work [36] shows the effect to depend on a real reorganization of the temporal pattern of firing; the response is abolished by barbiturates and is probably polysynaptic. Morrell is inclined to ascribe the phenomena to short-axon (Golgi Type II) cells which synapse on apical dendrites, fire with short spikes, and produce a field. Here is a truly dynamic neurophysiological response related to storage; Morrell's identification of the short-axon cells, diffusely distributed in the brain, as those responsible for the mnemonic response will await confirmation by other methods and in other laboratories.

Another neurophysiological phenomenon that is highly informative concerning the dynamic way in which information is processed is that of the conversion of incident light-quanta in the retina to the characteristic output of action potentials in the optic nerve. Through the application of new intracellular dye injection and histofluorescence techniques, together with electron microscopic and neurophysiological investigations of many vertebrate species, the five major cell types in the retina have been characterized structurally and physiologically. What has emerged is that the information processing in the retina is accomplished without generation of action potentials (spikes), but rather with slow-wave potentials.[37] Because the retina is an externalized bit of central nervous tissue, these experiments support the possibility that the slow-wave type of information processing may be more important in the central nervous system than is commonly supposed. One of the five types of retinal cells, the amacrine cells, which lack axons, apparently participates importantly in neurophysiological processing (as in the olfactory bulb) and does so without spike generation.[38]

Another window through which to view dynamic brain processes is by

[36] Morrell, personal communication.
[37] E. F. MacNichol, Jr., and H. G. Wagner, *Advances in Retinal Physiology, Neurosciences Research Program Bulletin* (in preparation).
[38] W. Rall and G. M. Shepherd, "Theoretical reconstruction of field potentials and dendrodendritic synaptic interactions in olfactory bulb," *Journal of Neurophysiology,* 31 (1968), 884–915; W. Rall, "Dendritic neuron theory and dendrodendritic synapses in a simple cortical system," in *The Neurosciences: Second Study Program,* F. O. Schmitt (ed.) (New York: Rockefeller University Press, 1970), pp. 552–565.

examination of the integration and coordination involved in the central control and mediation of skilled motor movement, i.e., how the sensory input is translated into appropriately timed and patterned efferent output underlying motor activity.

Behavioral Dynamism

Dynamism is the *Leitmotiv* of behavior. One is at a loss to choose some subjects as meriting mention above others: wakefulness, sleep, dreams, and the role of serotonin; the neural correlates of conditioning and learning; perception; drive and motivation; all these might well be chosen for discussion. Perhaps the problem of neural regulatory mechanisms and their relation to phenomena for which the concept of motivation becomes usefully relevant epitomizes the neural and behavioral dynamics as well as any other. As neural mechanisms involved in regulation of temperature, hunger, thirst, and sex are increasingly discovered, it becomes clear that there is a hierarchy of mechanisms ranging from simple reflex mechanisms (e.g., sweating and piloerection in relation to temperature) up to behavioral phenomena with motivational qualities (e.g., increased behavioral activity to maintain temperature).

Epilogue

Ceaseless dynamic activity is the hallmark of the brain at each level: whole brain, systems and subsystems; neurophysiological, metabolic, biochemical, and biophysical. It has been the chief purpose of this essay, by describing some of the known dynamic properties, to point the way to other, perhaps even more significant ones yet to be discovered.

Gone are the days when the role of the central nervous system during sleep could be characterized, as did Sherrington.[39] Visualizing activity in brain tracts as little stationary or traveling points of light streaming in serial trains in the neural nodes and networks at various speeds, Sherrington describes events during deep sleep and in arousal therefrom. Except for flashes of light due to the superintending of the beating of the heart and breathing, there is mostly darkness. The brain is released from the waking day and marshals the factors for its motor acts no more. Then, where hardly a light had twinkled or moved, the brain

[39] C. S. Sherrington, *Man on His Nature*, 2nd ed. (Garden City, N.Y.: Doubleday & Co., 1955), pp. 183–184.

becomes now a sparkling field of rhythmic flashing points with trains of travelling sparks hurrying hither and thither. The brain is waking and with it the mind is returning. . . . Swiftly the headmass becomes an enchanted loom where millions of flashing shuttles weave a dissolving pattern, always a meaningful pattern though never an abiding one; a shifting harmony of subpatterns.

In the history of neurophysiological research, some of the most outstanding work has been concerned with descriptions of stimulus-response type of activity, physiologic, anatomic, and behavioral; it is difficult because of technical limitations to investigate the brain in a more systems-oriented procedure. However, such work, even if vastly expanded and refined experimentally, could in its sum represent only an impoverished description of the brain as it really functions. What dynamic processes occur in addition to synapse-initiated neuronal firing in closed nets in the cortex, that thin outer layer of the brain which contains some 70 percent of all the neurons in the brain and which presumably accounts for at least some of its "higher" functions? The concept of connectionalism should be broadened to include the possibility of distributive pathways (perhaps numbering in the hundreds or thousands for particular tracts). In addition, the role of volume effects leading to global, holistic processes, including steady, polarization potentials and fields, oscillations, gradients, and other phenomena should be critically assessed.

In considering how excitation occurs in the sequential firing of neurons in the brain, we may tend to lose sight of the small nuances of changes of impedance, field, ion distribution and gradients, specific interactions of information-rich macromolecules with small molecules and with ions, and of other bioelectric parameters. These nuances may seem small when measured in bulk phase, but in microscopic compartments such topochemical reactions may be triggered and determined by strong and highly directional and specific forces.

If it were possible to analyze the brain—or perhaps at first only simplified systems, e.g., the *Aplysia* ganglion [40]—by systems and network theoretical methods, as have proved powerful in electrical engineering, we might get a glimpse of the significance of these topochemical and topophysical processes which, together with action waves and synaptic events in legions of neurons in nets, make up the ongoing activity of the brain. Without doubt, flows and forces could in principle be dealt with according

[40] E. R. Kandel, "Nerve cells and behavior," *Scientific American*, 223 (1970), 57–70.

to Kirchhoff's laws, as generalized in theorems such as that of Tellegen.[41] Unfortunately, we are probably still far from the time when such theoretical and experimental analyses will prove profitable.

I leave the discussion on a note of optimistic expectation: solutions of complicated problems of the brain by rigorous systems-network theoretical analyses may not be achieved in the near future, but the experimental and theoretical search will go on for even more dynamic processes that may eventually account for the individual as a self-aware entity possessed of all those qualities which make him human.

[41] P. Penfield, Jr., R. Spence, and S. Duinker, *Tellegen's Theorem and Electrical Networks,* Research Monograph 58 (Cambridge: M.I.T. Press, 1970), 143 pp.

Darwin
Versus
Copernicus

Theodosius
Dobzhansky

About three centuries ago, Pascal described the human condition with a lucidity and poignancy never since equaled:

> When I consider the short duration of my life, swallowed up in the eternity before and after, the little space which I fill, and even can see, engulfed in the infinite immensity of spaces of which I am ignorant and which knew me not, I am frightened, and am astonished at being here rather than there; for there is no reason why here rather than there, why now rather than then. Who has put me here? By whose order and direction have this place and this time been allotted to me? The eternal silence of these infinite spaces frightens me.

Whether the silence of the infinite spaces is more or less frightening to our contemporaries than it was to Pascal is hard to tell. The spaces still know us not, but we begin to know something about the spaces. By whose order this place and time have been allotted to me has, however, become, if anything, still more mysterious.

Objects most remote from us yet discovered in the universe are galaxies some five billion light-years away. The mysterious quasars (quasi-stellar objects), or some of them, may be as remote, but their nature and remoteness are still under dispute among cosmologists. This is a remoteness which staggers the imagination; the radiation from these objects reaching us today left its source billions of years ago. The universe is believed to have started in a "Big Bang," a cosmic explosion which made the universe "expand," or rather caused its different components to fly apart in all directions with colossal speeds. The date of the Big Bang, and consequently the supposed age of the universe, is estimated to be on the order of fifteen billion years. These estimates tend, however, to be lengthened rather than shortened by newer discoveries.

The number of galaxies in the universe visible in the 200-inch telescope is estimated to be close to one billion. Our galaxy is merely one of these, yet it may contain between one million and one hundred million planetary systems. One of these includes a medium-sized planet which we inhabit. The supposition that the planet earth is in any way unique or exceptional or privileged seems farfetched to many scientists. It is, however, the only one known for certain to have a tiny proportion of its mass involved in a process called life. Moreover, the diversity of living beings is very impressive. There are at least two million kinds, or species, of life on earth at present, and there were more in the past, which became extinct.

Speculation is rife concerning the possibility that there may be life of some sort on other planets, in other planetary systems, and in other galaxies. Some authorities go so far as to proclaim it a certainty that life not merely could, but must have arisen in many places in the universe. More than that, sentient and rational beings must have evolved on many planets where there is life. In other words, "We are not alone." The name "exobiology" has been invented for the study of the assumed extraterrestrial life. The problems of exobiology cannot be adequately discussed here; I realize that the following remarks may do injustice to the ingenious speculations advanced in this field. I cannot, however, help wondering if the exobiologists may not turn out to be high-powered specialists on a nonexistent subject. The stock argument in favor of the existence of life in many places in the universe runs about as follows: Although the critical step from the nonliving to the living may be a rare and improbable event, there are some one hundred million planets in our galaxy on which this step could be made, hence it must have been made on several or even on many. This argument is not really convincing, however, because nobody knows for sure just how probable or improbable the event may be under various circumstances. It is certain that the event happened at least once—on earth. The evidence that it was not a unique event is yet to be obtained—it cannot be taken for granted.

Let us, however, assume for the sake of a further argument that life did arise in many places, and moreover that it was life based on nucleic acids and proteins, in other words, life chemically of the same kind as that on earth. This granted, it far from follows that such life must have evolved elsewhere as it did on our planet, let alone that it must have produced humanoid organisms. Evolution is principally adaptation to the environment; however, even if the environments somewhere happened to be much like, though of course not identical with, those on earth, a reenactment or repetition of the terrestrial evolutionary history has a probability very close to zero. This is because biological evolution is not predetermined to achieve any particular form of adaptedness to the environment. It has a range of possibilities that is virtually unlimited.

Evolution is a creative process which is most unlikely to occur two or more times in the same way. Man was not contained in the primordial life, except as one of an infinitely large number of possibilities. What these other unrealized possibilities might have been we probably shall never know. And yet, the origin of man was not an accident either, unless you choose to consider all history, including biological history and that of human societies, states, and nations, as series of accidents. This is a possible view, but not an appealing one. It is far more meaningful to describe biological and human histories as successions of unique events, each event being causally related to what went on before and to what will follow in the future, and yet nonrecurrent. George Simpson gave arguments essentially similar to the above in a brilliant article entitled "The Non-prevalence of Humanoids," that is, nonprevalence anywhere except on our planet. Our species, mankind, is almost certainly alone in the universe. And to that extent, our planet is also unique.

To recognize this "aloneness" is not necessarily to experience the Pascalian "fright" and "astonishment." Quite the opposite. The space which mankind fills, and the duration of its existence so far, are indeed very small compared to the now known "immensity of spaces." The messages that we may wish to send describing human activities on earth may have to travel billions of years at the speed of light to reach the quasars and the remotest galaxies. And there is probably nobody there to receive these messages. Does it mean that all our doings, both those of individuals and of the human species as a whole, are mere whiffs of insignificance? Not at all; because it is unique, the career of the human species here on earth may be of cosmic significance. This idea need not be a wildly conceited delusion. Our species may well be alone in having discovered that the universe and all that it contains, including mankind, is a changing product of evolution. It is neither size nor geometric centrality in the solar system, or in our galaxy, or in the universe, that makes the planet earth so important. It is that the flames of self-awareness, of death awareness, and of evolutionary awareness have been kindled here on earth and probably nowhere else.

The image of man as seen by Pascal and his contemporaries and successors is different from that emerging from evolutionary science. The difference becomes understandable when viewed against the background of the history of science and of its philosophical implications since Copernicus, Galileo, Newton, and Darwin. Here again I am forced to be too brief and, I fear, too dogmatic. The pre-Copernican man felt certain not only that he was the heart of the universe but that the universe was created for him and because of him. The earth was the hub of several concentric spheres: those of the moon, of the sun, of the planets, and of fixed stars. God watched the smallest happenings on earth from somewhere up above. The interior of the earth contained an elaborately engineered hell; a man could avoid becoming its resident in perpetuity only by good behavior during his brief sojourn on the earth's surface, and by the intercession of the properly constituted ecclesiastic authorities. With travel difficult and slow, the earth seemed to be very large. It shrank progressively as it was gradually explored and as travel became easy and rapid. It is quite small in the age of jet aircraft. But whether large or small, the earth existed for man and for the realization of God's mysterious plans for man's salvation.

All these arrangements did not make man free of anxieties. He faced the *mysterium tremendum*—why has God arranged things as he has? This was, however, just one extra mystery—the greatest one to be sure—but mysteries were all around, from the vagaries of weather to the behavior of one's friends and enemies. All these things were the doings of spirits, good or evil. Though spirits were more powerful than men, men were not entirely defenseless against them, because one could secure the assistance of some spirits against others.

The development of science changed the situation. At first sight, the mystery began to recede; but in fact it was relegated to the beginning of the world. Copernicus, after him Kepler and Galileo, and still later Newton, together with their many followers and successors, changed the image of the universe and of man. The earth is a smallish planet revolving around a much grander sun. Instead of the celestial spheres there is only the endless void, in which other planets, suns, and galaxies are as tiny islets on an infinite ocean. Man is lost in cosmic spaces. It is not, however, the dimensional smallness of man that really matters. It is rather the mechanical and inexorably deterministic nature of the universe, and finally of man himself, that changes man's image. Celestial phenomena are calculable and predictable, provided that one has discovered the precise and eternal laws which they obey. Biological and psychological phenomena are less predictable, but only because they are much more complex and the laws governing them are yet to be discovered. Descartes decided that the human body was as much a machine as a clock or other "automation," although he still believed that man had a nonmechanical soul. Others found the hypothesis of soul to be superfluous. Man is a machine, and that is that.

God was found to be another superfluous hypothesis. To be sure, Newton and many other scientists tried to hold onto their religions. Newton thought that the planets were hurled into their paths initially by God. But subsequent to this divine act at the beginning, the planets follow their proper orbits, according to immutable laws and without further guidance. The deists thought that God was the original creator and lawgiver of the universe. Having created the universe and set it in motion, God found it so well made that his presence became no longer essential. Instead of mysteries, we have the laws of nature. Some people thought that God reserves the right of occasional miraculous intervention, temporarily abrogating the very laws which he himself has formerly established. To others such behavior appears unseemly for the all-wise and omniscient Creator. It is more convenient to imagine him as a sort of absentee landlord, who lets things take their "natural" courses.

Mystery driven out through the front door tends to creep in through the back door. Has the Creator and Lawgiver arranged things really well? If he is credited with the order, beauty, and goodness in the world, he must by the same token be responsible also for the disorder, ugliness, and evil. The machinery of the world has serious flaws, and this is a mystery defying comprehension. An absentee-landlord god can hardly be prayed to, since he is unable or unwilling to intervene to change the causal sequences which bring about events.

To this is added the hopelessness of determinism. As stated by Laplace, the doctrine of determinism is essentially that if one knew the position and speed of every particle in the universe at any single instant, and if one could submit this knowledge to analysis, then one could predict all future events and also retrodict all past events. Although this statement contains two pretty vertiginous "ifs," determinism is an explicit or implicit faith which is the basis of scientific activity. It leads, however, to an embarrassing inference: there is nothing new in the world, because all that ever happens was predestined to happen from the beginning. No human effort, or absence of effort, can change anything, because the effort or its absence is equally predestined. This is a far stronger fatalism than the fatalism sometimes (and mostly wrongly) ascribed to oriental philosophies.

Darwin has been called the Newton of biology, although the Copernicus or the Galileo of biology would perhaps be a better characterization. There is as yet nothing in biology analogous to, say, the laws of gravitation; the Newton of biology may be yet to come. To say this is not to underestimate Darwin's contribution. He has shown that the biological species, including man, have not appeared ready-made; their multifarious structures and functions are not mere whims of nature or of a Creator. Every living species is a descendant of ancestors unlike itself, and generally more unlike the farther back in time one looks. It is probable, though not certain, that all beings now alive are descendants of one primordial life which appeared some four billion years ago. Presumed remains of living beings three and one-half billion years old have recently been found. The organic diversity is a consequence of adaptation to different environments; the endless variety of bodily structures and functions makes possible an endless diversity of modes of life. There are so many kinds of organisms because they can exploit more fully the diverse opportunities which an environment offers for living than any single organism conceivably could.

The human species has evolved a unique way to cope with its environments. This way is culture. Culture is not transmitted from generation to generation by the genes, although its biological basis is so transmitted. Culture has been called "superorganic," although it surely rests on an organic foundation. Man is an animal, but he is so extraordinary that he is much more than an animal. Darwin and his successor evolutionists have thus extended to the living world, and even to the human world, the principles which were shown to be so supremely efficient in the study of the physical world. Biology has by now exorcised the ghost of vitalism, which wanted to see in life something radically incommensurable with the rest of nature. Mechanism has triumphed in biology. This triumph was what Darwin and the evolution theory were, and still are, mainly acclaimed for. There is, however, another aspect to evolutionism which may be at least equally and possibly more important. It sees the whole universe, and everything in it, in the process of change and development. The universe is on its way to somewhere. Where is it going?

The grandeur of the Newtonian image of the universe was in its serene constancy and the precision of its laws. Planets and their satellites follow their orbits again and again, in predictable fashion. Moreover, since Newton accepted the traditional creation date as well as the apocalyptic prediction of the end of the world, there was little opportunity for change either in the past or the future. The laws of the conservation of mass and of energy were discovered later; here was a break in the constancy, however—

although energy is conserved, it undergoes a directional change because of entropy.

What biological evolution is all about, however, is not constancy but change. Darwin and his successors have shown that the living world of today is different from what it was in the past, and that it may become different again in the future. Mankind proved to have a hitherto quite unsuspected kind of history. This is the history of its slow emergence from its animal ancestors in addition to the recorded history of patriarchs, kings, battles, and empires. And while recorded history goes back only a few thousand years, biological history extends somewhere between one and a half and two million years. But even this history is short relative to that of the life from which man came, which took perhaps four billion years. And back of that are more billions of years, when the universe existed without either life or man.

I do not wish to be understood as claiming that it was Darwin who made evolution into a universal principle. In point of fact, it was recognized before Darwin that the planetary system has had a history of origin from the primitive sun, or from a mass of matter which gave origins both to the sun and to the planets. Human history has been studied at least since Herodotus and Thucydides; late in the eighteenth century Condorcet ascribed to it a directional character—from a primitive barbarianism to an earthly paradise of perfect enlightenment. Darwin's theory of biological evolution is, however, the keystone of the evolutionary conception of the world, beginning with the evolution of the cosmos and culminating in the evolution of mankind. Modern cosmology is evolutionary cosmology. Even the atoms of the chemical elements, hitherto symbols of indivisibility and unchangeability, proved to have had an envolutionary history. In the homely language of some modern cosmologists, the atoms were "cooked" in the Big Bang at the start of cosmic evolution, and they are still being cooked in the furnaces of the interior of the sun and of the stars.

It has been urged by some authorities that the term "evolution" should be restricted to biological evolution only. I do not share this view, because it seems to me important to convey the idea that change and development are characteristic of nonliving as well as of living matter and of human affairs. This does not prevent one from recognizing that the processes of cosmic, inorganic, or geological evolution are different from biological evolutionary processes. The causes of biological evolution must be looked for in heredity, mutation, and natural selection. None of these is found in nonliving systems, and the analogies which some authors have attempted to draw are at best remote. Other analogues of heredity, mutation, and natural selection have been claimed in human social and cultural evolution with, I fear, even less success. These analogies are more often obfuscating than enlightening.

Nor can I see much of an advantage in the views expounded so brilliantly by such philosophers as Whitehead and Hartshorn. They like to ascribe to inorganic systems, and even to atoms and subatomic particles, some rudiments of life, individuality, and, further, of consciousness and volition. It is almost needless to say that there is no positive evidence, either compelling or presumptive, of any such biological and human qualities in nonliving systems. Even as a speculative possibility these views do not seem to me attractive. They really amount to a denial of anything substantially new ever arising in evolution. They are most nearly analogous to the early preformistic notions in biology; some eighteenth-century biologists believed that a sex cell contains a "homunculus," a tiny figure of man. This seemed to make the problem of development very simple—the homunculus had only to grow in size to become an adult man, and a corresponding miniature in an animal sex cell had to grow to become an adult animal of the proper species. But this simplicity was deceptive, since it made the problem of the development of succeeding generations insoluble. One had to believe that homunculi contained second-order homunculi, these had third-order homunculi, and so on, ad infinitum. An analogous difficulty arises with the "minds" of atoms. It might seem at first that human mind could simply evolve by growth of the atomic mind. Human mind is, however, somehow associated with the human brain, and where are the brains of atoms and electrons?

The most interesting aspect of evolution is precisely that it creates novelties. From time to time it transcends itself, i.e., produces novel systems with novel properties—properties which the antecedent systems did not have even as tiny germs. The emergence of the living from the nonliving, and the emergence of humanity from animality, are the two grandest evolutionary transcendences so far. Teilhard de Chardin was the evolutionist who had the courage to predict further transcendences, mankind moving toward what he called the megasynthesis and toward Point Omega, this last being his symbol for God. Here is evidently a borderland, in which Teilhard's science has collaborated with his mystical vision. I am not planning in the present discussion to take you on an excursion in this borderland of prophecy.

As already stated above, we do not know for sure whether the transcendences of the nonliving to life, and of animal to man, have taken place solely on this planet earth or in many places in the universe. Perhaps some positive information bearing on this issue will come from the progress in space travel. Be that as it may, we do have conclusive enough evidence that these three kinds of evolution, inorganic, organic, and human, have happened here on earth. These three kinds of evolution are not independent of each other; they are rather the three stages of the single Evolution of the cosmos. By calling them "stages," I do not mean to suggest that cosmic evolution stopped when the biological phase started, or that biological evolution stopped when the human phase began. On the contrary, the three kinds of evolution are not only going on, but what is more, they are connected by feedback relations. For example, geography influences the living things which inhabit a given territory; in turn, vegetation, animals, and especially human activities have now become geographic and even geologic agents. Human cultural evolution influences mankind's genetic endowment, and vice versa. In recent years there have been publicized some alarmist views, asserting that human genetic endowment is in a process of degeneration, and predicting dire consequences of this for the future. This matter cannot be adequately discussed in this article; I believe that the dangers have been exaggerated, and in any case the situation is not beyond possible control.

The evolutionary view of the world does not abrogate the classical Newtonian mechanistic view. The change which evolutionism makes is nevertheless of greatest importance for man's view of himself and of his place in the universe. The classical conception stressed the essential permanence of things, at least for the duration of the world's existence. The evolutionary conception emphasizes change and movement. The preevolutionary world view did not, of course, deny all change; but the changes were usually represented as cyclic, and the world as a whole did not go anywhere in particular. Spring, summer, autumn, and winter return again and again at the appointed times; people are born, grow, build families, get old, and die, and a new generation goes through the same succession of stages; plants and animals, like people, produce generation after generation; heavenly bodies follow their orbits again and again; mountains rise, are eroded away, become submerged in the sea, rise up again, etc., etc., etc. . . . . But to translate a French adage, the more things change the more they remain the same.

Constancy, lack of change, and regular recurrence seem to be reassuring and comforting to many people. "Like the good old days" is a compliment tinged with nostalgia. Change brings insecurity; one has to become adapted, adjusted, or reconciled to altered situations. Yet changelessness, or eternal repetition or return, is the acme of futility. A world which remains forever the same is senseless. It is what Dostoevsky called a "devil's vaudeville." All the strivings and struggles which a person, or a generation, has to go through are in vain because the next generation, and the one after that, and so on ad infinitum, will have to go through the same struggles all over again.

What difference does the idea of evolution make? Quite simply, it is this: the universe is not a status but a process. Its creation was not something which happened a few thousand years ago, before any of us were born and could have influenced it in any way. The creation is going forward now, and may conceivably go on indefinitely. The view that "there is nothing new under the sun" is in error. In the past there were an earth and a sun different from the present ones, and there will be a new earth and a new sun in the future. An important role in this forward movement belongs to the phenomenon called life, and to one particular form thereof called mankind, which exists as far as we know only on a single and not otherwise remarkable planet.

The evolution of life is remarkably rapid, measured on a cosmic time scale. Ten million years ago, the oceans and mountains, the moon, the sun, and the stars were not very different from what they are now, but the living beings inhabiting the earth were rather unlike the present ones. Ten thousand years ago mankind was quite different from what it is now, while except for the destruction of some biological species, the biological world was pretty much what we now observe. Evolution is a creative process; the creativity is most pronounced in human cultural evolution, less in biological, and least in inorganic evolution.

A creative process by its very nature always risks ending in a failure or being stranded in a blind alley. Every biological species is nature's experiment, essaying a new mode of living. Most species eventually prove unsuccessful and become extinct without issue. Yet some, a minority, discover new or superior ways of getting a living out of the environment which is available on earth. These few lucky discoverers inherit the earth and undergo what is technically known as adaptive radiation. That is, the surviving species differentiate and become many species again, only to repeat the process of discovery, extinction, and new adaptive radiation. Yet this is not another specimen of eternal return. New adaptive radiations do not simply restore what there was earlier; the new crop of species may contain some which have achieved novel or surer ways of remaining alive, or have discovered previously unexploited niches in the environment and have thus augmented the living at the expense of the non-living.

The trial-and-error process of proliferation of ever-new species and of disappearance of the old ones has achieved remarkable successes. Biological evolution has transcended itself by giving rise to man. Mankind as a species is biologically an extraordinary success. It has gained the ability to adapt its environments to its genes, as well as its genes to its environments. This ability stems from a novel, extragenetically transmitted complex of adaptive traits called culture. Culture leads to still another kind of discovery, discoveries of knowledge, which can be transmitted to succeeding generations again by means of the extragenic processes of instruction and learning. One of the discoveries which became known is the discovery of evolution. Man knows that the universe and life have evolved, and that mankind entered this universe by way of evolution. With perhaps a bit too much poetic license, it has been said that man is evolution having become conscious of itself. It is no poetic license, however, to say that having discovered evolution, man has opened up a possibility of eventually learning how to control it.

The enterprise of creation has not been completed; it is going on before our eyes. Ours is surely not the best of all thinkable worlds, and, we hope, not even the best of all possible worlds. Man is constantly asking whether his existence, and that of the universe in which he finds himself, has any sense or meaning. If there is no evolution, then all is futility— human life in particular. If the world evolves, then hope is at least possible.

An uncomfortable question inevitably presents itself at this point. Can science ever discover meaning in anything, and is a scientist entitled even to inquire about meanings and purposes? To a rigorous mechanicist who does not wish to think in evolutionary terms, such words as meaning, improvement, progress, and transcendence are meaningless noises. Everything in the world, including myself, is an aggregation of atoms. When this aggregation disaggregates, the atoms will still be there and may aggregate into something else. Is there an objectively definable difference between an object of art and a junk heap? If a virus and a man are nothing but different seriations of the nucleotides in their DNA's and RNA's, then all of evolution was a lot of sound and fury signifying nothing.

One of the exasperating phenomena of the intellectual history of mankind is politely called "the academic lag." This crudely mechanistic world view was acceptable in science chiefly during the eighteenth and nineteenth centuries. It had justified itself by having given a powerful impetus to scientific discovery. It is now being displaced by the evolutionary world view. Yet the representatives of what C. P. Snow has referred to as literary or nonscientific culture have only recently discovered that the world is nothing but an aggregation of atoms. It is a curious experience to hear an artist argue that a junk heap is, indeed, no less worthy of aesthetic appreciation than is the "Venus de Milo," because both are matter wrought into arbitrary shapes; or to have an eminent musician declare that the atonality and certain other characteristics of avant-garde music are merely recognition of the Copernican discovery that man is not the center of the universe; or finally to read in a book by an intellectual pundit that "something pervasive that makes the difference, not between civilized man and the savage, not between man and the animals, but between man and the robot, grows numb, ossifies, falls away like black mortified flesh when techne assails the senses and science dominates the mind."

In reality science is neither a villain debasing human dignity nor the sole source of human wisdom. In Toynbee's words:

> Science's horizon is limited by the bounds of Nature, the ideologies' horizon by the bounds of human social life, but the human soul's range cannot be confined within either of these limits. Man is a bread-eating social animal; but he is also something more. He is a person, endowed with a conscience and a will, as well as with a self-conscious intellect. This spiritual endowment of his condemns him to a life-long struggle to reconcile himself with the Universe into which he has been born.

The fact that the universe was evolved and is evolving is surely relevant to this reconciliation. The advent of evolutionism makes it necessary to ask a new question which simply could not occur to those who believed that the world is created once and for all, stable and changeless.

The question is, Where is evolution going? This question can be asked separately about the three known kinds of evolution—cosmic, biological, and human. It has also been asked about evolution as a whole, because the three kinds of evolution can be viewed as the constituent parts, or stages, of a single all-embracing process of universal evolution. This universe, so formidable and so beautiful, is in a process of change. It may be that evolution is merely drifting at random, and is going nowhere in particular. There is, however, also a possibility, for which no rigorous demonstration can be given, that universal evolution is one grand enterprise, in which everything and everybody are component parts. Whose enterprise is this, and with what aim and for what purpose is it undertaken? The four centuries of the growth of science since Copernicus have not dispelled this mystery; the one century since Darwin has made it more urgent than ever.

What role is man to play in evolution? Is he to be a mere spectator or, perchance, the spearhead and the eventual director? There are people who will shrug this question off, or will recoil from it, considering it an exhibition of insane arrogance. Since, however, man is one and presumably the only rational being who has become aware that evolution is happening, he can hardly avoid asking such questions. For the issue involved is no less than the meaning of his own existence. Does man live just to live, and is there no more sense or meaning to him than that? Or is he called upon to participate in the construction of the best thinkable universe?

The
Uncompleted
Man   Loren Eiseley

The nature into which Shakespeare's Macbeth dabbles so unsuccessfully
with the aid of witchcraft, in the famous scene on the heath, is unforgettable in literature. We watch in horrified fascination the malevolent change
in the character of Macbeth as he gains a dubious insight into the unfolding future—a future which we know to be self-created. This scene, fearsome enough at all times, is today almost unbearable to the discerning observer. Its power lies in its symbolic delineation of the relationship of
Macbeth's midnight world to the realm of modern science—a relationship
grasped by few.

The good general, Banquo, who, unlike Macbeth, is wary of such
glimpses into the future as the witches have allowed the two companions,
seeks to restrain his impetuous comrade. " 'Tis strange," Banquo says,

> And oftentimes, to win us to our harm
> The instruments of darkness tell us truths,
> Win us with honest trifles, to betray's
> In deepest consequence.

Macbeth who, in contrast to Banquo, has immediately seized upon the
self-imposed reality induced by the witches' prophecies, stumbles out of
their toils at the last, only to protest in his dying hour:

> And be these juggling fiends no more believ'd . . .
> That keep the word of promise to our ear
> And break it to our hope!

Who, we may now inquire, are these strange beings who waylaid Macbeth, and why do I, who have spent a lifetime in the domain of science,
make the audacious claim that this old murderous tale of the scientific twilight extends its shadow across the doorway of our modern laboratories?

143

These bearded, sexless creatures who possess the faculty of vanishing into air or who reappear in some ultimate flame-wreathed landscape only to mock our folly, are an exteriorized portion of ourselves. They are projections from our own psyche, smoking wisps of mental vapor that proclaim our subconscious intentions and bolster them with Delphic utterances— half-truths which we consciously accept, and which then take power over us. Under the spell of such oracles we create, not a necessary or real future, but a counterfeit drawn from within ourselves, which we then superimpose, through purely human power, upon reality. Indeed one could say that these phantoms create a world which is at the same time spurious and genuine, so complex is our human destiny.

Every age has its style in these necromantic projections. The corpselifting divinations of the Elizabethan sorcerers have given way, in our time, to other and, at first sight, more scientific interpretations of the future. Today we know more about man, where he has come from, and what we may expect of him—or so we think. But there is one thing, in my belief, which identifies Macbeth's "juggling fiends" in any age, whether these uncanny phantoms appear as witches, star readers, or today's technologists. This quality is their claim to omniscience—an ominiscience only halfstated on the basis of the past or specious present, and always lacking in genuine knowledge of the future. The leading characteristic of the future they present is its fixed, static, inflexible quality.

Such a future is fated beyond human will to change, just as Macbeth's demons, by prophecy, worked in him a transformation of character which then created inevitable tragedy. Until the appearance of the witches on the heath gave it shape, that tragedy existed only as a latent possibility in Macbeth's subconscious. Similarly, in this age, one could quote those who seek control of man's destiny by the evocation of his past. Their wizardry is deceptive because their spells are woven out of a genuine portion of reality—which, however, has taken on this always identifiable quality of fixity in an unfixed universe. The ape is always in our hearts, we are made to say, although each time a child is born something totally and genetically unique enters the universe, just as it did long ago when the great ethical leaders—Christ, the Buddha, Confucius—spoke to their followers.

Man escapes definition even as the modern phantoms in militarist garb proclaim—as I have heard them do—that man will fight from one side of the solar system to the other, and beyond. The danger, of course, is truly there, but it is a danger which, while it lies partially in what man is, lies much closer to what he chooses to believe about himself. Man's whole history is one of transcendence and of self-examination, which have led him to angelic heights of sacrifice as well as into the bleakest regions of despair. The future is not truly fixed but the world arena is smoking with the caldrons of those who would create tomorrow by evoking, rather than exorcising, the stalking ghosts of the past.

Even this past, however, has been far deeper and more pregnant with novelty than the short-time realist can envisage. As an evolutionist I never cease to be astounded by the past. It is replete with more features than one world can realize. Perhaps it was this that led the philosopher Santayana to speak of men's true natures as not adequately manifested in their condition at any given moment, or even in their usual habits. "Their real nature," he contended, "is what they would discover themselves to be if they possessed self-knowledge, or as the Indian scripture has it, if they became what they are." I should like to approach this mystery of the self, which so intrigued the great philosopher, from a mundane path strewn with the sticks and stones through which the archaeologist must pick his way.

Contemplating the Fish

Let me illustrate what I mean by a very heavy and peculiar stone which I keep upon my desk. It has been split across; carbon black, imprinted in the gray shale, is the outline of a fish. The chemicals that composed the fish—most of them at least—are still there in the stone. They are, in a sense, imperishable. They may come and go, pass in and out of living things, trickle away in the long erosion of time. They are inanimate, yet at one time they constituted a living creature.

Often at my desk, now, I sit contemplating the fish. It does not have to be a fish. It could be the long-horned Alaskan bison on my wall. For the point is, you see, that the fish is extinct and gone, just as those great heavy-headed beasts are gone, just as our massive-faced and shambling forebears of the Ice Age have vanished. The chemicals still about us here took a shape that will never be seen again so long as grass grows or the sun shines. Just once out of all time there was a pattern that we call *Bison regius,* a fish-like amphibian called *Ichthyostega,* and, at this present moment, a primate who knows, or thinks he knows, the entire score. In the past there has been armor; there have been bellowings out of throats like iron furnaces; there have been phantom lights in the dark forest, and toothed reptiles winging through the air. It has all been carbon and its compounds, the black stain running perpetually across the stone.

But though the elements are known, nothing in all those shapes is now returnable. No living chemist can shape a dinosaur, no living hand can start the dreaming tentacular extensions that characterize the life of the simplest ameboid cell. Finally, as the greatest mystery of all, I who write these words on paper, cannot establish my own reality. I am, by any reasonable and considered logic, dead. This may be a matter of concern to you reading these words; but if it is any consolation, I can assure you that you are as dead as I. For, on my office desk, to prove my words is the fossil out of the stone, and there is the carbon of life stained black on the ancient rock.

There is no life in the fossil. There is no life in the carbon in my body. As the idea strikes me—and believe me it comes as a profound shock—I run down the list of elements. There is no life in the iron, there is no life in the phosphorus, the nitrogen does not contain me, the water that soaks my tissues is not I. What am I then? I pinch my body in a kind of sudden desperation. My heart knocks, my fingers close around the pen. There is, it seems, a semblance of life here.

But the minute I start breaking this strange body down into its constituents, it is dead. It does not know me. Carbon does not speak, calcium does not remember, iron does not weep. Even if I hastily reconstitute their combinations in my mind, rebuild my arteries, and let oxygen in the grip of hemoglobin go hurrying through a thousand conduits, I have a kind of machine, but where in all this array of pipes and hurried flotsam is the dweller?

From whence, out of what steaming pools or boiling cloudbursts did he first arise? What forces can we find which brought him up the shore, scaled his body into an antique, reptilian shape and then cracked it like an egg to let a soft-furred animal with a warmer heart emerge? And we? Would it not be a good thing if man were tapped gently like a fertile egg to see what might creep out? I sometimes think of this as I handle the thick-walled skulls of the animal men who preceded us, or ponder over those remote splayfooted creatures whose bones lie deep in the world's wastelands at the very bottom of time.

A Question at Night

With the glooms and night terrors of those vast cemeteries I have been long familiar. A precisely similar gloom enwraps the individual life of each of us. There are moments in my bed at midnight, or watching the play of moonlight on the ceiling, when this ghostliness of myself comes home to me with appalling force, when I lie tense, listening as if removed, far off, to the footfalls of my own heart, or seeing my own head on the pillow turning restlessly with the round staring eyes of a gigantic owl. I whisper "Who?" to no one but myself in the silent, sleeping house—the living house gone back to sleep with the sleeping stones, the eternally sleeping chair, the picture that sleeps forever on the bureau, the dead, also sleeping, though they walk in my dreams. In the midst of all this dark, this void, this emptiness, I, more ghostly than a ghost, cry "Who? Who?" to no answer, aware only of other smaller ghosts like the bat sweeping by the window or the dog who, in repeating a bit of his own lost history, turns restlessly among nonexistent grasses before he subsides again upon the floor.

"Trust the divine animal who carries us through the world," writes Emerson. Like the horse who finds the way by instinct when the traveler is lost in the forest, so the divine within us, he contends, may find new passages opening into nature; human metamorphosis may be possible. Emerson wrote at a time when man still lived intimately with animals and pursued wild, dangerous ways through primeval forests and prairies. Emerson and Thoreau lived close enough to nature to know something still of animal intuition and wisdom. They had not reached that point of utter cynicism—that distrust of self and of the human past which leads finally to total entrapment in that past, "man crystallized," as Emerson again was shrewd enough to observe.

This entrapment is all too evident in the writings of many concerned with the evolutionary story of man. Their gaze is fixed solely upon a past into which, one begins to suspect, has been poured a certain amount of today's frustration, venom, and despair. Like the witches in *Macbeth,* these men are tempting us with seeming realities about ourselves until these realities take shape in our minds and become the future. It is not necessary to break the code of DNA in order to control human destiny. The tragedy is that men are already controlling it even while they juggle retorts and shake vials in search of a physical means to enrich their personalities. We would like to contain the uncontainable future in a glass, have it crystallized out before us as a powder to swallow. All then, we imagine, would be well.

As our knowledge of the genetic mechanism increases, both scientists and journalists bombard our ears with ingenious accounts of how we are to control, henceforth, our own evolution. We who have recourse only to a past which we misread and which has made us cynics would now venture to produce our own future out of this past alone. Again I judge this self-esteem as a symptom of our time, our powerful, misused technology, our desire not to seek the good life but to produce a painless mechanical version of it—our willingness to be good if goodness can, in short, be swallowed in a pill.

Once more we are on the heath of the witches, or, to come closer to our own time, we are in the London laboratory where the good Doctor Jekyll produced a potion and reft out of his own body the monster Hyde.

Nature, as I have tried to intimate in this little dissection, is never quite where we see it. It is a becoming as well as a passing, but the becoming is both within and without our power. It is this lesson, with all our hard-gained knowledge, that is so difficult to comprehend. All along the evolutionary road it could have been said, "This is man," if there had then been such a magical self-delineating and mind-freezing word. It could have immobilized us at any step of our journey. It could have held us hanging to the bough from which we actually dropped; it could have kept us cowering, small-brained and helpless, whenever the great cats came through the reeds. It could have stricken us with terror before the fire that was later to be our warmth and weapon against Ice Age cold. At any step of the way, the word *man,* in retrospect, could be said to have encompassed just such final limits.

Not Starry Influences

Each time the barrier has been surmounted. Man is not man. He is elsewhere. There is within us only that dark, divine animal engaged in a strange journey—that creature who, at midnight, knows its own ghostliness and senses its far road. "Man's unhappiness," brooded Carlyle, "comes of his Greatness; it is because there is an Infinite in him, which with all his cunning he cannot quite bring under the Finite." This is why hydrogen, which has become the demon element of our time, should be seen as the intangible dagger which hung before Macbeth's vision, but which had no power except what was lent to it by his own mind.

The terror that confronts our age is our own conception of ourselves. Above all else this is the potion which the modern Dr. Jekylls have concocted. As Shakespeare foresaw:

> It hath been taught us from the primal state
> That he which is was wished until he were.

This is not the voice of the witches. It is the clear voice of a great poet almost four centuries gone, who saw at the dawn of the scientific age what was to be the darkest problem of man: his conception of himself. The words are quiet, almost cryptic; they do not foretell. They imply a problem in free will. Shakespeare, in this passage, says nothing of starry influences, machinery, beakers, or potions. He says, in essence, one thing only: that what we wish will come.

I submit to you that this is the deadliest message man will ever encounter in all literature. It thrusts upon him inescapable choices. Shakespeare's is the eternal, the true voice of the divine animal, piercing, as it has always pierced, the complacency of little centuries in which, encamped as in hidden thickets, men have sought to evade self-knowledge by describing themselves as men.

Erich Fromm:

WHAT IS MAN'S STRUGGLE?

Ramon Xirau

In this essay I shall limit myself to three aspects of the theory of freedom
to be found in Erich Fromm's work: 1) freedom as seen from the viewpoint
of the history of human liberation, beginning with the biblical texts and
the oral tradition of Judaism—considering both as "radical humanism"; 2)
freedom as it has been sought and shunned by modern man, from the Renaissance to our day; and 3) freedom as the achievement of awareness and
the experience of choice between concrete alternatives (alternativism).
What links these two historical sequences and this vital, existential experience is the concept of man as a conflicted and contradictory being who is
nevertheless capable of progressing toward transcendence, freedom, and
greater rationality.[1]

I do not believe that Fromm's ideas are misrepresented if I say that his
thought—insofar as the evolution of freedom is concerned—is clearly
rooted in the concept of human progress which emerged in the Renaissance and was formulated by Feuerbach and several pre-Marxist socialists

[1] These pages should not be considered as an attempt to cover exhaustively the
theme of freedom in Fromm's work. I am here taking for granted the precise and
thorough analyses that Fromm devotes to the double theme of liberation and regression throughout most of his books. Among Fromm's books I have in mind, especially, *Escape from Freedom, Man for Himself, You Shall Be as Gods,* and *The
Heart of Man* which in my opinion state most clearly the subject matter we are here
concerned with. The theme I have selected seems to me to be fundamental and, at
the same time, one that has been rarely discussed elsewhere.

of the nineteenth century, and also by Spinoza, Marx, Freud and, to some extent, Nietzsche.

Erich Fromm believes, with Feuerbach, that the history of human religiousness—i.e., the history of the religious spirit—is the history of a progressive dealienation, and a progressive affirmation of free will, reason, and love between men. Like several of the socialists whom Marx somewhat unjustly called utopian (Fourier, Proudhon), Fromm believes that for most people the complete freedom of man lies in man's future, rather than in his present. Like the humanists of the nineteenth century, Fromm affirms that the history of man is a creative process. Unlike them, he has a more objective respect for various religious beliefs, even though his own is a nontheistic pattern of thought. Fromm regards the concept of God as a poetic expression of the highest value in humanism.

At first sight, the view of history as explained and analyzed by Fromm in *You Shall Be as Gods* seems to limit itself specifically to the evolution of the Jewish people; the reference points used by Fromm are the Bible and the oral tradition of the Jews. It is also true—and this point is of utmost importance—that in studying the Jewish texts and traditions as a unit, Fromm does not limit himself to relating exclusively the history of one people. What he does is to interpret the Bible and the oral tradition as "radical humanism." [2]

What is to be understood by this term? Fromm defines it clearly:

> By radical humanism I refer to a global philosophy which emphasizes the oneness of the human race, the capacity of man to develop his own powers and to arrive at inner harmony and at the establishment of a peaceful world. Radical humanism considers the goal of man to be that of complete independence, and this implies penetrating through fictions and illusions to a full awareness of reality. It implies, furthermore, a skeptical attitude toward the use of force, precisely because during the history of man it has been, and still is, force—creating fear—which has made man ready to take fiction for reality, illusions for truth.[3]

Several ideas in this quotation should be stressed. The first is the notion of a "global philosophy." True, in Fromm's biblical analysis there is a special love for the sacred texts of the Jewish people. At the same time—

[2] As a basis for his interpretation Fromm quotes the studies by Ludwig Krause, Nehemia Nobel, and very importantly, those of Hermann Cohen: *Die Religion der Vernunft aus den Quellen des Judentums.*

[3] Erich Fromm, *You Shall Be as Gods* (New York: Holt, Rinehart and Winston, 1966), pp. 13–14.

and perhaps mainly so—the Bible (and the Jewish tradition) interests him as a universal expression of the striving for freedom of the human race.

Fromm starts with a number of specific analyses and reaches principles that are applicable to all of human history. In this sense, *You Shall Be as Gods* is a philosophy of history, with close connections to the philosophies developed by Herder, Goethe, Marx, and that philosopher of the "art of living," Schweitzer; and the history Fromm analyzes is also the history of religious thought. Although Fromm defines his own attitude as that of a "nontheistic mysticism," [4] this does not prevent him from acknowledging that mystical experience may be equally valid for Judaism, Christianity, Brahmanism, or Taoism—for any religious or philosophical system, whether or not it includes a concept of God. He believes that mystical experience has the same validity for all truly religious men—however different their experiences and conceptualizations of such phenomena may be. Because the words "religious" or "spiritual" may be misleading, and because no two people's experiences are ever identical, Fromm designates mystical experience as the "x experience." We are dealing, in effect, with an experience and vision of love and reason within the reach of all men, provided they have freed themselves from *idolatry*—a term Fromm uses as synonymous with submission, alienation, and reification.

You Shall Be as Gods analyzes the history of the oneness of the human race from three biblical points of view: that of the concept of God, that of the concept of man, and that of the concept of history itself. I would like to discuss these viewpoints as they pertain to the progressive achievement of freedom.

First, Fromm denies the existence of original sin. Contrary to the Christian notion of Adam's Fall as a symbol of original sin, Fromm observes that the biblical text does not mention the word "sin," and he interprets the first part of Genesis as an act of rebelliousness which represents the "beginning of history, because it is the beginning of human freedom." [5] The more man unfolds the potential Godhood within himself, the more he frees himself from the supremacy of a merely authoritarian God. In fact, upon arriving at the concept of a covenant—that God made with Noah and his descendants—Jewish tradition converts God from an absolute ruler into a constitutional monarch: the right to live that man has won for him-

---

[4] This definition brings Fromm close to another tradition he has studied with great thoroughness: Zen Buddhism. The mystical experience of Zen is perhaps the clearest expression of a nontheistic mysticism.

[5] *Op. cit.*, p. 23.

self through his own effort can no longer be modified even by God. Because God is bound by rules of law and love, man is no longer his slave.

Subsequently, through the revelation to Moses, the concept of God as the God of nature—i.e., the ruler who made nature and man and who could destroy all his creations were he displeased—is no longer applicable. Instead, God becomes revealed only as the God of history, as when he states: "I am the God of your father, the God of Abraham, the God of Isaac, and the God of Jacob" (Exod. 3:6).

However, God does not mention a name. How shall he be named, this God who is both supremely present and supremely distant? Moses argued with God for a name because he felt that his people would not grasp the idea of a God who revealed himself only as the God of history. And for those Hebrews, accustomed to idols, a nameless God would indeed be meaningless. Accordingly, God conceded and said of himself: "I AM WHO I AM," expressed in the Hebrew *Eheyeh,* which is derived from the verb "to be." The significance of this term—which freely translated would mean: My name is *Nameless*—is that a living God, unlike an idol, can have no name. Only things have names. Thus, God cannot be respresented by name or image, and so cannot be translated into an idol.

This concept of a nameless God informed the twelfth-century thinking of Maimonides whose *The Guide for the Perplexed* described a "negative theology" in which it was not admissible to describe God's essence by listing (and hence limiting) God's positive attributes; but it was authorized to describe God in terms of his actions. We see, then, that the Jewish concept of God changed from the authoritarian God of creation to the nameless God of Moses to the God of Maimonides whom man can know only through his actions and not by a list of his positive attributes. In Judaism, then, there is—unlike Christianity—little significance attached to speculation about God's essence. Jewish "theology" is negative not only in the work of Maimonides but in another sense as well; that is to say, it negates idolatry, as did Maimonides himself, of course.

Whether or not this interpretation of the development of spiritual freedom would be acceptable to the various great religions—it could hardly be so for Christianity or for Mohammedanism—the conclusion to which it leads (and which resembles the conclusions reached by the prominent Catholic theologian Karl Rahner) is this: "The acknowledgement of God is, fundamentally, the negation of idols." [6]

[6] *Ibid.,* p. 42.

What is an idol? Why is the Bible so opposed to idolatry? First of all, an idol is a false object of adoration, a false god with which we identify in order to lose our fears while depending on an inert object which we endow with magical powers. Second, on a deeper level, as Fromm so well describes: "An idol represents the (regressive) desire to return to the soil-mother, the craving for possession, power, fame, and so forth." [7] By its intrinsic nature idolatry—whether of animals, stature, flags, or money—demands submission and requires an attitude of man's alienation from himself and his own powers. The importance of idols in purely authoritarian religions—and states—leads Fromm to contemplate a new science of "idology"; similar to Simone Weil, Fromm writes: " 'Idology' can show that an alienated man is necessarily an idol worshiper, since he has impoverished himself by transferring his living powers into things outside of himself, which he is forced to worship in order to retain a modicum of his self, and, in the last analysis, to keep his sense of identity." [8]

Whether Fromm's interpretation of the biblical tradition as charged with the revolutionary spirit of freedom is accepted or not, it is clearly possible for his conclusions to be accepted by all. And I believe it is precisely Fromm's intention that they be acceptable to all 1) when he holds that the "x experience"—the real religious, and especially the mystical, experience—implies that life be experienced as an existential problem faced by all men in their search to overcome their separateness and find harmonious relatedness; and 2) when he says, also, that the "x experience" implies a hierarchy of values according to which our individual aspirations should be guided; the supreme value—the highest development of one's abilities of love, reason and courage—is essentially a spiritual one; and 3) when he observes, finally, that religious experience is the experience of transcendence, in the human sense of transcending one's ego and going beyond one's selfishness and separateness in the spirit of love.

Parallel to the evolution of the changing concept of God and of reli-

[7] *Ibid.*, p. 43.

[8] *Ibid.*, pp. 48–49. We might add (1) that the idea of religion Fromm presents here is in agreement with the entire tendency to demythify which is today prominent among Protestant as well as Catholic theologians—a tendency that has its roots in Renaissance humanism, and especially in Erasmus and Juan Luis Vives; and (2) that our period tends toward idolizations that are more dangerous than the religious idolization of past periods. I refer to the tendency to make gods of violence, of progress, of science, and of persons whom contemporary man would like—due to the sense of his own powerlessness and the lack of faith in an authentic God—to convert into new gods. Simone Weil said that it is much easier to believe in idols than in the true God. Nothing could be more true.

gious experience, as only barely outlined here, there is the slow but progressive evolution of man. As the Bible describes, man was created in the image of God; and while man is not the God of whom he is the image, limits are not set on his evolution and, through inner growth, he is permitted to become ever more similar to God, through actions in the service of love and justice. Acting in this way is to know God in depth and authenticity.

Fromm conceives of human evolution and the growth of man as the passing from primary ties with nature and emancipation from incestuous attachments (not in the strict sexual sense as conceptualized by Freud) to reach his independence. This is difficult to attain, because it requires the experience of anxiety and separateness entailed in severing those primary bonds with his parents and society that bar man's growth. The obstacles that limit and at times eliminate man's progress toward individuation are formidable: narcissistic self-absorption, symbiotic pairings, clinging to an authoritarian structure—in short, regressive yearnings toward earlier modes of security.

Fromm summarizes the idea of how man's creation in God's likeness leads to human freedom in these terms: "The idea that man has been created in the image of God leads not only to the concept of man's equality with God, or even freedom from God, it also leads to a central humanist conviction that every man carries within himself all of humanity." [9] On this basis, the reading and interpretation of the Bible and the oral Jewish tradition, conceived of as a whole, lead to a universal concept of what, with Pascal, he would call "the human condition." [10]

We have reviewed the two concepts of God and man from Fromm's point of view. The third concept central to his thinking is that of *history*. History begins with the first act of human liberation, Adam's Fall, which Fromm understands not only as an expression of freedom, but also as a symbol of the separation between man and nature. With this first rupture of the ties between man and his matrix, man achieves awareness of his self and history commences. Man, having been thrown on his own possibilities, now creates his own history and *is also created* by this history: a process of solitude as well as of the quest for freedom. [11] As seen from the historical viewpoint, the Prophets, according to Fromm, describe man as a natu-

[9] *Ibid.,* p. 81.
[10] This term is more in agreement with Fromm's ideas than that of "human nature," where "nature" may lead to the thought of a fixed essence, or substance.
[11] *Op. cit.,* p. 88.

ral being who transcends nature,[12] yet who is also an historical being who makes his own choices and creates his own history, independently from God. And in a line of thought that once more reminds us of Feuerbach, Fromm states that Paradise is the golden age of the past which is in a dialectic relationship with the messianic time—the next stage in history, the golden age of the future.[13] These two stages are both states of harmony, but the unity of Paradise existed before the emergence of man while the unity of messianic time will exist when man is fully developed.

History thus is basically hope, but stemming from man's very nature, this hope is paradoxical: it is so because man *can* choose the way of freedom, but he can also—being conflicted, suffering, and yearning to return to prebirth harmony—choose the regressive path in which he abandons reason, responsibility, and awareness of himself and yields to necessity, passive waiting, and death-in-life.

Spinoza believed that every being makes an effort (*connatus*) to act according to his being. Every affect that contributes to this effort, that is to say, every affect based on love and joy is positive; while every affect that annuls or restrains "connatus," that is, every affect rooted in hatred and in sadness, is negative. Fromm's idea is not different when he insists: "The fundamental choice for man is that between growth and decay." [14]

This, then, is the framework of the human condition, from the viewpoints of God, man, and history. For Fromm the first act of freedom, for the individual as well as for the species, is the breaking of what he calls the "primary ties," or "primary bonds." Man, once separated, must fight to achieve his own freedom, a freedom he desires because he is alive and shuns because he is afraid. This ambivalent condition is exemplified in the changes of man's condition from medieval times through the Renaissance to the present.

Freedom in Modern History

Progress toward freedom versus the obstacles that man himself interposes between his potential to be actively free and his potential to be passively determined is the dynamic struggle described by Fromm in *Escape from Freedom* and *Man for Himself.*

[12] This idea resembles that expressed by Marx in the *Economic and Philosophical Manuscripts of 1844:* "Man is a natural being but a human natural being."
[13] *Op. cit.,* p. 123.
[14] *Ibid.,* p. 181.

"Human existence and freedom are from the beginning inseparable." [15] But it is necessary to distinguish between two meanings of the word "freedom": "freedom from"—that is, freedom from internal and external determination and constraints; and "freedom to"—the capacity to aspire to a positive freedom, to achieve the full realization of one's potentialities. Though man aspires to freedom, it is not less true that he also submits to a number of escape mechanisms that bar the way.

During the Middle Ages man lacked freedom, but he had the security derived from his religious faith. The feudal world together with the church constituted a double system of coordinates that afforded a stable life in the sense that man was not isolated, and had a fixed role in society. But with the spirit of the Renaissance, individualism was born, and man began to consider freedom as his most valuable possession. However, man's complex and contradictory nature makes this longing for freedom ambiguous: the move toward freedom takes man away from those ties that gave him security and this evokes doubts and the threat of loneliness implied by freedom. The greater the scope of his freedom, the more man loses his fixed place and the more isolation he experiences; with greater isolation there is more anxiety; and with more anxiety the more defensive processes come into play. In short, upon breaking the primary bonds that constitute freedom, man is inclined to develop a number of escape or security operations. Irrational forces leading to submission are thus grafted onto the positive striving for a life of freedom, productivity, and love. In other words, progress toward freedom is a dialectical process between the struggle for individuation against the desire to return to an embedded unity, autonomy versus acquiescence, growth in the face of solitude versus submission to irrational authorities whether external or internalized. The tendencies toward submission manifest themselves in not a few aspects of the Lutheran and Calvinist reformations; they also manifest themselves in the structures of capitalism and, above all, in the submission demanded by Nazism and Stalinism.

Fromm does not doubt that modern man has progressed toward freedom. But he emphasizes, especially in *Escape from Freedom,* that if man is not able to work toward greater self-awareness he tends to succumb to irrational processes that inhibit the attainment of liberation. These processes often involve submission to an authoritarian system, which is exemplified in sadistic and masochistic solutions to the fear engendered by sepa-

---

[15] Erich Fromm, *Escape from Freedom* (New York: Rinehart & Co., 1941), p. 32.

rateness; they lead to destructiveness or to automatic conformity.[16] How then is freedom to be understood and achieved?

Alternativism and Awareness

We know that man is by his very nature a contradictory being, both weak and strong, potentially free and potentially a slave. In stating the problems of the human condition, Fromm rejects the traditional concept of a fixed nature on which so many forms of authoritarianism have been based, and he rejects equally the more recent idea that man possesses no inborn nature whatsoever. Rather, human nature is seen as paradoxical and dialectical; in this context, let us look at the main terms Fromm uses to define freedom as a form of life and love of life, rather than as a theory about life.

In *The Sane Society* [17] freedom is described as involving the capacity to unite with others and be related to them; the capacity to transcend the state of being a passive person through creating, which requires activity and care; the achievement of a consistent sense of personal identity and the desire to become increasingly aware and rational. In short, freedom cannot be private and asocial; it must be achieved in a social world albeit limited in space and limited by the individual life span.

In *Escape from Freedom* Fromm equates one aspect of freedom with spontaneity, a creative freedom that recalls that described by Henri Bergson in *Time and Free Will*.[18] However, spontaneity is not a sufficient condition, even though it may be a necessary one, for the existence of true freedom. The concept of freedom that emerges from Fromm's work requires both the necessary awareness to experience given alternatives, and the capacity to choose between them.

Fromm has called this idea of freedom "alternativism." To develop this point of view, Fromm starts once more from his concept of the human condition. He writes:

> . . . as to the question of the nature of man, we arrive at the conclusion that the nature or essence of man is not a specific *substance,* like good or evil, but a *contradiction* which is rooted in the very conditions

[16] It is interesting to relate this discussion of human freedom to that developed by Teilhard de Chardin, for whom free men are not those who are timid, not the pessimists who renounce life, but the enthusiasts who love life, and in loving it love the God who gives sense to life. (See especially *The Future of Man.*)

[17] Erich Fromm, *The Sane Society* (New York: Rinehart & Co., 1955).

[18] Like Fromm, Bergson believed that freedom cannot be defined abstractly, and conceived of the free act as the relation between the I and the act performed by it.

of human existence. This conflict in itself requires a solution, and basically there are only the regressive or the progressive solutions.[19]

In other words, to choose freedom is to choose love of life; to escape from freedom is to choose the various forms negating life. Like Spinoza, Fromm believes that the development of human life toward greater rationality and a greater capacity for loving constitutes a free act; on the other hand, whatever leads to irrationality, primary ties, a closed system, and a narcissistic way of life is not a free act.

Fromm realizes, of course, that it is not sufficient to talk about freedom, nor to construct abstract systems apart from the facts. He carefully tries to avoid what Whitehead has called "the fallacy of misplaced concreteness," a fallacy that leads us unwittingly to think of the abstract as reality. Nothing could be more concrete than the concept of freedom Fromm presents. To be free consists, for him, in being capable of commitment and love; it consists also in being capable of choosing between real alternatives. It is, therefore, a true freedom that takes into account the actual conditions in which we live, a freedom that must be won at every moment, and through every act. What permits us to win our freedom is our capacity for awareness. To be free we must be aware of the ramifications of our actions, and of how the action we perform is suited to the end we propose to reach. We must be aware of the consequences of the act we choose to do and of the responsibility implicit in it.

To be free does not consist so much in *defining* a freedom in general terms; it is, rather, to be able to live it. Being largely determined by the physical and social worlds of which we are a part, we can be free only if we reach a clear awareness of the alternatives that appear before us, and if we are able to choose actively between them. While there can never be a pure indeterminism, there do exist definite possibilities between which we may choose. And to choose *well* means, for Fromm, in the words of Schweitzer, to choose with an attitude of reverence for life.

It is not necessarily so that freedom is a goal to be reached only in some distant future. Fromm believes, and he has expressed this especially in his more recent work, that a few men have at certain moments of their lives reached a clear harmony with the universe which is true freedom. In this context, Fromm agrees with Meister Eckhart, and he translates some sentences by this German mystic that convey this spirit of freedom, autonomy and independence.

[19] Erich Fromm, *The Heart of Man* (New York: Harper & Row, 1964), p. 120.

That I am a man
I have in common with all men,
That I see and hear
And eat and drink
I share with all animals.
But that I am I is exclusively mine,
And belongs to me
And to nobody else,
To no other man
Nor to an angel, nor to God,
Except inasmuch as I am one with him.[20]

[20] *You Shall Be as Gods, op. cit.,* p. 62.

The Dawn
of
Epimethean
Man   *Ivan Illich*

Our society is like the ultimate machine which I saw in a New York toy shop. This contraption is the opposite of old Pandora's box. It is a metal casket which snaps open when you touch a switch and reveals a mechanical hand. Chromed fingers reach out for the lid, pull it down, and lock the box from the inside.

The original Pan-Dora, the All-Giver, was an Earth goddess in prehistoric matriarchal Greece. She let all ills escape from her amphora, but she closed it before hope could slip out. The history of apollonian man begins with the decay of her myth and comes to an end in the self-sealing casket. It is the history of classical society, in which promethean citizens built institutions to corral the rampant ills. It is the story of declining hope and rising expectations.

I want to focus on the ability of man to survive this promethean endeavor, this attempt to escape the punishment of Zeus. I will let the myth speak about the awakening of man from a stable, archaic culture to the precarious balance of historic drama. I will describe the unbalanced attitudes, opinions, and sensitivities which underlie contemporary controversy, and compare this new consciousness with both primitive and classical self-awareness.

I will then outline the style in which we can hope to survive the threat of being smothered in the man-made pan-hygienic environment of a self-sealing box, and describe the self-chosen poverty we would have to live as Epimethean men.

For forty years, Dr. Fromm has pointed toward Bachofen's insight into the most significant revolution which can be historically studied: the transition from matriarchy to patriarchy in preclassical Greece. This essay represents the attempt of his pupil to meditate on the master's treatment of the Oedipus myth, and his attempt to suggest in mythical language that we might just now be going through a revolution no less profound.

Arche-pandora was sent to Earth with a jar which contained all ills; of good things, it contained only hope. Primitive man lived in this world of hope. He relied on the munificence of nature, on the handouts of gods and on the instincts of his tribe to enable him to subsist. Classical Greeks began to replace hope with expectations. Their version of Pandora let her bring and release both evils and goods. They forgot that the All-Giver (the Pan-Bringer) was the keeper of hope. They remembered Pandora mainly for the ills she had unleashed. They had become moral and misogynous patriarchs who panicked at the thought of the first woman. They built a rational and authoritarian society. They planned and built institutions from which they expected relief from the rampant ills. They became conscious of their power to fashion the world and make it produce services they also learned to expect. They wanted their own needs and the future demands of their children to be shaped by their artifacts. They became lawgivers, architects, and authors, the makers of constitutions, cities, and works of art to serve as examples for their offspring. Where primitive man had relied on mythical participation in sacred rites to initiate individuals to the lore of the society, the Greeks recognized as true men only the citizens who let themselves be fitted by paideia into the institutions their elders had planned.

The myth tells us about the transition from a world in which dreams were interpreted to a world in which oracles were made. From immemorial time, the Earth Goddess had been worshiped on the slope of Mount Parnassus. There, in Delphi, was the center and navel of the Earth, and there slept Gaia, the sister of Chaos and Eros. Her son Python the dragon guarded her moonlit and dewy dreams, until Apollo the Sun God, the architect of Troy, rose from the east, slew the dragon, and became the owner of Gaia's cave. His priests took over her temple. They employed a local maiden, sat her on a tripod over Earth's smoking navel and made her drowsy with fumes. They then rhymed her ecstatic utterances into hexameters of self-fulfilling prophecies. From all over the Peloponnesus men brought their problems to Apollo's sanctuary. The oracle was consulted on social options, such as measures to be taken to stop a plague or a famine, to choose the right constitution for Sparta or the propitious site for cities which later became Byzantium and Chalcedon. The never-missing arrow became Apollo's symbol. Everything about him became reasonable and useful.

In the *Republic,* describing the ideal state, Plato already excludes popular music.[1] Only the harp and Apollo's lyre would be permitted in towns because their harmony alone creates "the strain of necessity and the strain of freedom, the strain of the unfortunate and the strain of the fortunate, the strain of courage and the strain of temperance which befit the citizen." City dwellers panicked before Pan's flute and its power to awaken the instincts. Only "the shepherds may play [Pan's] pipes and they only in the country."

Apollonian man assumed responsibility for the laws under which he wanted to live and for the casting of the environment into his own image. Primitive initiation into mythical life was transformed into the education (paideia) of the citizen who would feel at home on the forum.

The world of the primitive was opaque, factual, and necessary. By stealing the fire from the gods, Prometheus turned facts into problems, called necessity into question and defied fate. Classical man crisscrossed the environment with channels, roads, and bridges, and even created man-made environments in the form of cities and cathedrals. He was aware that he could defy fate-nature-environment, but only at his risk. Only contemporary man attempts to create the world in his image, to build a totally man-made environment, and then discovers that he can do so only on the condition of constantly remaking man to fit it. We now must face the fact that man himself is at stake in his transition from Apollo to spaceman. Only those who have grasped this can grow beyond the processes launched by Prometheus, and the stage of Apollo, into the epoch of epimethean men.

That man can gamble on the survival of mankind to satisfy his fancy became manifest in the special supplement which *The New York Times* published for the first day of this decade. Every article bespeaks the perplexity of inhabitants in a totally man-made world. Life today in New York produces a very peculiar vision of what is and what can be, and without this vision, life in New York is impossible. A child on the streets of New York never touches anything which has not been scientifically developed, engineered, planned, and sold to someone. Even the trees are there because the Parks Department decided to put them there. The jokes

---

[1] Plato was conscious that "as the mode of music changes the fundamental laws of the state always change with them" and "if amusement becomes lawless the youth themselves become lawless."

he hears on television have been programed at a high cost. The refuse with which the child plays in the streets of Harlem is made of broken packages planned for somebody else. Even desires and fears are institutionally shaped. Power and violence are organized and managed: it is the gangs versus the police. Learning itself is defined as a consumption of subject matter, which is the result of a researched, planned, and promoted program. Whatever good there is, is the product of some specialized institution and it would therefore be foolish to demand something which some institution cannot produce. The child of the city cannot expect anything which lies outside the possible development of institutional process. Even his fantasy is prompted to produce science fiction. He can derive the poetic surprise of the unplanned only from the encounter with "dirt," blunder, or failure: the orange peel in the gutter, the puddle in the street, the breakdown of order, program, or machine, are the only takeoffs for creative fancy. "Goofing off" becomes the only poetry at hand.

Since there is nothing desirable which has not been planned, it soon becomes a verity for the city child that we will always be able to design an institution for our every want. He takes for granted the power of process to create value. Whether the goal is meeting a mate, integrating a neighborhood, or acquiring reading skills, it will be defined in such a way that its achievement can be engineered. The man who knows that nothing which is in demand is out of production soon expects that nothing which is produced can be out of demand. If a moon vehicle can be designed, so can the demand to go to the moon. Not to go where one can go would be a subversive act. It would unmask as folly the assumption that every satisfied demand entails the discovery of an even greater unsatisfied one. Such insight would stop progress. Not to produce what is possible would expose the law of "rising expectations" as a euphemism for a growing frustration gap, which is the motor of a society built on the coproduction of services and increased demand.

The Greeks replaced hope with expectations. They framed a civilized context for a human perspective. The modern city replaces the classical city with a world of ever-rising expectations, and thereby forever rules out all satisfaction. The state of mind of the modern city dweller appears in the mythical tradition only under the image of hell: Sisyphus, who for a while had chained Thanatos (death), must roll a heavy stone up the hill to the pinnacle of hell, and the stone always slips from his grip just when he is about to reach the top. Tantalus, who was invited by the gods to share their meal, and on that occasion stole their secret of how to prepare all-healing Ambrosia, suffers eternal hunger and thirst standing in a river of receding waters, overshadowed by fruit trees with receding branches. A world of ever-rising demands is not just evil—it can be spoken of only as hell.

Man has developed the frustrating omnipotence to be unable to demand anything because he also cannot visualize anything which an institution cannot do for him. Surrounded by omnipotent tools, man is reduced to a tool of his tools. Each of the institutions meant to exorcise one of the primeval evils has become a fail-safe self-sealing coffin for man. Man is trapped in the boxes he makes to contain the ills Pandora allowed to escape. The blackout of reality in the smog produced by our tools has enveloped us quite suddenly. Just as the rise of Apollo, of civilization and critical thought, happened suddenly, like a sunrise, so—quite suddenly—we find ourselves in the darkness of our own trap.

When I grew up in the thirties, the world was still permeated by the common sense of Apollo. I shared with my contemporaries certain notions of reality which lay beyond the reach of the scientist, engineer, or educator. We believed that there were some things not made by man, some things which could never be wished away. Whatever expectations we formulated, they were still rooted in the earth. Progress had not yet overtaken development—we still expected the engineer to increase our satisfactions while reducing our wants. We had not yet fallen victims to the new dogma that all men were insatiable consumers—and had a right to equal madness.

This has changed for those born after Hiroshima, those born right into the coffin. Reality itself has become dependent on human decision. The same president who ordered the ineffective invasion of Cambodia could equally well order the effective use of the atom. The "Hiroshima switch" has become the navel of the Earth, which could be cut by man himself. This new "omphalos" is a constant reminder that our institutions not only create their own ends, but also have the power to put an end to themselves and to us. The absurdity of modern institutions is evident in the case of the military. Modern weapons can defend freedom, civilization, and life only by annihilating them. Security in military language means the ability to do away with the Earth.

The absurdity underlying the nonmilitary institutions is no less manifest. There is no switch in them to activate their destructive power, but neither do they need a switch. Their grip is already fastened to the lid of the world. They create needs faster than they can create satisfaction, and in the process of trying to meet the needs they generate, they consume the

Earth. This is true for agriculture and manufacturing, and no less for medicine and education. Modern agriculture poisons and exhausts the soil. The "green revolution" can, by means of new seeds, triple the output of an acre—but only with an even greater proportional increase of fertilizers, insecticides, water, and power. Manufacturing of these, as of all other goods, pollutes the oceans and the atmosphere and degrades irreplaceable resources. If combustion continues to increase at present rates we will soon consume the oxygen of the atmosphere faster than it can be replaced. We can then calculate the day when we will wither like mice locked into a jar with a burning candle. We have no reason to believe that fission or fusion can replace combustion without equal or higher hazards. Medicine men replace midwives and promise to make man into something else: genetically planned, pharmacologically sweetened, and capable of more protracted sickness. The contemporary ideal is a pan-hygienic world: a world in which all contacts between men, and between men and their world, are the result of foresight and manipulation. School has become the planned process which tools man for a planned world, the principal tool to trap man in man's trap. It is supposed to shape each man to an adequate level for playing a part in this world game. Inexorably we cultivate, treat, produce, and school the world out of existence.

The military institution is evidently absurd. The absurdity of nonmilitary institutions is more difficult to face. It is even more frightening, precisely because it operates inexorably. We know which switch must stay open to avoid an atomic holocaust. No switch detains an ecological Armageddon.

One important reason for our perplexity is a lack of insight into the sudden emergence of a new style of social reality. It may help us to understand this reality if we compare it in a number of specific aspects with the respective worlds of primitive man and apollonian man.

Primitive man found himself in a world in which he lived in hope and trembling. His culture provided a stable balance, unchangeable within the horizon of one—or even several—generations. Apollonian man rendered this balance unstable; he discovered that he could increase his chance for survival, and he could increase his ability to develop into fuller manhood by creating institutions which would meet his new expectations on a new level of balance. For him the instability of culture became a valuable asset. Contemporary man has gone one step further. He objects in principle to the existence of a balanced world. Such a world for him would be worthless. He wants to build and manage institutions which can increase output indefinitely, which can coproduce goods and ever rising expectations, and which can insure all men of the world the status of consumers with equal rights.

Primitive man satisfied his hunger in a factual manner; he expressed his creativity in traditional forms. He cultivated—but did not conceive of the world as a project. Apollonian man learned to develop new appetites and the right to the satisfaction of new needs. For him society was itself the result of an endeavor which could reach its maturity only by acquiring and satisfying new civilized needs. Contemporary man believes in the constant progress of man in the world, and in the progress of the world itself. Progress swallows development, because continued improvement denies the possibility that any process leads to maturity. According to the contemporary world view, man can always profit from and therefore always and at all cost should seek further schooling, further medical service, further acquisitive power. Society can always profit from further expansion or improvement of a chance for some of its members. Contemporary man replaces the idea of civilized life, with equal rights, to make ever new demands for consumption which generate ever more ravenous needs.

For his sustenance, primitive man inescapably depended on the handouts or the caprice of gods, and on the instinct of the members of his tribe, and on the munificence of nature. He might try to propitiate the gods, to protect and shelter the hordes or family, to protect himself by observing the taboos. Fundamentally, he relied on hope.

Apollonian man did not accept an inescapable lot, but rather faced a tragic fate. In his struggle with necessities he or his peers might triumph or be defeated, but the struggle was always drama. He had to trust the virtue or morality of his neighbors and cocitizens who felt responsible for him. Even more important than protection from enemies was the preservation of the institutional order, the effectiveness of his institutions. He educated his children to fit them, revised his institutions in the light of principles he considered unchangeable, and interpreted the law according to traditional equity.

Contemporary man relies on science to permit him to define new puzzles and find new solutions. He depends on planned chance. Where primitive man could trust the instinct of others, and apollonian man their morality, he gambles on the enlightened self-interest of the functionary, the voter, or the majority, and insures his risks as best he can.

Observance of the taboo and obedience to the laws of the city are replaced by constant adaptation to progress. Trust in nature or the proven effectiveness of tried institutions is replaced by concern with the efficiency of the processes which engineer tools, goods, and services and their consumers; this trust in nature is replaced by the manipulation of the consumer, and laws which create the sense of increased efficiency.

The relationship of the self to the world is also distinct in the three situations: primitive man lived in a world without measure. He could neither measure the world nor could the world measure him. His initiation into reality—as perceived and maintained by his group—happened through initiation rituals. In primitive thought a member of the tribe grows into a man by sharing mythically in the lives of the gods as their doings—at the beginning of the world—become present in the rite.

In classical culture man's learning was a process of measurement; man measured the world with his body and discovered that the world was made to the measure of man. Distances were measured in feet—or in days traveled at the pace of man. Competition could occur, but only man against man, not man against some abstract measuring stick.

Contemporary man learns that he is measured by the same scale which can also be applied to things.

Clock time takes the place of life time; economic space overwhelms living space; speed makes human pace obsolete. Mass supplants weight and the Earth becomes just one of many centers of gravity. While primitive man was surrounded by immeasurable chaos and Greek man had projected the measure of his body into the cosmos, modern man lets measuring instruments impose the same law on things and himself. Mechanics provides the stuff out of which the myths of contemporary man are made. Schooling becomes a supernational measuring stick with its grade levels and test results. Health, welfare, and social service all become measurable.

As the Greeks discovered that the world could be made man's *opus proprium* they also perceived that it was inherently precarious, dramatic, and human. The world of the city child has lost this apollonian transparency. It has reacquired the facticity, necessity, and fatefulness which was characteristic of primitive times. But while the chaos of the barbarian was constantly maintained in the name of mysterious, anthropomorphic gods —today, only man's planning can be given as a reason for the world being as it is. Man has become the plaything of scientists, engineers, and planners.

In this new logic we grant a man the right to survive until the machohygienic environment will have come true, and man will have been re-engineered to fit it. But we grant him this right only if—in the meantime—he does not detain the coming of the reign of the machine.

We see this logic at work in us and in others. I know a Mexican village through which not more than a dozen cars drive each day. A Mexican was playing dominoes on the new hard surface road in front of his house —as he had probably done since his youth. A car sped through and killed him. The tourist who reported the event to me was deeply upset, and yet he said: "He had it coming to him."

At first sight the tourist's remark is not different from the statement of some primitive bushman reporting the death of a fellow who had run across the taboo and therefore had died. But the two statements carry opposite meanings. The primitive can blame some tremendous and dumb transcendence—while the tourist is in awe of the inexorable logic of the machine. The primitive does not sense responsibility—the tourist denies it. In both the primitive and the tourist the apollonian mode of drama, the style of tragedy, the logic of personal endeavor and rebellion is absent. The primitive has not become conscious of it, and the tourist has lost it. The myth of the bushman and the myth of the American are made out of inert, inhuman forces. Neither experience tragic rebellion. For the bushman, the event follows the laws of magic: for the American it follows the laws of science. The event puts him under the spell of the laws of mechanics which for him govern physical, social and psychological events.

The mood of 1970 is propitious to a major change of direction in search of a hopeful future. Institutional goals continuously contradict institutional products. The poverty program produces more poor, the war in Asia more Vietcong, technical assistance more underdevelopment. Birth control clinics increase survival rates and boost the population; schools produce more dropouts; and the curb on one kind of pollution usually increases another.

Consumers are faced with the realization that, the more they can buy, the more deceptions they must swallow. Until recently, it seemed logical that the blame for this pandemic inflation of dysfunctions could be laid either on the limping of scientific discovery behind the technological demands or on the perversity of ethnic, ideological, or class enemies. Both the expectations of a scientific millennium or a war to end all wars have declined.

For the experienced consumer there is no way back to the naive reliance on miracle technologies. Even Buckminster Fuller is not radical

enough anymore. Too many people have had bad experiences with neurotic computers, hospital-bred infections, and jams wherever there is traffic
on the road, in the air, or on the phone. Only ten years ago conventional
wisdom anticipated a better life based on an increase in scientific discovery. Now there is a propensity to dread the contrary. The moon-shots provide a fascinating demonstration that human failure can almost be elimi-
nated among the operators of complex systems—it does not allay our fears
that the human failure to consume according to instruction might spread
out of control.

For the social reformer there is no way back, either, to the assumptions of the forties. The hope has vanished that the problem of justly dis-
tributing goods could be sidetracked by creating an abundance of them.
The cost of minimum packages capable of satisfying modern tastes has
skyrocketed, and what makes tastes modern is their obsolescence prior
even to satisfaction.

The limits of the Earth's resources have become evident. Even if some
humanitarian and totalitarian egalitarianism succeeded in stopping any further increase in the standard of living of the rich, no breakthrough in science or technology could provide every man in the world with the com-
modities and services which are now available to the poor of rich
countries. For instance, it would take the extraction of a hundred times the
present amounts of iron, tin, copper, and lead to achieve such a goal, with
even the "lightest" alternative technology.

Finally, teachers, doctors, and social workers realize that their distinct
professional ministrations have one aspect—at least—in common. They
create further demands for the institutional treatments they provide faster
than they can provide them.

Not just some part, but the very logic of, conventional wisdom is becoming suspect. Even the laws of economy seem unconvincing outside the
narrow parameters which apply to the social, geographic area where most
of the money is concentrated. Money is, indeed, the cheapest currency, but
only in an economy geared to efficiency measured in monetary terms. Both
capitalist and communist countries in their various forms are committed to
measuring efficiency in cost/benefit ratios expressed in dollars. Capitalism
flaunts a higher standard of living as its claim to superiority. Communism
boasts of a higher growth rate as an index of its ultimate triumph. But
under either ideology the total cost of increasing efficiency increases expo-
nentially. The largest institutions compete most fiercely for nonmonetary
resources: the air, the ocean, silence, sunlight, and health. They bring the

scarcity of these resources to public attention only when they are almost irremediably degraded. Everywhere nature becomes poisonous, society inhumane, and the inner life is invaded and personal vocation smothered.

The suspicion that something is structurally wrong with the reality vision of *homo faber* is common to a growing minority in capitalist, communist, and "underdeveloped" countries alike. This suspicion is the shared characteristic of a new elite. To it belong people of all classes, incomes, faiths, and levels of civility. They have become wary of the myths of the majority: of scientific utopias, of ideological diabolism, and of the expectation to give goods and services with some degree of equality. They share with the majority the sense of being trapped. They share with the majority the awareness that most new policies adopted by broad consensus consistently lead to results which are glaringly opposed to their stated aims. Yet, whereas the promethean majority of would-be spacemen still evades the structural issue, the emergent minority is critical of the scientific *deus ex machina,* the ideological panacea, and the hunt for devils and witches. This elite begins to formulate its suspicion that our constant deceptions tie us to contemporary institutions as the chains bound Prometheus to his rock. Suspicion becomes vocation—a call to the task of exposing the Promethean fallacy.

Prometheus is usually thought to mean "foresight," or sometimes even "he who makes the North Star progress." He tricked the gods out of their monopoly of fire, taught men to use it in the forging of iron, became the god of technologists, and wound up in iron chains.

The brother of Prometheus was Epimetheus, or "hindsight." Epimetheus was infatuated when he beheld Pandora. The warnings of Prometheus could not stop his brother from taking Pandora to be his wife, and when the bride opened her amphora, the cycle of civilization started. Promethean Man began to *make* this world. Epimetheus stayed with hope-ful Pandora, and the couple continued to *"do* their thing," as one says today. Epimetheus fathered Pyrrha, who became the wife of Deucalion, the Noah of Greece. Except that his daughter was the second mother of mankind, Epimetheus was forgotten. Only now awakens the possibility that men of his boldness might survive the end of the promethean age.

Pandora was wed as *homo faber* began his ascent. We are now in the twilight of Apollo's day. The Pythia of Delphi has been replaced by a computer which hovers above panels and punch cards. The hexameters of the oracle have given way to twelve-bit codes and instructions. Man the helmsman turns the rudder over to the cybernetic machine. The ultimate machine closes in on us. Children dream of flying in their spacecrafts away from crepuscular earth.

We need a name for those few who love the earth, and on whom the earth's survival depends. Dom Helder Camara has suggested calling them an "abrahamic minority," because Abraham was the father of the faith of Christians and Jews. Dr. Fromm pointed out to Dom Helder that Noah was an even better symbol, since the helmsman of the ark was the father of believers and unbelievers alike, and his commandments did not demand an explicit belief in God but enjoined only the rejection of all idols. Even further in the background stands the father of Pyrrha, the woman on the ark of Noah-Deucalion, son of Prometheus. The grandchildren of Prometheus stand in the line of the forgotten brother Epimetheus. After the twilight of Apollo, hope beyond darkness lies in the dawning of epimethean man.

Homo faber has peopled the world with machines in his image and likeness, machines which make things, in the manner of the sorcerer's apprentice. Epimetheus robs his brother of his deceptions, takes unto himself the products which have been crowding him off the earth and its highways, and uses technology to build roads on which man can once again walk, opens channels by which men can put themselves back in contact with one another. Prometheus has replaced hope with expectations. Epimetheus tears down walls and builds access routes to pierce the darkness and shrink the distance separating the men of the modern city. He seeks after others, not to consume with them, but to live and act in communion.

The Platonic liberal has set minimum standards of manipulation which he imposes on all men to make them into what he considers more human. He needs schools, hospitals, and armies to bring all men under his benevolent control. Epimetheus seeks to guarantee freedom from all processes prescribed for improving or saving a person.

Man the producer spends more and more on tooling others to demand and then use his wares. Epimetheus removes restrictive licensing, credentialing, and all other limits on the free exchange of services.

Man as Sisyphus exhausts himself and the earth as he compulsively produces and consumes in an unending cycle of zealously progressive destruction. Epimetheus protects the munificence of nature by setting maximum per capita levels for the consumption of scarce resources.

Man as Tantalus sees his stolen ambrosia turn to poison as he engineers the production of self-satisfaction right into the organism of man.

Epimetheus knows he is the keeper of hope for others, and he can find hope only in the other he chooses for his neighbor.

In the morning hours of Apollo's day, man had to struggle with that nature he wished to conquer. As darkness falls on his pride, he has now to struggle with himself. The dawn awaits the hour when man will renounce his power to make things which shield him from the other. Prometheus taught us to shape iron. Epimetheus has but to learn to let his heart speak. The drama of Prometheus was a struggle with the gods. The drama of Epimetheus is the search for peace among men.

"The Protestant Ethic" with Fewer Tears

James Luther Adams

In much of current usage "the Protestant Ethic" is associated with the widely influential book of Max Weber (1864–1920), first published in Germany in 1904–1905.[1] No book of its kind has elicited such a wide range of scholarly discussion, much of it a vast misrepresentation.

One of the cruder oversimplifications is offered by William H. Whyte who, in a discussion of Weber, asserts that thrift and the survival of the fittest represent "the Protestant ethic in its purest form."[2] Another misconception epitomizes Weber's thesis by the formula, "Protestantism—or Calvinism—produced capitalism."[3] By others, the slogan "Capitalism produced Calvinism" is recited as an incantation, as if to imply that Weber was a Marxist. As summaries of Weber's thesis these formulas are, at the most, quarter-truths. They overlook the fact that Weber vigorously rejected

[1] Max Weber, *The Protestant Ethic and the Spirit of Capitalism,* tr. Talcott Parsons, Foreword by R. H. Tawney (New York: Charles Scribner's Sons, 1930). Weber's views on the Protestant ethic are also set forth in a later, companion piece, "The Protestant Sects and the Spirit of Capitalism," in H. Gerth and C. W. Mills (trans. and eds.), *From Max Weber: Essays in Sociology* (New York: Oxford University Press, 1946). The former will be referred to hereinafter as *PE.*

[2] William H. Whyte, *The Organization Man* (New York: Simon and Schuster, 1956), p. 14.

[3] An exaggerated version of this stereotype appeared in a conversation I had years ago in Paris with the Russian philosopher Nicolas Berdyaev, who wrote extensively on religion and capitalism. Speaking of the Protestant ethic, he said, "One could have predicted that American civilization would one day collapse, for it is grounded in Calvinism. We see this collapse not only in your greedy businessmen but also in your gangsters. Legs Diamond is a spiritual descendant of John Calvin." Following upon a few minutes' discussion, Berdyaev said in astonishment, "What a surprise to me. Why has no one ever told me that those gangsters are not Presbyterians?"

174

any monocausal theory of history, whether idealistic or realistic (Marxist).

I have chosen to present this essay in honor of Erich Fromm, partly because he has had a long-standing and systematic interest in the role of Christianity, and especially of Protestantism, in Western culture. It is, of course, not my purpose to recapitulate and assess Weber's entire intention and accomplishment in his studies of "the Protestant ethic" (I shall place this term in quotation marks when referring to his conception). That task has already been undertaken by a host of scholars.

My principal concern here is twofold: 1) to remind the reader that since Weber's study was concerned with "ascetic Protestantism" in its relation to economic behavior, he by no means intended a complete account of the Protestant ethic, and 2) to show that in Weber's presentation, even within this limit, he fails to take into account important aspects of "ascetic Protestantism," and that correspondingly he does not give attention to a significant influence of the Protestant ethic, particularly with respect to an indispensable feature of Anglo-American democracy, the voluntary association. In view of the fact that Weber with tears laments the end-result (as he sees it) of "the Protestant ethic," the import of this essay is to qualify his conception of that ethic and its influence, and therefore to view it with fewer tears.[4] This evaluation must take into account Weber's philosophical presuppositions and especially certain value judgments.

Weber is not a sociologist if by that term one refers to the specialist who examines human groups only by means of surveys and statistics. Weber must be classed with such seminal figures as Marx and Nietzsche, Adam Smith and Hegel. In a letter of his earlier years he wrote: "One can measure the honesty of a contemporary scholar, and above all, of a contemporary philosopher, in his posture toward Nietzsche and Marx. Whoever does not admit that he could not perform the most important parts of his work without the work that these two have done swindles himself and others." [5]

Weber, trained initially in law and economics, was a man of strong moral convictions. He was fundamentally concerned with the values of civilization and the ways these values have been formulated and implemented or perverted. As a social scientist, however, he distinguished fact state-

---

[4] The present essay is a considerably altered version of a lecture delivered at the University of Mainz, published in the *Zeitschrift für Evangelische Ethik*, XII, Heft 4/5 (1968), 247–267.

[5] Eduard Baumgarten, *Max Weber, Werk und Person* (Tübingen, 1964), p. 554. Cited by Arthur Mitzman, see Note 7 below.

ments from value judgments, asserting that the social scientist must confine himself to the former. Nevertheless, he not infrequently interrupts his exposition to render a value judgment, and then to apologize before returning to the matter in hand. Here we see an acute inner tension between commitment to scientific objectivity and the values of moral integrity and individual responsibility. A similar tension obtains between his concern for individual freedom and responsibility and his concern for a strong German state.

In examining civilizational values Weber presupposed a conception of man as a historical, social being. Indeed, in the end he developed a philosophy of history. Of crucial significance is his view that the sociologist, like anyone else who aims to understand human behavior, must be concerned with the *meaning* of that behavior. The sociologist, he says, examines behavior "when and insofar as the acting individual attaches a subjective meaning to it." [6] For Weber, as for Wilhelm Dilthey before him, the concept of meaning—a sense of the relation between the parts and the whole —enabled him to probe beneath the symbolism of religious and cultural myths, in search of "a meaningful 'cosmos,' " that is, in search of fundamental social and psychological sanctions and ultimate loyalties. These ultimate loyalties he held to be "religiously conditioned" insofar as they inform "a whole way of life." Precisely because of his concern with meaning (and meaninglessness), Weber as an "objective" social scientist dealt with the most "subjective" aspects of the human venture. In a special sense, then, he was a theological sociologist, though he spoke of himself as religiously "unmusical."

In explication of a doctrine of man, Weber held that ideas are not merely epiphenomena of social conditions and struggles, but decisively affect human behavior and history. At the same time, of course, he recognized that a reciprocal relation obtains between ideas and conditioning factors. His total work is, therefore, full of tensions, and it is a paradox that, despite his rejection of determinism and because of his recognition of conditioning factors (such as the unintended consequences of ideas), he was in contrast to Marx pessimistic in his assessment of present and future possibilities.

In examining "the Protestant ethic" Weber was mindful of his previous studies of the despotism of the Roman slave plantations, of the monopolistic practices of medieval trade associations, of the narrow self-interest and

[6] Max Weber, *Theory of Economic and Social Organization,* Talcott Parsons (ed. and tr.) (New York: Oxford University Press, 1947), p. 88.

political insensitivity of the Junkers, and also of Bismarckian authoritarianism. Indeed, in his view his own father was a well-kept lackey of Bismarckian authoritarianism as well as being an insensitive, domineering husband.[7]

All of these features figured in Weber's decision to study "the Protestant ethic," but as the book title indicates, his exclusive focus was to examine the relation between that ethic and "the spirit of capitalism." In his view, both this ethic and this spirit represent unique features in the history of religions and in the history of capitalisms; moreover, these historical entities enter into reciprocal relations. Without the ethic of ascetic Protestantism the spirit of modern capitalism could not have become so readily widespread. On the other hand, "the spirit of capitalism," in turn, affected the development, indeed the transformation, of "the Protestant ethic."

The unique features of the modern situation, as Weber views them, can be seen by examining his conception of "rational capitalism" and of "the Protestant ethic." These features of modern culture were but two aspects of an all-pervasive Western rationalism, manifest also in the arts, the sciences, and the forms of social organization. Rational capitalism came into being by cutting the moorings from the political capitalism and patrimonial order of the previous period. Rational capitalism not only promotes the free organization of labor and the idea of the intrinsic merit of work, but rejects the notion that acquiring money is a necessary evil. Instead, it views the earning of money as an ethical obligation; rejecting the notion that limits should be placed upon living standards, it promotes innovation by emphasizing impersonal considerations in accomplishing economic tasks efficiently. In these respects it is critical of the inherited tradition. In short, rational capitalism requires a functioning bureaucracy involving impersonal devotion to the task, specialized division of labor and a rationalized discipline. These ingredients call for, indeed they engender, a particular kind of mentality, which Weber identifies as "the spirit of capitalism."[8]

The uniqueness of this spirit Weber sees epitomized "in almost classical purity" in Benjamin Franklin's esteem for thrift and hard work, incumbent

[7] Arthur Mitzman in *The Iron Cage: An Historical Interpretation of Max Weber* (New York: Alfred A. Knopf, 1970) gives a detailed depth-psychological account of the political and family struggles with which Weber was concerned in the period immediately preceding his work on "the Protestant ethic."

[8] Weber's use of the term "spirit" (*Geist*) bespeaks not only his concern for meaning but also his awareness of a German semantic tradition in both religion and philosophy; we think especially of Hegel.

upon men as a profound duty—and in his case "free from all direct relationship to religion." [9] This sense of duty finds expression in virtue and
proficiency in a calling. The calling demands rationality in the sense of
relating means to ends, achieving a systematic, methodical performance,
and subordinating personal to impersonal considerations. Rationality and
calculation, then, become matters of duty. Moreover, ostentatious enjoy-
ment of rewards of success must be eschewed; it can serve only to damage
one's credit and one's standing. Similar characteristics are presented in
Weber's essay "The Protestant Sects and the Spirit of Capitalism," in describing Americans he encountered in the United States who "used" the
church as an accrediting agency in the business community and as a place
to "make contacts."

Alongside the already developing spirit of capitalism a new conception
of meaning, "the Protestant ethic," comes onto the scene. Weber musters
evidence to show that Calvinist theology and Anglo-American Puritanism
were conducive to rationalized, individualistic activity (particularly in the
economic sphere), activity undertaken not for the sake of gain but as a religious duty—to glorify God *in this world*. This vision of human existence
—this "ascetic Protestantism"—was supported by an ethic of vocation or
calling which issued in vigorous methodical activity, thus releasing a tremendous energy. This ethic was motivated by a doctrine of salvation predestined through grace, a doctrine that gave rise to an anxiety that led to
a redoubling of effort. At least initially, the dominant motive was "interest" in the salvation of the individual rather than the acquisition of wealth.[10]

In Weber's view, the central motifs of this vision of life had an independent origin in an interpretation of the Bible and of the disciplines of
the Christian life. Through the spread of these ideas in England when "the
spirit of capitalism" was already developing, they present a new attitude
toward worldly activity which, in essential features, is "congruent" with
that spirit. Accordingly, the ideas of the Puritans provide a milieu that is
both receptive to the spirit of rational capitalism and able to qualify that
spirit in terms of the "interest" of the Puritan in individual salvation,
wherein a sign of grace is righteous, industrious, methodical activity in the
world—labor in a calling. In time, however, ascetic Protestantism lost its

---

[9] *PE,* p. 48.

[10] Space does not permit our attempting even to summarize Weber's account of the
theological foundations of the Calvinist system, the absolutely transcendent, supramundane God, salvation by grace, the theory of predestination, the consequent
"inner isolation" of the individual before God and man.

powerful religious orientation and sanctioned a simple doctrine of work in the pursuit of wealth; indeed it even sanctioned the doctrine that wealth is a sign of grace, and finally that "piety is the surest road to wealth." These changes might be called Weber's account of the devil's toboggan slide of ascetic Protestantism.[11] To be sure, these developments are traced in detail and with considerable subtlety, but much of the evidence offered has been challenged by other scholars.[12]

Three other aspects of Weber's intention remain to be stressed. First, Weber says that he is "interested . . . in the influence of those psychological sanctions which, originating in religious belief and the practice of religion, gave a direction to practical conduct and held the individual to it." [13] In the main, therefore, he was interested not so much in sociological, structural features of the societal changes taking place as in the psychological sanctions for the legitimacy of a new pattern of the individual's conduct, that is, for the legitimacy of rational economic activity considered as a duty. To be sure, social-structural changes occurred, as in the emerging independence of economic and other activities from political control, a precondition of a pluralistic society. Weber focuses attention on the personality types attracted to the new patterns and their motivations. He also

[11] Having outlined the Weberian conception of the rise and decline of "the Protestant ethic," we should now observe that Erich Fromm's view of the advent and the consequences of Protestantism is quite different. For him Protestantism in the Reformation was not primarily a set of ideas initiating a new movement in history. Rather, the breakdown of the feudal medieval system which gave life a meaning through nourishing "a sense of security and belonging," left the individual, especially in the middle classes, isolated and free, and hence economically insecure and anxious. Luther and Calvin rationalized, intensified, and systematized this attitude, teaching men to accept their impotence and submit. One of the components of this Protestant ethos was the individual's compulsion to work, and this became one of the productive forces in capitalistic society (Erich Fromm, *Escape from Freedom* [New York: Rinehart and Co., 1941], Chap. III). Modern man, having been freed from the bondage of medieval economic and political ties, finds himself impotent and lonely in the midst of the supra-personal forces of capital and the market; he seeks escape from loneliness in the spurious and debilitating sense of belonging offered by Nazism or by the deceptions of "democratic" capitalism which make him into a compulsive, conforming automaton while seducing him into believing he is a free, self-determining individual. Although Fromm's view and that of Weber converge or overlap at certain points, their respective conceptions of the Protestant ethic and its role in the development of modern capitalist society differ quite markedly.

[12] See, for one example, Winthrop Hudson's documented critique of Weber's presentation (and distortion) of the ideas of Richard Baxter who serves as Exhibit A in Weber's "case": "Puritanism and the Spirit of Capitalism," *Church History,* 18:1 (March, 1949), 3–17.

[13] *PE*, p. 97.

indicates ways in which individual conduct is constricted by social forces it has released.

Second, Weber attempted, as part of his method, to construct "ideal types." This method, he insisted, had long been used (indeed is inevitable in analyzing human behavior); but he felt that it required clarification. Here again the concept of meaning is of crucial significance. The ideal type is an intellectual tool, a unified analytical construct, devised by the historian or sociologist in order to characterize unique, meaning-oriented phenomena of human action, and in such a way as to give them a quality of generality whereby comparison and contrast with other meaning-oriented phenomena become possible. The concept of meaning is involved here in dual fashion. Being a construct, the ideal type in the first place reflects the value-orientation of the one who devises or uses it as a tool. In the second place, it selects and accentuates concrete, individual phenomena in a onesided way so as to achieve precision, a precision that combines generality with individuality in a context of meaning. Weber thus combines insights regarding generality and particularity which may be traced respectively to the Enlightenment and to Romanticism. Since ideal types are made up of highly abstract patterns, he speaks of their being "utopian" (not to be found anywhere in concrete detail) and also of their "artificial simplicity." They serve as "conceptual points of reference" for "experiments" in comparative cultural analysis. Major illustrations of these ideal types are such concepts as otherworldly and this-worldly asceticism; a patrimonial traditionalist social order and a rational, innovating capitalist order; and, of course, the Protestant ethic and the spirit of rational capitalism.[14] In later writings Weber developed a whole series of ideal types, such as types of authority or domination (traditional, legal-rational, and charismatic) and types of prophetism (ethical and exemplary). It has been suggested that Weber's ideal types may be compared to Hegel's logically related concepts. Weber, to be sure, rejects any "emanationist" or dialectical theory of the sort espoused by Hegelian idealism. He was not only religiously but also metaphysically "unmusical."

Obviously, the particular form of an ideal type depends entirely upon the features chosen for accentuation. Hence, an ideal type is like a wax nose to be shaped in a variety of ways. Think of the protracted debate of the past generation regarding the question, What was the Renaissance? Similarly, Weber's ideal type of "the Protestant ethic," as we shall see, is not only made of wax; it is also a bone of contention.

[14] For references to ideal types in *PE,* see pp. 71, 98, 200.

Third, we must stress what we have already hinted at, namely that in Weber's view a crucial feature of Western culture is the element of rationality. He sees an anticipation of it in the universal ethical prophetism stemming from the Old Testament which in both Judaism and Christianity has served in principle to combat magic. Of course, he finds it in Greek science and logic. He also points out that, along with an ethos of work, it appears conspicuously in medieval monasticism in its methodical features.

Rationality "covers a whole world of different things." Moreover, for Weber it possesses a markedly ambiguous value: it is capable of obstructing as well as of promoting human freedom and fulfillment. If we spell out here its positive and negative aspects, we shall the more readily grasp the character of Weber's doctrine of man and his philosophy of civilization.

In its more positive aspects rationality appears in: the deliberate weighing of a methodical course of action; the process of intellectualization for the sake of clarity; self-control that overcomes instinct and "everything impulsive and irrational"; the rationalization of mystical contemplation; the shaping of means to ends; the method of scientific investigation (including the mathematization of knowledge); machine production, technology, and the mastery of the world; the division and coordination of activities for the purpose of achieving efficiency and productivity (which requires, for example, rational bookkeeping); the stability and predictability of bureaucracy; the organization of free labor to create or appeal to a market; the rational-legal acquisition of wealth by virtue of one's ability and initiative; the limitation of occupational effort to specialized work; military training; the system of counterpoint in music; the establishment of rational-legal authority; the logical ordering and rearrangement of the contents of the law; the conceiving of different types of order in society; the carrying through of radical social change; and, of course, the construction of ideal types. In all of these forms of rationality we see the combining of order and meaning. Many of these expressions of rationality have appeared in modern "rational capitalism" in its conflict with traditionalism, while many of them antedate the modern period. But rationality appears in unique fashion in "rational capitalism" and in this-worldly "ascetic Protestantism"—in its methodical and ethical conduct of life motivated by a coherent system of doctrine and commitment which is able to overcome an inherited traditionalist system.

On its negative side, rationality can be severely restrictive. It can appear in the conservative philosophy calculated to resist social change; it can claim to understand everything under a single perspective; it can reduce almost everything to specialization and to the rigidity of bureaucratic system, thus stifling individual decision and initiative; and it contributes to the "disenchantment" of the world and to the elimination of any vital sense of meaning and depth in existence. In these ways it becomes a threat to, indeed the destruction of, belief in the supra-empirical validity of an ethic rooted either in a humane sense of values or in a religious conception of the ultimate structure of things. Thus it can be the enemy of authentic personality and of commitment to "the daemon who holds the thread of its life." In these and in other ways rationality can lead to dehumanizing, compulsive behavior, to irrationality, and meaninglessness.

The positive aspects of rationality (along with individual freedom and responsibility) delineated by Weber are indispensable elements in civilization, and of course are cherished by him. The negative aspects, on the other hand, illustrate the axiom: the corruption of the best is the worst. It is no accident that the account given of the corruption of freedom and reason by Weber, a scholar learned in theological lore, should remind one of the Christian theologian's account of the corruption of the *imago dei*. In this respect one must say that Weber reveals a tragic view of history—in the Hebraic sense. Human freedom and reason are a heavy burden (as well as a gift) requiring constant vigilance; they are the pivot at once of meaning and of the possibility of the fall into unfreedom, irrationality, and meaninglessness. So fundamental for Weber is the negative dimension of rationality that it can be said to correspond to the concept of alienation in the thought of Karl Marx and Erich Fromm. Erich Fromm holds with Weber, however, that insofar as Marxism promotes monolithic bureaucracy it simply guarantees the continuation or creation of alienation. The dictatorship of the proletariat turns out to be the dictatorship of the bureaucrats.

Weber's most negative judgment on technical rationality and on the secularized, corrupted "Protestant ethic" appears in the famous passage near the end of his book:

> The Puritan wanted to work in a calling; we are forced to do so. For when asceticism was carried out of monastic cells into everyday life, and began to dominate worldly morality, it did its part in building the tremendous cosmos of the modern economic order. This order is now bound to the technical and economic conditions of machine production which today determine the lives of all the individuals who are born into this mechanism, not only those directly concerned with economic acquisition, with irresistible force. Perhaps it will so determine

them until the last ton of coal is burnt. In Baxter's view the care for external goods should only lie on the shoulders of "the saint like a light cloak, which can be thrown aside at any moment." But fate decreed that the cloak should become an iron cage . . . No one knows who will live in this cage in the future, or whether at the end of this tremendous development entirely new prophets will arise, or there will be a great rebirth of old ideas and ideals, or, if neither, mechanized petrification, embellished with a sort of convulsive self-importance. For of the last stage of this cultural development, it might well be truly said: "Specialists without spirit, sensualists without heart; and this nullity imagines that it has attained a level of civilization never before achieved." [15]

Then Weber goes on to make his usual apology for violating the principle that the social scientist should not inject value judgments into his presentation. "But this brings us," he says, "to the world of judgments of value and of faith, with which this purely historical discussion need not be burdened."

Despite the positive values of rationality, then, and despite the initial capacity of Puritanism to bring a new sense of meaning into life and to initiate a revolutionary process that displaced a restrictive social order, the outcome is an iron cage, a soul-less compulsive social system of specialization and bureaucratism without spirit and without heart—a nullity. This specialization and bureaucratism are closely linked with the joyless and impersonal character of work and with "its joyless lack of meaning." Moreover, capitalism, being today "in the saddle, . . . is able to force people to labour without transcendental sanctions." [16] The negative aspects of rationality have overwhelmed the positive.

In reading the long passage just quoted one is reminded of Nietzsche's prediction of the advent of "the last man," who will be a completely rationalized cog in a machine without creative vitality. This outcome, in Weber's view, is the working of the unintended consequences of initially noble impulses, and his comparative studies in the sociology of religion were intended to confirm this insight and to serve as a warning. In this connection one may think of Hegel's theory of "the cunning of reason." But whereas Hegel refers to the hidden instrument of the World Spirit unfolding and realizing a divine purpose, Weber's view is pessimistic—pessimistic also in contrast to the ultimate optimism of Marx. Weber leaves modern man

[15] *PE*, pp. 181–182.
[16] *PE*, p. 282.

in the iron cage; he questions whether there is a way out, hinting only at a variety of foggy possibilities.[17] Weber never loses his fear of perverted reason. It is strange, however, that despite his basic interest in economic forces, he says nothing here about poverty and the maldistribution of wealth. Nor does he explore the possible correction of bureaucratism. Yet, however dusty the answers he gives to the larger social issues raised, we must say with Benjamin Nelson that a major thrust of this whole study of "the Protestant ethic" is to be seen in his concluding protest against "conscienceless reason." [18]

While appreciating the immensity of Weber's accomplishment and the stimulus he has given to the study of the relations between religion and society, I want to offer three critical comments on his presentation of "the Protestant ethic."

First, let it be noted again that Weber's ideal type of "the Protestant ethic" is by intention a restricted one, in that by means of it he aims only to set forth the essential features of the relation between that ethic and economic behavior. On the last pages of the book he emphasizes this point and specifies the large areas of investigation which remain to be undertaken.[19] The ideal type constructed by Weber, then, is not an ideal type of the Protestant ethic as a whole. It excludes from consideration those types of Protestantism which do not belong under the rubric of ascetic Protestantism. Nor is it an ideal type of ascetic Protestantism as a whole.

Second, Weber stresses the point that the meaning of life in Calvinism and Puritanism was rooted in a belief in "a supramundane God" who is

---

[17] In his later writings Weber works out one of these possibilities in his conception of a nonrational, charismatic authority (initially a theological concept) in contrast to rational-legal and to traditionalist authority. *Charisma,* he says, rests in part "upon the belief in magical powers, revelations and hero worship," but it is destined to be routinized in the direction of bureaucracy. For a discussion of Weber's probable dependence on the church historian Rudolf Sohm for this view see the present writer's essay on "Rudolf Sohm's Theology of Law and Spirit," in Walter Leibrecht (ed.), *Religion and Culture: Essays in Honor of Paul Tillich* (Harper & Bros., 1959). The term *charisma* appears only once in *PE.*

[18] From a paper read at the 1964 Weber Centenary Conference held in Heidelberg, Germany, published in *Max Weber und die Soziologie Heute.* Otto Stammer (ed.), Tübingen, 1965.

[19] Noneconomic areas excluded from Weber's study have been investigated by Robert K. Merton (in the sphere of science), Michael Walzer (in politics), David Little (in law), and Ernst Troeltsch. Indeed, Weber himself said later on that because of Troeltsch's subsequent, massive accomplishment he did not retain his initial intention to explore other areas of social life in relation to "the Protestant ethic." *PE,* p. 284.

sovereign over the whole of life. Yet, due to his concentration on the "interests" and the conduct of the individual, Weber almost entirely ignores the Puritan concern for the social order as a whole. This deficiency in Weber's study is today receiving increasing attention. David Little, for example, has recast the Weberian thesis by directing attention to the Calvinist and Puritan demand for a new order of society.[20] In this connection we should add that Weber gives little attention to the internal life of the churches and the "pathos for order" rooted in the church fellowship.[21] Thus he fails to take into account the Calvinist view that the church and its members have the obligation to work for the establishment of a society of justice and mercy. For Calvin and for many of the Calvinists of the period, the Christian bears a *general* vocation in the world as well as having a specific calling in his daily work. This outlook is today referred to as "the totalistic impulse" of the Calvinists, and a recognition of it has given rise to a new phase of the controversy over Weber's thesis.[22] As a consequence of his not taking this "impulse" sufficiently into account, and of his centering attention on predestination and on the anxiety of the individual regarding his own salvation, Weber's finding with respect to "psychological sanctions" turns out to be inadequate.

The totalistic impulse of Calvinism is to be seen especially in the effort of the Puritans in England to take over the Establishment. When this effort failed, many of them became vigorous Dissenters, forming a variety of movements bent on reform. The totalistic impulse did not die. It was in wider commonalty spread (to adapt a phrase from John Milton). In this new situation sectarian doctrines of the church came to the fore, some of which developed into a proto-democratic doctrine of the free or voluntary church, but the demands for a new social order were not relinquished even

[20] David Little, *Religion, Order, and Law: A Study in Pre-Revolutionary England* (New York: Harper & Row, 1969).
[21] Because of this gap in Weber's investigation of Puritanism, Roger Mehl in his work on *The Sociology of Protestantism,* James H. Farley, trans. (Philadelphia: Westminster Press, 1970), questions whether Weber's study of "the Protestant ethic" can be "qualified as sociology of religion," for it fails to interpret religion as an "emanation of the social group" (p. 18).
[22] Cf. S. N. Eisenstadt, "The Protestant Ethic Thesis in an Analytical and Comparative Framework," in S. N. Eisenstadt, ed., *The Protestant Ethic and Modernization* (New York: Basic Books, 1968). In his essay Eisenstadt traces the stages of the controversy, the first stage being concerned with the question of the direct causal relation between Calvinist ethic and the development of capitalism, the second with the discussion of Protestantism's influence after it had "failed to carry out its first totalistic impulses."

though they were fragmented. In the middle of the century John Lilburne and the Levellers, for example, formed associations for political agitation, using rational techniques to appeal to public opinion. (Perhaps one can say that at that time "public opinion" as a factor in political life was born.) In some circles the idea of a democratic structure in the church was by analogy transformed into a demand for a democratic political order. Many of these efforts exhibit the continued working of the "totalistic impulses."

Of equal importance in this connection was another aspect of this development. The idea of the free or voluntary church, in order to vindicate itself in the face of the Establishment, called for a struggle for the freedom of religious association. In time this struggle was extended to a struggle for the freedom to form other voluntary associations. So noisy were some of these associations that Thomas Hobbes asserted that all such associations are subversive and dangerous—"worms in the entrails of the natural man" (Leviathan). Even the Anglicans began to form religious societies for the reformation of morals. These societies flourished for fifty years after the Restoration, and were able even to elicit cooperation from the Dissenters.[23] The Friends early in the eighteenth century refined the techniques of agitation toward the end of effecting legislation extending their religious and political freedom.[24]

Here we encounter, then, one of the most significant features of the Protestant ethic which Weber ignored by reason of the limits of his study. Ernst Troeltsch has asserted that the Calvinists were given "to an organized and aggressive effort to form associations, to a systematic endeavor to mold the life of society as a whole, to a kind of 'Christian Socialism.' "[25] Protestants in England and America in the eighteenth and nineteenth centuries formed associations to promote philanthropy, educa-

[23] Dudley Bahlman, *The Moral Revolution of 1688* (New Haven: Yale University Press, 1957).

[24] Norman Hunt, *Two Early Political Associations* (Oxford University Press, 1961). The author shows that the Friends at this time invented the essential techniques we associate today with "pressure groups." Shades of rationality!

[25] Ernst Troeltsch, *The Social Teaching of the Christian Churches,* tr. Olive Wyon (New York: Harper & Row, 1960), II, 602. We should note here that the earliest modern theorists of associations were Calvinists. Chief among them was Althusius. See Frederick S. Carney, "Associational Thought in Early Calvinism," in D. B. Robertson (ed.), *Voluntary Associations* (Richmond, Va.: John Knox Press, 1966). D. B. Robertson in his chapter on "Hobbes's Theory of Associations" characterizes Hobbes as "the greatest and most formidable enemy [of voluntary associations] in modern times."

tional reform, penal reform, factory reform, free trade, international peace, the extension of the suffrage, women's rights, the abolition of slavery and child labor, better working and living conditions, trade unions, cooperatives, the prohibition of alcoholic beverages, "municipal socialism," civil rights and liberties, lobbies, communitarian movements, know-nothing campaigns, and a multitude of other causes (including of course "antisocial causes" and "special interests").[26] Clearly, many of these associations have changed economic behavior.

In New England one can see the beginnings of these associations in the activities of the Friends in the seventeenth century, and later in the admonitions of Cotton Mather (*Bonifacius,* 1710) to form associations for philanthropic and moral purposes. Mather reports that he belonged to twenty such associations.[27] Benjamin Franklin makes it clear that in forming voluntary organizations he was initially inspired by Cotton Mather's book. Early in the nineteenth century when the United States was rapidly becoming a "nation of joiners" fairly elaborate theories of association came from the pens of leading clergymen.[28]

These associational movements for social change, anticipated in principle in seventeenth-century Puritanism, may be viewed as activities that in varying ways expressed a sense of vocation broader than that which Weber presents with respect to the vocation of daily work. They provide the citizen with the opportunity to emerge from the "iron cage" of specialization and to join fellow citizens in bringing under criticism economic as well as political and other institutions. They have served in both church and society as a principal means to promote criticism and innovation, individual and group participation and responsibility, and thus the dispersion of power. Although subject to manipulation and to rigid, soul-less bureaucratization, they have been a source of vital tension within the Protestant ethic. In the positive Weberian sense they represent a major form of ra-

---

[26] Denominational histories abound with examples of these associations. I give only one example which stresses the activities of Protestant Dissenters: Raymond V. Holt, *The Unitarian Contribution to Social Progress in England* (London: Allen & Unwin, 1938).

[27] Richard E. French, *Cotton Mather and the Development of American Values* (Harvard University Th.D. Dissertation, 1970), p. 163.

[28] For an account of three major American Protestant theorists of voluntary association, in the early nineteenth century, see the present writer's chapter on "The Voluntary Principle in the Forming of American Religion," in Elwyn A. Smith (ed.), *The Religion of the Republic* (Philadelphia: Fortress Press, 1971).

tionality in Anglo-American life, toward the end of "turning the flank of
recalcitrant institutions." [29] Moreover, for more than three centuries these
associations have provided a continuing critique of what Weber calls "the
Protestant ethic." They represent the institutional gradualization of revolution.

Why does Weber leave this whole dimension out of his delineation of
"the Protestant ethic"? The answer is that in tracing the development of
individualism he left out of account the residues of the "totalistic impulses" of original Puritanism. But there is an additional reason.

In a lecture of 1911 entitled "A Proposal for the Study of Voluntary
Associations," delivered in Frankfurt, Germany, at an International Sociological Congress, Weber said:

> The man of today is without doubt an association man in an awful
> and never dreamed of degree. Germany stands in this matter at a very
> high point . . . America is the association-land par excellence. In
> America membership in some middle-class association belongs directly
> to one's legitimation as a gentleman. The prototype of these associa-
> tions is the sect, a union of specifically qualified people. Today the as-
> sociation furnishes the ethical qualification test for the businessman,
> certifying that he is worthy of credit. American democracy is no sand
> heap, but a maze of exclusive sects, societies and clubs. These support
> the selection of those adapted to American life; they support it in that
> they help such people to business, political and every kind of success
> in social life. In these associations the American learns to put himself
> over. [30]

No one can deny that this kind of association has existed in wild variety.
But the association concerned with the public weal or with public policy,
so far from legitimating the qualifications of those who worship at the altar
of the bitch goddess Success, often elicits obloquy rather than enviable status for its members.

We have already observed that Weber views Benjamin Franklin as a
manifestation of the spirit of capitalism "in almost classical purity," devoted as he was to frugality and industry for the sake of personal success.
But Franklin was also the association-man par excellence. He probably

[29] A. D. Lindsay, *The Two Moralities* (London: Eyre & Spotiswoode, 1940), p. 85.
Lord Lindsay, Master of Balliol College, Oxford, has been one of the major scholars
concerned to trace voluntary associational efforts back to the Puritans.
[30] Manuscript translation by Everett C. Hughes.

formed more associations for the public good than any other American of his time: an academy for the education of youth in Pennsylvania, a voluntary fire department, the Pennsylvania Hospital, a society for the abolition of slavery, and the American Philosophical Society (which is still flourishing), and so on. If Franklin's secularized frugality and devotion to a methodical discipline of life and work were due to the influence of "the Protestant ethic," may we not say that his concern for the methodical discipline of associations calculated to promote the public good was also influenced by the Protestant ethic of "totalistic impulse"?

One might raise the question as to why Weber took such a narrow view of the voluntary association as we have just observed. The reason is perhaps that in Germany he could see few associations of the type concerned with public policy. In the lecture just cited he scores the singing academies for draining off the national energy into "warbling," thus distracting attention from public policies (a distraction which, he says, was much to the liking of the politicians in Berlin). Another reason is that in considering the sect as an agency certifying the qualifications of piety he selected characteristics belonging more exclusively to the *withdrawing sect* rather than to the Puritan *aggressive sect* bent on bringing in a new social order (the distinction is Troeltsch's).

We see, then, that "ascetic Protestantism" from the beginning possessed a more composite character than that which Weber attributes to it. No doubt it was because of the broad scope of the totalistic dynamic that Troeltsch spoke of Calvinism as the second social philosophy in the history of Christianity (the first being Thomism and medieval Catholicism). With similar perception Lord Acton was wont to say that the nerve of democracy as we know it was engendered in the small Puritan conventicles of the seventeenth century.

Weber has seen a different side of ascetic Protestantism. But by neglecting the features we have adumbrated here he has given us a lopsided conception of the Protestant ethic. With him we may properly lament the appearance of the degenerated, rationalized, "encaged" Protestantism he presents. But considering the vitalities he has failed to see, may we not be allowed to lament with fewer tears?

But that question is not the proper way to end this essay. Sixty-five years have passed since Max Weber published his study of the Protestant ethic and the spirit of capitalism. The nullity of which he spoke is more readily evident today than when he pointed to it. What Weber the prophet offers us is the shock of recognition—to enable us to see the cage of the so-called affluent society. Erich Fromm with more hope has for years effectively communicated the same shock, and has tried to find ways out of the cage for the authentic man whom Nietzsche calls the self-surpassing creature, the bridge to the future.

III *Social and Political Issues*

Notes
on
Educational
Reform *   David Riesman

Keeping in touch with efforts at educational reform in American universities has become increasingly difficult. Several years ago only a few pace-
setter institutions were experimenting with interdisciplinary courses, field
study programs, student-initiated courses, and independent study in their
undergraduate programs. But today these innovations have spread throughout academia in response to changed faculty attitudes and the newer
youth subcultures.[1] Exceptional places like St. John's Colleges at Annapolis and Santa Fe fight a continuing engagement in defense of traditional curricula resting on a program of Great Books which must be
accepted in its entirety. However, elsewhere students as well as faculty,
who have been in constant communication with each other, have helped
to spread experiments begun in one locale all over the academic map—
generally with the consequence of minimizing the traditional curricular
requirements or eliminating them altogether.

Understandably, educational reform is intertwined with other issues:
for instance, with the attack on science as stultifying, "irrelevant," or dangerous to mankind; with programs in black studies or in urban studies
which often have the highest priority on a campus, frequently with the aim

* I am indebted for helpful suggestions to Michael Maccoby, Edwin Harwood, and
Robert Bellah. Support for my research on higher education has come from the Ford
Foundation and the Carnegie Corporation.
[1] Both the sheer magnitude of change and the degree to which it may promote ho-
mogeneity are suggested by Harold L. Hodgkinson, *Institutions in Transition: A Study
of Change in Higher Education,* a publication of the Carnegie Commission on
Higher Education, 1970; for discussion of change in some pioneering liberal arts colleges, see Morris Keeton and Conrad Hilberry, *Struggle and Promise: A Future for
Colleges* (New York: McGraw-Hill Book Co., 1969).

of doing something about white racism or ghetto poverty. In many colleges the proponents of participatory educational democracy—carrying into (more or less) voluntary associations the national principle of "one man, one vote"—contend that participation per se is a more important reform than any substantive changes in styles of teaching and learning. Correspondingly, whatever else may be happening on a campus, a drastic delegitimation of authority is proceeding, whether this be the authority of experts or professionals, of curricular programs, or of traditions of scholarship and learning. In the place of the older authority there has arisen what Erich Fromm in *Escape from Freedom* and *Man for Himself* described as anonymous authority: the authority of whatever is defined as relevant and consonant with an epoch of rapid social change, in short, with whatever extracurricular preoccupations students and faculty now press upon their institutions.

Though I do not agree with Erich Fromm in some of his specific comments on education today, notably in connection with Summerhill, I believe that the implications of his general thought for the understanding of education are very important. My own thinking about education and my work over many years as an educational reformer are the beneficiaries of Erich Fromm's work and example. For instance, the distinction he makes between rational and irrational authority, analogous to the one he draws between rational and irrational affects, is helpful to me when I reflect on the present battle over authority in higher education.[2] When he first made his distinction between rational and irrational affects—thus arguing that there can be rational love and rational hate—the intellectual climate tended to regard rationality as affect-free (and therefore, as good and trustworthy); while we move unevenly into an era which regards irrationality as life-giving and rationality as merely a hang-up, the distinction, with values reversed, remains.[3] Fromm's thought is syncretic, not only with respect

[2] Many social critics, when they encounter what they regard as excesses of reason, are tempted to turn against reason itself and to defend irrationality as somehow more deeply human. Fromm's distinction preserves reason as essentially human, undercutting the despair that leads to praising irrationality per se. Cf. the candid, troubled discussion in George P. Elliott, "Revolution Instead—Notes on Passions and Politics," an essay principally concerning education, *The Public Interest,* 20 (1970), 65–89, especially pp. 85 ff.

[3] The distinction is not a simple one, and there is no space here fully to explore Fromm's meaning. He considers rational those affects which are conducive to the optimal functioning of human beings, to the growth and unfolding of life; irrational affects are those which diminish or weaken the capacity for the art of life. Love

to this ancient dualism of thought and feeling, but also with respect to the differences among the great world religions and such civil (or nonreligious) religions as patriotism, socialism, or humanism. Characteristic also is his insistence that the past should not be junked (an almost impossible effort in any event) even while one tries to move toward a more hopeful future; thus he has recently written: "For many of the younger generation who belittle the value of traditional thought, I should like to stress my conviction that even the most radical development must have its continuity with the past; that we cannot progress by throwing away the best achievements of the human mind—and that to be young is not enough!" [4]

Beyond such conceptual clarifications, his influence has led me in my thinking about education and teaching to appreciate the importance of moral qualities in the scholar and teacher. Just as he asks investigators in scientific research to be open to observation and impressions and hunches, so also he argues in teaching and in psychoanalysis for openness that lessens defensiveness and the need to impress others. Contrary to the ideology of many Americans, perhaps especially males, he stresses the importance of vulnerability as one of the qualities of humaneness.[5] While I know that in dealing with sullen or actively hostile students my own resiliency leaves much to be desired and my good humor often deserts me, Fromm's model of unsentimental vulnerability is something I try to attain. Generally speaking, he sees the importance for creative intellectual work of such moral qualities as this, as well as courage and faith; intelligence unanchored in the affective life is not enough. Indeed, I have observed that it is the cultivation of these moral qualities which often makes the difference between interesting, potentially significant work, and conventional academic gamesmanship. (Needless to say, gamesmanship can take many forms: increasingly it takes the form of desire to shock and to appear properly rebellious, a member of what Harold Rosenberg once termed "the herd of independent minds.")

---

might then be rational if not based on masochism or possessiveness. Hatred would generally be irrational, markedly so when it is of an idling kind, as in an idling motor, waiting for targets of opportunity—but arguably rational when reactive to a specific threat to life. Whether an affect is rational or not says nothing about its comprehensibility through reason: both alike can be in principle understood.

[4] See Erich Fromm, *The Revolution of Hope: Toward a Humanized Technology* (New York: Harper & Row, 1968), Foreword, p. xvii.
[5] See *ibid.*, p. 85 and elsewhere.

Current Themes of Educational Reform

During the academic year 1968–1969, while on leave from Harvard, I had the opportunity to discuss ideas and ideals of educational change and reform with students and faculty at a number of places widely differing from each other: Stanford University (then engaged in a large self-study); the University of California at Davis and at San Diego; the University of North Carolina (where the first two undergraduate years were being examined by a student-faculty committee); the new College of the State University of New York at Old Westbury which had just opened that year; Oakland University in Michigan; and, more briefly, Pitzer College in the Claremont group of colleges. In addition, I perused the student press at a number of colleges and followed the discussions of reform in the educational journals. I have already indicated the similarity of concerns that one meets from coast to coast. Everywhere one encounters the desire for a more egalitarian university. Meritocratic distinctions are under attack and so is the apparatus of grades, course prerequisites, and selective admissions. One often finds encounter groups or sensitivity training sessions praised as the optimal situations for learning, in part on the ground that faculty authority and expertness could be reduced and true mutuality encouraged. While some encounter groups do succeed in opening people up to themselves and others, at times intrusively and at other times with greater care and tact, there may be a general tendency to focus on the intrapsychic in such settings. But one also finds a widespread effort to get students and faculty out into field situations, such as community organizing or experiments in communal living.[6] The range of field settings that is envisaged is likely to be narrow: pockets of poverty, inner-city ghettos, the exotic and the deprived; less often will students involve themselves in the life of a church, a business corporation, or a small town.

In all these areas, the trend is away from what is regarded as alienated learning and toward first-hand experience. An amateur spirit prevails, which has its benign sides but also certain dangers. There is a frequent belief that theoretical work gets in the way of experience: a naive underesti-

[6] Of course, I am not implying that learning could not occur in field settings! I do my best to encourage my own students to do manageable pieces of empirical work, for instance some enterprise of participant-observation or a small-scale interview study. However, many newly developed programs that boast of putting students out into the field do not provide the kind of preparation that a good anthropology department would. For further note on encounter groups, see footnote 20.

mation of the epistemological problems of experience itself. Related to this on many campuses is a rejection of rationalism and of the search for objectivity in scholarship, an attitude which identifies spontaneity with irrationality and regards cognition as necessarily deadening, and the effort to categorize as a sign of necrophilic tendencies. This view finds support in the various drug subcultures on the campus, as well as in the continuing attack on research as a sophisticated support for the status quo, and thus for war. If one asks students of this persuasion why they wish to be in the university at all, apart from the imperatives imposed by the draft, they will sometimes say that this is where their friends are, where they can be away from home, and where they can use the resources of the university as a base for their extramural activities.[7] These ideas of educational reform originated in the elite colleges and among articulate critics, and often had the support of the student press. But they have spread to many campuses in what were once provincial parts of the country, including the "provinces" of large cities, where most students are the first generation in their families to attend college.[8] The vocal students who have been the carriers of educational change are apt to be the more affluent, to be majoring in the humanities or the "softer" social sciences, and to be male and white.[9] These students contend that the educational system oppresses them, though

[7] The term "community" comes up constantly in these discussions: there is the academic community, the black community, the student community, etc. The term carries none of the tentativeness with which Erich Fromm speaks of the formation of Groups in the last chapter of *The Revolution of Hope* (pp. 158–162). There is instead in these discussions a naiveté in assuming that people who share contiguous turf will have anything in common and that they already form a community rather than a series of competing barrios or fractionated sects.

[8] The same is true in the high schools. See *How Old Will You Be in 1984: Expressions of Student Critique from the High School Free Press,* Diane Divoky (ed.) (New York: Avon Books, 1969).

[9] Black students on the white campus may come together to demand Black Studies programs and greater "relevance" to the urban scene or to the problems of blacks; but in general, in my observation, they do not favor radical educational reform, but feel more secure with traditional "collegiate" structures both in the curriculum and the extracurriculum; they are often at odds with white radical students who, the blacks feel, can afford to dispense with universities whereas they, as members of a previously deprived group, need all the educational benefits they can get.

I know no coed campus where women have taken the leadership in educational reform, and I believe they suffer as blacks do from some of the current temptations of reformers, since the women need to make full use of their undergraduate years to establish quasi-professional competence if they are not to remain dependent on the chances and mischances of marriage and to have the opportunity to enter careers outside the prevailing range of "women's jobs." *See* David Riesman, "Observations on Contemporary College Students—Especially Women," *Interchange,* vol. 1, pp. 50–63.

most are not so despairing as the violent activists who see in the university the symbol of "the corrupt society" and seek to stop its operations altogether. Nonetheless, even moderate student reformers and their faculty supporters share with antiuniversity activists an ignorance of the history of American higher education.[10] They are seldom aware of the irony that many in other industrial societies are seeking to incorporate the American practices now under attack in order to strengthen their own systems of higher education. This lack of historical knowledge helps sustain the mythology that American higher education was once uncorrupted by commercialism, careerism, or other worldly constraints.[11]

Many students, however, do read. When I have asked them what books have influenced their ideas of educational change, they mention the writings of John Holt, George Leonard (*Education and Ecstasy*), Herbert Marcuse, Norman O. Brown, A. S. Neill, Edgar Friedenberg, Paul Goodman, and a number of others.[12] The students draw from this body of literature a critique of prevailing educational practice and particularly an attack on the research-oriented university as run for the benefit of the faculty and not of the undergraduates. And their reading leads many to suppose that there are no problems of scarcity, either of talented teachers or of other human resources; the faculty are seen as willfully refusing to teach, and the society is sometimes seen as willfully insisting on dehydrated and irrelevant learning.[13]

[10] There are some notable exceptions. Thus, three years ago Ira Magaziner and Christopher Coles at Brown University compiled a massive dossier on educational reform; impressing many faculty members with their seriousness, they succeeded in many of their aims of loosening the curriculum, abandoning traditional grading, etc.

[11] The best historical work I know is that of Laurence Veysey, *The Emergence of the American University* (Chicago: University of Chicago Press, 1965); Thorstein Veblen's *The Higher Learning in America: A Memorandum on the Conduct of Universities by Businessmen* (New York: Viking Press, 1918) is a caustic account of philistinism and seemly pedantry.

[12] A few mention the writings of Judson Jerome, Professor of Literature at Antioch College; see for instance, "Portrait of Three Experiments," in *Change* 2 (July–August, 1970), 40–54, and other writings in that journal and *Life*. Some students draw from my own writings on education what I would regard as overgeneralized or misapplied conclusions. Thus, they scan Christopher Jencks and David Riesman, *The Academic Revolution* (Garden City, N.Y.: Doubleday & Co., 1968) in order to find ammunition—there is plenty there!—to throw against the graduate schools and the hegemony of academic departments. (Others read the book, also too simplistically, as a complacent defense of the educational status quo.)

[13] There is a more somber note that occasionally crops up in the discussions I have had with students, especially on the more avant-garde campuses: this is an insistence that the heights of culture are in themselves an offense to the impoverished masses

Many faculty members, and not only the younger products of the graduate schools, agree with these condemnations. Bored by their own research in many cases, excited by the cultural revolution, eager to identify with what seems to be youthful and energetic, they read into the student movement support for their own educational ideals. Students can also find in Fromm's writings passages which support the way they view matters; consider the following from his contribution to a symposium on Summerhill School:

What is the student rebellion all about? The phenomenon is somewhat different within each country. In some, it represents socialist demands; in others, a fight for greater student participation in the deliberations and the decision-making of the university establishment. In these struggles, some groups have rejected violence; in others, various degrees of force have been employed. In some cases, institutional methods have been attacked; in others, particular individuals have been damned. Yet behind all these apparent differences, all the marching, sitting, and shouting students have something in common: *they are all experiencing a deep hunger for life.* They feel that their education is being bureaucratized, and that at best, they are being sufficiently prepared to enable them to earn a good living. But paramountly, they also feel they are not being offered stimulating intellectual food in large enough portions to enhance their sense of aliveness. These students insist that they do not want to be dead in the midst of plenty; they insist that they do not want to study in institutions which, in their yielding to the vested interests of professors, administrators, and governmental forces, pay too little attention to their generation's need for a critical examination of today's conventional wisdom.

The campus rebels, even though sometimes misled through political naiveté and lack of realism, and even though sometimes motivated by destructive drives, at least draw attention to the fact that today's processes of higher education are deemed unsatisfactory by a large number of the young element.

The educational failure of our high schools is even worse. By his very action, each drop-out casts a vote against the education he has

---

of the so-called Third World, and that the heights should be pulled down in the hope (a vain hope, in my judgment) of filling up the abysses. Sometimes the theme is explicit: if not everyone can share in the joys and illuminations of high culture, then no one should.

been receiving. Who would deny that juvenile delinquency is related to the failure of our educational system to provide stimulation and meaning for our adolescents.[14]

The passage just quoted exhibits only one aspect of Fromm's thought concerning students and education. Furthermore, he might not make the same statement today. Taken as they stand, these remarks seem to me a considerable overgeneralization. It is common for reformers to suppose that protesters largely share their agenda, especially if they say they do. The litany of attack on bureaucratized education and on the vested interests of academia got a good deal of its start among the campus rebels of the Free Speech Movement at Berkeley in 1964–1965. But careful studies of the protesters show that they were more appreciative of their courses and their education and less critical, except for public relations purposes, than the inactive students; what originally led them into action was neither a demand for greater student participation in university affairs nor a search for "stimulating intellectual food," but the civil rights movement in the Bay Area and their desire to use the campus as a platform for it.[15] When, after the Movement began, a new Acting Chancellor (Martin Meyerson) came in who was quite open to change, asking students for suggestions about educational reform, hardly any responded.

Similarly, I regard it as an error to declare that each dropout can be seen principally as a vote against our high schools, although surely many are just that. Such a notion is likely in practice to lead the dedicated and idealistic high school teacher toward the pedagogic equivalent of therapeutic despair because it is a vast overestimation of the role of formal education as against the more compelling influences of the home and the street. The *Coleman Report* on equality of educational opportunity suggests how little of the variance in educational outcomes can be explained in terms of school settings in comparison with home and family and peer settings.[16]

[14] See Harold H. Hart, ed., *Summerhill: For and Against* (New York: Hart Publishing Co., 1970), pp. 251–252.

[15] There is a large literature. See, e.g., Robert H. Somers, "The Mainsprings of the Rebellion: A Survey of Berkeley Students in November, 1964," in Seymour Martin Lipset and Sheldon S. Wolin (eds.), *The Berkeley Student Revolt: Facts and Interpretations* (New York: Doubleday-Anchor Books, 1965), pp. 530–558; see also the discussion in Nathan Glazer, *Remembering the Answers* (New York: Basic Books, 1970).

[16] For a full discussion, see Christopher Jencks, "The Coleman Report and the Conventional Wisdom," prepared for *On Equality of Educational Opportunity*, Frederick Mosteller and Daniel P. Moynihan (eds.), to be published by Random House.

Many students and many teachers experience a deep hunger for life and many resist conventional notions of career and consumerism. But many in my observation, in rejecting what they see as mindless and puritanical work for meaningless ends, have relied on a countercultural repertoire which also turns out to be limited. Decency, ingenuity, sensitivity can often be found. But I see a fair amount of psychedelically tuned aliveness which, though sometimes angry, commonly turns sullen and despairing. Indeed, so rapidly do the student movements change their mood and style and so intermittent has been the interest in educational reform (as distinguished from reforms in governance and politics) that it is hard to know what the impact has been on the great majority of uninvolved students, or what the consequences have been for the majority of uninvolved faculty.

Were Fromm writing about the student movements today he might well put even greater emphasis on destructive drives than appears in the quotation above. Indeed, toward the close of his contribution to *Summerhill: For and Against* he writes very critically:

> And then there are many of the young who believe that freedom means absence of tradition, absence of structure, absence of plan: what is desirable is unstructured, spontaneous action. They often believe that "the old ideas" and values are of little or no use today, that to know tradition, not to speak of accepting some of it, is in itself an obstacle to freedom.*

Similarly, the Fromm who writes in *The Revolution of Hope* about the literacy campaigns of Professor Paolo Freire in Latin America would not be sympathetic to affluent white student radicals such as those I have heard say to black underprivileged students that, since the latter have a great oral tradition, they should not bother with "whitey's hang-up of writing" and other academic binds. Many students have missed Fromm's dichotomy, in his contribution to the Summerhill compendium, between order, which he regards as mechanical and dead, and structure, which he defines as the property of all living (and indeed, nonliving) things and as essential for growth and creativity.[17]

---

* One can hear this expressed in a very primitive form by many young students; and also expressed in a veiled, highly sophisticated form, in the writings of H. Marcuse. [Cf. the critique of Herbert Marcuse in *The Revolution of Hope*, pp. 106–107, and the critique of relativism on pp. 87–88.]

[17] See *Summerhill: For and Against, op. cit.*, pp. 262–263; note also in Fromm's Foreword to A. S. Neill, *Summerhill: A Radical Approach to Child Rearing* (New

In a recent discussion at Harvard with student educational reformers, I suggested that students could actually become more free by learning tangible skills and accomplishments, so that they might be able to do things and not continue to remain dependent. To counter this, one reflective student cited *Summerhill,* saying that it didn't matter if a student sat around for a year or so because eventually he might want to do something, and then he would do it under his own motivation and without pressure. Another student cited Erich Fromm to support his contention that contemporary social science consisted of a series of pigeonholes for compartmentalized disciplines which bear no relation to the problems of the great world.[18]

What is evident to me in many discussions is an idealism about the way learning should go on which can find some support in Fromm's work. It is an idealism that tempts us to believe that we can get rid of all the mixtures of motives with which most of us live, and that then we can find our way to a purity of humane experience unmediated by ordinariness or routine. Any education is worthless which is in any degree compromised by imposed schedules or by the desire to win approval or to get into graduate school; and the fear of having a "corrupt" or impure motive leads to a great watchfulness rather like that of the Puritans. But unlike the Puritans, work is not therapeutic or seen as indicative of election: it is apt to be seen as repressive. Thus, this idealism appears in some students to lead to vacillation between self-contempt for not living up to the ideal and a somewhat passive waiting to be captured by some all-encompassing activity.

The ways in which such students scrutinize themselves and each other have been influenced by the popularization of psychoanalytic thought. For many young people it is one of the forms of debunking, along with a vulgar Marxism and an old-fashioned American cynicism. Many people today regard psychoanalysis as having demonstrated the primacy of the buried emotional life and the ways in which rationalizations masquerade as rea-

York: Hart Publishing Co., 1960), p. xvi, his emphasis on the importance of Neill's own extraordinary qualities as a caution against assuming that a school like Summerhill can be built anywhere, any day. On the peer pressures that may exist at Summerhill at the present time in the relative absence of adult controls, see the account by a visiting educator: Mary Keohane, "A. S. Neill: Latter-Day Dewey?" *Elementary School Journal,* 70 (1970), 401–410.

[18] Fromm is not always seen as an ally by critical students. An SDS leader at a state university, on being introduced to me, launched into a vehement attack on Fromm's "revisionism" of Karl Marx. This student said that Marx was lulling the bourgeoisie in his early humanistic writings; these were purely propagandistic in intent; Fromm was robbing Marx of his toughness and turning him into a soft bourgeois romantic!

son. Things are never what they seem: they are always worse than they seem. Many students and faculty consider encounter groups as ideal settings for education because they supposedly get away from "excessive" cognitive emphases and formal relations and allow people of different ages and backgrounds to experience each other directly. These devotees are generally unfamiliar with Erich Fromm's insistence that what is repressed and what is evoked in a particular setting is not some pan-human flow of sex and aggression, but what a particular culture and a particular social character find no way to categorize or to use.[19] Fromm is critical of the common notion that what is "real"—as in the expression "the real me"— is an underlying aggression or racism or rampant sexuality; in encounter groups it often happens that people manipulate their aggressions or, indeed, their sexuality, sometimes in fake humility in order to establish a new moral hegemony in which the most apparently candid come out on top. What then may be repressed is sensitivity of feeling, delicacy (or snobbery) of reactions to other people, since one would be made to feel guilty for such reactions.[20]

Many of the adult and student educational reformers have had expensive secondary and university educations (I include myself here) and start their critique from their own backgrounds of cultivation and literacy. Many have had an interest in ideas since childhood and could have managed to educate themselves in the absence of requirements. In talking in recent years with such reformers, I have recognized that many are aware that their own college careers are unlikely to be affected by their proposed reforms; they are seeking to be generous to their successors. Yet they may not fully appreciate how high is the platform on which they themselves are standing and how hard it is to reach if one comes from a family that is not only nonaffluent but also skeptical of ideas and of education gen-

---

[19] Cf. Fromm, *Beyond the Chains of Illusion: My Encounter with Marx and Freud* (New York: Pocket Books, 1962), chap. 9, "The Social Unconscious."

[20] I do not intend here to be making blanket statements about all encounter groups in all sorts of social strata and contexts. I am talking about liberal arts colleges where the manipulative tend to get involved with the shy. Consequences might be quite different among a group of older people of lower-middle class origin where everyone is inhibited, if not always shy. Furthermore, I do not speak out of personal experience with such groups, but out of observing instances on television, reading some of the literature, and talking with many devotees. The evangelism of some proponents of the movement reminds me of the similarities of some encounter groups, at the extreme, to Chinese thought reform sessions as described in Robert J. Lifton, *Thought Reform and the Psychology of Totalism* (New York: W. W. Norton & Co., 1961).

erally. The reformers' insouciance, though often antielitist in rhetoric, may paradoxically turn out to be a way of insuring some affluent students against downward social mobility.

Because these students come from families that have arrived, and, indeed, at times from professional and intellectual families, they are apt to say to themselves that they want to "be" rather than to "do." They have a point when they declare that America and perhaps the whole Western world have been undone by an excessive emphasis on performance and achievement, but given the populous world we inhabit, it is an ambivalent and complicated point. To reject competence will not help the Western world survive or become more humane. Sometimes I have asked such students whether they believed that there are any skills at all that their culture is justified in asking them to acquire, or whether in their own development there is any point up to which they believe that they need the counsel of adults in the matter of their own further education. Frequently, they don't think there is such a point.

The analogy sometimes offered me is the finding that neonates will, like other animals, know how to feed themselves properly, to find the right amount of salt and other nutriment, when faced with a choice of possible edibles. Similarly, the students claim that they will know what it is they want and need and that in due course they will provide it for themselves. At the extreme to which these students often push the issue, there is implicit here a denial of the concept of culture itself: a belief that people will grow up into some pan-human protoplasm able to communicate with other protoplasm without either the freedoms or the restraints of our cultural inheritance. The unanthropological and unhistorical nature of such a view is striking.[21] The rejection of competition with peers and of the old-fashioned mania for success has admirable features, but it is a common fallacy of student and faculty critics to lump together rivalry with others and what might be called competition with the *ding an sich*—with the damned

---

[21] In the discussion of educational constraints that harass them, students quite commonly attack the language requirements in colleges and graduate schools, and everywhere these are being abandoned. My response has sometimes been to say to the students that their criticism of the inadequacy of most language requirements is quite correct and that they should insist on a language-immersion program in Peace Corps style in which they will be exposed to another culture so intensely that they will for a period not be able even to swear or to make love in their mother tongue, and in which all aspects of the non-American culture will be available to them from its high art to its vernacular slang or music. Students tend instantly to reject such a demanding alternative; no doubt many faculty would also.

thingmanship of a violin, for example. Such students tend to wait to fall in love, as it were, with a topic or a vocation, just as Erich Fromm has noted in his writings that they wait to "fall" in love with another person, rather than making an active effort out of which a genuine relatedness might actually come.

The Cultural Revolution: Authority Delegitimized

In pondering such discussions with students, I have kept looking for settings in which they are faced with an authority that cannot easily be personalized and, hence, where issues of fighting against fears of being dependent would be less likely to interfere with education. One example is the responsive reaction many students have to a coach of a non-big-time athletic sport whom they see as their ally in improving their skill or pleasure in the sport, even if he may also be critical of them for indolence and failure to practice. Another is the response of students performing in orchestras or chamber music groups, where the conductor may be seen as the transmitter of the imperatives imposed by the score, rather than as an authority in his own right (and, therefore, wrong). Of course, a coach or a conductor may exercise irrational authority and subordinate players to himself rather than to the rules of the game or to the score. Yet, at their best, musical groups get sorted out by competence so that the first violinist or solo French horn does not have to be elected or chosen by lot.[22]

Perhaps as late as 1967, one could still have said that students in the better colleges were seeking to perform well in regular academic terms because they did not really question the curriculum, and because even if they did, they wanted to be able to enter good graduate and professional schools.[23] Students were coming to a growing number of avant-garde col-

[22] To be sure, such settings also come under student attack for their competitiveness and their insistence on equality of opportunity rather than equality of outcome. Students tell me that in some schools which recently had active madrigal and chamber orchestra groups, the only performed music that now prevails is that of the guitar, plucked and sung to in an untrained and casual way. And in some colleges of music and art, there are students who will insist that their creativity would be stunted if they had to submit to supervision and criticism—they declare that no one is entitled to evaluate them except themselves.

[23] At Harvard College, for example, the "gentleman's C" of the insouciant aristocrat was no longer an admired goal but a deprecated legacy. For a picture of Harvard College in this period, critical of its complacencies while aware of its advances, see McGeorge Bundy, "Were Those the Days?" in *Daedalus,* 99 (Summer, 1970), 531–567.

leges with ever more precocious intellectual equipment. In the middle-1960s, college presidents of such institutions saw their task as a struggle to recruit college professors in a market extremely favorable to the latter. Few, if any, observers suspected that major institutions would by the end of the 1960s face financial bankruptcy, and more to the point here, moral delegitimation and loss of authority.

However, when in June, 1970, I attended the annual Institute for incoming college presidents run by the American Council on Education, most of the men and women in attendance were deeply troubled concerning the issue of legitimacy. They were aware that many state legislatures expected them to act like other corporate executives (or, rather, as the latter are in fantasy supposed to act) and to be able to control campus turmoil and to fire dissident or destructive faculty and students. Inside the institution, in contrast, they are supposed to be egalitarian and infinitely accessible, and they are constantly being told that they must maintain "dialogue," or that "better communications" are the answer to all conflicts of interest. Most shrink from the accusation of being authoritarian or high-handed. The distinction Erich Fromm makes in *Man for Himself* between rational and irrational authority is almost impossible for them, as for many other Americans, to make—understandably, of course, when it involves their own conduct. And like most people, perhaps especially Americans, they consider it part of their job to be well liked as well as to be respected.

If authority is not to lie in themselves and their own behavior, does it then perhaps lie in the curriculum which has been handed down to them? Can they defend the curriculum even while recognizing its undeniable biases and limitations? A handful of the men and women at the Institute were of this persuasion, believing that in the prevailing vogue of irrationalism, they had to defend the authority of scholarship and of cultural traditions, even if the particular carriers of these traditions on their campuses are all too human, fallible in their pedantry, their vanity, their rationalism, and all the other sins charged over the centuries against scholarship. In being prepared to make such a defense, these presidents are only too well aware that they can readily be defeated and ousted, and they know that they will be attacked as reactionaries. An increasing number of presidents is taking quite a different road, namely, to form an alliance with radical young faculty and students in opposition to that segment of scholarly faculty who insist on the authority of the curriculum over students and of the academic professions and their standards over faculty members. The convictions of such presidents in favor of participatory democracy outweigh such convictions as they have about the claims of scholarship or the importance of inherited cultural traditions. Indeed, within this small but growing group, many presidents, like many faculty, believe that to take any other position would be elitist—and the accusation of "elitism" has in many university circles become almost as damaging as the accusation of racism (the two are often interchangeable).

Increasingly, students and many faculty vehemently insist that lectures are by definition authoritarian and that they compel the listeners to be passive receptacles. In contrast, encounter groups or rap sessions are praised as active and participative. Yet it is a misjudgment to suppose that one can tell a priori what is active and what is passive. The assumption that listening to a lecture or a concert is necessarily passive, while "rapping" is active, seems to derive from an old-fashioned American judgment about muscularity and strenuousness: ironically, a judgment voiced by many who regard themselves in politics and culture as "anti-American." In the absence of any effort to learn a skill or to discipline oneself in a cultural tradition, the new, more groovy forms of teaching and learning can become vehicles for that narcissism which, in *The Heart of Man,* Erich Fromm sees as endemic but redeemable.[24]

Some Personal (Perhaps Quixotic) Strategies in Undergraduate Education

In an earlier draft of this paper I examined some attempts at undergraduate educational innovation, briefly reviewing the two St. John's colleges at Annapolis and Santa Fe,[25] Shimer College in Illinois, and Ben-

[24] See Erich Fromm, *The Heart of Man: Its Genius for Good and Evil* (New York: Harper, 1964), chap. 4. See also, for a penetrating analysis of many of the issues dealt with in this paper—one which appeared after the text was written—Walter P. Metzger, "The Crisis of Academic Authority," in *Daedalus,* 99 (Summer, 1970), 568–608.

[25] In *The Revolution of Hope, op. cit.,* p. 115, Erich Fromm has a passing comment on such a program, speaking of "our college students [who] are literally 'fed up' because they are fed, not stimulated." He continues, "They are dissatisfied with the intellectual fare they get in most—although fortunately not in all—instances, and, in this mood, tend to discard all traditional writings, values, and ideas. It is futile simply to complain about this fact. One has to change its conditions, and this change can occur only if the split between emotional experience and thought is replaced by a new unity of heart and mind. This is not done by the method of reading the hundred great books—which is conventional and unimaginative. It can only be accomplished if the teachers themselves cease being bureaucrats hiding their own lack of aliveness behind their role of bureaucratic dispensers of knowledge; if they

nington; I also discussed some ventures in setting up enclaves within major universities, notably the Experimental College at Berkeley.[26] The article grew much too long, and I decided to eliminate the detailed discussion of these experiments. Yet I want to emphasize a point I was making there, namely that any viable educational reform must be tied to its base of faculty and students and to the particular cultural context; it is thus (unlike pilot models in industry) not readily transferred to diverse sorts of institutions. What may be transferred is a mode of thinking about educational reform.

I can offer no solution, even a partial one, to the educational problems that beset us. The great social and cultural shifts of our time have unsettled educational institutions as they have unsettled the churches and many individual families. In such a fluid setting my own recommendations tend to be conservative. I am often asked about starting a new experimental college, and having observed a good many such colleges in recent years, my inclination is to say that in the present climate they are apt to attract both faculty and students who are visionaries with competing sectarian visions, and that one needs an extraordinarily firm leader to avoid disaster. As I have just said, I am more sympathetic to innovations within relatively stable settings. I have seen student-led courses which have been useful because of the particular group involved and their dedication; I have seen others turn into therapy sessions or rapidly disintegrate. I have seen some of the most hopeful innovations occur in denominational colleges, such as Immaculate Heart in Los Angeles or Florida Presbyterian in St. Petersburg, although such colleges are certainly not untroubled.

In general it seems to me wrong to tear down given educational structures and curricula, no matter how inadequate, unless one has something

---

become—in a word, by Tolstoy—'the co-disciples of their students.' " I think that indeed there are problems in the Great Books formula and that the textual analysis that colleges have built on that formula can become routinized. In discussions at both St. John's colleges, I have made similar criticisms. Nevertheless, the seriousness, even solemnity, with which students and faculty read and analyze the set texts can be a refreshing contrast to the many other small, experimental liberal arts colleges where the students principally spend their time on pot and each other. I am prepared to defend the two St. John's colleges, despite my criticisms, until I see a number of better models around.

[26] See Joseph Tussman, *Experiment at Berkeley* (New York: Oxford University Press, 1969); for Shimer as it was in an earlier day, see Christopher Jencks and David Riesman, "Shimer College," *Phi Delta Kappan* (April, 1962), pp. 415–420; and more generally, David Riesman, Joseph Gusfield, and Zelda Gamson, *Academic Values and Mass Education* (Garden City, N.Y.: Doubleday & Co., 1970).

better to put in their place. The attack on arbitrary custom and inherited tradition, in education as in other spheres of life, has gained an extraordinary momentum in our time. One approach is to insist that schools and colleges are inherently stultifying, "total institutions," and that young people would be better off without them. Another approach is to set against the existing institutions the vision of new ones, which would be staffed by wholly devoted, wholly empathic teacher-learners, not committed either to the political or the pedagogic status quo. However, proponents of the counterculture tend to oppose institutions as such, and to believe that free-form education requires no planning, no organization.

In our secondary schools and our colleges, there are many demoralized instructors who realize that the reforms of which they are capable seem miniscule in the face of a cultural revolution whose sources lie in large measure outside the schools, and which has the support of the highbrow centers with their sympathy for Dionysian styles of life. That sympathy is now to some degree being carried into the secondary schools by young teachers who are themselves the products of permissive private or luxuriant public schools and for whom rigid order and necessary structure are not distinguishable from each other: they oppose both. Naturally, what has been said just now can readily become an alibi for complacency; one has to examine the social context before coming to a decision as to the appropriateness and the tone of criticisms. Since a system of higher education with 600,000 faculty members and seven million students is not capable of making quantum jumps, the effort at instant transformation will bring chaos rather than creativity.

We are presently moving from a system of mass higher education in which half the age-grade goes beyond high school to some form of college and in which enrollments more than doubled between 1960 and 1970, to a system of near universal higher education up to the fourteenth grade. Our problems would be somewhat less grave if it became general practice after high school to enter on a period of employment or of voluntary service and to rely on adult education rather than on an automatic assumption of post-secondary education for many students who are neither mature enough nor eager enough to profit from college. The majority of these students are pursuing vocational or preprofessional curricula which will lift them socially from blue collar to (often more poorly paid) white collar work;[27] the status of students, their families, and their prospective occupa-

[27] The decline of blue-collar work that was assumed to follow upon the rise of automation has been greatly exaggerated. See Robert S. Weiss, David Riesman, and

tions (along with the draft) all press in the direction of college. For most of these "first-generation" students, college is seen as a somewhat less boring option than its alternatives, and the programs and prospects for educational reform seldom come from them. Intensive teaching and advising might in some cases help such students redefine their aims while they are in college without necessarily pulling them away from attainable post-college goals. Just this occurs in some fortunate encounters. But while such colleges often have devoted teachers and hard-working counselors, the matching between these and any particular student is usually fairly accidental. The advice such students get often depends on the tilt of the curriculum and the everpresent grapevine.

In more favored settings with carefully selected student bodies and the cushion of private endowments, I am inclined to think that it makes sense to shift resources toward more intensive advising, even at the expense of course work. I have in mind here Erich Fromm's comment in *The Revolution of Hope*,[28] already quoted, concerning the futility of complaining about student dissatisfaction and the need for faculty members to become, in his term, "vulnerable," and responsive to student interests. By "vulnerable" I do not mean "apologetic." Many students are capable litigants and rhetoricians, used since childhood to discovering and exploiting adult weaknesses. What I have in mind is the openness to listen to a student in order to catch the latter's concerns and preoccupations as possible foci for more systematic learning and exploration. "Vulnerability" may also mean recognizing how threatened one is by student antagonism and attack without having to suppress these reactions to appear to oneself impregnable and unaffected. Vulnerability might require a decision that other faculty members, less threatened in this particular way, could be more help to particular students. At the same time a college of modest size whose faculty took seriously the demanding enterprise of teaching would also need to ask itself how students could be helped to become more vulnerable, more open to an awareness of their limitations as well as their strengths.

Given the narcissism that leads many students to play always from their strengths and to conceal what they regard as their weaknesses, I am not sure that many could be persuaded to listen to a faculty adviser in a

Edwin Harwood, "Work and Automation: Problems and Prospects," in Robert K. Merton and Robert A. Nisbet (eds.), *Contemporary Social Problems,* 3rd ed. (New York: Harcourt, Brace & World, 1971), pp. 545–600.

[28] *Op. cit.,* p. 115.

one-to-one discussion on the uses they might make of a curriculum. Yet I would like to see them asked to take part in an assessment of their capacities in a variety of areas of cognitive and emotional functioning, so that they would confront areas they had previously protected themselves from. The aim here would be less to make them "well rounded" in some abstract and standardized sense than to encourage them to develop their potentialities and to discover new modes of enjoying their own activity. If students were simultaneously given the chance to continue in areas of achieved competence, they might better be able to endure seasons or areas of vulnerability. Such an adviser might help students focus on their possible career aspirations, and I would like to see many begin at once as freshmen on a professional program studied in a broad, liberal way. (I recognize the bias against preprofessional education prevailing among both elite college faculties and their students; however, much education in the liberal arts is actually preparation for a career of an academic or literary sort, and need not in fact be "liberal" in the sense of emancipating, whereas preprofessional work in medicine or engineering or law does not have to be narrow.)

Ideally, the adviser would help students become aware of ways in which they can learn from educational settings previously defined as utterly dismal or boring. Especially today, when there is such an animus against all large and allegedly impersonal milieus, students need to learn how to listen to lectures with what in *The Revolution of Hope* Erich Fromm terms "activeness," mixing their own thought with that of the lecturer and attending to what the anthropologist Edward Hall calls "the silent language" as well to the spoken words.[29]

Most colleges have long since given up the hope that faculty members could or would serve as advisers in any intensive fashion (such as is done, for example, at Sarah Lawrence College). *Faute de mieux,* they have divided the advising function between academic or curricular advising done

---

[29] A few colleges such as Sarah Lawrence and Bard approach the model here sketched. There, the personal authority of the don or counselor takes the place of the complete absence of formal curricular requirements. The don seeks to encourage students to explore the curriculum and to abandon self-protectiveness. Since until just now Sarah Lawrence has been a woman's college, and since a great number of the faculty have been lively and talented young men, the dons have had a certain authority; they have only rarely met students whose mask of independence truculently declares: "You can't make me . . ." In my own observation of coeducational settings, women students have been more responsive and responsible—though these qualities sometimes are disadvantageous to their education and development, and frequently are too easily dismissed as mere docility.

by faculty, and more personal advising which tends to be left to a para-academic category of counselors, sometimes trained in Rogerian methods of sympathetic reassurance and occasionally in a more psychoanalytic mode. This division of labor, unavoidable as it may be, tends to rob faculty members of feedback concerning the extent of their impact, perhaps especially on the shy and unself-confident students who feel more at ease in talking about their dilemmas with unthreatening counselors than in talking back to preoccupied faculty members. And the counselors, because they are clearly not academic, can only at best bind up the wounds, not change the rules of the game or give their counselees more resilient ways of playing the game.[30] In the present climate on the campus, counselors may join with other academically marginal people such as campus ministers to support students in opposition to faculty expectations and curricular demands. They may thus serve less to bind up wounds than to show themselves as swingers, in sympathy with student hedonism and a variety of antirational cults.

Of course, it would be wrong to make a sharp dichotomy between faculty scholars and antiacademic counselors: as pointed out earlier, many faculty have themselves become antiacademic, and there are many counselors who take seriously the academic side of college life and seek to show students what it takes to profit from that side.[31]

In most colleges it may not be possible to persuade faculty to resume the advising function, especially for students who have not yet decided on a major and hence are not in the province of any one department. But it seems to me important to make the attempt. However, if faculty are to serve successfully as advisers, they will have to learn more than they now know from hearsay about how they and their colleagues perform as teachers. In most colleges the privacy of the classroom protects faculty members from each other's scrutiny. And even if this were not the case, faculty members might be hesitant to be candid in talking with students about other faculty, since this power could so easily be exploited in a vindictive

---

[30] Cf. Michael Maccoby, "The Game Attitude," Ph.D. Thesis, Department of Social Relations (Harvard University, 1960).
[31] See William G. Perry, Jr., *Forms of Intellectual and Ethical Development in the College Years* (New York: Holt, Rinehart and Winston, 1970), describing the work of the Harvard Bureau of Study Counsel; the Bureau not only seeks to help students grapple with the demands of their academic work but also offers faculty members the opportunity to have their classes recorded and played back under the sympathetic criticism of a counselor, in the hope of helping them to become better teachers.

or self-serving way. I am not sure how feasible it is or what the costs would be of breaking down the privacy of the classroom and encouraging mutual visiting and criticism. Certainly, faculty members who wish to be retained or promoted because of the quality of their teaching cannot rightly insist on privacy, yet there have not been enough assessments of the side-effects of visiting to give me confidence that the tact and generosity requisite for such a procedure will be found.

I had the benefit of such a program as a member of the Social Science staff of The College of the University of Chicago, where all members attended each other's lectures and discussed each other's modes of learning and teaching in jointly taught, interdisciplinary courses.[32] We worked with students in small sections, though we did not monopolize the advising function. When I came to Harvard in 1958, I recruited a staff of graduate students and young faculty to work with me in a large undergraduate course whose one requirement for students would be a long term paper, work on which would facilitate a closer student-faculty relation than is common in universities. In recruiting a staff of ten or a dozen men and women for the course, I have looked for those with an interest in problems of learning and teaching, and with an intense curiosity about self and society; they come from sociology, political science, history, law, clinical and social psychology, comparative literature, and the American Civilization program. While most graduate students have little or no supervision of their initial forays in undergraduate teaching, we encourage visiting of each other's sections and critical discussion of each other's lectures; we meet weekly to discuss books read in the course and the long papers of the students to which we respond with extensive advice and commentary.

In our advising of students in this course—and each section leader became an adviser, as I also did—it was difficult to persuade Harvard undergraduates that, in writing their papers for the course, they could make any original contribution. A great many had had the disheartening experience of finding themselves no longer the brightest stars of their respective high schools, but surrounded with hundreds of outwardly impressive fellow valedictorians. Some came to doubt their own powers; they reacted guardedly to their courses and to each other; their curiosity concerning the world was dimmed by the fear of revealing their inadequacies. We published three volumes of student papers, not necessarily the most elegant, in order to

[32] See for a contemporary discussion, David Riesman, "Some Problems of a Course in 'Culture and Personality,' " *Journal of General Education*, V (1951), 122–136.

suggest that it was possible for a neophyte to do something original, to describe something new, especially if he could draw on his own access to a particular segment of our society: of school, job or locale.[33]

The political and cultural revolutions on the campus have in the last few years altered what many students bring to such a course and what they expect from it. I would say that whereas our principal problem once was to encourage student self-confidence, a growing problem today is to broaden student curiosity about society. Paradoxically, too much self-confidence inhibits curiosity: some precocious students arrive at college believing that they already know what society is like—and that it is utterly vicious. To spend any energy exploring the details appears to them a delaying tactic at best, at worst a kind of counterinsurgency. Many of these students have been exposed to ideas of liberation from very early on; some have been taught in secondary school by young radicals avoiding the draft or by young anticareerists avoiding what they regard as the rat race of university life. They may not actually have read Nietzsche, Sartre, Camus, Fromm, Fanon, but they have been exposed to the ideas of such writers osmotically in a kind of post-McLuhan way. They arrive at college believing themselves sophisticated; one of the problems we face as teachers is the actual provincialism of young men and women who regard themselves as fully cosmopolitan. Because their emotional and, hence, intellectual interest is so largely focused upon America's underclass, it is difficult to evoke their interest in the full range of human experience. Many say that they want to share "the black experience," assuming that there is only a single experience and that in any case it is only of suffering and debasement on the one side and joyful naturalness on the other. It is hard to get such students to extend their disciplined empathy and curiosity to a wide variety of life in this country (though the tiny minority of active revolutionaries among them talk about contacts with the "working class").[34]

No longer do we have a problem of persuading students to do some piece of empirical work outside the library—our problem now is the op-

---

[33] Space forbids discussing the many, undoubtedly overambitious, aims of the course which for many students will be their only exposure to the social sciences. In readings and lectures as well as small group discussions, we focus both on problems of methodology and of substance, illustrating how a great generalizing writer like Tocqueville or Veblen proceeds, and also how a meticulous clinician or participant-observer works.

[34] Michael Lerner, a former Harvard College student, describes such elite student snobberies in "Respectable Bigotry," *The American Scholar,* 38 (Autumn, 1969), 606–617.

posite, of getting students to look at books at all, if they do not fall within the current canon. Reactions to our reading Alexis de Tocqueville's *Democracy in America* are especially revealing. Many students and some staff members tend to dismiss him as a French aristocrat, a liberal-conservative, who is abstract and out of another century. They cannot identify with this young Frenchman and his remarkable experience of America. Some resent his detachment, not seeing that he was passionately arguing with his fellow French aristocrats and conservatives as to how they might respond creatively to the coming democratic world rather than dig in their heels for rear-guard action.

Tocqueville would not be astonished at some aspects of the cultural revolution insofar as it is a reaction against hierarchy, tradition, and elites. Because egalitarianism has always been stronger in America than in other industrial societies, the cultural revolution forces faculty members to confront not only resistant students, but also ambivalence within themselves to the degree that they identify with students. Indeed, if one looks around the world at the student movements elsewhere, one might surmise that the cultural revolution is strongest in the United States. It is a postindustrial phenomenon in the quite concrete sense that affluent American students believe that hard scientific and technical work, or work in organizational harness, is no longer necessary in the affluent society. Here they share Herbert Marcuse's view of surplus repression.

Even at an avant-garde institution like Harvard College, however, such judgments, at once hedonistic and despairing, are widely voiced but less widely shared. My colleagues and I have continued to find students who are interested and alert. It may not be extravagant to say of some of the staff and students who have been involved in the course, that they are "people who have deep convictions without being fanatical, who are loving without being sentimental, who are imaginative without being unrealistic, who are fearless without depreciating life, who are disciplined without submission." [35]

Again and again, from *Escape from Freedom* in 1941 to *The Revolution of Hope* in 1968, Fromm contends that there are no easy formulae by which an individual can live his life. Reason is a frail but essential resource; it helps him interpret the concrete demands of the human situation

[35] Erich Fromm in *The Revolution of Hope, op. cit.*, p. 160. See also the discussion of the infectious quality of interest (which, however, Fromm distinguishes from curiosity, which he defines as passive, whereas in the text I have used the two terms interchangeably), *ibid.*, pp. 80–81.

in which he finds himself, and partially to transcend these. In every society and in every stratum of a differentiated society, the human situation imposes its requirements on all men: in Fromm's terms, all need to assimilate in order to survive, and to be related to others in order to preserve their sanity. These requirements are not responded to in a random way, but by the formation of a social character which provides for its possessors a temporary and necessarily more or less truncated solution to life. The potential wholeness of man is only adumbrated in any extant society: in some groups, rationalism (as distinguished from reason) conquers all; in others, irrational hatred or masochism conquers.[36] Fromm believes that many possibilities are in principle open for less inharmonious relations between man and his own powers, man and nature, man and other men. It is the ambitious task of education to help students explore these possibilities. The great world religions, history and biography, anthropological investigation, and self-examination can all serve to reduce man's alienation from himself and his lack of "at homeness" in the world.

Ambitious tasks can become frustrating and self-defeating if pursued with fanaticism and quixotic disregard for the local landscape. When utopian thinking becomes, not a guiding principle, but a reason to condemn all existing structures, the result is likely to be a growing impatience and despair. In my judgment it is necessary to protect from attack efforts at small-scale experimentation of the type illustrated in what I have written here. However, I frequently run into an all-or-nothing approach: if an educational reform does not even propose to cure all deficiencies for all levels of students—if, for example, it only deals with a few well-prepared students in a prosperous academic milieu—it is for many not worth doing at all.[37]

In the present climate, educators like other Americans need to have what I have sometimes called the nerve of failure. I do not mean that failure is romantically desirable or that I am asking people to become heroes or martyrs, but rather that they decide what are the essential issues on which they are prepared to stand firm and if necessary be defeated, and

---

[36] For a discussion of the various kinds of violence which, in the animal world, are species-specific to man, see Fromm, *The Heart of Man: Its Genius for Good and Evil, op. cit.*, chap. 2.

[37] One does of course encounter the recurrent strategy of "the worse, the better": if structures such as universities can be destroyed and if anarchy occurs, then there is a chance that the Revolution may triumph. Under American conditions, it seems to me far more likely that the Right will triumph or that disintegration will indeed spread.

what are the areas where they can compromise and temporize without giving way to the excesses of the cultural revolution. At many points, my own position, immersed in ambiguities, lacks the solace of clarity. My hope is a modest one that what can be discovered will become cumulative, and that even our failures, if we do not deceive ourselves as to why they occurred, may help our successors avoid our errors before they invent their own.

The
Paradox
of
Culture   Edward T. Hall

The best minds of each age inevitably come to grips with alienation in its
various forms. The explanations keep changing, but there can be no doubt
that it represents one of the core issues in man's life. Today one can observe at least three areas in which serious alienation occurs: in the self;
between men; and between man and nature. In light of these explanations
which keep shifting with time, it would be misleading, presumptuous, and
wrong to take serious issue with the basic psychoanalytic explanations pro-
mulgated by Freud in his lifetime *in the context in which they were formulated*. Instead, I would wish first to add a dimension to a small portion of
the Freudian scheme, and second to build on some of Fromm's thinking as
it can be applied to culture and its effect on man's intellectual processes.

Thinking of Erich Fromm's work over the years, I have been increasingly amazed by his ability to bridge two completely different types of intellectual processes, the world of myth and the dream, and the linear, "logical" written word of the Western world. In the final analysis, I would
rather suspect that while Fromm is best known for his ideas, one of his
main contributions will prove to be the way in which he has cut through
the complexity of uniting these two disparate worlds. How did Fromm do
this? For one thing, he has always been deeply involved in the human situation. He values man for what he is, in a culture that has done everything
it could to reduce man to nothing. And that is where the root of the problem lies. That is why one must strive to go beyond, building on the theories constructed by Freud and Fromm, and include at least the foundations
of the hidden cultural matrix in which human thoughts are set. It is an understanding of this hidden matrix that psychoanalysis lacks as an essential
component in its theoretical underpinning.

The latent level of culture appears to be the source of much of the difficulty that we see in the world today. In my opinion, Western culture has produced a split in man by channeling his physical, mental, emotional, and social energies in contradictory ways. Western man is controlled by hidden rules—the nature of which he is only vaguely aware of at best, and completely oblivious to most of the time. What is more, until these patterns are known and understood, not only will man be alienated from himself, but he will be forever limited by hidden binding constraints.

In many long conversations with Fromm, he taught me most of what I know about psychoanalysis, and in particular his own contributions to psychoanalytic theory. There was no way at that time for me to repay my debt to him, for I was unable to put into words the idea that under the deceptive superficiality of surface culture, of which Fromm was fully aware, there lay hidden some deep and dangerous mental and moral traps. Historically, these traps were first identified in language. Edward Sapir, writing forty years ago, observed that in language (an important part of culture) man had created an instrument which was quite a different thing from what is commonly supposed. He states:

> The relation between language and experience is often misunderstood . . . (it) actually defines experience for us by reason of its formal completeness and because of our unconscious projection of its implicit expectations into the field of experience . . . language is much like a mathematical system, which . . . becomes elaborated into a self-contained conceptual system which *previsages all possible experience* in accordance with certain accepted formal limitations . . . categories such as number, gender, case, tense, mode, voice, "aspect" and a host of others, . . . *are not so much discovered in experience as imposed upon it* . . . (italics mine).[1]

Working with other cultural systems, I have found evidence that it is not just in language that one finds such constraints, but elsewhere as well, provided of course that one is fortunate enough to have studied cultures sufficiently different from his own to bring its latent aspects into focus. Two widely divergent experiences, psychoanalysis and work with other cultures, have convinced me of several things concerning man's intellectual processes. First, thinking itself is greatly modified by culture; second, Western man only uses a small fraction of his mental capabilities; third,

[1] Edward Sapir, "Conceptual Categories in Primitive Languages," *Science,* 74 (1931), 570.

there are many different and legitimate ways of thinking; fourth, we in the West value one way of thinking above all the others. The one that we favor we call "logic," which is a linear system that has been with us since Socrates. For Western man, his system of logic is synonymous with the truth, it is the only road to reason, all of which makes Freud's discoveries even more remarkable. When Freud educated us to the complexities of the psyche, forcing us to look at dreams as a mental process that evaded the linearity of manifest thought, in so doing he shook the very foundations of the scientific world. Fromm has added to Freudian theory, and with his characteristic brilliance, managed to bridge the gap between these two systems of thought [2]—the linear world of logic and the integrative world of dreams.

Since the interpretation of dreams, myths, and acts is always to some degree an individual matter,[3] I cannot help asking myself what Fromm would have added to my own interpretation of a *New York Times* news item [4] about a police dog that had been discovered on an uninhabited island near New York.[5] Visible only from a distance, the dog, nicknamed "the King of Ruffle Bar," had managed to sustain itself for an estimated two years, was apparently in good health, and presumably would have survived his semiwild state, barring accidents, for the rest of his natural life. However, some well-meaning soul sighted the dog and reported him to the ASPCA, thereby setting the bureaucratic wheels in motion. Since "the King" could not be approached by people, a baited trap was set. According to *The New York Times* report: ". . . everyday a police launch from Sheepshead Bay takes off for Ruffle Bar, the uninhabited swampy island of the dog. Everyday, a police helicopter hovers for a half hour or more over Ruffle Bar." A radio report of the event broadcast at the time, detailed descriptions of how the helicopter harassed the dog in futile efforts to catch him (he refused to enter the trap), or at least to get a better view of him. Police were quoted as saying the dog "looked in good shape." When questioned, representatives of the ASPCA said: "When we catch the dog, we

[2] Erich Fromm, *The Forgotten Language* (New York: Rinehart and Co., 1951).
[3] No matter what point of departure one uses, symbols inevitably have both a shared and an individual component. No two people ever use the same word in exactly the same way, and the more abstract the symbol, the greater the likelihood of a sizable individual component.
[4] *The New York Times,* February 20, 1970.
[5] The island, Ruffle Bar, is situated in Jamaica Bay, about five miles southwest of JFK International Airport.

will have it examined by a vet, and if it is in good health, we will find a *happy* home for it." [6]

If the above story had been a dream or a myth instead of a news report, there is little doubt as to its interpretation. Both the latent and the manifest content are quite clear, which may explain why this local news item was given national coverage. I find, as I go over the story, that free associations come to mind on different levels. The story epitomizes the little man against the big bureaucracy. There is also a delusional side which cannot be overlooked. I refer to the ASPCA which became obsessed with capturing the dog. Once triggered, the ASPCA involved the police with a remorseless, mindless persistence terrifyingly characteristic of twentieth-century bureaucracies once they are activated. Interestingly enough, the police, having known about the dog for an estimated two years, had been content to leave him on the island. Emotionally they sided with "the King," even while carrying out their orders. "Why don't they leave the dog alone?" said one policeman; another observed, "The dog is as happy as a pig in a puddle." [7]

The delusional aspects have to do with the institutionalized necessity to control "everything," and the widely accepted notion that the bureaucrat knows what is best—never for a moment does he doubt the validity of the bureaucratic solution. It is also slightly insane, or at least indicative of our incapacity to order priorities with any common sense, to spend a thousand or more dollars for helicopters, gasoline, and salaries for the sole purpose of bureaucratic neatness. Even more recently, a *New York Times* news item [8] reported a U.S. Park Police campaign to stamp out the time-honored custom of kite flying on the grounds of the Washington monument. Their charter to harass the kite fliers lies in an old law written by Congress supposedly to keep the Wright Brothers planes from becoming fouled in kite strings.

The psychoanalyst Laing is convinced that the Western world is mad.[9]

[6] Remarks attributed to a representative of the American Society for the Prevention of Cruelty to Animals (ASPCA), (italics mine). A *New York Times* dateline of February 23, 1970, describes the capture of the dog and repeated the statement about the "happy home."

[7] Note the imagery, not commonly the type reported coming from the mouths of New York's finest. I am also sure that there was no thought of the implications of the metaphor.

[8] *The New York Times*, April 23, 1970.

[9] R. D. Laing, *The Politics of Experience* (New York: Ballantine Books, 1967). Erich Fromm also speaks of "the dark period of . . . insanity we are passing

These stories of the dog and the kite fliers symbolize man's plight as well as any recent events I know,[10] and bolster Laing's view. However, it is not man who is crazy as much *as his institutions* [11] *and those culture patterns that determine his behavior.* It is my opinion that we in the Western world are alienated from ourselves, and from nature, and that we labor under a number of delusions, one of the important ones being that life makes sense, i.e., that we are sane. We persist in this view despite massive evidence to the contrary. We live fragmented, compartmentalized lives in which contradictions are carefully sealed off from each other; we think linearly rather than comprehensively,[12] and we do this not through conscious design, or because we are not intelligent or capable, but because of the way in which our culture structures life in subtle but highly consistent ways which are not consciously formulated. That is, culture has components that influence us in ways that are outside or beyond our awareness. The cultural currents referred to are like the invisible jet streams in the skies that determine the course of a storm; they shape much of our lives, yet their influence is only beginning to be identified. Given our linear, step-by-step, compartmentalized way of thinking,[13] it is virtually impossi-

---

through," in *Sigmund Freud's Mission* (New York: Harper & Brothers, 1959). The notion that the world is mad is not restricted to the psychiatrists and psychoanalysts. Ada Louise Huxtable, the architecture critic, writes in *The New York Times,* March 15, 1970, ". . . one *practical* decision after another has led to the brink of cosmic disaster and there we sit, in pollution and chaos, courting the end of the earth. Just how practical can you get?" (italics mine). Joseph Heller's *Catch-22* is devoted to the same theme.

[10] The other insanities, like the war in Vietnam, spending more on space than on the cities and housing, or more on an unwanted supersonic transport (keeping 30,000 people awake for each passenger carried), are so vast and grandiose that the mind boggles at the enormity of the outrages that man can commit against himself. Somehow, the dog's plight not only symbolizes man's drive to be himself, but it is also on a scale that one can comprehend.

[11] John Kenneth Galbraith holds that the New Economics will also reflect the view that it is not the consumer but business and government bureaucracies that determine the economic state of the nation.

[12] "Linear" and "comprehensive" are not being used as synonyms for "irrational" and "rational." Quite the opposite—sequential or "linear" statements are suited to solving certain kinds of problems, whereas comprehensive processes are better adapted to other kinds. *What is irrational is using one where the other is required,* just as it is irrational to use a sports car to pull a plow or a tractor to race with. See note 13 below.

[13] Marshall McLuhan, *The Gutenberg Galaxy* (Toronto: University of Toronto Press, 1962), and "The Effect of Printed Books on Language in the 16th Century," in *Exploration in Communication* (Boston: Beacon Press, 1960). Buckminster Fuller and Marshall McLuhan both in public utterances and their writings have distinguished be-

ble for man to consider complex events comprehensively, or to weigh priorities according to a system of common good.

Because our welfare—perhaps our survival—depends on our understanding these cultural currents and their hidden patterns, I should like to discuss some interrelated facets of these recently discovered components of culture. I refer to only four of an unknown number of disparate topics, patterns, and events which are mutually reinforcing (synergistic) in their effects when they occur together in a single culture.

1 Man's tremendous success in evolving his extensions.

2 The manner in which time and space are unconsciously structured and used.

3 The structure of the relationship of: (a) information to (b) context in order to derive (c) meaning.

4 The manner in which our institutions, particularly our schools, compartmentalize virtually everything.

The world we live in has an internal dynamic which must be analyzed. The following quote briefly summarizes a few of its relevant features:

> In the United States we allow individuals to do virtually anything: pollute the lakes, contaminate the atmosphere, build a high-rise next door that makes our own living space uninhabitable because it shuts off the view, create walled-in slums in public housing high-rise, transform a potential recreation area on a lake into a run-down industrial waste, plow up the countryside, bulldoze trees, and build thousands of identical prefabricated bungalows in open country. Peter Blake in his book, *God's Own Junkyard,* has documented this aspect of our anarchic and anomic approach to planning. I have discovered (to my sorrow) that in building a house, plumbers and electricians often make important decisions overruling the owner and the architect: they change walls with abandon, run pipes where they should never be, and arrange interior spaces at will. Similarly, important decisions on the

tween two different ways of thinking. McLuhan talks about linear and nonlinear thinking; Fuller about comprehensive and noncomprehensive thinking. The distinction, while popularized by McLuhan and Fuller, is also made by less widely known, but thoroughly respected academicians. A recent article in *Science*, November 28, 1970, by Beryl L. Crowe comes to the same conclusion that I have reached: namely, that the answer to some of our most basic problems lies in the way we think. Crowe also quotes Aaron Widnvsky (1964) concerning a comprehensive study of the budgetary process whereby the government "proceeded by a calculus that is *sequential* and *incremental* rather than *comprehensive*" (italics mine).

national scene are often made by officials, both public and private, who have little or no knowledge of the consequences of their actions.[14]

In addition to the historical features of our culture, there are synchronic processes at work which must be considered. If some mad scientist had set out to develop a cultural system for confusing and controlling man, he could hardly have done better. Let us examine how we are captives of our own systems of handling time and space—beginning with time. American time is what I have termed "monochronic," that is, Americans usually prefer to do one thing at a time, which requires some kind of scheduling, either implicit or explicit. Not all people conform to monochronic norms, some being more resistant than others. Nevertheless, there are social and other pressures that tend to keep most Americans within the monochronic frame. However, when Americans interact with people of foreign cultures, those cultures with polychronic time systems cause Americans great difficulty.

Monochronic time (M-time) and polychronic time (P-time) represent two radically different solutions to the use of both time and space as organizing frames for activities. Space is included because the two systems (time and space) are functionally interrelated. M-time emphasizes schedules, segmentation, and promptness. P-time systems are characterized by several things happening at once. Emphasis is on involvement of people and completion of transactions rather than adhering to preset schedules. P-time is treated as much less tangible than M-time. P-time is apt to be considered a point rather than a ribbon or a road. What is more, the point is sacred.[15] Americans overseas are stressed in many ways when confronted by P-time systems such as those in Latin America and the Middle East. In the markets and stores of Mediterranean countries, one finds himself surrounded by other customers vying for the attention of a clerk. There is no apparent order as to who is served next and confusion and clamor abound. On another level, within the governmental bureaucracies of these countries, a cabinet officer may have a large reception area outside his private office. There are almost always small groups waiting in this area, and these groups are visited by government officials who move around the room, conferring with each group. Much of their business is

[14] Edward T. Hall, "Human Needs and Inhuman Cities," *The Fitness of Man's Environment, Smithsonian Annual II* (Washington, D.C.: Smithsonian Institute Press, 1968); reprinted in *Ekistics*, vol. 27, no. 60 (March, 1969).
[15] Edward T. Hall, "The Voices of Time," in *The Silent Language* (Garden City, N.Y.: Doubleday & Co., 1959).

transacted in public instead of having a series of private meetings in an inner office. Particularly distressing to Americans is the way in which appointments are handled by polychronic people. Appointments just don't carry the same weight as they do in America. Things are constantly shifted around, nothing seems solid or firm, particularly plans for the future. There are always changes in the most important plans right up to the very last minute.

In contrast, within the Western world, man finds little in life that is exempt from the iron hand of M-time. In fact, his social and business life is completely time-dominated. Time is so thoroughly woven into the fabric of existence that we are hardly aware of the degree to which it determines virtually everything we do, including the molding of relations with others in many subtle ways. By scheduling, we compartmentalize; this makes it possible to concentrate on one thing at a time, but, it also *denies us context* (to which I will return later). Since scheduling by its very nature selects what will and will not be attended and permits only a limited or fixed number of events within a given time period, one can see immediately the outlines of a system of priorities for both people and functions. Important things are taken up first, and allotted the most time; unimportant things are left to last or omitted if time runs out.[16]

Space and its handling also signals importance and priorities. The amount of space allocated and where a person is placed within an organization tells a lot about him and his relation to the organization. Equally significant is how he handles his time. In fact, discretion over scheduling —the ability to choose when one will be in the office—is an indicator of success in our culture. The exceptions are salesmen, whose jobs demand that they be away from their desks, and those who hold unusual positions.

---

[16] Anyone who wants to study priorities in the United States at virtually any level has but to examine time allocations. The point is not to be fooled—some things that we *say* are important are not so important as they seem. (Time fathers spend with children, for example.) Furthermore, the relationship of the number of events to time is linear, sequential, and fixed. You can only increase the number of events by decreasing the time allotted to each, since each event is a transaction and has both an attack or warm-up phase as well as a decay or terminating phase. A theoretical point is reached where productive time (the time between warm-up and terminating) drops to zero and the whole day is devoted to greeting and saying good-by to people with whom no business is done. To get around this M-time, executives are forced to delegate responsibility to others who are in the grip of the time process, except that time must be taken out for them to interact and pass on the information they were hired to gather. This not only forces M-time people to add layers to bureaucracies, *but* sets a theoretical limit on the size of all bureaucracies.

An example of the latter is the city editor of a newspaper; his job is inherently polychronic.[17] The importance of place—where activities are permitted to occur—has become so much a part of modern bureaucracy that some employees whose performance would be enormously enhanced if they could get away from their desks are seldom permitted to do so.

For M-time people reared in the North European tradition, time is linear and segmented like a road or a ribbon extending forward into the future and backward to the past. It is also tangible. They speak of it as being saved, spent, wasted, lost, made up, accelerated, slowed down, crawling, and running out. These metaphors should be taken very seriously, because they express the basic manner in which time is conceived as an unconscious determinant, or frame on which everything else is built. M-time scheduling is used as a classification system that orders life. With the exception of birth and death, all important activities are scheduled. It should be mentioned that without schedules, and something very much like the M-time system, it is doubtful if our industrial civilization could have developed the way it did. Schedules were certainly important; in fact, they were crucial to industrial development in the initial stages.[18] Monochronic time seals off one or two people from the group and intensifies relationships with *one* other person or at most, two or three people. M-time in this sense is like a room with a closed door that ensures privacy. The only problem is that you must vacate the "room" at the end of fifteen minutes or an hour, a day, or a week, depending on the schedule, and make way for the next thing in line. Failure to make way by intruding on the time of the person waiting is bad manners as well as a special way of being inconsiderate.

The point is that monochronic time is arbitrary and *imposed,* that is, *learned,* but because it is so thoroughly learned and so thoroughly integrated into our culture, it is treated as though it were the only natural and "logical" way of organizing life. Yet, it is neither inherent in man's own rhythms and creative drives nor is it existential in nature. Furthermore, the

[17] Polychronic time (P-time), as the term implies, is nonlinear. Everything happens at once. Some jobs and occupations are more polychronic than monochronic. Whole cultures, such as those encountered in the Middle East and Latin America, are polychronic (Hall, *The Silent Language, op. cit.*).

[18] Sebastian de Grazia in *Of Time, Work and Leisure* (New York: Simon and Schuster, 1969) describes how the early English industrialists had to contend with a work force that was not schedule oriented and did not keep or maintain commitments on time until a generation of children raised in factories and conditioned to the whistle began ordering their lives according to this new synthetic system.

functional-structural aspect of organizations, particularly business and government bureaucracies, is the *subordination of man to the organization,* which is accomplished largely by the way in which the time-space systems are handled.

In a very real sense, time and space are functions of each other. How can you meet a deadline if you are constantly interrupted? How can you listen deeply and carefully to a patient's account of his life without proper architectural screening? [19] It is in this respect that the cultural systems also contrast with each other, for polychronic people like the Arabs and the Turks are *almost never alone,* even in the home.[20] They interact with several people at once and are continually involved with each other. Scheduling is difficult if not virtually impossible with P-time people unless they have mastered M-time technically as a very different system, one which they do not confuse with their own, but which they use when it is situationally appropriate, much as they use a foreign language.

Theoretically, as far as bureaucracies are concerned, P-time systems should demand a much greater centralization of control and be characterized by a rather shallow or simple structure. The top man deals continually with many people, most of whom stay informed as to what is happening, because they are around in the same spaces, are brought up to be deeply involved with each other, and continually ask questions to stay informed. In these circumstances, delegation of authority and a buildup in bureaucratic levels should not be required to handle high volumes of business. This is actually the way it works out for people like the Arabs and the Latin Americans. Administration and control of polychronic peoples in the Middle East is a matter of job analysis: taking each subordinate's job and isolating the important functions that go to make up the job. Functions are then specified and often indicated on elaborate charts with checks

[19] I am referring here to ideal patterns. Many people have to put up with spaces that cripple them in the performance of their jobs. Some of this comes about because of the tight way in which space, as well as time, is locked into the bureaucratic ranking system. It is quite clear, for example, that case workers in welfare departments require the privacy of an office, yet the rank of their activity and the low status accorded the needy are such as to make the office bureaucratically unfeasible (offices are for important people and their activities). Incongruities of this type at all levels, where the requirements of the activity call for one thing and the organizational needs for something else, endow much of life with the Alice in Wonderland quality that Lewis Carroll described so beautifully. It also accustoms us to the bureaucratic insanity and reinforces the notion that you really can't beat City Hall.
[20] Edward T. Hall, "Arab Concepts of Privacy," in *The Hidden Dimension* (Garden City, N.Y.: Doubleday & Co., 1966).

that make it possible for the administrator to be sure that each function has been performed. In this way it is felt that absolute control is maintained over the individual. Yet, *how and when the scheduling is done, is left up to the individual.* To schedule for him would be considered a violation of his privacy. In contrast, M-time people schedule the activity and leave the analysis of the parts of the job to the individual. A P-type analysis, even though technical by its very nature, keeps reminding the subordinate that his job is a system, and is *also part of a larger system.* M-type people, by virtue of compartmentalization, do not see their activities in context as part of the larger whole. In their thinking they are pushed in the opposite direction because the schedule compartmentalizes, segments, isolates, and above all it stresses organizational goals. Again, this is epitomized in our allowing the TV commercial, the "special message from our sponsor," to break the continuity of even the most important communication. By way of contrast, in Spain I once counted twenty-one commercials lumped together at the end of an hour's program. The polychronic Spanish put the commercials *between* the major programs.

Both systems have strengths as well as weaknesses. There is a limit to the speed with which jobs can be analyzed, although once analyzed, proper reporting can enable a P-time administrator to handle a surprising number of subordinates. Nevertheless, organizations run on the P-type model are limited in size and depend on having gifted men at the top. P-type models proliferate bureaucracies as a way of handling greater demands on the system. The M-type organization goes in the opposite direction. They can and do grow much larger than the P-type, however. M-types combine bureaucracies, as in the consolidated school and the business conglomerate. The particular blindness of the M-type organization is to the *humanness* of its members. The blindness of the P-type is to the capacity of the top man to handle contingencies and stay on top of things. M-type bureaucracies as they grow larger turn inward, becoming blind to their own structure, grow rigid and are even apt to loose sight of their original purpose as seen in context. A prime example is the Army Corps of Engineers and the Bureau of Reclamation that wreak havoc on our environment in their dedicated efforts to build dams.

This brings us to another important topic—*context in relation to meaning*—which can be illustrated in the context of education, where much of our M-type compartmentalizing takes place and where it is inculcated in the young.

To understand the role of context as it relates to meaning, one must at least partially understand Marshall McLuhan's [21] point that the media is the message. Linearly oriented Americans have difficulty with McLuhan's thinking, because our culture is what I have termed a "low context culture" [22] in which there is great emphasis on content but very little emphasis on context. The idea of context as a function of meaning is basically very simple, yet like many simple ideas, it carries tremendous implications for understanding a wide range of communication events. It also makes it possible to talk about and relate in a single frame some events which had previously been treated as unrelated. In a word: meaning (M) —any meaning—is a function of information (I) in a context (C). At this point, it is possible to write it as a simple formula $IC = M$. What I have just written is the "I" part of the formula. The context portion is minimal at this point, so the reader provides his own context until the writer further expands on what he means. Contexting the reader takes time, particularly when one is using a linear system such as writing. So, it may help to set down a few basic propositions: 1) Nothing has meaning when stripped of context. Subproposition: it is virtually impossible to strip any event of context, because of man's propensity for providing context whenever it is missing. 2) The relationship of information to context varies. In general, where there is a lot of emphasis on the *information part,* there will be less on the *context part.* Also where there is a lot on the *context* side, very little *information* is required. This can be illustrated by a simple diagram in which C stands for context, I for information, and M for meaning. At the

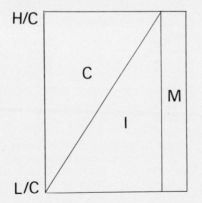

[21] Marshall McLuhan, *Understanding Media* (New York: McGraw-Hill Book Co., 1964).
[22] The notion of high- and low-context communications was first developed and presented by me in a paper delivered at the American Anthropological Association meeting in Pittsburgh in 1966 as part of a program on Interactional Anthropology.

top, high-context (H/C) information is featured, at the bottom, low-context (L/C) information is featured.

An example of a high-context communication situation is a couple who have lived together successfully for 25 years or more. Neither one has to say very much for the other to know what is going on (they talk for other reasons, which is an entirely different subject). An example of a low-context situation is any set of technical instructions, descriptions, or even a computer program.

When people from two different cultures meet, they share a common background of information, *but they do not share contexts;* therefore, the *meaning* of what is happening is different for each of them. What is more, some cultures rely more heavily on context than others (these I term high-context cultures). This affects the way people think as well as how they communicate.[23]

If one looks at the content part of our educational system, some of it may make sense, but most of it makes very little sense. A striking example is found in our method of teaching foreign languages—our way does not work and it has not worked for generations; yet we continue to use it. The claim made by many students today that their education is not relevant is in most instances justified, as are the claims made by critics like John Holt,[24] George Dennison,[25] Nat Hentoff,[26] and others.[27] Nevertheless, if one forgets about manifest content for a minute and looks at what schools are really teaching (the latent content), one finds that the schools are highly effective instruments of society. Indeed, perhaps, they are too good at what they really do and not good enough at what they are supposed to do. Few people have identified or even looked at the context (media-latent)

[23] Thinking and communicating may very well be inseparable. Benjamin Lee Whorf (*Language, Thought and Relating* [New York: The Technology Press and John Wiley & Sons, 1956]) and Sapir (*Selected Writings* [Berkeley: University of California Press, 1949]) both thought so. There is much to support this if one takes the CI = M view—that is, adds context to the total situation. Until now, context has been treated in a variety of ways, but seldom as inseparable from meaning. In fact, much of our "science," most of our bureaucracies, our entire system of justice, in fact, do their best to dispense with context because no one knows how to deal with it.

[24] John Holt, *How Children Fail* (New York: Pitman Publishing Corp., 1966), *How Children Learn* (New York: Pitman Publishing Corp., 1967), *The Underachieving School* (New York: Pitman Publishing Corp., 1969).

[25] George Dennison, *The Lives of Children* (New York: Simon and Schuster, 1969).

[26] Nat Hentoff, *Our Children Are Dying* (New York: Viking Paperback, 1967).

[27] John Holt has compiled a list of forty-two authors and film makers who have documented the state of our schools. This list may be obtained by writing Mr. Holt at 308 Boyleston Street, Boston, Massachusetts 02116.

aspects of education in the United States. Several messages are unmistakably clear: most schools can be counted on to teach students the fundamental fact that all things are subservient to time. Schedules dominate the school day, the week, the month, the year—in fact, the entire process of education. What is happening in the classroom, no matter how vital, is inevitably interrupted by the bell, the quarter, the semester, the school year itself. Educators assign priorities to subjects by the amount of time allotted to them as well as their placement in the overall schedule.[28] Equally important is the educational message that *bureaucracies are real* and that students must learn to deal with them. Furthermore, bureaucratic solutions and bureaucratic thinking can usually be depended on to circumvent the issue of external reality. Bureaucratic feasibility and bureaucratic survival are the *guiding principles in educational decision-making* and students and teachers learn this early in their school experience. A student finds in many of his teachers the models for the bosses whom he will encounter later in his life. If he does not learn to deal effectively with different teachers, he will never be able to handle his future bosses.

What happens in the classroom is a *game* in which the teacher sets the rules. If the student happens to have a good auditory memory and he is articulate, he can learn to be quite good at the game. This makes the teacher happy. Students whose capabilities and talents lie in other sensory modes (*i.e.*, they may be visually or kinesthetically talented) or those who do *not* meet the auditory and verbal norms, have a very difficult time because their teacher is unhappy with their lack of verbal skills. Part of the academic game is that we pretend that all students remember and image in the same way, and therefore those who image or remember differently are classified as "dumb." [29] This enables the verbally talented to feel superior as well as loved by their teachers, but it also deprives our society of some sorely needed talents.

[28] Another way of assigning priorities to subjects would be through the choice of people who instruct. "English is such an important subject, we could not possibly do with anything less than the *best* person available." It often develops that the man who is good is frequently at odds with the system. And while there are exceptions, given the choice, the United States educational establishment can be counted on more often than not to favor the system over excellence, particularly if it means tampering with either time or bureaucratic procedures.
[29] People like Buckminster Fuller who think in systems terms, and who use what I term kinesthetic imagery (they experience relationships with their bodies). I was privileged to have industrial and visual designers as students for several years. Teaching them was an experience entirely different from teaching the usual liberal arts student.

On the bureaucratic side, the lesson most students must learn if they are to survive is that most teachers have to be successful bureaucrats above all else, otherwise, the teachers won't survive. The teacher's primary mission is to keep order. What is more, the reward for keeping order, as in all bureaucracies, is a free hand to keep order in his own way. One of my graduate students was recently fired from his position as student teacher in a public school. Up to the time of his dismissal he had received superior ratings. Yet, when it was discovered that not only was he not keeping "order," but he did not really believe that "straight rows make straight lives," he was fired—despite the fact that his students were doing better than average work.

In light of the above remarks the United States educational system, instead of being irrelevant, is remarkably relevant for the way in which its latent functions serve to prepare the young for real life. It could not have survived as long as it has if it had not been relevant. It is only irrelevant to those who expect schools to truly *educate* people. Since I intend to address myself to this subject at greater length elsewhere,[30] I will not develop the topic further here, except to summarize the implications in terms of context:

Our educational system, like most school systems, is a function of both content and context, on the manifest and the latent level. Our particular delusion is that the former is reality and that the latter does not count. An educational system which presents material in fragments produces a citizenry with great vulnerability to circumstances requiring comprehensive thought or action. On the individual level it produces people who have great difficulty planning their own lives. Such crucial decisions as choice of mate and career are quite often left to chance. People just drift into things. On the national scale our inability to plan and to see the implications of our actions has resulted in a failure to recognize and stop the destructive assaults on our environment. We have great trouble conceptualizing any system. For example, in considering economic systems, we just don't see the connection between a government or business policy and the impact on people's lives. Galbraith[31] has made this point patently clear. One can

[30] Education as an expression of culture constitutes an important section in a forthcoming book.
[31] John Kenneth Galbraith, *The Affluent Society* (Boston: Houghton Mifflin Co., 1958). Galbraith's thinking has not been accepted by many economists, particularly those who are content to work and think either without context or in very low context situations in which masses of data make the very interpretation of those data difficult and controversial. Witness the controversy as to whether it is purchasing power or money that determines the temperature of an economy.

also cite numerous examples in the political realm—Vietnam is the most obvious. This war can only make sense to someone who ignores the larger context, which is the drastic and devastating consequences of the war for our young people, our poor, our cities, and the welfare of the country as a whole.

In twenty-five years of systematic observation of Americans (including myself) [32] interacting with other cultures in *real life situations,* I have developed an analytic system for making observations of very small events and analyzing their patterns.[33] This has forced me to look on the context side of the equation and has put me in the position of intermediary between cultures where people continually bring me different sides of the same story. Hundreds of these encounters have convinced me that the basic patterns of those parts of culture that are out of awareness are so stable, persistent and ubiquitous that only a few people recognize them and only a very few of these are capable of changing them. To summarize, there are two crucial points:

1. Cultures evolve as highly specialized adaptations to the environment. Cultures adapt internally to their own structure as well, molding members through their institutions to perform the requisite tasks.[34] It follows, therefore, that all cultures are vulnerable to those situations that were not prominently featured in the process of their own evolution. Since cultures evolved in different environments and developed personalities and institutions that are specialized adaptations to environmental pressures, they are therefore to some extent vulnerable to each other.

2. By its very nature, cultural vulnerability is much more serious and more difficult to deal with than political or economic vulnerability, because it always involves not only the character of the people themselves, but how life and institutions are organized. What is at stake, therefore, is frequently a matter of life and death, or life with meaning versus life without meaning. The tragedy of the American Indian is an example of cultural vulnerability. Members of any culture sense their own vulnerability when confronted with another culture. Yet one cannot deal with one's own cultural vulnerability by conquering or eliminating someone else. The vulner-

[32] There are a few social scientists who use themselves as controls or subjects in transactions with other cultures. For the past fifteen years I have made it a practice to do this systematically, some of the advantages being that there is always a context and the subject is always available.
[33] See Hall, *The Silent Language, op. cit.,* and *The Hidden Dimension, op. cit.*
[34] That is, cultures adapt to themselves. All over the world, people develop adaptations to bureaucracies, to social organization, to mechanization.

ability remains and may even be exacerbated when a political cure of a cultural condition is attempted.

For example, the Japanese actually learned this lesson as a consequence of their defeat in World War II. Certain characteristics and strengths of their cultural system enable them to plan their entire economy in a comprehensive way and to integrate different facets of their political, economic, and cultural systems in a way that puts the United States to shame.[35] Of course, the Japanese have other problems—like pollution, a direct consequence of their economic success. However, given the Japanese capabilities, their capacity for controlling special interests, and their *high-context* culture, I would favor them over us in any race to solve both environmental problems and human problems.

For a nation, survival depends on the capacity to adapt and to develop new institutions and new personality types to deal with changing times. There is an old law of biology that states that in order to survive a species must adapt. The same is true for culture. *Culture is man's major adaptive mechanism* (he changes his body very little). But, paradoxically, culture is also the major environment in which man develops and with which he must contend. That is, man must adapt to himself, both as a member and product of his own culture and in a world of other cultures. Cultural adaptations were successful in the past when changes were taking place at a slower rate. Today, given our highly developed technical systems and speeded-up communications, changes are taking place at a rate that is apparently faster than it is possible for our institutions to assimilate. What is more, the faster the change, the wider the generation gap.[36] The cultural processes that are at work, however, are much the same, except that the young are more aware of the implications of the split between real life and what happens in the schools than their parents are. Nevertheless, it is not enough for the young to say that the whole structure is rotten and must be destroyed. This is like the neurotic who says that suicide is the only answer. Admittedly, there are people who do commit suicide because they cannot stand the reality of their own lives, but there are more creative ap-

[35] The Japanese gross national product was $43 billion in 1960; and $164 billion in 1969. Automobile production increased by a factor of 10 (481,000 in 1960; 4.6 million in 1969). UPI, December 19, 1969—dateline Tokyo. See also, Howard F. VanZandt, "The Japanese Culture and the Business Boom," *Foreign Affairs,* January, 1970.
[36] Margaret Mead, *Culture and Commitment: A Study of the Generation Gap* (Garden City, N.Y.: Natural History Press / Doubleday, 1970).

proaches, albeit psychically painful ones. No change in one's own psyche is accomplished without giving up one's illusions of one's self.

To summarize, my basic position is that American culture, once vigorous and viable, has become much less so today. If we are to survive and adapt successfully, we *must* change, and this change will not be easy. It involves, among other things, a recognition of the fact that life is rooted both in context and in content, and that without both, life makes little sense.

In Fromm's words, Freud's discovery of the unconscious ". . . bogged down because it was applied solely to man's libidinal strivings." [37] It is paradoxical that Freud, who changed an age with his thinking, founded a movement that eventually became bureaucratized and ritualized.[38] As Fromm points out, Freud tried to unite in a synthesis the two divisive forces of nineteenth-century Western thought—Romanticism and Rationalism. Actually, the issue is not Romanticism versus Rationalism, but the deeper issue of an expanded concept of the unconscious (to include all other areas of life) and integrating this with the conscious. We must see the unconscious as present in all cultural events and then take the next and most difficult step of integrating the latent and the manifest—the media with the message, and the context and information—in order to arrive at true meaning. So far, Western man has only been capable of dealing with the *content* part of the equation, as "the King of Ruffle Bar" discovered when he entered the trap set by the bureaucrats of order. The context part of their behavior had escaped the bureaucrats entirely.

The paradox is that, in his strivings for order, Western man has created chaos, denying that part of himself that integrates, while enshrining the part that fragments experience.

[37] *Sigmund Freud's Mission, op. cit.*
[38] *Ibid.*

Can
Modern Civilization
Escape
Self-Destruction?

Jerome D.
Frank

History is dotted with the relics of extinct societies, but the destruction of a society has usually been compatible with the survival of most of the individuals composing it. A society may be said to cease to exist when the institutions and values that characterize it change radically. Thus it could be said that the Roman Republic died when Octavius turned it into an empire, and today the American political system seems likely to destroy itself by abrogating its most significant characteristic, the right to dissent. While these forms of social death may be accompanied by considerable loss of life, usually there are enough survivors to form the membership of the society that rises from the ashes. In this sense every successful revolution can be looked upon as the suicide of a society, to be succeeded by the birth of a new one. Whether societies die of old age, suicide or murder, the survivors soon form a new social system. Rarely have civilizations, such as Carthage, been permanently destroyed.

Today, however, all human civilization can destroy itself beyond the possibility of rebirth for a long time to come, either through slowly poisoning the biosphere—the environment that sustains life—or through a nuclear war.

Social suicide through destruction of the ecosystem would be analogous to those forms of unintended individual suicide that are consequences of self-indulgence. In this it resembles the slow suicide of some alcoholics or heavy cigarette smokers. Pollution of the biosphere is the unwanted and incidental by-product of the incredible achievements of industrialization; it therefore presents the most immediate threat in heavily industrialized countries, but is certain eventually to endanger people everywhere.

To take just one example, a subtle form of air pollution which may have the most inexorable effects is the gradual increase of atmospheric carbon dioxide resulting from industrial use of fossil fuels, on the one hand, and the progressive destruction of vegetation to make room for expanding cities, on the other. Furthermore, as nations pour increasing amounts of industrial wastes and pesticides into the seas, the day may come when they will poison plankton, a major transformer of atmospheric carbon dioxide into oxygen. In any case, the increasing concentration of atmospheric carbon dioxide affects heat and energy transfer between the earth's surface and outer space, producing alterations in the earth's climate, with unpredictable effects, such as the possible melting of the polar ice caps.

There are both perceptual and motivational reasons for our failure to grasp the gravity of the danger of slow suicide through biospheric poisoning. From a perceptual standpoint, most of the dangers are remarkably unobtrusive; in fact, they are undetectable by the senses. Radioactive isotopes and pesticides in our tissues and the slowly rising carbon dioxide content of the air cannot be seen, heard, tasted, smelt, or felt, so it is easy to forget about them. When pollutants do impinge on our senses in the form of eye-burning smog or brown water, they are experienced as part of the general background of living rather than as a sharply focused threat. In this same connection, although environmental poisons are constantly increasing, the increments are very small compared to the base level, so, in accord with the well-known psychophysiological law, they do not rise above the threshold of awareness. Humans may be in much the same plight as a frog placed in a pan of cold water which is very slowly heated. If the rise in temperature is gradual enough, he will be boiled without ever knowing what happened to him.

These perceptual obstacles to appreciating the dangers created by technological advances play into strong motives for not doing much about them, based on the fact that the rewards yielded by technology are large, tangible, and immediate, while the penalties are remote and contingent. It does not take a learning theorist to know which will determine behavior. For a cigarette smoker the immediate gratification of a smoke far outweighs the probability that it will shorten his life twenty years hence. Similarly, at the social level, the prospects of increased revenue to a community from a new industry dwarf the long-term hazards to health it might create.

Looked at in another way, the cost to an individual of reducing his contribution to atmospheric pollution is out of all proportion to the benefit, because the latter is spread over the entire population. The millions an electric utility company spends to purify the smoke from its power plant yield no tangible benefits to the stockholders except slightly cleaner air to those who happen to live in the vicinity. The converse also holds—the benefits an individual gains by adding a tiny increment to the poisoning of the ecosystem are obvious, while the costs to him are infinitesimal. The pleasure and convenience afforded by a second family car are vastly greater than its cost—an infinitesimal increase in danger to the owner's health produced by the mite it adds to air pollution. So one can safely predict that, despite bursts of rhetoric and enthusiasm, every concrete effort to reduce damage to the ecosystem will meet strong covert or overt resistance from those who must foot the bill.

The dangers created by these unintentionally suicidal activities are still remote and increase only gradually, so there is yet time to overcome them. Of more immediate concern is the danger of self-destruction of human society through intentional acts, except that the intention is not suicide but murder. In group conflicts the primary aim is to destroy the enemy while surviving oneself; but after the intensity of conflict passes a certain level, the drive to kill the enemy becomes stronger than that of self-preservation. In Bertrand Russell's sardonic words, humans are more anxious to kill their enemies than to stay alive themselves.[1] When this state of affairs is reached, all remaining inhibitions against killing are thrown to the wind and humans resort to the most powerful engines of destruction at their disposal. All that has saved mankind from destruction so far has been the inefficiency of even the most powerful weapons. With the creation in the past few years of enormously deadly biological and chemical poisons and, of course, nuclear weapons, this safeguard has been removed.

It is now possible for small revolutionary groups within a society to wreak enormous havoc. For example, poisons exist so powerful that small amounts introduced into a city's water supply could kill all its inhabitants. After the Chicago Democratic Convention in 1968, the news media carried a story that two hippies had attempted to "turn Chicago on" by pouring several pounds of LSD-25 into the water supply. Had they succeeded, the chemical would have been neutralized by the chlorine in the water. However, nations have stockpiled huge supplies of other undetectable poi-

[1] B. Russell, "Can Scientific Man Survive?" *The Saturday Review*, 40 (December 21, 1957), 24.

sons, effective in submicroscopic amounts, which cannot be so easily inactivated—for example, botulinus toxin, one large glassful of which contains enough doses to kill everyone on earth.

The domestic danger posed by nuclear bombs is also very great. It takes only fourteen pounds of enriched plutonium, about the size of a grapefruit, to create a bomb about as powerful as that used on Hiroshima. Largely as the result of the growth of nuclear power, enriched plutonium is in abundant supply, and thousands of engineers now know how to fashion bombs from it. It does not require much imagination to envisage a militant radical group hijacking some plutonium and hiding bombs in major cities —one each would be enough. Even one such bomb, hidden near the nation's capitol and timed to go off during a State of the Union message, would simultaneously kill the President, his cabinet, Congress, and the Supreme Court and destroy most of Washington, thereby decapitating the federal government.

With respect to external dangers, it is common knowledge that Russia and the United States have enough nuclear weapons to destroy each other many times over and are still continuing to accumulate and "perfect" them.

So if humans are to avoid self-destruction via mutual murder, they must learn to place restraints on the violent conduct of group conflicts. This task, in the last analysis, is a politico-military one. That is, its solution depends on the creation of new institutions for handling domestic and international conflict; but students of human nature can contribute to it through bringing to bear their knowledge—still pitifully inadequate—of psychological determinants of group and individual violence, as a first step toward bringing it under control.

Like all forms of human behavior, violence has biological and environmental determinants, the latter including psychological as well as physical factors. The evidence for biological components is that certain brain centers when stimulated lower the threshold for violence, as does increase in blood levels of the male sex hormone. The evidence is clear in all infrahuman mammals, and is highly suggestive in humans. It must be stressed, however, that neither of these bodily interventions automatically produce violent behavior—the proper environmental instigators must also be present.

It is also highly probable that, since human groups have been fighting each other since time immemorial, the survivors of these endless battles have been genetically selected for their fighting propensities.[2] As a result, humans are very easily instigated to violent behavior by a wide variety of stimuli as diverse as physical attack, threats, insults, and a sense of grievance.

Were this all there were to the story, control of human violence would be virtually hopeless. Fortunately, however, social sanctions and group codes are more powerful determiners of human behavior than individual biological or psychological drives. During World War II hundreds of thousands of citizens of Leningrad starved to death in the midst of plenty because the abundantly available food supply happened to have a human shape—for almost every one of the inhabitants the taboo against cannibalism was stronger than the instinct of self-preservation.[3] Gandhi in India and King in the United States were able to create group standards that restrained their followers from violence in the face of extreme instigations, including direct danger to their lives.[4]

Paradoxical as it may seem, the human attribute that poses the greatest threat to survival is probably not aggression but altruism (or, as Arthur Koestler terms it, self-transcendence [5])—that is, the remarkable willingness of humans to die and kill for the sake of something greater than themselves. At the simplest level, this larger entity is the group of which one is a member. For humans, as for all social animals, the group, not the individual, is the survival unit; and when it is threatened, its members sacrifice their lives in its defense. In this, humans closely resemble baboons and are not too different from ants. But the human group gains the allegiance of its members not only because it is the biological survival unit, but because it embodies and preserves certain ideals, values, and symbols that give meaning to the lives of the group members, and this is uniquely human. When Kamikaze pilots committed suicide for their emperor, they had more in mind than the little man sitting on the throne of Japan; and when men offer up their lives for the Flag or the Cross, it is for the concepts these bits of cloth or wood represent.

Though in a war members of each side are prepared to die as a last resort, their main task is, of course, to destroy the enemy. Enemies pose real

[2] K. Lorenz, *On Aggression* (New York: Harcourt, Brace & World, 1966).
[3] H. Salisbury, *Nine Hundred Days: The Siege of Leningrad* (New York: Harper & Row, 1967).
[4] J. D. Frank, *Sanity and Survival: Psychological Aspects of War and Peace* (New York: Random House, 1967), chap. 12, pp. 257–286.
[5] A. Koestler, *The Ghost in the Machine* (New York: Macmillan Co., 1967), chap. 15, pp. 225–266.

threats and must be fought, but the crucial question is: what is there about enemies that removes all restraints on their killing each other? As with self-transcendence, this disinhibition is made possible mainly by the capacity of humans to symbolize.

Konrad Lorenz has made a persuasive case that, with the possible exception of rats, humans are the only creatures with powerful attack equipment who do not have inhibitions against killing members of their own species.[6] It may well be, however, that humans do have such inhibitions but escape from them by using their conceptual powers to define enemies as nonhuman in some crucial way. The enemy never consists of individual fathers, brothers and sons but is a symbolic entity that partakes of the nonhuman and is absolutely evil. Thus the word "enemy" is characteristically preceded by "the"—not "our"—as if to imply that his evil qualities make him a threat to all humanity.[7] Since each society believes its own worldview or ideology to be the only true one, persons who hold a conflicting one are seen as either irrational or wicked, but in either case not as human as we are.

The ideological component is both an important instigator of wars and a cause of their destructiveness. Groups perceive each other as enemies when they find themselves striving for goals that one can obtain only at the other's expense. These are often material—domestically, a greater share of the society's goods; in international affairs, the resources, territory, or manpower of another nation—but they always have an ideological overlay. Abstract ideals are always invoked to justify resorting to war. The American government justifies its intervention in Vietnam in the name of preserving Freedom; the North Vietnamese claim to be struggling against Imperialism. Ideological formulations may serve to cloak other less acceptable aims—for example, simple grabs for power—that might dampen the fighting ardor of those called upon to risk their lives in battle. The transparent hypocrisy of the professed ideological aims of the United States in Indochina has undoubtedly intensified the resistance of the young to this war.

Fights over possessions or territory have a natural end-point, but fights for freedom, justice, democracy, communism, and the like do not. The only way to be sure an idea is dead is to kill every last person who holds it.

In addition, ideologies are often more important sources of psychologi-

---

[6] Lorenz, *op. cit.*

[7] J. G. Gray, *The Warriors* (New York: Harper & Row, 1969).

cal security than possessions, so a challenge to them is a greater threat. Because of their power to conceptualize, humans are forced to recognize the insignificance of their individual lives, which appear to be nothing more than brief, tiny flashes of experience in a universe that does not seem to care. This is intolerable to many people, and to counteract it they create ideologies which give meaning to existence. For them, the loss of their ideology, as might follow defeat by a group that maintains an incompatible world-view, may be worse than biological death, so they prefer to die.

The prospect that man will destroy himself either through heedless self-indulgence or through mutual suicide in the guise of mutual murder is a gloomy one, and in all conscience it is hard to find much grounds for cheer. However, there is some comfort in the old adage that while there is life there is hope, and with respect to the international scene, some straws in the wind are faintly encouraging. For one thing, strategic nuclear weapons, while they have not prevented wars, seem to have contributed to the growing ineffectiveness of violence as a means of resolving political disputes. The danger that any local war may escalate into a world conflagration may partly account for the fact that no war has been fought to clearcut victory since World War II. These weapons have also forced a new concept on the nuclear powers—deterrence by weapons whose *sole* purpose is to prevent war. In the past, weapons of deterrence were used to wage war if the threat of their use failed. Strategic nuclear weapons can be used only to threaten—they cannot be used without destroying the user. The policy of mutual nuclear deterrence is wildly expensive and has created a highly unstable mutual menace, which raises the hope that it will become so burdensome and so obviously absurd that it will eventually lead to moves toward disarmament.

The beginnings of the decline of the sovereign state and the emergence of world government, on which the preservation of peace must ultimately depend, are also discernible, even though in many ways the power of certain nations has never seemed more absolute. On the one hand, even the largest and richest nations are increasingly incapable to perform one of their major functions—protecting the security of their citizens. On the other, the service functions of the United Nations, which contains the germ of world government, are becoming increasingly valuable, especially to the smaller, underdeveloped nations. The core of its strength lies not in its political arms—the Assembly and the Security Council—but in the World Health Organization, the Economic and Social Council, the World Labor Office, and the World Monetary Fund. The allegiance of citizens to their government depends on its perceived ability not only to provide security but also to enhance the general welfare. The United Nations is beginning to do the latter for many people throughout the world. The creation of effective international peace-keeping institutions is a task outside the scope of psychology; but the workability of these institutions depends on changes in the attitudes of the individuals composing national populations, and here students of human behavior may have something to offer. Perhaps one of their major contributions may be to elaborate how the same technological advances that have created the new dangers to survival have also created new means of mobilizing psychological forces to combat them.

First of all, technology has provided new constructive alternative means for satisfying the needs of individuals formerly met by violence, notably the need of young men to establish their masculinity by testing themselves against adversity, whether the adversary be natural or human. In the past the warrior represented the epitome of the virile, courageous man, and still does, but some men have achieved the same sense of identity through risking their lives on cliffs or in gliders, and today some of the antics of the violent student groups seem to be at least partly motivated by the same need.

New possibilities for meeting some of these needs have been provided by the advent of the Space Age. Space travel abounds in opportunities for heroism and self-sacrifice and spacemen are the new heroes.

Outer space also provides a new arena for constructive international competition—constructive because, whatever its military implications, the conquest of space is sensed as a project of all mankind and people everywhere share in its victories and defeats. Russians and Americans sincerely congratulate each other on new space triumphs and share the grief over tragedies experienced by spacemen of either nation. Practically the whole world breathlessly followed the perilous journey of Apollo 13.

To be sure, only a few can actually make space flights, but thanks to the human capacity for identification, millions of youngsters gain vicarious satisfactions by identifying with them, just as they do with star athletes. Obviously outer space, the ocean floor, and other new realms of competition and yet-to-be-discovered adventure can provide only a small part of the needed substitutes for violence, but their potentials are considerable.

Modern technologies also make possible a rapid amelioration of the conditions of life that instigate violence, which can be summed up for our purposes by the term "frustration." This requires, first of all, a sharp check on the rate of growth of the world's population, since it is impossible to satisfy expectations for a better life as long as new mouths gobble up gains faster than they can be achieved. One of the most hopeful new technological advances, therefore, has been the invention of cheap, reliable methods of birth control which have become technologically feasible for the first time, and still more effective methods are on the way.

Finally, technology has created powerful new ways to cultivate the sense of world community—the recognition by all the world's people that, to use Adlai Stevenson's phrase, they are all travelers on the same crowded spaceship, a recognition which at present very few humans possess. A dream of philosophers and divines for millennia, but never more than a dream, the Brotherhood of Man has suddenly come within human grasp.

I have suggested earlier that humans, like other predators, do have inhibitions against killing their own kind, whom they define as members of their own group. Without such inhibitions social living would be impossible. These inhibitions find expression in, and are powerfully supported by, laws and institutions for their enforcement, but these work only to the extent that persons under their dominion perceive themselves as members of the same community. If they do not, they no longer feel bound by its laws. Today we are witnessing this phenomenon in the United States, especially among Negro poor, on the one hand, and affluent, educated youth, on the other, both of whom for different reasons feel alienated from the power structure and lack confidence in its institutions.

Just as domestic tranquility in the United States depends on restoring the sense of community of all Americans, so world peace requires the creation of a sense of community of all the world's peoples transcending their national allegiances.

To achieve this goal, at the individual level nothing is as effective as personal contact, and today's cheap mass transportation has made possible personal meetings of people from different countries on a hitherto undreamed of scale. Of course, personal contacts can exacerbate misunderstandings as well, but much is being learned about how to increase the chances that they will promote mutual good will. As an example of what is now feasible, a practical plan for interchanging tens of thousands of Russian and American high school students to attend each other's schools for a year can be activated at any time that both nations agree to do so.[8] The youngsters would be especially suited to promote mutual understanding be-

[8] S. D. James, "Exchange Plan Gains in Acceptance," *War/Peace Report* (October, 1964), p. 15.

cause they are at an impressionable age in which they readily form friendships, and are too young and inexperienced to be good spies, and so would be less likely than adults to arouse the suspicions of their hosts.

But the most powerful new potential for improving international attitudes lies in the electronic mass media, especially the transistor radio and television. These jump cultural and literacy barriers and have an emotional impact far exceeding that of the written word. As an impetus to the fight against pollution and a means of fostering a sense of world community, the photos of the living Earth from Apollo 12 are worth thousands of articles and speeches.

The power of television to influence behavior may be illustrated by some examples. An article that appeared in a journal with 15 million readers elicited seventy-five letters of comment—the same points made on a television discussion program elicited one thousand letters in a week. A broadcast on chemical and biological warfare paved the way for the Presidential renunciation of biological weapons and a pledge of no first use of chemical ones.[9] Examples could be multiplied indefinitely.

Television, properly used, can break down stereotypes, restore individuality to members of depressed groups, and force their plight on the attention of and consciences of dominant ones. The television series on hunger in America gave a powerful impetus to the passage of food legislation stalled in Congress.

By bringing the realities of the Indochinese war into the living room, television has made it difficult for Americans to maintain the stereotype of the enemy as nonhuman and has undoubtedly contributed to the growing revulsion against this war, reflected in the precipitous drop in the sale of war toys, and the mounting pressure on the government for bringing our men home. In short, by individualizing members of other groups and making their aspirations and sufferings as vivid as one's own, it can mobilize concern, compassion, and other feelings of human solidarity to an extent and degree never before possible.

Of course, mass electronic communication is only a means. It can be used to heighten as well as to reduce group enmities and it is powerless to resolve the conflicts of interests underlying them, but its potentials for fostering international attitudes that increase the chances for peaceful solutions of such conflicts have not even begun to be exploited.

Finally, modern science and technology have created opportunities for

[9] N. Johnson, "Big Brother Is Watching You," *The Key Reporter*, 26 (Spring, 1970), 3.

activities at the group level which, by improving the attitudes of groups toward each other, will inevitably produce similar changes in the attitudes of the individuals composing these groups.

Social psychologists have shown that the most powerful antidote to enmity among groups is cooperation toward a goal that both groups want but neither can achieve alone.[10] At first glance survival would seem to be such a goal since all people desire it and its achievement requires international cooperation. Under some circumstances, however, survival takes a back seat compared with the urge to destroy the enemy. Moreover, the long-term measures, required for national survival, such as general disarmament, appear to increase the short-term risks of destruction by an enemy, so mobilizing the urge to survive works both ways.

Modern science, however, has created many opportunities for cooperative activities among nations to attain goals that all of them want but none can achieve alone. We know from the experience of one such activity, the International Geophysical Year, that this fosters habits and attitudes of cooperation which gradually become embodied in institutions. Scientists have devised dozens of such projects which can be activated as soon as the world's leaders are willing.

To recall the other major threat to human survival, destruction of the environment, combating pollution provides an ideal goal for international cooperation. The threat it presents is worldwide, and since problems cannot be solved on a scale smaller than that on which they arise, pollution can be overcome only by worldwide cooperative actions. It makes no difference, for example, where DDT finds its way into the ocean since oceanic creatures everywhere absorb it, and radioactivity spewed into the atmosphere from any source circles the globe. Moreover, a cooperative attack on pollution, in contrast, for example, to an international effort to halt the arms race, involves no risks. While certain outcomes of negotiations might be financially more advantageous for some groups than others, the losers would not be endangered and they would be better off than if no agreement had been reached. Persistent rumors that "Soviet and Western representatives have been holding secret discussions on the establishment of a large scale, internationally staffed 'think tank' to study common problems of industrial societies" [11] suggest that this very hopeful form of international cooperation may not be far off.

[10] M. Sherif and C. W. Sherif, *In Common Predicament: Social Psychology of Intergroup Conflict and Cooperation* (Boston: Houghton Mifflin Co., 1966).
[11] D. S. Greenberg, "Soviets, West Discuss 'Think Tank,'" *Science,* 166 (December 12, 1969), 1382.

For the first time, in short, we have the means to create a sense of community among peoples of different nations, and we must do so if mankind is to survive its own destructive ingenuity.

To conclude, from a philosophical viewpoint, for the first time humans have taken the power of life and death into their own hands. We cannot prevent death, of course, but we are learning to postpone it—how long, nobody knows. It is conceivable that the average life span may go up to 150 years as we learn to combat not only diseases but the aging process. Although how much we can prolong life is uncertain, it is perfectly clear that we can drastically shorten it. Barring a cosmic accident, if the human race is destroyed in the foreseeable future, it will be by its own hand, not by natural forces beyond its control. This may in part account for the gloom and despair expressed by so many contemporary poets and playwrights, who keep hammering away on the related themes that life is meaningless and absurd, a kind of bad joke, and that man is capable only of making himself and his fellows miserable. Could such viewpoints spring in part from a feeling of terror at our inability to live up to the appalling responsibilities of our new power? In any case, while this power is frightening, it is also hopeful. We have succeeded in subduing a host of natural dangers whose origins were initially obscure. The dangers that face us today are man-made, and many of their causes are well known. The remedies, unfortunately, are only beginning to emerge, but at least we know that their potential exists for the first time. By exerting every effort along the lines I have mentioned (and along many others I have not been able to imagine), humans may yet be able to avert race suicide and move forward to enjoy exciting new adventures and possibilities for fulfillment.

Democracy
in a
Changing
World
Erich Kahler

Our entire world, its very existence and consistence, is in crucial jeopardy. It would be a desperate task to list the innumerable faults of innumerable people and the crimes of whole nations, at the source of this condition, rather than attribute all evil to the nature of man. I am tempted to presume that the present deplorable state of humanity derives—at least partly, but decisively—from changing circumstances, which we must examine carefully.

In doing this, we may, I think, safely choose the case of the United States as representative, in general, for the most advanced stage of world civilization—especially considering its size and power, and its having started from humanitarian and progressive principles that embodied the hopes of the modern world.

The concept of democracy is complex, having changed along with human evolution. But there are two basic distinctions that seem to me relevant to our inquiry.

1   The first concerns a *radical difference between ancient and modern democracy*. The initial form of explicit democracy, the Athenian, originated in an oligarchic structure within a patriarchal monarchy. It was made up of a limited number of free citizens of the *Polis,* who exercised the power of government personally and directly. The leisure necessary for this task was made possible by the primeval institution of slavery. Government, vested in this elite, which was identical with indigenousness, was their prerogative and sacred duty; government carried the affirmative value of nobility. This ancient, limited democracy was *active democracy*.

Modern democracy evolved from a fight of people in whom a sense of individual identity and independence had begun to rise, in opposition to the age-old oppressive rule of feudal monarchies and privileged nobilities. It was therefore primarily a fight *against* being ruled; government was to be as restricted as possible, limited to the indispensable requirement of keeping the civic order functioning properly, a task for which authority had to be delegated to officials and deputies by a more and more numerous and dispersed population. The duties and preventive limitations of government had to be laid down by *law*. The arbitrary personal ruler was superseded by impersonal, suprapersonal rules. The "rights of man" and "civil liberties" were established through explicit constitutions, instituting equality of all citizens, "justice for all," and protection of individual independence. *Legality, equality, justice,* and individual *independence* are, accordingly, the elementary principles of modern democracy, which is primarily *defensive democracy*.

The defiance and distrust of government found its expression in the original conceptions of "liberalism," capitalism, "free enterprise" and, more specifically, in the American Bill of Rights. It laid the foundation of the traditional attitude of the American people toward government: the protection of the people against undue "interference of government" in private affairs and, within government, the safeguard of Congress as representatives of the people against encroachments of the Administration.

This attitude was bound to become more articulate, when the Administration had to expand so as to be bureaucratically more effective in regulating the life of a rising population in more complex circumstances, a task that necessarily implied an increasing autonomy of special departments and agencies.

The tendency of defensively guarding against government is an impediment to timely adaptation of people's frame of mind to changing conditions. This attitude still appears as, what it was originally intended to be, a protection against authoritarianism. The situation, however, is more intricate. The reluctance, and increasing incapacity, of the people to concern themselves with government unless it touches their private interests is precisely what can now bring about tyranny.

2   The second distinction is subtle, yet most important to keep in mind. It is the distinction between *form and spirit*. The American people are inclined to rely all too complacently on formal institutional safeguards. They want to believe that, for example, introducing elections and parliaments among liberated colonial peoples—some of them tribal peoples,

who for centuries have been subject to ruthless exploitation and neglect—
is the way to introduce democracy among them. Winston Churchill has
provided the formula for such a belief in his 1944 speech on Greek events:

> My idea of [democracy] is that the plain, humble common man who
> keeps a wife and a family . . . goes off to fight for his country when it
> is in trouble, that he goes to the polls at the appropriate time and puts
> his cross on the ballot paper showing the candidate he wishes to be
> elected to Parliament—that is the foundation of democracy . . .

Now, at this stage in history, after the experiences we have endured,
this formula cannot but appear as a gross, hypocritical simplification. We
know too well what utterly undemocratic practices have been engineered
and supported all over the world under the cover of formal constitutional
proceedings. We have, before our eyes, the sham elections, which the
South Vietnamese junta has dressed up as representative of the people, to
soothe the easily reassurable qualms of the American public. We have witnessed what happened at the 1968 Chicago Democratic Convention and
the subsequent trials. Fundamental changes of the structure of American
society and of the conditions of its global involvement have by far ex-
ceeded the scope of constitutional provisions. These changes have created
loopholes and have left wide stretches of public life—uncovered by
even an attempt at "law and order"—open to arbitrary practices, permitting a misrepresentation of the letter and disregard of the spirit of the
Constitution.

Even if the letter of the Constitution, e.g., the First Amendment, were
more faithfully observed than it is, this would not be sufficient to guarantee the preservation of democracy. No document alone, be it the noblest
and most carefully worded, can provide such a guarantee. It is the spirit of
the people, the people that created it and the people that uphold it. And
this very spirit seems to me imperiled by the change of conditions in our
century.

It is useful to recall what we all know, but easily forget. After the
American Revolution, the population of the country was about 3,250,000
people, of whom approximately one third was unfree. Not counting the
women, who had a limited status and no vote, and the many settlers in remote regions, about only 120,000 Americans could meet the religious,
property, and other qualifications for full citizenship; moreover, those who
did qualify were mostly farmers, cities being still rare. This was the people
for whom the Constitution was designed. To be sure, the later amendments

added some most important provisions, like women's right to vote, and the formal abolition of slavery, among others; but the established order remains fragmentary and profoundly inadequate to the present situation.

Today, the population of the United States has grown past 200 million and is increasing rapidly. Industry, technology, and science have recast the structure and texture of society. A nation of rural individuals has turned into a nation of principally urban, indeed megalopolitan, highly industrialized, and technically organized masses, and even agriculture is being industrialized. Mechanical mass production is correlated with standardized mass consumption; they have mutually created and promoted each other. Science and its technological applications—expanding, changing, ramifying incessantly—have outgrown the control of the individual, have functionalized, instrumentalized, our way of life; and the computers are on their way to taking even crucial human functions and decision-making out of man's mind to handle them mechanically and automatically. *The apparatus of life encumbers its substance.*

The interference of the power of advertising, in conjunction with the development of mass media, has invalidated the law of supply and demand, by constantly producing artificial demand; supply is correspondingly manipulated. Advertising, in the form of novel methods of propaganda and persuasion, has also falsified the democratic process. For a candidate who does not have the millions to buy costly television time is doomed. Russell Baker stated in *The New York Times*—and it was not a joke, but thoroughly documented—

> As everyone should know, but probably doesn't, political candidates are no longer elected. They are sold. In 1966, to cite a case, Governor Rockefeller was put in the hands of an agency (Jack Tinker and partners) whose other accounts included Alka-Seltzer, and their work converted him from a sure loser to the hottest product since Bufferin.

In addition, modern means of communication and mass media have contracted our world, have made it into one, closely interdependent, if ununified, unit, and have immensely accelerated and multiplied happenings. Daily, indeed hourly news and its reactions produce daily, indeed hourly events. We live in a constant turmoil of happenings that benumbs and befogs our consciousness. The borderlines between national and international politics have become fluid.

When we look for a valid concept by which to measure the huge divergence of the prevailing condition from the requirements of a commensurate, human democracy there is no better one than Lincoln's classical formula: Government of the people, by the people and for the people. Taking this formula as a yardstick, we shall find that the nations, which most closely approximate this standard, are the small European ones, like the Swiss, Dutch, and the Scandinavian, all of them long civilized and homogeneously cultured, whose populations, due to their limited size, are able to remain in close touch with—that is, to know, judge, and control —the personalities they elect for government. They are—again because of their size—less relevant to the course of world events, and their concerns therefore are mainly domestic and well-defined economic problems, which can be grasped by their direct impact on everybody's life. This illustrates the crucial role that the size of population plays for the maintenance of democracy and underscores the threats inherent in an excessive population growth.

In addition, America has inherited a special fateful predicament. All important Western nations have indulged in the shameful custom of slave trade, but all of them have been able to liquidate these remnants of the past through colonialism. They supplanted slavery by colonialism, which is external, remote, in a superficial sense legitimized collective slavery. America is a unique case, having herself issued from a colony and from a colonial war of liberation. This laid the seeds of a deep contradiction in principle from which America could hardly extricate herself. She created a colony within a colony, thereby converting slavery into a *domestic colonialism,* a colonialism within her own borders. The basic, constitutional principle of democracy induced her to a nominal liberation of the slave population that has developed into a full-fledged compact people, with customs and aspirations of their own, an ethnic group that, however, was held in the same state of misery and degradation as all colonial peoples everywhere in the world, only in the midst of their own masters, not in faraway regions.

This "colony" cannot be liberated by eliminating it from the make-up of the country. The black people have become, like other ethnic groups, part of the United States. This is their home, in spite of all that has been done to them. However, in the face of universal liberation movements, they can no longer be peaceably reassured by further procrastination, nor by surreptitious means of suppression, or "benign neglect," lest the democratic foundation of this nation be fully destroyed. As matters stand, their rightful, abrupt claims are apt to clash with all sensible attempts at reform, and so threaten to tear the country asunder.

Now let us look a little closer into our situation and examine how the tremendous changes have affected the democratic process.

Take the *government*. The Constitution provided for checks and balances, for a division of powers—legislative, judicial, executive. It did not make provisions for the formation and activities of parties. To be sure, the development of parties is a natural consequence of the democratic process; it is fully implied. Hence party politics started with the initiation of modern democracy itself. But parties further grew with the population, and in the process became institutionalized.

Inevitably an administrative party officialdom, the party machines, developed, whose overwhelming influence is sufficiently known. Since an increasing population has less and less opportunity to know the personalities eligible for national government, nominations of candidates are presented to, and sometimes forced upon, the constituency by party officials; because of party competition, the charisma and vote-getting capacity of the candidate is all-important, and hardly any consideration is given to his governmental capacities: a broad view and knowledge of the world, perspicacity, independence, and clarity of mind.

This state of affairs appears to have been an inevitable result of the expansion of democracy, but its further development under the American party system carries particular dangers for the democratic process. We have witnessed in large democracies two extreme alternatives: the uninhibited *multiparty system,* based on full parliamentary control of the administration, and the dogmatically protected American *two-party system,* based on the division of powers, with its checks and balances, and fixed terms of office. The two-party system has obvious advantages over the excessive proliferation of parties—often brought about by no other reason than the reckless ambitions of would-be leaders—a system that ruined democracy in France, Italy, and Weimar Germany. The two-party system affords the democratic process a protective stability, which functions fairly well in a time of relative calm. In our rapidly changing, revolutionary world, however, it hinders the adjustment of new developments and conceptions, and obstructs their open expression, clinging as it does to the status quo. The European democracy before, and partly after the Second World War, died of too much flexibility. The American democracy is on the point of dying of extreme rigidity and formalization.

The two ruling parties in this country have grown all-powerful. They are deeply, traditionally entrenched, and shielded from any potential competitor by preventive measures in various states, such as making recognition of a new party dependent on a size of membership that cannot possibly be reached in the initial stage, and on the approval of State Attorneys, who belong to either of the ruling parties. The Democrats used to be identified with social progressivism, and the Republicans with social and economic conservatism. But these traditional differences are dwindling. Both parties are "umbrella parties"; they include progressive as well as reactionary elements. The progressives in each party are forced to harmful compromises and timid, tactical expedience. As far as foreign policy is concerned, we have in fact a one-party system. What there is of critical opposition operates within, but not between, parties. This state of affairs makes voting along general party lines of political conduct hardly possible.

The emergence of a third party which could become one of the ruling parties, as in England, or a vertical split of the existing parties, is prevented by the insurmountable strongholds of the traditional parties. Since the terms of office of the Administration are fixed, and the unity of the parties is sacrosanct, conscientious people are made temporary prisoners of the ruling administration, whatever its failures. In England, for instance, after revelations such as the Tonkin resolution hearings produced, a Prime Minister could not have stayed in office one day longer. Indeed the whole investigation would have happened much earlier, and all the blood and toil and suffering, all the subsequent pernicious influences of an irresponsible regime, might have been spared. Americans, however, have to wait at least for the end of the four-year term, and chances are that by that time most of the people will have forgotten to ask how it all came about and will have been carried farther into a condition that "has to be accepted now we are in it." This is an unhealthy, frustrating situation that obstructs a timely expression of change through regular channels and induces stagnation of the democratic process.

Accordingly, the competition between the two parties has been voided of substance and degraded to a functional contest, like that of the Mets and the Cardinals. The two-party system was originally meant as a means of mutual control, part of the general system of checks and balances. But, since dirty spots and failures can be found everywhere, any electoral campaign tends to degenerate into a balance of abuses.

It is widely held that a party division based on general attitudes and orientations would not fit the complexity of American conditions. But in reality, this very complexity, this growing and ever-changing complexity, has arrived at a point of exploding the hollow shells of the parties. Recently, the conflict between doves and hawks cut deeply into the official parties and, paradoxically, both these unofficial parties were sometimes united in their opposition to the ruling party's administration.

Another practice that has a degenerative effect on the democratic process by blocking change is the seniority system prevailing in the congressional committees. This favors the established, older, frequently segregationist politicians and bars younger, more alert contenders from leadership. This is most harmful in the case of the Rules Committee, which is able to allow or deny any proposed legislation access to the floor, and thus constitutes a usurped power. As Duane Lockard has observed in the *Nation:*

> . . . the gatekeepers are chosen not by any overt act of political parties . . . indeed not even by the members of Congress. They are chosen by the lottery (not even a lottery, but the comfortable assurance of perpetual re-election) of the Seniority System . . . Public acceptance of this dispersal of authority is a fact . . . The great majority (of the people) have no strong feelings one way or the other, for the simple reason, that they are not given to assessing the operation of Congress or of any other major institutions of government.[1]

All this is symptomatic of the growing inattention of the people to government, and the resigned trust in *technical experts,* due to their inability to cope with the bewildering intricacies of modern conditions. The modern situation demands *active democracy,* increasing popular participation in the irresistibly expanding government, but the people as well as Congress in its majority is still geared toward *defensive democracy*—that is, restricting public administration, as well as the people's attention to its control.

As a result of this state of affairs, the political life of the nation has abandoned the constitutional channels of democracy. The legal process of democracy runs idle, and the direction of the crucial concerns of the nation is left to uncontrollable influences and undercurrents. Political determination has shifted to authorities of constitutionally different competence (like the courts handling the race issue, and the initiative to legislation coming from the Administration instead of from Congress) or to wholly illegitimate sectional and functional forces: lobbies, pressure groups of all kinds, administrative agencies like the Pentagon, in concurrence with the interests of industrial corporations and the millions of people in their service (Eisenhower's "complex," which indeed has expanded to a military-industrial—and labor union complex), the *AEC,* the *CIA,* the *FBI,* the *AAM,* the *AMA,* and so forth. These have become the decisive factors in public affairs.

[1] The *Nation*, March 24, 1962.

In the initial stages of American democracy, congressmen were meant to represent the common interests of the nation, and in a small community with a fairly homogeneous population, the interests of sectional groups were, in spite of the divergence of agricultural and business interests, still conformable to the interests of the nation as a whole. Today, the immense dispersion, variety, and specialization of regional and occupational group interests make it almost impossible for congressmen to attend both to the dominant concerns of their constituencies and to the true interests of the nation, which more often than not run counter to the immediate interests of sectional groups, and which "the folks at home" are utterly unprepared to understand and care for. It takes exceptional courage and self-sacrifice to stand for the nation, and even for humanity at large, against one's district; there are very few men in Congress who so risk their political lives and they usually do not survive the next election.

In this context, most congressmen have to worry perpetually about re-election. From the moment a congressman is elected, he starts steering for reelection. There is hardly a year left to him to devote himself comparatively unencumbered to his government duties. In his second year, again an election year, his every action is geared to vote-getting. More and more, with memorable exceptions, *a congressman appears to be elected for the main purpose of being reelected.*

The changes in the character of government since the establishment of the Constitution correspond to the changes in the structure of the *people,* which are even more fundamental. In point of fact, the changes in government and the changes in the people are one interacting process and should be seen as one.

Up to the end of the nineteenth century the people consisted of "rugged individualists," carrying on their personal trades. (The collectivistic trend, though, was noticed even by Tocqueville in 1840, in a period that was technically not ripe for it.) Free enterprise meant personal enterprise, freedom of the human individual. Today, the people consists of innumerable and manifold collectives—corporations, unions, associations, organizations, bureaucracies—and of economic, professional, administrative, academic, and scientific groups. Accordingly, the personal interests of people predominantly *coincide with the interests of the collectives* to which they belong and on which they depend. Views and purposes are, to an ever-diminishing degree, their personal own; they are directed by their collectives.

In the daily turmoil of our mass society, under the impact of an uninterrupted stream of inflated news, offers, displays, inventions, and new findings, people are unable to form stable reasoned opinions. So, as far as they do not follow the lines of their specialized group interests—the ones they can best grasp and judge from experience—*they take in the predigested material of our largely coordinated newspapers, journals, and commentators.* They have hardly time and strength left for careful thinking and for obtaining thorough information. Our tremendous apparatus of mass communication, with those panel discussions of experts who pour out heaps of diffuse arguments, is unable to convey a correct and organized picture of the problems and their background. All this is too much and not enough; it augments the confusion instead of resolving it. Even discussions of scholars hardly produce more clarity; one of them remarked after a meeting: "We are still confused, but on a higher level."

What is worse, factual truth is submerged under more or less palpable *indoctrination.* We do not have a consistent, critical opposition press of wide distribution. How many people read the *Nation,* the *New Republic,* the *Progressive,* or *I. F. Stone's Bi-Weekly*—not to speak of foreign newspapers; who takes the trouble to look up the *Congressional Record* for occasional oppositional speeches, delivered before empty houses? The newspapers, again with notable exceptions like *The New York Times,* are a chorus, echoing with slight, obliging variations the official versions. Conscientious reporters and commentators, like Walter Lippmann, are scarce. The dependence of radio and TV networks on commercial sponsors and the consequent cautiousness of program producers are common knowledge.

Democracy is a two-way process. Guidance in the form of thorough, coherent information has to reach the people so that they can develop valid opinions. It is useless to poll people on questions which they never have reasoned out properly. Their answers would be random emotional reactions, or current clichés. What goes under the name of public opinion is often what the government itself, and what the collectives—either directly or indirectly, through their influence on the government, the press, and mass media—have publicized, and what then, in turn, the Administration heeds in its political conduct.

We are today at a crossroads where the well-being of the nation, and indeed of humanity, often stands in opposition to the requirements of sectional groups; it is thus bound to demand sacrifices from them. The worst of it is that these demands are determined by complex global interrelationships, which are not immediately apparent and can be grasped only through extensive information.

These circumstances require for the presidency a man with wide knowledge of the social, psychological, and intellectual currents of our age, a man whose mind is firmly independent and capable of forming concepts and convictions, yet still is resilient enough to learn from experience; a man who has traveled extensively in foreign countries and not just on "good-will" tours; who has made himself truly familiar with foreign peoples, their conditions and aspirations, so as to gain a broad view of the world, unencumbered by propaganda.

To summarize: the domestic situation of the United States shows us *the perilous gap that has evolved and keeps widening between the people and their government.* This is not like the ordinary "generation gap" that has always developed between the young and their elders. (To be sure, the young sense both the defects of an inveterate system and the hypocrisies with which the government tries to conceal them much sooner and more sharply since their own future—life or death—is involved.) The gap I have in mind is a much deeper, *constitutional gap* that can no longer be patched up by single reforms, even if the people were amenable to radical reforms at all.

The determination of policies has abandoned the constitutional channels of democracy. Relations between the people and the government are formalized, and the actual power of Congress is paralyzed between the inordinate demands of sectional collectives from below, and the uncontrolled pressures of power groups from above. Complicating matters, a gap even worse has developed between the perceptive capacity of the common man and the technical and global complexities of problems he faces as he tries to cope with the stress of urgent decisions—which, to be beneficial, need to be taken, not according to particular preferences or compromises, but in accordance with the welfare of the whole nation.

As we will see, the failure of the cumbersome, superannuated apparatus of the old democratic system has suddenly been made apparent by the awakening of humanity to the overriding and worldwide problem of pollution with its immense implications and ramifications; the fateful condition of man's natural environment by far surpasses in gravity all the special problems of single nations and ideologies. To grapple with world problems we first have to deal with "national interest," the crucial concept on which the policies and conflicts of the nations hinge.

"National interest" has never been defined, not even by international law. Like many other crucial terms, as for instance, "aggression" and "defense," it has been left comfortably open to casuistic interpretation, adaptable to all kinds of national and privately usurped purposes. The term could be stretched to the claim for "Lebensraum," as in the cases of the Third Reich and Japan; indeed it has been stretched by America to apply at least 10,000 miles away from the homeland. Most fatefully, however, this unlimited concept is held up as the legitimate basis of government. Now, however, we are suddenly confronted with a universal interest that only conflicts with the "national interest."

Today, even under a dictatorship, every person has an inescapable share in the conduct of national affairs. Whether he wills it or not, he is made an accomplice of his government. Reckless behavior in "foreign affairs" finds its response in the spread not only of criminal violence in the street, and in the outbreaks of despondent protesters, but in civic groups that have dropped all public responsibility: doctors who, oblivious to their Hippocratic Oath and with the support of the AMA, leave hospitals unattended; striking hospital personnel, fire departments, garbage collectors, grave-diggers. A nationwide mail strike in open distrust and defiance of the government threatened chaos as it has existed before only on the international scene. Even a national guerrilla war seems under way. *All of this signifies the breakdown of the old boundaries between domestic and foreign issues, which are now so interwoven.*

All nations, even the most powerful ones, are inextricably entangled in a world that *combines technical unity with an unprecedented political anarchy*—unprecedented precisely because of the underlying, unacknowledged technical unity of the world which conflicts with its political anarchy. No superior authority exists, capable of keeping the discordant political, economic, and ideological "national interests" in bounds. On the other hand, no disengagement of a nation from the rest of the world is possible any longer.

There are other, even more consequential factors breaking down the barriers between domestic and foreign policy. *Transnational economic forces* and giant industrial corporations determine our policies everywhere, and their conglomerately allied, if occasionally rival, interests span half of the globe. The Standard Oil Corporation of New Jersey, whose assets in the United States amounted to about $11½ billion during the early sixties, sold its products in more than a hundred countries and owned 50 percent or more of the stock in 275 subsidiaries in fifty-two countries. Similar figures are available for corporations dealing in steel, rubber, aluminum, chemical, and other commodities; they far exceed the gross national income of more than half of the existing nation-states. The impact of these firms in determining national policies is notorious. One need not be a Marxist to realize that the Cuban Sugar Export Corporation had something to do with the American policy toward the Batista regime and its successor; that the Union Minière and British Petrol were rather sizable factors in the Congo crisis; and that Anderson Clayton and United Fruit were not totally disinterested in what happened in Guatemala and Brazil. In fact, the American ambassador openly prided himself on having brought down the progressive regime in Guatemala. It need not be stressed that the CIA is the clandestine harbinger of these forces which make havoc of the concept of "national sovereignty" and "national interest."

This intervention by alien enterprises, over which the people at home have no control, carries the most serious implications. For the crimes committed by these unscrupulous transnational forces—their wanton, atrocious wars and interventions—are enacted in the name of the people by national governments who present them to the people as required by the national interest when, in fact, "national interest" means private interests.

All this is taking place while problems of utmost exigency, supranational, supra-ideological problems threatening the very existence of all humanity, call for immediate action and international cooperation. The most pressing of these problems is the rapidly increasing *overpopulation of our planet,* almost too late to solve; and it is not only an overpopulation of people, but also—as a result of all these people's incessant urge to make money—of the proliferation and acceleration of technology; it is an almost instant massification of everything—of objects, projects, procedures, of all the residual trash of life, even massification of rarities.

Into this most critical state of our world there has erupted that revolutionary event I mentioned before: the wholly unprepared emancipation of the colonial peoples, which, by creating a host of quasi-independent new nations, made the structure of the U.N. obsolete and signaled a new climate of international democracy. At present this development has increased the prevailing anarchy and made all international problems more intricate.

Many nations in Asia, Africa, and Latin America now struggle against insuperable odds; they will never be capable of reaching prosperity and full independence unassisted. Yet, as their population grows, foreign aid —minimal in comparison to the colossal need—seldom passes the ruling cliques to benefit the people; in any case, it is mostly military and has political strings attached.

And now, when anarchy mounts throughout the world, new sources of conflicts are plainly before our eyes: the arms race is starting a new round with the production of ABM and MIRV; suppression, and this means perpetuation, of civil wars of liberation is sought; and the United Nations, our first faint attempt at the institution of a peaceful world order, is arbitrarily being bypassed or misused by the important powers.

To avert such catastrophe, we need a global antipoverty program, a pooling of aid, indeed, a sharing of resources among all nations. Who would be able to organize and administer such common aid, but a world organization? National governments will never be prepared to do this, neither the capitalistic governments, elected to further their "national interests" at the expense of others, nor the Soviet-dominated regimes, blinded as they are by the despotic maintenance of group orthodoxy. But how can one expect an uninformed, in fact ideologically misinformed, at best apathetic, public to understand that today the true national interest, and any partisan interest, has become identical with the interests of humanity at large.

Here we are at the crucial point, or rather at the crucial vicious circle. Only when 1) in the opposing camps the awareness of perils threatening all arises, and 2) an intense common anxiety produces the necessary feeling of human solidarity—only then would we come close to establishing an effective world organization, one equipped with a strong judicial executive, and with nuclear arms in its permanent custody.

This dilemma in which we are caught makes the interconnection between national and an incipient global democracy quite evident. For a genuine democracy at home—a rule of legality, equality and justice for all, as projected by the American Constitution—is not sustainable in a world of anarchy, lawlessness, and carelessness. The whole world is present everywhere, at all times. The curtain has vanished, and the violence, intrigues, and corruption that go with the power struggle abroad disintegrate the domestic order.

I have no illusions about the prospects of near-utopian aims. They could only be approached by what Gunnar Myrdal calls "the courage of despair." And yet, we have no choice. They constitute, taken all together, the unique, ineluctable challenge of our age, and the purpose of this approximate survey of our paradoxical circumstances was to show the extent and the dimensions of these circumstances.

Our hope goes to our young people, who feel vaguely that there is something profoundly wrong with our civilization. In March, 1969, Harvard biologist Dr. George Wald, in a memorable speech, spelled out this common cause, underlying the directionless unrest of young people in our days. It is their feeling of being cheated not only of their youth, their present, but indeed, for the first time in history, of their *whole imaginable future, including posterity.* No establishable goal seems left to them, no common human aim, even beyond their own life.

"We are on the road to extermination," another great biologist, Dr. Albert Szent-Gyorgyi says, "American society is death-oriented . . . All our ideas are death-oriented . . . According to very respectable scientists," he adds, "man's chances of survival are dropping toward 50 percent, and by the end of the century will be below that." Why, then, should we be surprised at the sight of young people who have begun to enact the foreseeable destruction that the adult world has in store for them anyhow?

There exists for them, however, a final way to save their own future and that of humanity: *an ultimate attempt to unify.* What cannot be achieved by dispersed groups with scattered purposes may be accomplished by joining forces, by creating a unified youth movement, a strong international movement of young people, beyond ideological and parochial boundaries. The prerequisite of such an undertaking would be setting aside, if only provisionally, minor differences of opinion, remaining perpetually and firmly aware of the one superior task, and the dangers of ruinous divisions. It would be also imperative to forget all previous patterns, and start afresh to think things through, to build a new up-to-date socialism out of our present circumstances and our most pressing needs.

This movement should refuse to serve as a lightning rod to channel away the revolutionary temper of young people. It should not accept an assignment from the old order to concentrate energy in just fighting pollution —as if pollution was something that could be isolated from the rest of the gigantic task. It should insist on taking on the whole revolutionary mission, all the while exercising self-discipline, renouncing violence, seeking thorough factual information, pursuing patiently, soberly, systematically, the various salvaging goals and their coordination. It should strive to prevent the computerization, this consummate dehumanization, of our whole life. What should inspire it is the pride of the awful responsibility that today lies upon it, and the unique, singular joy of being intensely, actively, undeceivably alive.

10^5 Per Square Mile   *Isaac Asimov*

By A.D. 2550, less than six centuries from now, at the present rate of population increase, the density of Earth's population will be 100,000 per square mile. In other words, if, in 2550, all the Earth's population were spread out evenly over all the continents, including the Sahara, the Himalayas, and Antarctica, and including also the bottoms (or surfaces) of all the oceans, every spot on Earth would be as crowded as Manhattan today at lunch hour.

In *The Revolution of Hope* Erich Fromm raises another specter (and a frightening one it is, too) of a completely mechanized society in which "man himself is being transformed into a part of the total machine, well fed and entertained, yet passive, unalive and with little feeling." This is something to be vehemently fought against, for surely it is impossible to accept the dehumanization of man.

Is this the only imminent crisis that we face?

May not man be in less immediate danger of being dehumanized than Earth itself is in danger of being crowded with too much humanity?

To see what I mean, let us put the present day in the context of the grand sweep of human history.

Human history might, in its very broadest sense, be divided into: 1) Man the hunter, 2) Man the farmer, 3) Man the burner.

In the beginning, when the first creatures we can call hominid evolved in Africa about two million years ago or so, the result was not particularly impressive. The early hominids were food-gatherers, scavengers, carrion-eaters. Their numbers were few and they could not have shown much more promise of success than the modern gorilla does.

Intelligence, of itself, does not seem to have much survival value, certainly not as much, in the long run, as does sheer fecundity. Nevertheless, the early hominids had enough intelligence to make environment-controlling inventions and that, apparently, was what put them past the critical point and onto the path toward the present uniqueness of man.

The discovery of flint and the methods for handling it, the technique of starting a fire, the invention of the spear and bow-and-arrow, all made hunting more efficient and broadened the scope of human activity.

By 8000 B.C., man, with the use of fire and clothing, had spread out of the tropical areas to which he was adapted and had occupied all the major land areas of the Earth (excepting always Antarctica). The total world population may have been about eight million. Nor could it have gone very much higher in a hunting and food-gathering economy.

About 8000 B.C., however, somewhere in the Near East, a fundamentally new way of life was worked out in the form of agriculture and herding. Food, both plant and animal, was cultivated and tamed. It no longer had to be hunted and it could be produced in greater concentration.

The technique of farming spread slowly out from the discovery center, and behind it like concentric ripples came other important advances: basketry and pottery, the use of metals, the invention of writing. Each advance made a considerable population increase possible.

By A.D. 1800 all the major land areas of the world were dominated by economies based on agriculture. There remained hunting and food-gathering societies but they could be exploited at will by those nations based on agriculture. Man the farmer ruled the world and population was then about 900,000,000 (0.9 billion). Nor could it go very much higher in a purely agricultural economy.

By A.D. 1800, however, again a fundamentally new way of life was worked out. Man had always burned fuel of one sort or another for warmth, light, and protection. By the end of the eighteenth century, however, he was burning it to lend power to the steam engine. He was burning wood, then coal, then oil and gas, finally uranium to place the vast energy sources of the nonanimal world at the disposal of mankind. With the Agricultural Revolution, Man the farmer had concentrated his food resources; now with the Industrial Revolution, Man the burner concentrated his energy resources.

Once again population was able to increase, and now, in 1970, we stand at something like 3.3 billion. Though there are scraps of hunting societies, and quite large sections of agricultural societies, it is the industrialized nations that effectively rule the world. Man the burner is king.

Judging by the past, we might say we are approaching the point where once again population is about as high as it can comfortably be under a given basic form of economy and that it is high time for a new radical innovation; an innovation that will again open a new horizon illuminated with a greater glory.

This is the optimistic view: the cheerful extrapolation from two cases to a general rule; the feeling that since twice before new horizons opened when needed, this will happen over and over again in response to necessity.

But why must that be so? The existence of horizon beyond horizon is not unlimited; there is an end, and a hard one too.

Our situation now is very much like the man who, wanting to fly, jumped off the Empire State Building. He did indeed have the sensation of flying and as he fell faster and faster the sensation grew more satisfying. By the time he passed the tenth floor, moving downward, he felt he had every right to extrapolate from what he had already experienced to a future in which he would outdo the jet planes in speed and maneuverability. Except that the truth was that ten floors below was the sidewalk—and the end.

What is equivalent to that sidewalk in the course of human history is —population increase.

Throughout the history of mankind, population has increased steadily. Why, then, ought we be more concerned with population increase now than we were previously? Since population increase has not destroyed us in the past but has served to increase our mastery over nature, why find doom in it now?

To see the answer, consider the length of time it takes the human population to double itself. If we take the estimates of world population at various times in history, we can come up with the following (admittedly very approximate) table for the length of time it took the population to double itself:

up to A.D. 100	1400 years
100–1600	900
1600–1800	250
1800–1900	90
1900–1950	75
1950–1970	47

What we are facing now, then, is not just the fact of population increase, but the additional fact that the *rate* of increase has itself been increasing steadily.

It took nine hundred years from the time, say, of Marcus Aurelius to that of William the Conqueror, for Earth's population to double. In the *next* nine hundred years, even assuming that the rate of increase goes no higher but merely remains where it is today, Earth's population would multiply 500,000 times!

The reason for this steady rise of the rate of increase is not because more children are being produced. If anything, the birth rate has decreased over the centuries. It rests almost entirely with the decline in death rate. Fewer and fewer infants die, and those who survive live longer and longer until now the general life expectancy is over seventy years in the more advanced portions of the globe. The reasons for this are not hard to see either. Advances in agriculture increase the food supply, advances in transportation insure more efficient distribution, advances in the knowledge of nutrition, in medicine, in surgery—

Granted that we see the reason, let us also underline the fact itself. The population is not merely still increasing; it is increasing *at a faster rate than ever before*.

Does this fact alone presage doom? Isn't it possible that science, which is *also* advancing at a faster rate than ever before, will come up with ways of handling that population increase, so that the increasing numbers will continue, nevertheless, to live better and better?

Don't think it. It is quite easy to calculate the year in which at the present rate of increase, the total mass of human flesh and blood will be equal to the total mass of the known Universe (not only our own Earth and Solar system, but the mass of all the stars in our Galaxy and in all the billions of other galaxies beside). Such is the power of a geometric progress that this ridiculous extreme is not something to be attained in the far and misty never-never land of an impossibly-distant future. It will come to pass (in theory) in the quite prosaic year of A.D. 8700.

Obviously, science, no matter how advanced, cannot deal with a mass of humanity equal to that of the Universe, especially when that mass is only a little over six thousand years in the future. If present conditions point to that ridiculous end, it is at least as obvious as $1 + 1 = 2$ that these conditions must change drastically.

For a second time, let us draw in our horns and consider the population changes that will take place not in millennia or even centuries, but in mere decades.

At the present rate of increase (assuming no further increase in that rate) the Earth's population will double in forty-seven years. By A.D. 2017, in other words, Earth's population will be 6.6 billion. That, at least sounds bearable, if possibly uncomfortable, so that we have a clear half-century in which to do nothing. But wait—

The rate of energy consumption, the burning rate of Man the burner, has been increasing and will continue (for a while) to increase at a rate greater than the increase of population itself. Not only does population increase but per capita consumption of energy does, too.

It has been estimated that if things continue as they are, then by the time the population of the United States doubles, its energy consumption will have increased sevenfold. Presumably this is true for the world generally, too.

It seems reasonable to suppose that the rate of energy consumption can be considered a rough guide to the rate at which Earth's nonrenewable resources (coal, oil, exploitable ores, etc.) are being consumed; that it also parallels the rate at which Earth is being polluted by the products of burning and of industry generally.

In that case we see that by A.D. 2017, assuming that present trends continue, the rate of resource consumption and of environment pollution will be seven times what it is today.

But at the present moment we are already consuming Earth's resources at a dangerous rate. A recent estimate, for instance, states that Earth's readily available supply of nonferrous metals will be squandered within twenty years. If a half-century from now the demand for such metals is seven times the present quantity, where is it to come from? (We may, of course, learn to extract poorer ores and make more use of scrap for recycling—but will we develop such sources in half a century to supply seven times the present annual quantity?)

At the present moment, moreover, we are polluting the Earth's environment at a critically dangerous rate and are visibly poisoning the Earth to the point where many doubt whether mankind can rally its powers and its will to save the situation *even at its present level of danger*. What will we do a half-century from now if pollution reaches seven times its present level?

Clearly, our way of life must change drastically within the next half-century, then.

But have we even that much time? Let's consider conditions as of today.

The United States consumes as much energy, right now, as the rest of the world put together. It consumes at least half of all the Earth's production of nonrenewable resources, and produces at least half of all the environmental pollution on Earth.

The other nations of Earth have as their goal (and who is to say them

nay) the achieving of a standard of living equal to that of the United
States. If by some miracle they were all to achieve it instantaneously, then
right now, without the addition of a single individual to Earth's population, the rate of resource consumption and environment pollution over the
planet as a whole would increase eightfold.

The planet could not endure this, so we are forced to the conclusion
that we have already passed the point of no return. The Earth has already
reached the point where it cannot possibly support even its *present* population at an average standard of living equal to that of the United States
today.

Nor, in assessing our present danger, need we confine ourselves to
physical factors only. What about the psychological difficulties that attend
increased population?

There have been experiments on crowding among rats, and it has been
clearly shown that physical and psychic failures attend such crowding. Is it
possible to get some idea of how the intensity of such troubles increases as
crowding gets worse? Does the intensity merely double when the numbers
are doubled?

It seems reasonable to me to suppose that tension rises not merely with
the number of people in one's vicinity, but with the number of different interactions possible with the people. And it is quite possible that the number of different interactions increases much more rapidly than the number
of people.

Suppose, for instance, you have five men and five women and you set
about pairing them in different ways. How many different combinations of
one man and one woman can you produce among the ten individuals? The
answer is $5 \times 4 \times 3 \times 2 \times 1 = 120$.

Now double the population and make it ten men and ten women. The
number of different combinations is $10 \times 9 \times 8 \times 7 \times 6 \times 5 \times 4 \times 3 \times 2 \times 1 = 3,628,800$.

Without making too much of the exact figures, we can at least conclude
that even a small increase in crowding can enormously increase tensions.
Where the world as a whole is generally uncrowded, the tensions of crowding in limited areas can be (and have been, in the past) relieved by emigra-
tion. With the frontier escape valve gone, however, and with the world
generally crowded, matters have changed, and have done so spectacularly
for the worse.

Considering that already, at the present moment, the level of tension
among the population generally (as evidenced in alienation, violence, drug

addiction, and other social ills) is the despair of concerned sociologists, what can we expect to be the result of even a *small* further increase in population?

It seems to me we must conclude then that the Earth is *already* seriously and dangerously overpopulated. If society exists now in a seemingly stable and even apparently still-improving condition, that must be only because 90 percent of the Earth's population is in a depressed condition which makes it possible for the remaining 10 percent to live well.

Mankind, then, would seem to be facing a situation quite unlike any it has ever faced before. Its problems now are by no means merely different in degree from any that have existed before; they are different in kind.

Until World War II (at latest) mankind has lived in an essentially infinite world—one in which it could multiply at will, waste at will, poison at will, with the comfortable knowledge that in the foreseeable future, and certainly in the generation's lifetime, it would not be held to account. The suffering planet was large enough to absorb the man-made insult.

Now that has changed. Now we live in a finite world. Our numbers and our kind and level of technology are bringing us to chaos within the lifetime of those now living!

The consequences?

I think that before A.D. 2017 when Earth's population is expected, at present rates, to have doubled, the death rate will have begun its inexorable increase. As the food supply fails to keep up with the bounding population, as it even begins to decline absolutely through the poisoning of the environment, the great famines will start. Undernourishment will set up the foci of the great epidemics and with the withering of resources, industrialization will decline.

When the last dregs of population increase are added to the sharpening battle for food and survival, tensions will exacerbate to the point of thermonuclear war, perhaps, or to the lesser but more prolonged agony of worldwide anarchy.

The first half of the twenty-first century would therefore see a precipitous drop in population and a total, or nearly total, dismantling of man's technology. The second half of the century will then see a new equilibrium, with perhaps a few hundred million human beings scratching a living out of the soil amid the ruins of a past civilization already fading into the dimness of the past.

Can we console ourselves with the thought that however horrendously evil the process, mankind will have an opportunity to recover and build again, and using the experience of the past as guide, develop a second and far better Golden Age?

I'm afraid not.

The new and very low equilibrium achieved by the wild destruction that is sure to come if our present direction is not drastically changed, will not only have destroyed most of the human race—it will have, by then, destroyed many other forms of life as well. The entire fabric of ecology will have been dangerously weakened and torn; the very habitability of the planet will have been compromised.

The Earth will be as it has never been before; its soil destroyed and poisoned in such a fashion as may take not decades or centuries but millions of years to restore; its resources squandered and scattered to the point where it will take not millions of years but hundreds of millions to reconcentrate.

Can mankind make a comeback with its technology gone and with the planet utterly ruined into the far-distant future? How?

For those dedicated and concerned with righting man's inhumanity to man and to nature, it is a painful irony that such a love can never come to pass if no one lives.

It is not man's humanity alone that is threatened with disappearance, but man himself!

To stave off the doom, we must first recognize something fundamental about the important problems that face the world today. The population increase, the squandering of resources, the prevalence of pollution, the exacerbation of tensions—are problems that are each planetary in nature, problems that can each be solved only on a planetary basis.

Not even the most powerful single nation can solve any of these problems by itself, or solve them within its own borders alone. A solution, even a good one, applied to only a small portion of the Earth's total area and population is no solution at all if the problem remains unsolved elsewhere.

Will it do any good, for instance, for the United States (within its own borders only) to achieve population stability, resource conservation, depollution, and tension ease, if the rest of the world continues as at present? The chaos will come anyway and overrun us.

And even if we succeeded in holding off the forces of ruin flooding in from all sides and maintained ourselves as a kind of island of technology in a surrounding ocean of barbarism and death, how long will this remain possible? Even today we maintain ourselves only at the expense of half the resources of the rest of the world. Remove that rest of the world and force us to live on our own fat, and our technology will wither and join the rest of the world in the dust heap.

No, the major problems must be solved everywhere or not at all. This means cooperation between the various nations (the various industrialized nations at a bare minimum). The cooperation must be sure and unfailing, for we have no time for games.

To put it briefly, we need a world government; some body which is powerful enough to enact a course of policy that will apply over the Earth generally and with sufficient police power to enforce compliance.

In the end, if there were time, this is exactly what would happen. In general, the history of man (particularly in its more progressive periods) has seen a more or less steady increase in the area and population of the dominating political units. Given enough time, then, we would expect a world government to be the final flowering of political evolution.

The trouble is that we don't have enough time for its "natural" evolution. Its evolution must be hastened. However strong an emotional attachment we may have to our various nations, we must recognize that their independence has been an illusion for a long time, now. When an oil tanker of Nation A can foul the beaches of Nation B; when an exploding nuclear test bomb of Nation C can spray the air of Nation D with radioactivity; when DDT used by Nation E ends up in fish caught by the ships of Nation F—how independent is any nation?

And at the present moment in history, to cling to a mythical national independence that doesn't exist is suicide.

But suppose we do achieve a world government. How do we go about solving, through world action, the dreadful problems that face us?

We must continue to use resources; but we must use them with utmost economy and we must reclaim all we can of those used.

We can't help polluting, but we must do so minimally and with every effort to remain within the environment's capacity for self-renewal.

We can't relieve tensions altogether, but we must do all we can to soothe and bring together.

The delicacy of the task is so enormous under even the most favorable conditions that it is clear we could not possibly succeed if that task were made steadily more mountainous by increasing population.

To make everything else possible, then, the first task is to stabilize the population and to look forward to a system of planned population decrease.

But how?

Here again it would seem that mankind faces a problem different in kind but not in magnitude from every problem that has ever faced it before. Never at any time in history has motherhood been anything but an honorable and revered estate. Never at any time in history has a baby been anything but the dearest being one can imagine.

Yet it is now going to be forced upon us, however much against our will, to consider motherhood and babies, more often than not, as antisocial.

This must be so because if we are to decrease the Earth's population without increasing the death rate, we must insist that each woman leave behind her less than two children (on the average).

But how can we force a woman to have very few children? Shall we simply pass a law saying that every woman must be sterilized after she has had her second child? It is conceivable we might come to that, but is there no other way out?

For thousands of years social pressures have favored conception. Women have been carefully educated into believing that their highest fulfillment was as wife and mother; parents of many children have been honored; the sex act has itself been regulated by defining as perverse every action which yields satisfaction without danger of conception.

All this has been sensible enough in an empty world and in one where the death rate was so high and life expectancy so low that it took maximum fecundity to insure even a small population increase.

In our present crowded world, with its low death rate and long life expectancy, the old notions, hallowed though they be, are, when put into practice, a crime against humanity.

Women must not be encouraged to think of themselves as baby factories. Birth-control devices and methods must be further improved and made available to all; their use taught matter-of-factly in the schools; and their employment encouraged as a positive social good.

Perhaps there ought to be a complete turnaround in our attitude toward the sex act itself. No longer must we insist that only that is wholesome and "natural" which will have the greatest chance of leading to conception. Shocking as it may seem, why not encourage those practices which do no physiological harm, give relief from sexual tension, and run no risk of conception?

The aging rulers of Church and State, who are certain to live out their lives before the ruin engulfs mankind, have no right to condemn a younger generation to that ruin by insisting on the mores which they had to live by in another and long-dead world.

But can we, in the space of a generation or so, so utterly overturn our long-accustomed political system as to accept effective world government, develop effective methods of population control, and accept a nonconception-oriented sexual outlook?

The chances would seem small indeed. The alternative is so ultimately horrible, however, that I can only hope that the initial tastes of the disaster-to-come will drive us headlong into the less distasteful out of urgent respect for our lives.

And if we come through? If we manage to establish a rational society (even if at the cost of serious losses), what will the characteristics of that society be? Can we avoid computerization?

I think not.

We must understand what computers (or at least the computers of this century) are. They are problem solvers. They are mechanical devices that do merely what slide rules do (or pen and paper), only much, much faster. If we turn to computers, it is only because we need answers faster than the human brain can supply them, and in the world of the future, when we are hoping to draw back from the brink of catastrophe by tiptoeing across an ice-coated tightrope, quick answers, *very* quick answers, are exactly what we'll need.

To be sure, we mustn't make a god out of the computer; a computer can't give us an answer that is more correct than the material and instructions we feed into it. But let us not make a demon of the computer, either. The human brain cannot always give an answer more correct than the material and instructions fed into it, any more than the computer can.

To be sure, the computer can't take into logical account those factors that can't be made quantitative—like sympathy, love, generosity, concern. But then neither are our brains infallible under emotional challenges.

The question is, finally: Can a computerized society coexist with human individuality? Can mankind at one and the same time have its computers and avoid dehumanization?

In our present society—right now—perhaps not.

It is the essence of my argument, though, and my hope, that if there is to be a computerized society, it will be of a nature far removed from our present one. A computerized society should be one that has recognized the dangers about to fall upon us today and has been able to draw back at the cost of an enormous self-directed change in precisely those things it had always held most dear. It will be a society that had proved itself capable of placing reason and intelligent concern before ingrained fixity of thought and feeling.

Such a society will be mature enough, I am quite certain, to be able to handle computers as tools and not as masters; to appreciate people as human beings and not as cogs.

And then, if we can but come through the nearly totally black prospect of the near-future, we may find that what has opened up to us will be a bright and hopeful far-future.

The
Possibilities
for
Radical Humanism

Mihailo
Marković

I

Modern industrial civilization has increased man's possibilities to live a richer, freer, more creative life worthy of his potential. But man has not yet learned how to use them; slavery and poverty, both material and spiritual, still predominate in our age.

As the result of technological development, enormous social forces and controls over natural phenomena have been set in motion. Instead of being rationally directed by man, they govern him. States, parties, churches, armies, ideologies, nuclear institutions, have their own logic of functioning which, in a way that is still mostly unknown to man, generates processes whose outcomes are unpredictable and independent to the rational human mind. While these forces have enabled man to begin to conquer outer cosmic space, they have not yet been mobilized on earth to conquer misery, hunger, wars, most simple diseases, illiteracy, and infant mortality.

Paradoxically, although an ever-increasing number of people in the civilized world are now able to satisfy their basic needs, new artificial needs have been widely stimulated: in the first place, desires to possess useless objects largely for the sake of possession, a need for *having* more on account of *being* more. Another subtle yet crucial social change is that the old gap between intellectual and physical work is being gradually replaced by a new one, that between the creative work done by a few and the utterly dull, routine work done by a vast majority.

Thus, the standard of living has greatly increased but in most cases this has not made for more humane relationships between social groups. For example, while productivity increases rapidly, higher wages are still tied to

275

a higher degree of exploitation (defined as the usurpation of value produced by unpaid work). It does not make an essential difference to the worker whether the usurper is a capitalist or a bureaucrat.

Again, technical civilization has provided means to shrink distances among individuals both in space and time: big cities, fast transportation, highly efficient media of communication, etc. At the same time, this development tends to destroy, without providing substitutes, all the emotionally loaded links which connect an individual with his original natural milieu. That is why modern man is so uprooted, condemned to experience utter loneliness in the midst of a crowd. The more he belongs to a mass society the less he is a member of any genuine human community.

Ever since the Renaissance there has been a strong integrating trend in the civilized world: a spreading of the same technology, economic cooperation and exchange, a mixing of cultures, the creation of an international political organization, reciprocal influences in the arts, and scientific collaboration. But simultaneously, strong disintegrative factors are at work: nationalism, racialism, ideological wars, religious intolerances, narrow specialization and excessive division of labor, sustaining of sharp boundaries between various spheres of social activity such as politics, law, science, philosophy, morality, and the arts—in general, an atomistic way of thinking and approaching things. The result is: far less solidarity among people and fewer connections between social institutions than is desirable and possible.

Due to modern technology and the development of democracy, human freedom has been greatly increased, at least insofar as we mean by freedom the possibility of choosing among alternatives. However, every choice depends on the criteria for choosing, and in our time these criteria are more successfully than ever pressed on individuals by highly elaborated and efficient propaganda and advertising techniques. It is tragic how often modern man is enslaved when he has the illusion of being free.

This discrepancy between illusion and fact is especially evident in the international political arena. Most nations like to cherish the illusion that their governments are striving for peace; nevertheless, we have been living on the brink of war during the last two decades. Most statesmen cherish the illusion that their decision-making is rational, and optimal under given circumstances. However, the result of so many "rational" decisions is a completely irrational situation: the collective suicide of mankind has become a real possibility and it can happen at any moment by pure accident.

II

The idea of making the world more humane presupposes definite anthropological conceptions as to what is man, what is his nature, what does it mean to exist in an authentic way and to live a true, human life.

Any analysis of human behavior in history would lead to the conclusion that, as a matter of fact, man has given evidence of very different and even *contradictory* features. To illustrate: man has always tended to enlarge his *freedom,* to overcome historically set technological, political, and social limits. However, slavery is the invention of man. And even to a liberally minded person, a vision of complete individual freedom has always been unbearable, both because of the fear of the irresponsibility of others and the reluctance to accept responsibility himself. That is why he sets limits and establishes various kinds of *order* of all forms and at all levels of social life: morality, law, discipline at home, at school, at work, in political organization, strict rules in art, methodological principles in science, etc.

One of the most distinctive characteristics of man is his *creativity.* In contrast to other living beings man constantly evolves his tools, his methods of work, his needs and objectives, his criteria of evaluation. That is why human history, in spite of its retrogressions and oscillations, can, on the whole, be considered as a rather rapid process. Still, in contradiction to this, there is also a tendency in man to resist work and to avoid the effort of creating new things and new forms. The majority of people have always dreamed of happiness as a state of affairs without work and without change. Even more of a contradiction, no other creature in the world can compete with man in destructiveness. The exceptionally great endeavors in developing this side of his being have in our time given notable fruit: man's capacity today for destruction by far exceeds his capacity for creation.

Man is a *social being* not only in the sense that he prefers to live in a community but also in a more profound sense: all the features by which he is constituted are social products—language, forms of thought, habits and tastes, education, values, and so forth. Nevertheless, there is also a strong tendency in most individuals to behave occasionally in an *antisocial* way, to pursue selfish private ends, to isolate themselves from others, to break links with people without any discernible reason, to be possessive, power hungry, and, even in the arts and philosophy, to get rid of all socially established rules, to make their thoughts and feeling hermetic and minimize communication with others.

Man is surely a *rational* being. He is able to analyze things and situations, to weigh alternatives, and to derive consequences. He can predict the outcome of a chosen course of action and adjust his behavior to achieve desired goals. But his goals are too often *irrational*—they correspond to his immediate interests, urges, drives. And even when his long-term goals are rather rational in the sense that they have been selected after careful deliberation over his genuine needs and real possibilities of the given situation, his short-term goals and his actual behavior may greatly deviate from them. As a matter of fact, man frequently acts in complete disregard of his knowledge, even knowing that his course of action is self-destructive. It should be noted that this basic irrationality of human behavior is only partly the consequence of atavistic impulses, primitive passions, deeply rooted egotistic impulses, or even mental disorders. Partly it is the effect of a fundamental human need for an immediate, spontaneous reaction, a need which is in obvious peril in an age of science, technology, and overplanning in which those who are not able to calculate and reason coldly look unfit and unlikely to survive.

One could go on expounding such antinomies.[1] They are obviously statistical middle values of very large populations in different times. What seems to be essential about them is the fact that one or the other pole of each antinomy may predominate, depending on the given historical conditions. But historical conditions are not something simply given and predetermined; they are the result of practical human actions taken in partly different previous conditions. The question, then, arises: *which are the constitutive characteristics of human nature that we should prefer and whose predominance in the future we should secure by our practical action in the present?*

First, we must differentiate two concepts of human nature. When we analyze history to establish certain general tendencies of human behavior, we arrive at a *descriptive* notion of man that can be expressed by a series of factual empirical statements. But when we prefer some human features over others—such as being social, productive, creative, rational, free, and

---

[1] For example: Man is both peace-loving and belligerent; he tends to belong to a movement and to have a common cause, but also he often prefers to be left alone; he is very conservative and reluctant to modify traditional patterns of life, but on the other hand, no pattern of life satisfies him permanently.

peaceful—and when we classify these characteristics as "truly human," "genuine," "authentic," "essential," "natural," etc., we arrive at a *value* concept of man, indicating that man is essentially a being of praxis, which can be described by a set of value statements.

These two concepts of human nature have to be justified in different ways, and are open to different types of criticism. The descriptive notion of man has to be supported by factual evidence. Someone who wants to challenge it can try to show that there is no evidence to support it, or that the evidence is too meager for such an inductive generalization, or that facts at our disposal lead to an entirely different inductive conclusion. In other words, this is an issue that can be settled by applying scientific method.

The value concept of man, on the other hand, can, at best, be supported by factual information only to the extent that 1) the human traits entering it must correspond to at least *some* observed general tendencies in the past and that 2) their realization in the future must not be incompatible with the social forces acting in the present. These conditions, however, can also be met by alternative value concepts: these can express the preference for *some other* tendencies in the past, and can correspond to some other real possibility in the present. The choice among such alternative value concepts cannot be made in a purely theoretical or purely scientific way. We must make our decision on the basis of our fundamental, long-term practical orientation to life, which obviously depends not only on knowledge but also on interests and needs, and on a willingness to act in a certain direction. The crucial problem here is: whose interests and needs are here in question—those of an individual, of a particular social group, or of mankind in general?

A value concept can be justified by showing that it not only expresses certain private needs but also general social needs and interests. This can be done, first, by establishing that the vast majority of people really have preferences conveyed by the value concept in question, and second, by showing that this concept corresponds to a humanist tradition, expressed by the best minds in the past.

Nothing will be proven in this way; it is impossible to convince someone that he ought to accept a value simply because it has been accepted by others. However, this could be a sufficient basis for *rational* discrimination among various proposed solutions.

Taking into account the great humanist tradition during the last twenty-five centuries as well us the actual contemporary preferences that underlie all moral judgment, there can be little doubt that, *other conditions being equal,* and with all necessary qualifications and exceptions, there is a strong tendency to prefer: freedom to slavery, creative action to destruction and passivity, consideration for general social needs to egotism, rationality to any behavior governed by blind emotional forces, peacefulness to belligerency. It would be dogmatic and incorrect to say that only these desirable qualities constitute human *nature* and human *essence* or human *being,* as against another ontological level of human appearance to which all evil in man would be relegated. In order to establish a sense of direction and a general criterion of evaluation in a humanist philosophy and practice, it is sufficient to claim that these qualities constitute what is most valuable in man and what can be considered the *optimal real potentiality* of human being. To fulfill these potentialities is to live a "true," "genuine," "authentic," "humane" life. Failure to fulfill them leads to what is often called *alienation.*

III

The characterization of modern civilization given at the outset of this essay indicates that the vast majority of people, in spite of all achievements, still live a rather alienated and inhumane life.

Unfortunately, the process of developing a more humanistic approach to life is often construed in a superficial way, as simply a greater consideration for the weak, the backward, and the helpless. Humanism is then reduced to a program of aid to overcome material misery, eliminate hunger and illiteracy, and bar the brutal forces of political oppression. All this certainly constitutes a part of such a broad concept but a rather nonessential part. For this idea of "humanization" does not challenge the very roots of contemporary society; it is acceptable by all those who are interested in preserving its status quo. The best spokesmen of the great powers, interested in keeping certain smaller countries in a subordinate position, do not urge excessive and brutal forms of exploitation; they recognize that sooner or later such behavior inevitably leads to violent revolts of the oppressed. In advocating small liberal reforms and humanitarian programs of aid in terms of consumer goods, they are far more rational and efficient defenders of a basically inhuman system.

If we are really dissatisfied with the human condition today, if we are ready to search for the deepest causes of human degradation, if we are convinced that a much more fundamental change is needed than the growth of concern for the poor and underdeveloped, then we must further qualify the broad and rather vague concept of "humanism," and would do better to speak in terms of *radical humanism*.

Marx once said that: "To be radical means to take things from the root. And the root of man is man." This sentence is not a tautology if we interpret the term "man" as a descriptive concept in the first case and as a value concept in the second.

To be radical means, then: to take care of what is most valuable to man, to create conditions in which man would become increasingly a creative, social, free, rational being. The main problem, however, is: what are those conditions, and what is their order of importance?

It is true that contemporary man is enslaved by alienated social forces such as states, political organizations, armies, and churches. But the question is: what factors produced these forces and what keeps them so powerful?

It is true that contemporary man leads a poor life even when he is materially rich, because his needs are irrational, focused on an urge to possess as many objects as possible. But what is the social mechanism that creates such irrelevant, artificial needs?

It is true that modern man feels more isolated than ever, even in a crowd. But the question is: what is there in society which frustrates his desires for friendship, love, and membership in a genuine human community? Also, what are the objective social causes of all other disintegrative and regressive processes, such as growth of nationalism and racialism, atomization of society into professional groups, hegemony in politics, and monopoly of the mass media?

I believe that almost all contemporary forms of alienation are rooted in the existence of social groups that have a monopoly on economic and political power. This kind of monopoly is based either on the private ownership of the means of production (in the case of capitalism) or on the privileged position in the political organization of society (as in the case of a bureaucracy), or both.

To be sure, monopoly implies various kinds of usurpation. The usurpation of the unpaid work of other people is usually called *exploitation*. The usurpation of other people's rights in social decision-making is *political hegemony*.

Contrary to common assumptions, according to which it does not make sense to speak about exploitation when workers' wages and the standard of living have reached certain levels, exploitation is the function of two additional factors. One is the productivity of work; if productivity increases faster than wages, the degree of exploitation may also increase. The second is the social distribution of surplus value; if in society there are individuals and groups whose income exceeds the value of their (past and present) work, the greater part of surplus value goes to such groups for their surplus income and the greater is the degree of exploitation. This means that one has the right to speak of more or less concealed forms of exploitation not only in an advanced country where the material misery has been greatly reduced, but also in a postcapitalist society to the extent that it contains strong bureaucratic tendencies.

Contrary to the claims of professional politicians in both capitalist and socialist countries, there is very little democracy in the contemporary world (if this excessively misused term still means anything). The fact is that almost nowhere do the vast majority of people have any real possibility to influence decision-making on essential matters. The representatives of people in higher-level social institutions are elected either because of very large financial investments and the support of powerful party machines or the election itself is so formalized to be simply a ritual. In both cases the situation is clearly one of the political hegemony of certain privileged groups over the rest of the people who feel powerless and sometimes directly oppressed.

The existence of any such group—which usurps the position of the political and economic *subjects* and leaves all other individuals and groups in the position of *objects* to be manipulated—is the basis of all other contemporary forms of dehumanization.

State, army, political organization, and so forth are the instruments of such manipulations. The function of most ideologies is both to conceal this process and justify it.

As public opinion is the opinion of the ruling elite, and as power over people and things is the fundamental value of every exploiting group, the consequence is that ordinary people tend to follow and base their needs on a hunger for power and things.

Ideological and commercial propaganda plays a great role in molding human souls, attitudes, tastes, preferences, making freedom of choice an illusion, especially when the criteria of choice are widely determined by those who possess the mass media of communication. Monopolistic control of mass media is one of the essential means of preserving and perpetuating all other monopolies.

Once a particular group with a special interest in acquiring a monopoly of power starts speaking in the name of the whole society (and that is what has always happened with ruling groups, including bureaucracies in the postcapitalist society), it stops pursuing general social goals, values, and interests: these very concepts arouse strong suspicion. Accordingly, the society loses integrity and its sense of wholeness. This trend, together with the trend in increased division of labor, gives rise to innumerable sharp boundaries where links would be desirable: for example, among nations, races, professions, and spheres of social consciousness (morality, law, politics, science, philosophy).

Therefore, to *humanize radically* the contemporary world means to create conditions in which each individual could be an historical subject, able to participate in the control of enormous social and natural forces that have so far been produced. An essential condition of such fundamental human liberation is the *abolition of any concentration of political and economic power in the hands of any particular social group*.

The supersession (*Aufhebung*) of private ownership of the means of production and the abolition of capitalists as a class is the decisive first step in this direction. The supersession of politics as a profession which enables a social group permanently to monopolize all accumulated work, and the abolition of bureaucracy as a privileged elite—is the second decisive step.

Each is a *necessary* condition of a radical humanization but only both taken together constitute its *sufficient* condition.

IV

What are the historical possibilities of such a radical humanization in our epoch? First, what is meant in stating that an event or trend is *historically possible?*

We should distinguish between an a priori and an a posteriori concept of historical possibility. The former is our *hypothesis* about the future based on our theoretical analysis of observed general tendencies in the past. The latter is our *knowledge* about the present based on practical experience.

In both cases, to say that a course of events is *historically possible* means that it is compatible with actually given features of an historical situation. There are three essential components of a given situation that are relevant for the concept of historical possibility.

The first is made up of the objective social facts of the system under consideration. Many future events are excluded by the present state of affairs—e.g., the level of technological and scientific development, the state of the economy, the nature of existing political institutions, the level of education, prevailing traditions, etc. Simply on the basis of these factors one can, for example, speak about the possibility of a peaceful socialist revolution in Italy, a violent one in South America, and the impossibility of revolution in the United States in the near future, which does not preclude the possibility of important social changes there, especially in connection with a much wider introduction of automation, and the growing revolt in the universities.

The second factor relevant for the concept of historical possibility is the observation of past trends. Since these trends are not as simple and strict as laws, even those statistical laws evident in comparatively simple systems of nature, exact prediction of future events is not possible. Nevertheless, there are good reasons to speak about *social determinism* in the weaker, more flexible sense of *excluding certain alternatives and allowing certain others,* with a greater or lesser degree of probability. For example, taking into account the trend since 1937, one can say that no economic crises in the capitalist world comparable with those up to 1929 are possible. At the same time, one can say that regular recessions are highly probable and even inevitable. Also, the trend in the socialist world since 1953 makes a return to Stalinism very improbable, if not impossible.

To be sure, in all such estimates both previously mentioned moments must be taken into account: only when the initial conditions of the system are given (by the description of relevant facts), can a set of future possible states of the system be determined.

The third factor is unknown, or only partly known and predictable: human behavior. History is full of events which would have been thought highly improbable, in the light of objective conditions and past trends. However, unexpected outbursts of energy, the unpredictable action of many people, as well as the sudden occurrence of mass irrationality, fantastic blunders or genial solutions of the most difficult problems—have caused almost impossible things to happen.

Both the Russian and Chinese revolutions had little chance to succeed, in view of existing technology and economic conditions, social structure, and the power of foreign intervention. Still they came true. It would have been easy to prevent Hitler's coming to power. However, Nazism was sadly underestimated, and up to his final takeover German social democrats and communists saw the enemy in each other instead of Hitler. The antifascist coalition during the Second World War was a considerable deviation from the logic of international politics between two world wars. It was due, in the first place, to a substantial blunder in the Anglo-American estimate of Russian ability to resist German attack.

Recent Yugoslav history is full of events whose realization—from the point of view of objective conditions—was rather improbable. The overthrow on March 27, 1941, of Cvetković's government (which signed the pact with the Nazis), was clearly a choice of war against a formidable enemy without a glimmer of hope to survive as a state. The new government thereupon surprised many by acting in a completely confused and cowardly way, and lost the war in a few days. Whereas such a collapse usually leads to a general demoralization, in this case it was followed instead by a mass uprising. In the context of our discussion, two things about this uprising should be noted: first, it cannot be explained by objective conditions, which resembled those in other occupied European countries; second, a cold, scientific analysis of all objective factors would have demonstrated that the uprising was doomed. Nevertheless, it succeeded, due to the extraordinary behavior of the thousands of individuals who took part in it.

True, history, tradition, social character, and prevailing moral beliefs provide clues as to the future behavior of a specific people or nation. Nevertheless, this is insufficient to make very reliable forecasts. An essential quality of man is that he is able to rise above every norm and habit and to deviate from any predetermined pattern of behavior. Only in these terms can man be considered a free being, and history an open process.

The unexpected role of subjective factors is the main reason why we cannot draw a sharp boundary line between historical possibility and impossibility. Between those human projects which are clearly possible (although in individual cases they might fail) and those which are clearly impossible (being incompatible with existing natural and social laws in a historical moment) there is an area of vagueness that includes cases where we cannot know if a project is possible until we try it. From this it follows that the two extreme views as to the epistemological and ontological status of possibilities should be rejected: 1) the positivist one that the possibilities are *given* and can be known *before* practical action, and 2) the other, characteristic of existentialists like Sartre, that man's future is quite *open* and independent of the past, that we are absolutely free to choose, and only *at the end* do we come to know what really was or was not possible. While, in every historical moment, the objective features in a given system of social phenomena do allow us to project a set of possible future states of the system, the boundaries of this set are vague. Such is the a priori concept of historical possibility. After action is taken, practical experience helps us make the necessary revisions and build up the a posteriori concept which is more precise and whose boundaries are sharper.

V

When we think about the actual possibilities of overcoming any existing concentration of economic and political power, we may take into account general historical trends as well as the practical experience of various social movements in the recent past.

A scientific study of capitalist society in our century shows clearly that the role of the capitalist class, in the organization and management of production (let alone other spheres of social life), has been decreasing steadily. There can be little doubt that the very institution of private ownership of the means of production—which has played such a great role in the creation of modern industrial society—has now become redundant, especially in the most developed capitalist countries, and can be successfully replaced by various forms of collective ownership. The experience of successful socialist revolutions demonstrates that modern society (in spite of difficulties where social preconditions are not yet ripe) can still be organized to develop a comparatively high rate of technological and economic development.

Nevertheless, alienation (in many forms) survives in present-day, post-capitalist societies to the degree to which power is concentrated in the hands of a bureaucracy. By "bureaucracy" is meant a coherent and closed social group of professional politicians, that keeps all decision-making in its hands and enjoys considerable political and economic privileges. The growth of bureaucratic tendencies is related to a number of regressive processes such as: the decrease of initiative in the basic cells of economic life, formalization of political activities, followed by the induction of passivity in the people, subordination of all kinds of creative work to politics, growth of careerism, and moral disintegration.

There is a certain historical justification for the existence of a political elite in an underdeveloped country, especially in the initial period in which foundations for a new social order have to be laid down. When this has been done, however, there is no historical need for its survival as a particular social entity. This does not imply either a denial of every kind of elite or a utopian belief that no rulers or social organizations exerting a certain amount of power in directing and coordinating social processes are needed.

The existence of a moral and intellectual elite is *conditio sine qua non* of a progressive and humanist social process. But it must not lead to the creation of a closed social group with special rights. There is a vast difference between a ruler who considers himself indispensable and uses force to make his subjects happier against their will, and an ordinary competent man who, having *temporarily* left his profession to perform certain political functions, considers his office nothing more than an honor, and uses force only against those who break democratically established norms of social behavior. Likewise there is a fundamental distinction between the institution called *state* which has always been the coercive instrument of a particular social group whose interest it was supposed to protect and promote by force, and a truly democratic social organization which needs force only to secure the general interests of the given community against antisocial behavior of certain individuals. This model might be better named *self-management*.

There is no historical need for a special social group of professional politicians in a developed postcapitalist society with a high level of technological development, productivity, and culture. Among a large number of gifted people of various professions who have acquired a certain political experience and skill, it would not be difficult to elect excellent people to political office for a limited amount of time. Strict responsibility to their voters, observance of democratic procedures in all decision-making, obligatory rotation, lack of any material privileges (salaries for political functions should not exceed those for any other creative work), and various other measures should discourage any excessive political ambitions, and effectively prevent their realization.

Time is perhaps not yet ripe for a complete deprofessionalization of politics and for a rapid replacement of the organs of the state by those of self-management, both at the *micro* and the *macro* levels. However, the first experiences demonstrate clearly that even in a semideveloped country (like Yugoslavia) it is possible to move in this direction, and the result is a large-scale liberation of initiative, and creativity even among those people in the most degraded social layers who have traditionally been kept in utter ignorance and passivity.

Humanism and Revolution

Gajo Petrović

I

Marxist philosophy, as interpreted by Stalinists, was conceived as a combination of 1) "dialectical materialism," an abstract philosophical ontology-epistemology, and 2) "historical materialism," an unphilosophical, economistic view of history. The task of the first was to formulate the most general, "dialectical" laws of nature, society and human thought, and also to clarify the relationship between "mind" and "matter" ("spirit" and "nature," "thought" and "being"). The task of the second was to ascertain the relationship between the "social being" and the "social consciousness" (or between the social "infrastructure" and "superstructure"), and to discover the basic "laws" of historical development. Neither of the two contained an explicit theory of man. However, while explicitly rejecting the very possibility of a philosophical concept of man, the Stalinists have in fact elaborated a vulgar, "economistic" concept of man, according to which man is basically a "toolmaking animal," a being whose whole activity is determined by his economic production.

A number of Marxists who criticised Stalinism in the fifties and at the beginning of the sixties maintained that this was a misinterpretation of Marx's views, that there was a different concept of man in Marx, a concept according to which man is not an economic animal but a free, creative being of praxis, a being who to be sure can be alienated from his creative possibilities, but who can also dealienate himself and realize his true human nature. Such a concept of man, according to this view, played an important part in the thinking of Marx, so that his thought could be regarded as a new form of humanism. Not all who have conceived Marx as a humanist agree on all points of their interpretation, but many do agree that Marx's philosophy is neither pure ontology concerned with the general

288

"objective laws" of the universe without regard to man, nor a concrete social theory dispensing with the general concept of man. And some interpret Marxism as a humanistic "ontology-anthropology" concentrating upon the concept of man as a free and creative being and requiring a revolutionary change of existing society.

Such an interpretation of Marxist philosophy has given it new life both in theory and practice. Not only has it opened up new vistas for many interesting theoretical problems which were suppressed or "forgotten" in Stalinism, it has also inspired many people in their practical struggle against Stalinism, for a truly human form of socialism. Naturally it has provoked bitter attacks from the ranks of international Stalinism. Thus the representatives of a humanistic interpretation of Marxism have been accused of being "revisionists," "abstract humanists," "idealists," "bourgeois liberals," and the like. Coming from a viewpoint of crude dogmatism these assaults cannot be regarded as a theoretical danger for the new conception of Marxist philosophy. However, during the sixties the humanist interpretation of Marxism has come to be criticized not only from the "right" (from Stalinistic dogmatism), but also from the "left"—from a number of Marxists construing an opposition between humanism and revolution and maintaining that Marxism is a theory of revolution, and not humanism.

Those who think that "revolution" (and not "humanism") should be taken as the key concept of Marxism argue that the world we live in is so entirely perverted that it could be "improved" only by being destroyed and replaced by a basically different world, in other words through that radical change we call "revolution." "Humanization" in the sense of the gradual improvement of the existing inhuman world can only increase its chances for survival. And "humanism," as the theory preaching such gradual "humanization," is essentially a conservative and even reactionary ideology.

Such criticisms have been rejected by those who think that the concept of "humanism" is essential to Marxism. In defending their own humanistic interpretation of Marxism, some of them have been inclined to dispense with the concept of revolution. And some have even maintained that revolution as a violent overthrow of social relations is necessarily inhuman, and cannot serve as a means for a transition to a new, higher form of human society. Thus we now seem to be confronted with a choice: either we have to reject humanism in the name of revolution, or we must condemn revolution in the name of humanism. Is this an inescapable alternative? Or can we try to elaborate a viewpoint which would find place for both "humanism" and "revolution"?

In a number of papers which I have published since the beginning of the fifties, concepts of "humanism" and "revolution" both play an essential part. That "humanism" and "revolution" are not incompatible is implicit in these papers. However, this view has not been explicitly discussed and elaborated. Thus the question about the relationship between humanism and revolution, as it poses itself for the present author, is essentially a self-critical question. Have we been right in joining concepts of humanism and revolution or was this due to inconsistency and lack of critical thinking?

II

Whether revolution is desirable depends on questions of definition and on matters of fact. It depends on how we use the word "revolution," but it also depends on how we see the situation in the contemporary world.

To begin with, I do not think that the term "revolution" should be used, as it sometimes is done, as simply another name for the violent change of persons or groups in power. If the shift of power is produced within one social class, it would be more adequate to talk of "putsch" or "overthrow."

I am certainly much closer to those who regard revolution as a transition of power from one social class to another. Nevertheless, not every passage of power from one class to another can be regarded as revolution. If power passes from a progressive class to a regressive, this should rather be called counterrevolution.

However, seizure of power by a progressive class, if not used to change the social order, hardly deserves the name of revolution.

The passage of power into the hands of a progressive class accompanied by the construction of a new, higher social order can more rightly claim the name of social revolution. However not every replacement of a lower social order by a higher one is revolution; revolution applies only to the creation of a qualitatively different society. What is more, even the "qualitative difference" can have "degrees." In other words, not all revolutions are equally "revolutionary." Only socialist revolution, which is directed not at the replacement of one form of exploitation by another, more progressive, but at abolishing all kinds of exploitation, at overcoming all forms of self-alienation of man, is revolution in its deepest and fullest sense.

Can a radical change of society be effected only by a transformation of social structures? I believe it is wrong to think that the transformation of social institutions can be separated from the change of man, or that the change of the social order can precede the change of man, which should follow automatically. The transformation of society and the creation of new man are possible only as two closely connected sides of the same process. Therefore it is unjustified to reserve the term "revolution" for only one aspect of this unique process. "Revolution" should be reserved for a radical change in both man and society, and only socialist revolution creating a dealienated, really human man and society (social community) is revolution in the fullest sense.

Given this concept of revolution, the question arises whether in the contemporary world revolution is still possible and desirable. Of course I cannot undertake here a detailed analysis of the contemporary world and can only indicate some relevant aspects.

If socialism in the sense of a free community of free men were a reality, all talk of revolution would be deprived of meaning. But socialism in this sense does not exist anywhere. On the contrary, we live in a time in which inhumanity in its most brutal forms is practiced on a world scale. Colonial wars, exploitation of underdeveloped countries, and oppression within the most developed countries are all too well documented. To be sure, there are countries which claim to be "socialist," or successfully "constructing socialism"; were these claims true, some countries would only require further improvements. Unfortunately, a number of too convincing analyses have shown that these claims are unfounded. Thus we maintain that social revolution is still an open question on the world scale.

Certainly, the question about the possibility and desirability of revolution could also be asked in the context of whether the time for revolution has come, and what its most appropriate forms might be.

Without disputing the importance of such concrete questions (which are by no means simple and easy), I would like to insist that they cannot invalidate the basic thesis that revolution is in principle necessary for the contemporary world. Difficulties on the way may be very great, but they cannot change the fact that there is a profound need for revolutionary transformation of the existing world if man wants to remain and fully become man.

III

How does humanism fit into the above concept of revolution? Shall we try to fuse it somehow with the revolutionary viewpoint, or shall we reject it in the name of revolution?

Among the objections which could be made to humanism from a revolutionary standpoint, we shall briefly discuss only those which say that humanism is incompatible with a revolutionary attitude because it is 1) philosophically unfounded, and therefore uncritical, 2) scientifically not
elaborated, and consequently abstract, 3) anthropologically naive, and
hence idealistic, 4) socially superficial, which means opportunistic, 5) tacti-
cally pseudoneutral and universally tolerant, i.e. conservative, and 6) ideologically illusion-spreading, and thus reactionary. Our answers to these
objections are meant not as a defense of all existing forms of humanism,
but rather as the attempt to show the potentialities of revolutionary, Marxist humanism.

1   One sometimes encountered objection to humanism is that it is
"philosophically unfounded" or "uncritical" because it concentrates upon
the concept of man and remains within the limits of philosophical "anthropology" and "psychology," ignoring great "metaphysical" questions about
the nature and modes of Being—as if man could exist (and be understood)
outside the world, by himself and alone.

This objection holds in some cases. There really are humanists interested in man only and who also think that great metaphysical controversies
are irrelevant for the understanding of man. However, "uncritical," philosophically unfounded humanism is not its only possible form. If humanism
is understood as creative thought directed at grasping and co-creating the
essence of man, there is no reason why it should abstain from those profound metaphysical questions whose clarification is necessary for the understanding of man. Far from being confined to an "agnostic" or "skeptical" attitude toward the great ontological questions, humanism is naturally
"driven" to them. And this natural "drivenness" ("Angewiesenheit," as the
Germans would say) has not remained a pure possibility. In Marx's
thought humanistic intentions are interwoven with investigation of the
deepest "metaphysical" questions and the problems of everyday life.

2   Another objection to humanism is that it remains too far from the
real problems of living. Man does not exist as Man in general or as unified
Human Nature. He is a complex being possessing many different aspects
(biological, economic, political, artistic, scientific, religious, etc.). He is an
historical being whose nature changes from one historical epoch to another. He is a socially diversified being, divided into social classes and
other groups. And he is also an individual, every "specimen" having
unique characteristics. Thus only a scientific investigation of man, which
takes into account his complex and differentiated nature, could help both

to elaborate an adequate picture of man and to change the world in a human way. In other words what we need is not abstract humanist hair-splitting, but concrete scientific study.

This objection is also based on a misunderstanding of humanism. The recognition of a common human nature does not deny that human nature is complex, nor of the fact that it may assume different historical and social forms. Nor does a philosophical, "ontologico-anthropological" analysis of man require repudiation of a scientific investigation of various aspects or forms of man's being. On the contrary, such a philosophical analysis makes possible and requires further concrete investigation of man. In other words, the idea that humanism should be strictly separated from scientific inquiry is as unfounded as the seemingly opposite idea that it should be separated from the realm of ontology. Both ideas are based on the same ungranted assumption that humanism must remain confined within the province of a pure anthropology.

3   A further objection to humanism is concerned not with its subject-matter or approach, but with its "content." It says that humanism is too naive and optimistic because it sees merely the "positive," "good," "virtuous" side in man, and overlooks its "negative," "bad," or "sinful" side. Humanists regard man as a free, creative being, progressing to ever higher forms and enriching his own life by transforming himself and the nonhuman world in a human way. However, the objection says, man is not only good, kind, virtuous, free, and creative, he is also bad, demonic, immoral, dangerous, and destructive. Both sides are equally parts of human nature and it is not justified to ignore the latter.

However convincing this objection about naïveté might sound, it is perhaps naive itself. Those who say that man is basically a free and creative being do not want to dispute that he can be (and as a matter of fact has been) unfree and uncreative. Uncreativeness and unfreedom are modes of being of a free and creative being. In other words, only a being which can be free and creative, can be also unfree and uncreative. A being which cannot be free, cannot be unfree either. Far from denying the self-alienated existence of man, Marxist humanism sees alienation as a permanent possibility and threat. If man were merely "good," and if he had no "inhuman" side, the humanistic requirement for a radical change of man would be devoid of meaning.

4   A fourth objection to humanism is directed not against its theses on the nature of man, but against its analysis of contemporary society and its basic social goals. Without going to the roots of present social problems

(says the objection), humanists see only small shortcomings in the existing system and accordingly require a series of small reforms, gradually "humanizing" the existing social system. However, existing society is not merely insufficiently human, it is seriously dehumanized and perverted. Thus for its humanization a radical, revolutionary change is necessary.

True, some humanists have really been reformistic and opportunistic, but this is not a necessary consequence of humanism as such. A consistent humanist should require the overcoming of all inhumanity and this can be achieved only by a qualitative change. Thus, far from being opposed to the requirement for a radical revolutionary change, a humanistic viewpoint logically leads to it. On the other hand, those who insist on the radical "inhumanity" of the contemporary world and call for its revolutionary humanization cannot themselves dispense with the concept of humanism.

5   A fifth objection to humanism is concerned with the methods with which it would achieve its goals. According to this objection humanism preaches love, respect, understanding, and toleration for and toward everybody, because every man, according to humanism, regardless of his individual properties, possesses a common human nature. Recommending equal love for all as a universal medicine it refuses to make any difference between social groups or individuals and it does not want to show preferences or harm anyone. Such a "neutral" attitude, which disregards the difference between the rich and the poor, the exploiter and the exploited, the oppressor and the oppressed, the happy and the unhappy is really an option to tolerate oppressors and exploiters.

This again is an appropriate objection to some forms of humanism and an inadequate criticism of others. If the humanistic requirement for equal love toward everybody is taken seriously, it cannot mean toleration of exploitation and oppression. If every man should be treated with respect, this means that those social structures should be abolished in which men are treated as objects of exploitation and oppression, as things to be mercilessly used and abused in the interests of a privileged minority. Love and the requirement for a revolutionary change of the world are thus directly linked.

6   Nevertheless, the sixth objection says, the preaching of love, respect, and goodness, even if it is conceived as allowing or recommending revolutionary change, remains conservative and even reactionary if it refuses to participate in that revolutionary change. And this is really the case with modern humanism. It indulges in nice phrases on man, freedom,

creativity, and honesty, while it ignores reality where there are no traces of these niceties. Thus it creates and spreads illusions about the world we live in, conceals the truth, and helps to preserve the existing.

There is no doubt that humanist phraseology can serve and has already served such purposes. But humanism is not the only theory that has been abused in this way. Every philosophical theory, if reduced to mere phraseology and emptied of its real content, can be misused for reactionary purposes. Thus if revolutionary humanism is abused in this way, it is not its fault; it is the responsibility of those who thus abuse it.

IV

Most of the above objections to humanism from an allegedly revolutionary standpoint were based on a misunderstanding of humanism and on its reduction to some of its historical forms. In a similar way various objections to revolution from an allegedly humanistic viewpoint are mainly based on the misunderstanding of the essence of revolution.

Among many imaginable objections to revolution we shall briefly consider only those which say that revolution is 1) bloody and therefore inhuman, 2) minoritarian, and hence undemocratic, 3) necessary, but not sufficient, 4) possible, but not necessary, 5) occasionally helpful, but often harmful, 6) phraseological and thus abusable. There are certainly many other possible objections to revolution, but a complete listing is not our purpose.

1   One objection argues that revolution as a violent overthrow involving bloodshed and cruelty is inhuman, and therefore to be avoided. To be sure, the objectors concede, not all revolutions were equally bloody, and most of them did not regard violence as a goal in itself. Terror and brutality were most often regarded as tools for constructing a new society. But inhuman tools cannot be of much help for human goals.

This objection starts from the right historical observation that many social revolutions in the past have, as a matter of fact, involved bloodshed and cruelty. It overlooks the fact that epochs of counterrevolution and of "peaceful" conservative dominion have often involved even more bloodshed and inhumanity. The objection also rightly maintains that high human goals cannot be achieved by low inhuman means. But it uncritically assumes that terror and brutality are essential to revolution. However, not cruelty but the creation of a qualitatively different man and society is the essence of revolution. Its goals cannot be achieved without the use of power, but they cannot be achieved with violence either.

2   Another objection to revolution says that even if it is not brutal, it is undemocratic, because it is a radical social change executed by a minority against the will of the majority. All changes in which the majority is interested can be achieved by gradual evolution without force, violence, and revolution.

This objection again disregards the historical fact that throughout centuries minorities have ruled over majorities and that for their overthrow the use of power by the majority was necessary. Thus there is no ground for maintaining that revolution is of necessity a minority action. On the contrary, revolution in its full sense is a creative collective activity in which the majority of people takes part. Only the majority through their own self-activity can fundamentally change their own social relationships and themselves.

3   A third objection to revolution says that although it may be a necessary precondition for the construction of a truly human society, it is not sufficient. A revolution may overthrow a conservative government or destroy oppressive institutions, but this is not enough. The period of revolutionary destruction should be followed by "positive" or "constructive" development creating new human relationships.

This is certainly a requirement with which we could agree, but the concept of revolution cannot be reduced to a political change. What in the above objection is taken as the postrevolutionary period of constructive development is really the essence of revolution. As has already been said, "revolution" if not followed by the creation of a new man and society is not revolution but a political "putsch." None of the great revolutionaries was prepared to reduce revolution to a mere "putsch." Revolution, as Lenin conceived it, is an "incredibly complicated and painful process of the withering away of the Old, and of the birth of a new social order, a new way of life for scores of millions of people."

4   A fourth objection would be that although revolution can be one way for overcoming human alienation and establishing a really human society, it is not the only way. A really human society could also be established via slow evolution, through a number of continuous small changes. Therefore the insistence on revolution as the only possible way to a humanist society may prove extremely harmful, preventing the use of forms and methods which might be more efficient in some historical situations.

But revolution as an "incredibly complicated and painful process" does include small, continuous changes. Thus there is no necessity to construe unbridgeable opposition between "revolution" and "evolution." The decisive question is, however, whether a series of small changes remains within the limits of the existing social order, or whether it negates it and inaugurates a basically different community of men. In the first case we have a process helping to improve and strengthen the existing social order, in the second case a qualitative change or revolution. It is impossible to have qualitative change without revolution simply because revolution *is* such a qualitative change.

5   A fifth objection to revolution would say that, although revolution might be necessary in principle, it might be undesirable in a concrete historical situation, when the conditions for revolution are not yet ripe. Revolution on all conditions leads to an avanturism which brings great damage to progressive social forces, by giving a welcome excuse to reactionaries.

A simple answer is that a revolutionary attitude does not require revolution under all conditions. The thesis that only revolution can create a new man and society is not equivalent to the thesis that the time for a social revolution is always ripe. A revolutionary attitude and an avanturistic preaching of social revolution regardless of situation have nothing in com‐ mon. Revolutionaries have often stressed that a "revolutionary situation" is a necessary precondition for revolution. But a revolutionary attitude is certainly also opposed to that opportunistic attitude for which the time for revolution will never come. There can certainly be no guarantee for a revolution's success but it is not possible to be man without being prepared to take some human risks.

6   A sixth objection to revolution is really directed against the misuse of revolutionary phraseology. Although revolution itself might be desirable, the objection says, the talk on revolution might be a veil used to hide the opportunistic position of some people who, maintaining that they are preparing themselves for a great revolution in the future, abstain from allegedly "small" progressive actions in the present.

Here again we are not confronted with an objection to revolution, but with the possibility of abusing a theory, a possibility which exists for every theory and for which no theory as such can be made responsible. A theory can be responsible only for the consequences, which follow from it. Thus revolution cannot be responsible for the counterrevolutionary distortions and misuses of the revolutionary theory. On the contrary, opportunistic and counterrevolutionary theories and practices can be exposed only with the help of a true revolutionary theory and activity.

V

We can now go back to the central question from which we started: Are we to reject humanism in the name of revolution, or shall we condemn revolution in the name of humanism?

I hope the above discussion has shown that this is a false alternative. Consistent humanism which does not want to stop half-way demands a radical negation of existing inhumanity and the creation of a qualitatively different, truly human society. In other words it demands revolution. On the other hand true revolution cannot be satisfied with small social changes, it requires the creation of a qualitatively different, really human man and society. In other words it requires a radical humanization of existing man and society.

The whole meaning of this paper could thus be summed up in the thesis that there can be no genuine humanism without a real revolutionary attitude, nor a truly revolutionary attitude without real humanism. Revolutionary humanism is the only full humanism, and humanist revolution is the only true revolution. In other words, revolutionary humanism and a humanist revolutionary attitude are one.

All our replies to objections were directed in the same basic direction: to demonstrate the inseparability of humanism and revolution, and to show that revolutionary humanism and humanistic revolution are the only alternatives for our time. There has been considerable repetition in these answers. But at a time when humanity is repeatedly endangered and violated by aggressive inhumanity, a repetitive insistence on both humanism and revolution seems indispensable.

What Does It Mean to "Be a Marxist"?*   *Adam Schaff*

Erich Fromm is a thinker who has consciously and manifestly drawn inspiration from Marxism. But he is not, and in view of his interests could not be, simply an interpreter of other men's ideas; on the contrary, he is an original thinker who, regardless of the sources that may stimulate him, goes his own way and breaks new ground. In consequence, he has frequently been a center of controversy, and never more so than when attempts are made to "classify" him into this or that school. These have inevitably run into difficulties, and the same can be said of the dispute over Erich Fromm's relationship to Marxism. For every argument used to prove he is a Marxist, another has been found to prove the contrary.

Obviously, pigeonholing a thinker is not the most important issue. Nor is it particularly simple when faced with a creative and innovating mind; indeed it usually proves quite impossible. However, the attempt may still be a rewarding exercise insofar as it sheds additional light on a body of work and on contemporary intellectual currents. This is the basic idea behind my essay. I do not propose either to "classify" Erich Fromm or judge him by the standards of Marxist orthodoxy. That would be pointless. I am one of those people who think very highly not only of his work as a philosopher but also of his stance as a man. I am convinced that not only has he drawn inspiration from Marxism but also that he has opened up new avenues of inquiry with a Marxist approach. So it would seem both fruitful and justified to consider the work of Erich Fromm from this vantage point—especially for one who is himself a Marxist. The following remarks are offered as a theoretical contribution toward making an analysis of this kind.

Questions like "What is meant by being a Marxist?" or its complement, "What is meant by being a revisionist?" are not new. They have resurfaced in every new period and whenever the word "Marxist" was not given the crude, oversimplified interpretation of an adherent to certain "orthodox" doctrine, in the sense of absolute fidelity to the teaching of the masters.

Anyone who rejects such a dogmatic and, in practice, useless conception of "being a Marxist," who regards Marxism as a science and so as an open system which must be augmented and modified along with the development of reality and its apprehension by mankind, must also encounter the problem of determining what are or are not Marxist views. When new issues arise, it is no use going back to the classic writings, since their authors did not and could not—since they were scholars, not prophets—foresee new problems and situations; thus the question "What does it mean to be a Marxist?" and its counterpart, "What is meant by revisionism?" always reassert themselves.

In our time these questions need asking not only in view of the appearance of new problems, but also because of the great confusion caused by the propaganda warfare waged by various groups within the international movement which invokes Marxism as its theory and ideology; as a result, concepts like "Marxist" and "revisionist" are robbed of their scientific meanings and serve, instead, as emotive descriptions for immediate targets in the political struggle. Naturally, this does not help to clarify ideas which are complex and vague enough as it is. Still, "being a Marxist" does have a rational meaning which is worth tracking down in view of the gravity of the arguments taking place.

When we say that someone is a Marxist, we mean that he has opted for a certain body of ideas known as "Marxism." This emphasis on the subjective aspect of "being a Marxist"—stressing the idea that to *be* a Marxist a man must *want* to be one—is, I believe, extremely important. Simply to proclaim certain propositions which accord with, or are even historically derived from, Marxism does not make someone a Marxist. After all, he may disagree with other parts of the doctrine or even—a very common occurrence nowadays, especially among sociologists and historians—be unaware that his views derive from Marx, so thoroughly and organically have his theories been absorbed by modern science. In other words, no one can be counted a Marxist against his will, since this term implies a deliberate act of commitment to Marxism as an intellectual movement.

Wanting to be a Marxist—that is, declaring one's allegiance—is a necessary condition for being counted as a Marxist. It is equally certain, however, that this is not a sufficient condition. There is an obvious distinction between subjectively wanting to be something and objectively being it. Good intentions are not enough to make someone, say, a pianist, a tennis player, or a scholar—and the same is true of being a Marxist. In this case, too, what is needed is not only the *will* but also the *capacity,* and that is an objective and verifiable qualification.

Thus to be a Marxist in the field of theory, it is necessary to have a certain skill, and this skill—a certain sum of knowledge—must be genetically connected with the views of Marx and his successors, since these constitute the whole known as "Marxism." *But what kind* of skill is needed, and *how* is it to be exercised to validate the name "Marxist"?

The simplest answer would seem to be: as thorough a knowledge as possible of the writings of Marx, Engels, and the other classics, and a faithful cultivation and continuation of their views. But such a dogmatic interpretation of Marxism as a kind of creed must itself be criticized since, as the historical vicissitudes of Marxism have shown, even such an absurd position would not be without supporters. The classics of Marxism, however, insisted that Marxism was not a system, in the sense of an enclosed doctrine but only a guide to action. Marx himself made Cartesian skepticism a basic element of his scientific outlook. Asked by his daughters for his favorite motto, he replied *de omnibus dubitandum est.* Accordingly, for a Marxist there can be no hesitation between scientific method and pietism.

To be a Marxist, therefore, one must know the views of Marx, Engels, and other classics and—realizing that the postulate of perfect knowledge is always only a model—uphold them unless they have been invalidated or modified by the development of society and science. Under this definition anyone who claims to be a Marxist not only need not dogmatically believe in whatever is written in the classics of Marxism, but should check their views and, if necessary, modify or even reject them as obsolete. This is an extremely important point to be borne in mind before classifying someone as either a Marxist or a revisionist.

So far so good: the designation of Marxist can legitimately be claimed by someone who has declared his allegiance to Marxism, has a sufficient knowledge of its principles, and stands by them unless they have been overtaken by the historical development of social life and science. But from here on, the matter is neither as simple nor as straightforward as it might seem. For example, one might reflect on some questions that arise in this context and demand an answer if the term "Marxist" is to have some operative sense:

Who is authorized to decide that a Marxist proposition needs to be modified or even discarded?

How far can one go in this direction before claims of adherence to Marxism cease to make sense? Or, to put it another way, are there some basic propositions which may not be rejected without forfeiting one's right to call himself a Marxist? If so, what are they?

Is the problem of allegiance to Marxism a purely theoretical question or a practical and political one as well? Or, to put it another way, can the term "Marxist" be applied to someone who adopts the Marxist position in theory without acting on it in practice, or only to someone whose theoretical views are consistent with his practical activity in the political sphere? How are we to assess and describe those who agree with Marxist theory, but disagree with the policies of the communist movement in general, or of some communist party in particular?

Questions like these—and there are others—need a reply before any general answer will be found of value.

But first we must come to grips with the question of revisionism which, though a correlate of the positive definition of "Marxist," needs to be broached explicitly if we are to avoid difficulties later on.

First of all, we should describe as a revisionist someone who is a Marxist insofar as he is familiar with the principles of Marxism and has avowed his allegiance to it. Anyone who simply rejects these principles because he disagrees with them is an opponent of Marxism, not a revisionist. Nor is someone a revisionist (in the historically accepted sense of the word) who, while recognizing the value of a certain tenet, proposes some change or amendment since, in its original form he believes it is—or has become historically—inconsistent with the empirical facts. By definition then, a revisionist is (only and always) a Marxist who advocates certain appropriately qualified alterations in Marxist theory. To use this term, as is sometimes done, to denote an opponent of Marxism who proposes a partial or complete rejection of this theory is imprecise and illegitimate.

But what kind of changes in Marxist theory have to be proposed in order to call someone a revisionist, seeing that Marxism is an open system, which means that it can be reinforced not only with new propositions but also by changing or even eliminating those that have been made obsolete by the development of science and social reality? Since, as we know, the classics of Marxism *insisted* on just such a critical and open-minded approach, when and under what circumstances can this procedure be found improper and so warrant the pejorative description of "revisionism"?

In the light of our previous remarks, the answer to this question should not be difficult: the only legitimate change is one justified by the incompatibility of the theory with reality; an illegitimate change ("revisionist" in the bad sense) is one that is not justified by the development of our knowledge of the world or by the altered circumstances of the social reality we investigate.

This general formula seems simple, but a moment's reflection, however, requires us to put forward at least three additional questions which complicate the picture:

1   Is *every* change of this kind liable to the charge of "revisionism"?

2   What is to be adopted as the *criterion* of compatibility when it is proposed to make changes, not in theoretical propositions that describe reality and state its laws, but in ideological norms and postulates?

3   What is to be done if *opinions differ* about the adequacy of the theory and the need for change? Whose opinion should prevail? What should the standards of judgment be: how many people stand behind each of the contradictory propositions, or their content?

My answer to the first question is firmly in the negative: not *every* change in Marxist theory, even if it is shown beyond all doubt not to be justified on the grounds of incompatibility with reality, is to be condemned as "revisionism." There must be no blurring of the difference between error—to which a Marxist is also entitled—and "revisionism," since there can be no search for truth without the risk of error; as we know from historical practice, the fear of being called a revisionist can be a deterrent to creative inquiry. In any case, it would be ludicrous in assessing the Marxism of a thinker not to be guided by the *entirety* of his views when they are beyond reproach from this point of view but, in error, perhaps, in a theoretically insignificant way. Thus it is certainly not *any* change in Marxist theory mistakenly proposed by a person that entitles us to criticize him as a revisionist; this would depend instead on his *system of views* regarding some major part of Marxism. But what are these *major* parts of Marxism? Here is a problem which requires an answer to our previous question about the basic propositions of Marxism, and the limits of the changes that can be made without forfeiting the right to be called a Marxist.

To run ahead a little, I believe that there is no clear-cut answer to any of these questions. This enormously complicates the issue of whether it is legitimate to describe someone's views as "orthodox" Marxist or "revisionist." A glance at the history of the problem indicates that, in the past, the term "revisionist" was used sparingly, and then only when theoretical divergence was accompanied by departures *in political practice* from the principles of the revolutionary struggle for power or its retention. For example, when Lenin attacked Plekhanov's hieroglyph theory, he did not describe it as revisionism, though he regarded it as mistaken and inconsistent with Marxism. The prodigal use of "revisionism" as a term of abuse, leading to its increasing devaluation, is a product of later times.

Again, as to whether every change in Marxist theory can be assessed as "revisionism," one must also bear in mind the individual *frame of reference*. After all, "revisionism" designates the action of revising—in the sense of changing—certain views and its consequences. But since Marxism is an intellectual system which has evolved historically, and to which various people have contributed, one must always be aware of the time and specific stage of development of the theory when talking of its revision.

Which of the views of Marx and Engels are to be respected in the sense of being obliged to uphold them on pain of the charge of revisionism? From what period? Should it always be assumed that the later views are more correct? What other thinkers, apart from Lenin, have the same status? History, as well as the ideological disputes now in progress in the working-class movement, indicate that these are not minor questions and that they complicate the task of someone wishing to reach a rational judgment about whether to classify certain views as revisionist, rather than simply use the word "revisionist" as an insult.

The matter becomes even more complicated when we come to the second question: what is to be done if there are differences of opinion regarding the validity of ideological norms and postulates? For despite the difficulties we have mentioned, it is still clear what is at issue when we accept the compatibility of Marxist theory to reality as the criterion of admissible changes. But this applies to propositions predicating something about reality—that is, its description in the broad sense of the word. On the other hand, when we construct an ideology—a system of views and attitudes which, on the basis of a certain system of values, guides human behavior towards a recognized goal of social development—we are dealing not only with descriptions but with assessments and standards of conduct which are not *logically* deducible from descriptive propositions; even if we agree that they are *genetically* deducible—I myself would support this view—we must admit that there is no question here of an obvious inference from predicative statements.

From a certain description of reality, from its *apprehension,* there arise through a complex social process certain assessments—that is, systems of values recognized by certain groups—and, in consequence, accepted norms of conduct. But if I conclude that, in certain conditions, they need to be modified, my argument with someone who opposes this suggestion cannot be decided by a simple appeal to reality but only by reference to its cognition; this implies a subjective factor. The criterion of the compatibility of the theory with reality cannot be applied in this case, at any rate not in its simple and direct sense. Thus if I say, for instance, that in the altered circumstances of our time the development of socialism calls for teaching people to think for themselves, and this entails a radical extension of freedom of thought and speech, and if someone disagrees with this assertion, then to label either of the parties to this dispute as "revisionist" *is meaningless*—unless one follows the dogmatic interpretation of this term which involves comparing whatever is said with the statement of some recognized authority. Appealing to reality is of no use in this case. In a normative statement what is involved is a certain recommendation, in other words, something that is not embodied in any description of reality.

The third question is, in my view, the most fruitful from the pragmatic point of view, since it reveals the shakiness of any answer. As we know, a general consensus is not to be recommended as a criterion of truth, still less the consensus of one or another group. The decision of an authority is even less acceptable. Thus, when there are no clear objective criteria and there is also controversy among the people involved, we must reconcile ourselves to admitting humbly that the situation is controversial and the problem cannot be settled unambiguously.

Our digression over the concept of "revisionism" will have injected us with a sizable dose of skepticism and wariness in approaching the problems that concern us. Let us now, with this lesson in our minds, revert to our difficulties with the definition of "Marxist."

We have seen that the only concept of Marxism justified by its own principles is one of an open theory. As we have said, its propositions can be supplemented and altered if the need arises. But who is to decide that one has actually arisen?

Naturally, *anyone* who has come up against this question in the course of inquiry. A variety of reservations can and should be added: he must observe maximum caution in the changes he makes, carefully examine the differing views of those who are qualified and experienced, etc. But the final result cannot be altered: the decision rests with anyone who has seriously pondered some issue—and this right belongs to everyone. To think otherwise is a sad remnant of the personality cult, in its literal sense.

All this might seem commonplace were it not for a certain "but" which arises when we remember the twofold function of Marxism: scientific cognition and the binding agent of a movement fighting for specific social goals. Obviously, these functions are organically related and complementary, but they nevertheless form two aspects of a complex phenomenon and to appreciate this difference is a help in understanding our problem.

From the point of view of its cognitive function, Marxism cannot and should not be afraid of any changes proposed within its framework: if they prove mistaken, they will be criticized and rejected. This is a normal and accepted procedure in all fields of science, and as a *science* Marxism is not —and should not be—an exception.

But the position changes when we consider the function of Marxism as an ideology welding together a movement fighting for certain social goals. Durkheim once called this function of ideology a religious function; he had in mind the factor of faith, in the sense of a profound and unquestioned belief in the justness of something, as the cement of social movements. This factor undoubtedly also appears in the social movement based on Marxism, often determining the strength of people's convictions and their readiness to make sacrifices for the ends specified by this movement.

Now, in this field, a change of principles, opinions, recognized goals, and their attendant norms is not a neutral matter. On the contrary, their relative invariability, and their simplicity as well, guarantee (at least in certain circumstances) the maintenance of the emotional tension on which faith and militancy depend, especially where mass movements are concerned. Hence the pragmatic politician will be extremely cautious in accepting such changes, and his disposition toward them, as is psychologically only natural, will be suspicious: they complicate the situation and may weaken the militancy of the masses. This consideration should not be minimized, for it is extremely important. And it is here that the confusion begins: if experimentation and innovation are extremely useful and even desirable in the field of theory, where the dangers are negligible, in the sphere of practical politics the matter is far more involved. For in view of the possible risks, even the most fervent advocate of innovation will tread warily if he has a minimum of political experience and a sense of responsibility for action undertaken in the social field.

These two functions—the scientific and the ideological-political—are not only organically related but are also linked by feedback; that is, they control and stimulate each other in their historical development. This gives additional weight to the observation that, though they form a single whole, they display, within certain limits, varying and even contradictory tendencies. Here is a dialectic straight out of the textbooks. But unfortunately it tends to be overlooked, which is all the more dangerous since both functions of Marxism, because of their relative independence, have in social life relatively different and separate groups of representatives: theorists-scientists and practical ideologists-politicians.

Of course, the boundaries between them are not clear-cut; obviously, there may be cases of a personal union—the most favorable arrangement —but unfortunately such examples are increasingly rare and attesting to, in this case, an unwelcome tendency toward a "division of labor" and specialization. Such a division becomes dangerous, both ideologically and in practice, not only when the "incumbents" of these different functions of Marxist ideology cease to perceive and understand their unity, but also when they overlook their differences. One observes Marxist intellectuals who, while they are right in calling for freedom of discussion and creation, overlook the social implications of their work, often displaying a quite childish lack of political judgment and responsibility (which, naturally, does not help to raise their standing with the politicians). On the other hand, there are Marxist politicians who, preoccupied with the social consequence of such changes, forget about the unity of theory and practice and of their responsibility for the development of theory.

Even though the stability of the ideological factors that bind a group might seem to strengthen its emotional capacity for struggle and sacrifice, in actual fact such protection of unity at any cost, to the point of sectarianism and dogmatism, leads in the longer run to a profound crisis of ideological disillusionment; it causes a correspondingly more serious disintegration of the group, a process which may often be incurable and irreversible. Those men are poor politicians indeed who, while loudly professing to be defending unity, are most radically and dangerously working for its disintegration by failing to appreciate the importance of the advancement of theory, both for progress and the consolidation of the influence of their ideology.

But let us come back to the point in hand: who is authorized to decide that changes and modifications need to be made in Marxist theory to adapt it better to reality, in the broad sense of the word? With the reservations set out above, let us repeat the answer we have already given: *anyone* who reflects on these issues. Whether or not these proposed changes prove tenable is another matter; it depends on how well substantiated the changes are, and on the results of their social appraisal. But one thing is certain: there are no privileges in these matters; no individuals, groups, or institutions enjoy a special status. And there is no other way of assessing the merits of these changes except by the force of their arguments based both on the theoretical premises of Marxism and on an analysis of the social practice.

This answer to the first question emphasizes the significance of the next one: how far can these changes be carried before calling oneself a Marxist ceases to make sense?

In answering this question we must distinguish at least three different forms it can take.

First and foremost: what questions are legitimate with regard to Marxism? In the light of its own principles, *every* question is legitimate; and equally legitimate, or even necessary, is *every* change in its propositions if they collide with the properly researched evidence of reality. Marxism is a science, not a religious creed, and so is subject to the general laws of science. But if in making these changes we reach a point where Marxism as a *system* ceases to exist, it would make no sense to call oneself a Marxist. This raises the question of a body of views whose survival is essential if we are to talk seriously of Marxism.

Marxism, as theory, is a historically shaped system of views composed primarily of its philosophy, sociology, political economy, political theory, and specific research method. It is a system in the strict sense of the word; when the classics of Marxism said that their views "are no system" they had in mind the special meaning of this word developed by metaphysics. In other words, Marxism is a set of elements—in this case, whole theories —in which to change one is to change the others. This is why rejection of any of the basic components of Marxism is the same as rejecting Marxism as a whole. Consequently, it is not possible to be a "partial" Marxist, acknowledging only certain of its areas or aspects; if one does not accept the *system* of Marxist thought, one does not accept Marxism and is not a Marxist. Here then is the first distinct boundary which may not be crossed if one wants to keep the right to be called a Marxist.

In practice, however, in what might be called the day-to-day routine of science, research is specialized and one is usually a philosopher, economist, sociologist, psychologist, psychiatrist, etc., who is not concerned with the other fields, often remote from his own interests, which form part of

the Marxist system. Take a social scientist who in his sphere accepts the
research method and basic theoretic principles of Marxism, draws his inspiration from it, and is avowedly one of its supporters; is he a Marxist or
not? Obviously a rhetorical question: of course, he is. But in a slightly different sense than if he simply displays a lack of interest in the fields of
Marxism outside his immediate province. The matter becomes more complicated if he actually rejects Marxism in these other areas. In this case we
are dealing not with a Marxist but with a researcher who employs the
methodological and theoretical guidelines of Marxism in a certain sphere.
These are quite different situations, as are the theoretical and practical
conclusions to be drawn from them.

But this being so, where is the boundary whose crossing implies the
surrender of the right to be called a Marxist even in this second, narrower
sense?

Each component of the Marxist system is a relatively independent
theory of philosophy, sociology, economics, etc. Each of these theories has
the shape of a more-or-less rigorously structured intellectual system. As in
every such system, the various propositions can be graded according to the
degree of their importance to the structure of the theory. On the other
hand, as has been said, Marxism—both in the sense of the entire system
and its component elements—is an "open" system; since it is not a dogmatism, it develops, absorbs new elements, alters old ones, etc. In principle
there is nothing to stop such changes being made if they are justified by
the development of man's knowledge of social and physical reality. However, there are limits to these changes; if these limits are crossed, it would
no longer make sense to talk of Marxism as a specific theoretical system;
the system would cease to exist and the author of these changes could not
claim to be called a Marxist. The general rule would be that these limits
are determined by the basic theses of the theory. It is not possible to pre-
scribe in detail which propositions play this fundamental role, but the idea
can be illustrated with examples, and in such a situation this is enough.

For instance, rejection of materialism as a view of the world in favor
of spiritualism means renunciation of Marxism as an intellectual system
and thereby takes away the right to call oneself a Marxist. This is clearly
not a question of degree. The point is not whether we can put various con-
structions on the principles of materialism, but whether we accept or reject
its basic proposition in the field of epistemology (the objectivity of existence) and ontology (the materiality of existence) which decide the materialist character of a given school. Anyone who does not acknowledge this

principle and adopts any kind of spiritualist admixture is simply not a materialist, and *by the same token* not a Marxist, since he dismantles Marxism as a specific theoretical system.

The same applies to historical materialism, the Marxian analysis of capitalism and its sociopolitical model (including the ethical aspects of human attitudes) of the socialist society.

To grasp the full meaning of this answer, we must turn to the third version of the question posed earlier: can one make changes and modifications in the position of the Marxist classics with regard to *these,* for us, key issues? The answer, of course, is positive: one can and should change and modify the propositions of the classics in accordance with the needs of the developing social and scientific reality. It was Engels himself who said, for example, that materialism must change its form together with every great scientific discovery which revolutionizes our view of the world. A fortiori this applies to social problems.

In other words, the key problems in Marxism are neither an exception nor taboo for the researcher. Nor was this what I had in mind when I insisted on their exceptional position in Marxism. But it is one thing to make changes and modifications, however far-reaching, in theoretical propositions (for instance, by saying that the theory of reflection in one of the forms in which it has been stated is not tenable in the light of modern knowledge about the role of the subjective factor, and above all, language in cognition; or by showing that the theory of the three levels of cognition is mistaken for similar reasons; or by rejecting the Hegel-Engels concept of movement as an objective contradiction; or by discarding the Morgan-Engels concept of prehistory on the evidence of modern anthropology). It is another thing entirely to *renounce* them (for instance, by replacing materialism with spiritualism, the dialectic with crude evolutionism, the materialist concept of history with the idealistic concept of great individuals as the sole and autonomous makers of history, etc.). In the former case, we are working "inside" the propositions of Marxism—whether the changes are justified or not is another matter; in the latter, "outside" them, in the sense of simply dismissing them as wrong, thereby rejecting Marxism itself.

By way of precaution, let me end with one reservation: in all that has been said here we have ignored the problem of truth and falsehood. It is obvious (and I have emphasized this often enough) that science knows no taboos *whatsoever* and that we cannot hesitate to criticize any proposition if it is contradicted by scientific truth. What we were concerned with here was another question: is there a corpus of propositions whose negation would 1) mean the end of Marxism as a theoretical system—even though certain true propositions might survive—and 2) would thus deprive anyone who discarded them of the right to call himself a Marxist? The answer to *this* question is a positive one, which involves a variety of consequences for the meaning of the terms "Marxist" and "revisionist."

Finally, the last question of this series: can the designation "Marxist" be claimed only be someone who links theory with practice, drawing revolutionary practical conclusions from the Marxist theory, or also by someone who upholds Marxism in theory but is either not politically active or, if active, draws from Marxist theory different conclusions from those embraced by the communist movement.

This is primarily a question of *definition*. We can assume *ex definitione* that we will only qualify as a Marxist a revolutionary who is active and bases his political practice on Marxist theory. But the question then arises: what are we to call those supporters of Marx who do not draw such practical conclusions from their convictions? For instance, a social scientist (I have met many such academics in the United States) who declares himself a Marxist and does indeed follow the Marxist method in his research, but is not and does not intend to be, for one reason or another, politically active. So radical an extension of definitional requirements (i.e. to reserve the name "Marxist" only for those who not only adhere to Marx's thought in theory but are also politically active revolutionaries) seems to be not only incompatible with the conventions of language, but would also introduce an unnecessary confusion of concepts. It would be better to leave the term "Marxist" as a description of certain beliefs and *theoretical* attitudes, and reserve for *practical* attitudes some other name, such as "communist" or the like.

This is all the more advisable in that the matter is by no means as simple as it once seemed; the same is also true of the question whether the same theoretical premises always lead to only one possible directive for practical action. Today we can see clearly that this is not the case, that there are various possibilities, and that proceeding from a *common* theoretical base we can arrive at various practical interpretations and conclusions—which does not give us the right to dismiss as non-Marxist people who think differently from us.

What conclusions can be drawn from these remarks? Though they may seem vague and modest, they are nevertheless important for the purpose we set ourselves. For we have found that although the issues are enormously complicated and require much discussion, we can with a fair degree of accuracy define what is meant by "being a Marxist" and therefore what we understand by revisionism. But the most important result is the conviction that a researcher who professes Marxism and draws creative inspiration from it is by no means condemned to sterile dogmatism and exegesis of the established texts. On the contrary, the more creative he is the more "orthodox" he is in his Marxism. In other words, he is completely free to bring into the perspective of Marxist theory new lines of inquiry and the new horizons opened up by the development of science; he is entitled to make changes in the traditional form of the theory where dictated by these advances; and in doing so he does not cease to be a Marxist, as long as he stops short of changes so fundamental that they destroy the system of Marxist theory; and finally, in creatively developing Marxism he cannot be accused of "revisionism," though he might well level this charge at his opponents who, confusing fidelity to Marxism with dogmatism, betray one of the basic principles of Marxism: treatment of the body of its propositions as a science, that is, as an open system.

The
Prospect
for
Radicalism   Tom Bottomore

Erich Fromm has the distinction, among others, of being one of the small
number of people who helped to keep radical ideas alive in the unpropi-
tious climate of the 1950s, and thus to prepare the way for the renewal
and diffusion of such ideas in the following decade. It will not be inappro-
priate, therefore, for us to consider what the new radicalism has so far
achieved and what is the prospect for the future.

There is evident, at the present time, in all the industrial countries, not
only a strong reaction against radicalism but also a loss of vigor and a proliferation of internal divisions in the radical movement itself. Indeed, there
has been a very rapid and bewildering fluctuation in the character and for-
tunes of the new social movements ever since they first emerged in the late
1950s, after the Anglo-French attack upon Suez and the Hungarian revolt.
The "New Left" which developed at that time in the European countries
was still deeply involved with traditional radical and socialist movements,
through membership of labor organizations and through participation in a
community of ideas derived from Marxism and other socialist doctrines; it
possessed, therefore, many elements of continuity with earlier forms of
radicalism, and particularly with those of the 1930s.

A notable change occurred with the rebirth of radicalism in the United
States of America. This began with the civil rights movement of the early
1960s, in which there appeared the two elements which were afterward to
dominate the whole movement: the students and the Negroes. At the outset
the two groups cooperated in what was essentially a militant reform movement, but divisions soon appeared as the more radical Negroes moved on
to "black nationalism" and "black power," while the students became in-

creasingly involved in the antiwar movements and in the confrontations within the universities. By the end of 1968 the separation of the two movements was almost complete. At the same time each movement came to represent quite a striking departure from previous forms of radicalism: in one case, radicalism as an ethnic, "nationalist" movement, loosely connected with ideas about revolution in the Third World; in the other case, radicalism as a youth movement, associated with cultural dissent and innovation which encompassed such phenomena as pop and folk music and the cult of "mind-expanding" drugs.

In the following discussion I shall concentrate upon the student movement which has an international character and is less specifically tied to American conditions.[1] Some aspects of its development were foreseen and given an intellectual justification by C. Wright Mills, who argued from the absence of a radical labor movement in the United States of America to the need to envisage possibilities of radical change in terms of a cultural criticism animated by the young intellectuals. This American style of radicalism assumed a definite form in the Berkeley Free Speech Movement of 1964, and soon thereafter it spread widely in many countries. Its influence resulted to some extent from the world involvement of the United States of America; without question, the single most important unifying element in the radical student movement has been the opposition to the Vietnam war. But there were also other factors at work. One, which has itself to be explained, was the growing sense of a generational identity among young people in the industrial countries, and the particular feeling, among university students, that with the accelerating technological revolution and the rapid increase in their own numbers which is a part of this process, they were coming to occupy a position of crucial importance in society. Another factor was the apparent decline of some older kinds of radicalism, which manifested itself in what the students regarded as the spread of "consensus politics," whether this took the form of an actual coalition of parties (as in West Germany) or simply the diminishing radicalism of left-wing parties. During the 1950s there seemed to be spreading in Europe a style of nonideological politics resembling that in the United States of America, and insofar as this could be attributed to changes in the charac-

[1] Some important features of the Negro movement have been well analyzed by Harold Cruse, *The Crisis of the Negro Intellectual* (New York: William Morrow & Co., 1967). Quite recently, the movement has taken another new direction with the emergence of the Black Panther party, which seeks to establish a broad alliance with white radical groups and has proposed an economic program which is closer to socialist ideas than most of the new radicalism has been.

ter and role of the working class in the European countries the conclusion followed that a new basis for dissent and opposition had to be found in other social groups.

The student movement, as the new animator of political conflict, developed with extraordinary rapidity between 1964 and 1968, reaching a climax in the revolt of May, 1968, in France. Since then it has suffered a decline. In the United States the principal radical organization, Students for a Democratic Society, has become divided into a number of conflicting groups; in France the student movement has reverted to the pre-1968 welter of campus sects (largely along the lines of left-wing groups outside the university) and has lost much of the public support it enjoyed for a time; the German SDS has recently been dissolved and its erstwhile leaders have dispersed; in Britain there is no longer an effective radical student organization. It is possible that this represents no more than a temporary setback. If it is true, as some have argued, that the "scientific and educational estate" now occupies a crucial place in society and is in the process of elaborating an ideology and forms of political action appropriate to its situation, as the industrial working class did in the nineteenth century, then recent events may be seen as the first tentative steps toward organization and action of a more durable kind. On the other hand, the decline may correspond with a characteristically rapid fluctuation of mood, interest, and orientation in student movements, resulting from the high degree of mobility of their members.

However we interpret these phenomena it is important to recognize some of the weaknesses in the student movement, which tended to be overlooked in the excitement of the late 1960s when students presented in a dramatic way new ideas and attitudes, helped to produce a much needed revival of intellectual and political controversy, and animated the protest movements. One of the weaknesses arises simply from the fact that the student movement is a *youth* movement. The social influence of a younger generation may be considerable, as Karl Mannheim noted, in bringing a novel approach, a new mode of thought and experience, to the assimilation, use, and development of the cultural heritage which it encounters. But it is highly improbable that the structure and course of development of any society at any time will be determined mainly by the ideas and aspirations of its very young and inexperienced members. In most spheres, the "young Turks" who bring about important innovations do not belong to the age group of university students, but are in their late twenties or early thirties, having passed beyond the period of confused seeking and striving which characterizes younger age groups. Moreover, this kind of innovation is very largely a matter of individual discoveries, rather than an activity of a whole generational group. When we consider the nature of broad social movements and of major changes in the structure of society it becomes apparent that these depend upon quite different bonds from those of an age group—upon nationality, economic interest, class membership, or religious community. Thus, even the argument about the growing importance of the "scientific and educational estate" as an active social and political group (which I mentioned earlier) concerns the future role of the scientific and academic professions much more than it concerns the students.

These disabilities of the student movement are enhanced by other factors. One is the rapid circulation of members, which renders difficult the maintenance of a consistent political style or organization. Others arise from the connection between the student movement and some aspects of a wider "youth culture" including pop and folk music and drugs, which have very little radical significance at all. It is true that these phenomena have sometimes been regarded as forming part of a general movement of liberation, but this is largely to misinterpret them. Pop music expresses, generally in the most banal language, the universal doubts and uncertainties of adolescence. It has little critical content, and what it had at the outset has diminished with the growth of commercial interests. The most that can be said for it as a cultural innovation is that it may reflect, especially in such activities as pop festivals, a desire for greater community, or even, in a religious sense, communion, and thus a drift away from acquisitiveness and self-aggrandizement. In folk music there is a larger element of social criticism and protest, but by comparison with earlier periods the protest is vague, ill-formulated, individualistic, and sometimes counterfeit, as in the case of those folk singers who use protest songs merely in order to further their own careers.[2]

The cult of drugs can also not be regarded as liberating; for what enlargement of human freedom can possibly result from making one's mental states and experiences totally dependent upon chemical substances? It is rather the ultimate alienation of one's human powers to a world of objects. Like alcoholism, the use of drugs is an action expressing despair, revulsion, withdrawal from the public world of social issues into a private

[2] See the discussion in R. Serge Denisoff, "Folk Music and the American Left: A Generational-Ideological Comparison," *British Journal of Sociology,* 20:4 (December, 1969).

world of personal troubles and fantasies. It reflects, no doubt, a dissatisfaction with the state of society as seen from an individual point of view, and at the same time a malaise of society itself; but it does not lead to any kind of movement for the radical reconstruction of society.

It is not very clear, at present, how closely these different aspects of the "youth culture" are related, but insofar as the student movement lays stress upon its own generational character it is certainly affected by the prevailing outlook of the whole age group to which it belongs; and there is evidently a considerable degree of cultural exchange between the "hippy" and the "activist" groups within the younger generation (though more obviously in the United States of America than elsewhere). This mingling of radical and nonradical tendencies undoubtedly adds to the ideological confusion which reigns in the student movement; but the confusion is in any case a phenomenon which, on more general grounds, we should expect.

The student movement became active at a time when radical social thought was passing through its still unresolved crisis, which originated in the criticisms and revisions of Marxist thought,[3] in the confrontation with doctrines elaborated by revolutionary movements in peasant societies (for example, in China, in Cuba, in North Africa, and in other areas of the Third World), and in controversies with the exponents of new theories about the nature of modern industrial societies.[4] The students, consequently, drew their ideas from very diverse sources; from the thought and experience of revolutionaries in the Third World as well as from the extraordinarily varied interpretations of present-day society offered by social critics in the Western industrial countries. It is not to be supposed that students themselves are capable of producing a coherent social theory from this mishmash, although they may, as they have shown, raise critical questions and shadow forth a new social outlook which will help to direct the work of critical social thought. Unfortunately, this valuable activity has frequently been perverted into purely political campaigns, carried on with the aid of simple slogans, which have brought the movement into conflict

---

[3] It is impossible, here, to review all the criticisms and reinterpretations of Marxism during the past twenty years. Among the important contributions to this debate are the writings of Leszek Kolakowski, Stanislaw Ossowski, Gajo Petrović, and others associated with the Yugoslav journal *Praxis,* C. Wright Mills, Herbert Marcuse, Jürgen Habermas, Jean-Paul Sartre, and Eric Fromm himself.

[4] For example, Raymond Aron, *18 Lectures on Industrial Society* (New York: Praeger, 1967), and J. K. Galbraith, *The Affluent Society* and *The New Industrial State* (Boston: Houghton Mifflin Co., 1958).

with most of the rest of society, including a large part of the labor movement,[5] and have considerably reduced the effectiveness of the social criticism which emanates from universities.

The future of radicalism—in thought and in action—depends upon
whether or not the limitations imposed by the recent predominance of the
student movement can be overcome. The student movement has to be seen,
and to see itself, as only one section of a growing intellectual movement,
best described as socialist humanism, which is directed (unlike most earlier
forms of dissent) against a multiplicity of enemies—against capitalism,
against technocracy, and against totalitarian socialism. In this movement there are several important objectives which students can help, and
in some degree have already helped, to attain. The first is to equip
themselves—and this applies above all to those in the social sciences—as
effective critics of society. The second is to establish this critical, and so
far as possible radical, outlook securely enough for it to persist and develop outside the university, in the scientific and professional occupations
which students will enter. The third is to defend intellectual freedom and
autonomy in the universities, or to reestablish it in those societies where
universities have fallen under the domination of businessmen, civil ser-
vants, or party officials. In this area, though, I think the main responsibility falls upon university teachers, and it has been their defection in many
cases which has thrust an impossible burden upon students. There is a further objective, closely connected with this, which is to examine carefully
and thoroughly what are the alternatives to the "multiversity" or "knowledge factory." It is somewhat surprising, in view of the importance which
students themselves attribute to their opposition to bureaucratization, that
there has been so little serious consideration of what needs to be done in
order to create a human atmosphere in the university, and to restore its
character as a community of scholars in which critical thought can flourish
unhindered—if indeed that is what is wanted. One necessary step would
obviously be to limit the size of universities, another (in many countries)
to reform the system of university government; but beyond this there is the
task of thinking profoundly about the proper character of universities in

[5] This has occurred in many West European countries, where the radical student
movement has had strained relations, and sometimes open conflicts, with socialist
parties and with the trade unions. This was particularly evident in West Germany in
1968. In the United States the gulf between workers and students has been even
more marked; the most recent illustration is the demonstration of New York construction workers against the peace movement.

the twentieth century, in the context of a rapid expansion of higher education of very diverse kinds, and at the same time experimenting with different forms of organization. Far from aiding this process of reflection and transformation, some student activism in the last two or three years has seemed more likely to destroy the universities, by its contempt for intellectual life, its intolerance of divergent opinions, and its obsession with purely political questions. This has been extremely damaging to the radical cause, not least because no good society is conceivable without universities, or equivalent institutions, in which men can practice and exemplify free intellectual inquiry for its own sake.

Even if intellectual dissent flourished, as it began to do in the 1960s, and even if it took shape in a coherent critical theory, as it has not yet done, this would still be inadequate for the transformation of society. In order to bring about radical change there is needed a social movement which embodies the practical experiences and interests of large numbers of men. In most of the Western industrial countries the labor movement still occupies this place, and outside the labor movement there can be no radical politics. There are, in fact, many signs that this movement is itself becoming more radical again—the rapid extension of a general strike in France in May, 1968, which, far more than the student movement, threatened the Gaullist regime; the wave of militant trade union activity in Italy at the end of 1969; the increasing militancy of workers in the most technologically advanced industries in many countries; the considerable revival of interest in the ideas and practices of workers' control. It is not at all improbable that the intellectual radicalism in the universities and the new orientations in the labor movement will come together to produce great social changes in the course of the next decade.

In the United States of America it is much more difficult to foresee the development of a broad radical movement. Since the end of the First World War there has been no mass labor movement committed to bringing about radical changes in the structure of American society. Is it conceivable that this should change now, in conditions of growing prosperity and declining trade unionism? There are, as radicals have frequently pointed out, many groups in American society which do not share in its material advantages, and which constitute potential nuclei of opposition. Some of them, notably the Negroes and the Mexicans, have engaged in increasingly militant, though not necessarily radical, action. There is also a revolt of at least a considerable part of the younger generation against the condition of American society. But the American working class remains aloof from any kind of radical politics. I do not think this state of affairs will change quickly. Nevertheless, if the present intellectual dissent, and the various opposition movements, could be brought together in a political organization—a new radical party—it does not seem impossible that such a party could eventually attract many workers to its policies and actions, especially those workers in the more advanced industries, who are likely to have a growing interest, in the United States of America as elsewhere, in directing more fully the work process in which they are engaged. These possibilities can only be tested in practice; at all events, the endeavor to create a new radical party would offer greater hope than a continuation of the present fragmented dissent and sporadic protest.

Equally difficult is the assessment of possible changes in the Soviet societies of Eastern Europe. It is clear that there has been, since 1956, growing intellectual dissent, and it can scarcely be doubted that the kind of social outlook which was formulated by Czechoslovak intellectuals and students during the socialist renaissance of 1967–1968 would also find expression in the other Soviet countries if the opportunity presented itself. We should note, however, that in the instances where there has been a radical movement in these countries—in Hungary and Poland in 1956, and in Czechoslovakia in 1967–1968—it has arisen out of a conjunction between intellectual dissent and working-class, trade union opposition to the regime. If there is to be progress, on the basis of an economy which is already collectivized, toward a socialist society in which men are genuinely liberated, not subjected to the rule of censors, party officials, and the secret police, then both these elements will be necessary—the intellectuals who demand freedom to speculate and to criticize, and the workers who demand control over their working conditions and a real voice in the determination of social policy.

In all modern radical movements there has been this close link between ideas and interests, most fully developed when a theory of society such as Marxism becomes inextricably involved with a powerful social movement. The contribution of radical intellectuals to this process is both negative and positive. On one side it is to show, in a critical way, the character of existing society; its injustices, limitations, and conflicts. This work of criticism, when it becomes sufficiently widespread—when the established order is largely deserted by the intellectuals—is one of the elements which prepare the way for a new society. But it is not complete unless it can also show the possible directions of change, interpret the emerging social movements, and prefigure the new social order. It has to accomplish the work which Marx, as a young man, set himself when he wrote: "We develop new principles for the world out of its own existing principles. . . . We may sum up the outlook of our Journal (the *Deutsch-Französische Jahrbücher*) in a single phrase: the self-knowledge (critical philosophy) of the age about its struggles and aims."

This positive vision, the development of new principles out of existing principles, is what appears weakest and most obscure in present-day radical thought. If we search out the reason for this weakness we can hardly fail to reach the conclusion that it is above all the disillusionment with socialism, which began at the end of the 1930s and has been intensified by the development of the Soviet version of socialism since the end of the war, through the closing years of the Stalinist terror to the *Realpolitik* of the military occupation of Czechoslovakia. Radical thinkers have now to criticize both capitalism and socialism as existing forms of society, and they are often tempted to direct their main criticism against industrialism itself. The idea of an alternative form of society becomes faint and shadowy, because what was once the ideal—socialism—now exists as a problematic reality. What we have to do in order to meet this situation, as some are already attempting, is to rethink socialism, both in terms of the institutions appropriate to an egalitarian society,[6] and in terms of the social movements and political actions which are capable of bringing it about without the disfigurement which it has suffered from violence and repression.

[6] I have in mind, particularly, the serious study of problems of management and participation in large-scale industry, of reforms in social administration which would bring the social services more under the control of those affected by them, of changes in educational institutions which would diminish the authoritarian elements in them and provide a better early experience of self-government. Too little thought has been devoted to the possible forms of new institutions, and too little attention has yet been given to the available practical experience of more egalitarian types of organization, such as workers' self-management, communities of work, and some community development projects.

Appendix I
Bibliography of Erich Fromm

Books

Die Entwicklung des Christusdogmas: Eine Psychoanalytische Studie zur Sozialpsychologischen Funktion der Religion. *Internationaler Psychoanalytischer Verlag.* Vienna: 1931. Reprinted from *Imago* 16, Heft 3/4, 1930, pp. 305–373. English translation *The Dogma of Christ,* 1963.

Escape from Freedom. New York: Farrar & Rinehart, 1941.

Man for Himself: An Inquiry into the Psychology of Ethics. New York: Rinehart & Co., 1947.

Psychoanalysis and Religion. New Haven: Yale University Press, 1950.

The Forgotten Language: An Introduction to the Understanding of Dreams, Fairy Tales and Myths. New York: Rinehart & Co., 1951.

The Sane Society. New York: Rinehart & Co., 1955.

The Art of Loving. New York: Harper & Bros., 1956.

Sigmund Freud's Mission. New York: Harper & Bros., 1959.

Zen Buddhism and Psychoanalysis (with D. T. Suzuki and R. de Martino). New York: Harper & Row, 1960.

Marx's Concept of Man. New York: Frederick Ungar Publishing Co., 1961.

May Man Prevail. Garden City, N.Y.: Doubleday & Co., 1961.

Beyond the Chains of Illusion. New York: Simon and Schuster, 1962.

The Dogma of Christ and Other Essays on Religion, Psychology and Culture. New York: Holt, Rinehart and Winston, 1963.

The Heart of Man. New York: Harper & Row, 1964.

Socialist Humanism (ed.). Garden City, N.Y.: Doubleday & Co., 1965.

You Shall Be as Gods. New York: Holt, Rinehart and Winston, 1966.

The Revolution of Hope. New York: Harper & Row, 1968.

The Nature of Man (Co-ed. with Ramon Xirau). New York: Macmillan Co., Problems of Philosophy Series, 1968.

The Crisis of Psychoanalysis: Essays on Freud, Marx and Social Psychology. New York: Holt, Rinehart and Winston, 1970.

Social Character in a Mexican Village (with Michael Maccoby). Englewood Cliffs, N.J.: Prentice-Hall, 1970.

Selected Articles and Essays

"Der Sabbath." *Imago,* 13 (1927), 223–234. Reprinted in *The Forgotten Language,* 1951, pp. 241–249.

"Dauernde Nachwirkung eines Erziehungsfehlers" (Lasting after-effects of a mistake in education). *Zeitschrift für Psychoanalytische Pädagogik,* 10 (1927), 372–373.

"Psychoanalytische Trieblehre" (with F. Reichmann), (Psychoanalytic theory of drives). *Zeitschrift für Psychoanalytische Pädagogik,* 3 (1929), 266–268.

"Psychoanalyse und Soziologie." *Zeitschrift für Psychoanalytische Päedagogik,* 3 (1929), 268–270.

"Review of *Die Schulgemcinde"* by S. Bernfeld. *Zeitschrift für Psychoanalytische Pädagogik,* 4 (1930), 116–117.

"Oedipus in Innsbruck. Zum Halsmann-Prozess" (Oedipus in Innsbruck. On the Halsmann Trial). *Vossische Zeitung* (January, 1930), and in *Psychoanalytische Bewegung,* 2 (1930), 75–79.

"Der Staat als Erzieher: Zur Psychologie der Strafjustiz." (The state as educator: on the psychology of criminal justice.) *Zeitschrift für Psychoanalytische Pädagogik,* 3 (1930), 5–9. Also in *Almanach,* 1931, 119–125.

"Zur Psychologie des Verbrechers und der Strafenden Gesellschaft" (On the psychology of the criminal and of the punishing society). *Imago,* 17 (1931), 226–251.

"Politik und Psychoanalyse." *Psychoanalytische Bewegung,* 3:5 (1931), 440–447.

"Über Methode und Aufgabe einer Analytischen Sozialpsychologie" (The methods and tasks of an analytical social psychology). *Zeitschrift für Sozialforschung,* 1 (1932), Doppelheft 1/2, 28–54. Published in English in *The Crisis of Psychoanalysis,* 1970.

"Roger Briffault's Werk über das Mutterrecht" (Roger Briffault's work on matriarchal law). *Zeitschrift für Sozialforschung,* 2 (1933), Heft 3, 382–387.

"Die Psychoanalytische Charakterologie und Ihre Bedeutung für die Sozialpsychologie" (Psychoanalytic characterology and its significance for social psychology). *Zeitschrift für Sozialforschung,* 1 (1933), Heft 3, 253–277. Published in English in *The Crisis of Psychoanalysis,* 1970.

"Die Sozialpsychologische Bedeutung der Mutterrechtstheorie" (The social-psychological significance of the theory of matriarchal law). *Zeitschrift für Sozialforschung,* 3 (1934), Heft 2, 196–227. Published in English in *The Crisis of Psychoanalysis,* 1970.

"Die Gesellschaftliche Bedingtheit der Psychoanalytischen Therapie" (The social background of psychoanalytic therapy). *Zeitschrift für Sozialforschung,* 4 (1935), Heft 3, 365–397.

"Theoretische Entwürfe über Autorität und Familie." (Theoretical models of authority and family). *Studien über Autorität und Familie,* Sozialpsychologischer teil, Max Horkheimer (ed.). Paris: Felix Alcan (1936), pp. 77–135; 230–238.

"Zum Gefühl der Ohnmacht" (The feeling of powerlessness). *Zeitschrift für Sozialforschung,* 6 (1937), 95–119.

"The Social Philosophy of 'Will Therapy.' " *Psychiatry,* 2:2 (May, 1939), 229–237.

"Selfishness and Self-Love. Psychiatry, 2:4 (November, 1939), 507–523. Reprinted in *Man for Himself,* 1947, pp. 119–141.

"Faith as a Character Trait." *Psychiatry,* 5:3 (August, 1942), 307–319. Reprinted in *Man for Himself,* 1947.

"Should We Hate Hitler?" *Journal of Home Economics,* 34 (1942), 220–223.

"What Shall We Do with Germany?" *Saturday Review of Literature,* Vol. 26 (May 29, 1943).

"On the Problems of German Characterology." Transactions of the N.Y. Academy of Science, 1943, Vol. 5, pp. 79–83.

"Sex and Character." *Psychiatry,* 6:1 (February, 1943), 21–31. Reprinted in *The Family—Its Function and Destiny,* R. N. Anshen (ed.). New York: Harper, 1949.

"Individual and Social Origins of Neurosis." *American Sociological Review,* 10:4 (August, 1944), 380–384. Reprinted in C. Kluckhohn and H. Murray, *Personality in Nature, Society and Culture,* New York: Alfred A. Knopf, 1953.

"Introduction." *Oedipus: Myth and Complex: A Review of Psychoanalytic Theory.* Patrick Mullahy. New York: Hermitage Press, 1948.

"Sex and Character: The Kinsey Report Viewed from the Standpoint of Psychoanalysis." In *About the Kinsey Report,* D. Geddes and E. Curie (eds.). New York: The New American Library, 1948. Republished in *Sexual Be-*

havior in American Society, J. Himelhoch and S. Fleis Fava (eds.). New York: Norton, 1955, pp. 301–311.

"The Nature of Dreams." *Scientific American,* 180 (May, 1949), 44–47.

"The Oedipus Complex and the Oedipus Myth." In *The Family: Its Functions and Destiny,* R. N. Anshen (ed.). New York: Harper & Bros., 1949, pp. 321–347. Reprinted in *The Forgotten Language,* 1951, under the title "The Oedipus Myth."

"Psychoanalytic Characterology and Its Application to the Understanding of Culture." *Culture and Personality,* S. S. Sargent and M. W. Smith (eds.). New York: Viking Press, 1949, pp. 1–12.

"Freud and Jung." *Pastoral Psychology,* 1:7 (1950), 11–15.

"Man-Woman." In *The People in Your Life: Psychiatry and Personal Relations,* Margaret M. Hughes (ed.). New York: Alfred A. Knopf, 1951, pp. 3–27.

"The Contribution of the Social Sciences to Mental Hygiene." Proceedings of the Fourth International Congress on Mental Health, Mexico City, 1951. A. Millan (ed.). La Prensa Medica Mexicana, Mexico, 1952, pp. 38–42.

"The Art of Dream Interpretation." *Pastoral Psychology,* 2 (1952), 17–25.

"The Psychology of Normalcy." *Dissent,* 1 (Spring, 1954), 39–43.

"The Humanistic Implications of Instinctivistic 'Radicalism.' " *Dissent* (Autumn, 1955), pp. 342–349.

"The Present Human Condition." *The American Scholar,* 25 (Winter, 1955–1956), 29–35.

"Selfishness, Self-Love and Self-Interest." *The Self: Explorations in Personal Growth.* Clark E. Moustakas (ed.). New York: Harper & Bros., 1956.

"Remarks on the Problem of Free Association." *Psychiatric Research Reports,* Washington, D.C.: American Psychiatric Association, 1956, Vol. II, pp. 1–6.

"Love and Its Disintegration." *Pastoral Psychology,* 7:68 (1956), 37–44.

"A Counter-Rebuttal to Herbert Marcuse." (An exchange.) *Dissent* (Winter, 1956), pp. 82–83.

"Man Is Not a Thing." *Saturday Review,* March 16, 1957.

"Symbolic Language and Dreams." In *Language: An Inquiry into its Meaning and Function.* Ruth Nanda Anshen (ed.). New York: Harper & Bros., 1957.

"Psychoanalysis—Scienticism or Fanaticism?" *Saturday Review,* June 14, 1958.

"Values, Psychology and Human Existence." *New Knowledge in Human Values,* A. Maslow (ed.). New York: Harper & Bros., 1959, pp. 151–164.

"The Limitations and Dangers of Psychology." *Religion and Culture,* W. Leibrecht (ed.) (Essays in Honor of Paul Tillich.) New York: Harper & Bros., 1959, pp. 31–36.

"The Case for Unilateral Disarmament." *Daedalus* (Fall 1960), pp. 1015–1028.

"Let Man Prevail—A Socialist Manifesto and Program." *The Call Association,* New York: 1960.

"The Prophetic Concept of Peace." In *Buddhism and Culture:* A Festschrift in honor of D. T. Suzuki. S. Yamaguchi (ed.). Kyoto, Japan: Norkano Press, 1960.

"Foreword to *Summerhill—A Radical Approach to Child Rearing,*" by A. S. Neill. New York: Hart Publishing Co., 1960, pp. i–xvi.

"Foreword to *Looking Backward,*" by Edward Bellamy. New York: New American Library, 1960.

"Afterword to *1984,*" by George Orwell. New York: The New American Library (Signet Classic), 1961, pp. 257–267.

"A Debate on the Question of Civil Defense" (with Michael Maccoby). *Commentary,* 33 (January, 1962), 11–23.

"Disobedience as a Psychological and Moral Problem." In *A Matter of Life,* Clara Urquhart (ed.). London: Jonathan Cape, 1963. In the U.S. by Little, Brown and Co., 1963.

"C. G. Jung: Prophet of the Unconscious." A discussion of *Memories, Dreams, Reflections* by C. G. Jung, recorded and edited by Aniella Jaffé. *Scientific American,* 209:3 (1963), 283–290.

"Our Way of Life Makes Us Miserable." *The Saturday Evening Post,* July 25, 1964.

"Creators and Destroyers." *The Saturday Review,* January 4, 1964.

"Foreword II" to *Escape from Freedom.* New York: Avon Books, Hearst Corp., 1965.

"The Application of Humanist Psychoanalysis to Marx's Theory." In *Socialist Humanism.* E. Fromm (ed.). Garden City, N.Y.: Doubleday and Co., 1965.

"Memories of D. T. Suzuki." In *Proceedings of the Eastern Buddhist Society,* Otani University, 1966.

"The Psychological Problem of Aging." *Journal of Rehabilitation,* September/October, 1966.

"Prophets and Priests." In *Bertrand Russell, Philosopher of the Century: Essays in his Honor,* Ralph Schoenman (ed.). London: George Allen & Unwin, 1967.

"The Psychological Aspects of Guaranteed Income." In *The Guaranteed Income,* Robert Theobald, (ed.). New York: Doubleday & Co., 1967.

"The Condition of the American Spirit: Are We Fully Alive?" *Newsday,* January 13, 1968.

"In the Name of Life." *Psychiatry and Social Science Review,* July, 1968.

"The Present Crisis of Psychoanalysis." *The Reach of Mind: Essays in Memory of Kurt Goldstein,* Marianne L. Simmel (ed.). New York: Springer Publishing Co., 1968.

Essay. In *Summerhill: For and Against.* New York: Hart Publishing Co., 1970,
    pp. 251–263.

"Introduction." *Celebration of Awareness,* by Ivan D. Illich. Garden City,
    N.Y.: Doubleday and Co., 1970.

Appendix II

Notes on the Contributors

Bernard Landis Dr. Landis received his Ph.D. in psychology from the New School for Social Research and his training in psychoanalysis from the Postdoctoral Program at New York University. Since 1963 he has been at Cornell University Medical College where he is an Associate Clinical Professor as well as Associate Attending Psychologist at New York Hospital (Payne Whitney Psychiatric Clinic). He is also engaged in private practice. His book *Ego Boundaries* was published in 1970.

Edward S. Tauber Dr. Tauber received his medical degree from Johns Hopkins University. He is a member of the American Psychoanalytic Association, and he is a Fellow and a supervising and training analyst of the William Alanson White Institute of Psychiatry, Psychoanalysis and Psychology, and has previously served as the Institute's Chairman of Faculty. In addition, he is Adjunct Professor of Psychology at Yeshiva University. He has been actively engaged in conducting studies in perception and sleep research, and has coauthored a book on dreams—*Prelogical Experience: An Inquiry into Dreams and Other Creative Processes*. He maintains a private practice in New York City.

James Luther Adams Distinguished Professor of Social Ethics at Andover Newton Theological School and Professor Emeritus of Divinity at Harvard University, James L. Adams earned his Ph.D. at the University of Chicago, his D.D. at Meadville Theological School and, in addition, a Doctorate of Theology at Marburg University in Germany. His special interests are in the application of religion to social life, and religion and the arts. Among his books are *Taking Time Seriously* and *Paul Tillich's Philosophy of Culture, Science and Religion.* He is the translator of several volumes of Tillich and has also translated Erich Fromm's early study, *The Dogma of Christ.*

Aniceto Aramoni   In addition to his private practice of psychoanalysis in Mexico City, Dr. Aramoni is Director and Professor at the Mexican Institute of Psychoanalysis, which is part of the Faculty of Medicine at the Autonomous University of Mexico. He is the author of two books: *Mexico, the Land of Man* and *New Psychoanalysis?*

Isaac Asimov   Professor of Biochemistry at Boston University School of Medicine, Dr. Asimov has written successfully to a broad audience, while presenting advanced ideas in mathematics, biology, astronomy, physics, chemistry, mythology, and the Bible. His *Biographical Encyclopedia of Science and Technology* is a standard reference work. Among the best known of his one hundred books are *Genetic Code* and *The Intelligent Man's Guide to Science.*

Tom Bottomore   Tom Bottomore is Professor of Sociology at the University of Sussex, Brighton, England and president of the British Sociological Association (1969–1971). His books include *Karl Marx: Selected Writings in Sociology and Social Philosophy* (with Maximilien Rubel); *Karl Marx: Early Writings; Sociology: A Guide to Problems and Literature;* and *Classes in Modern Society.*

Theodosius Dobzhansky   Russian-born and educated, Dr. Dobzhansky is a world-renowned geneticist and humanist, currently a professor at the Rockefeller University. A holder of many awards, including the National Medal of Science, he is the author of *Genetics and the Origin of the Species, Biological Basis of Human Freedom,* and *Heredity and the Nature of Man.* His major research is in the field of heredity and cultural evolution.

Loren Eiseley   Dr. Loren Eiseley is Benjamin Franklin Professor of Anthropology and the History of Science at the University of Pennsylvania, and Curator of Early Man at the University Museum. He is the author of *The Immense Journey, The Firmament of Time, Darwin's Century,* and *The Unexpected Universe.*

Jerome D. Frank   Professor of Psychiatry at the Johns Hopkins University School of Medicine, Dr. Frank has written extensively on both psychotherapy and on issues of disarmament and peace. His books include *Group Psychotherapy: Studies in Methodology of Research and Therapy* (with F. Powdermaker); *Persuasion and Healing: A Comparative Study of Psychotherapy;* and *Sanity and Survival: Psychological Aspects of War and Peace.*

Harry Guntrip A psychotherapist and researcher in long-term psycho-therapy at the University of Leeds Medical School in England, Dr. Guntrip experienced a training analysis both with Dr. W. R. D. Fairbairn and Dr. D. W. Winnicott. Among his books are *Personality Structure and Human Interaction;* and *Schizoid Phenomena, Object-Relations and the Self. Psychoanalytic Theory and Therapy* is in press.

Edward T. Hall Professor of Anthropology at Northwestern University and former director of the State Department's Point Four Training Program, Dr. Hall has authored two books that develop the concept of culture as a system of communication: *The Silent Language* and *The Hidden Dimension,* and has defined the new field of "Proxemics," the study of man's experience of distance and his use of space as being a function of culture, status, and personality.

Ivan Illich Founder of the Center for Intercultural Documentation (CIDOC) in Cuernavaca, Mexico, where he now lives and works, Dr. Illich is the author of *Celebration of Awareness: A Call for Institutional Revolution* and is widely known for his iconoclastic approach to both educational and religious institutions.

Erich Kahler A cultural historian and philosopher, Professor Kahler was a member of the Institute of Advanced Study at Princeton University. He was born in Prague and came to the United States in 1938; it was Thomas Mann who suggested that he be invited to the Princeton faculty. His books include: *Man the Measure: A New Approach to History; The Tower and the Abyss: An Inquiry into the Transformation of the Individual;* and *The Meaning of History.* Professor Kahler died June 29, 1970.

Mihailo Marković Professor of Philosophy at the University of Belgrade, Dean of the Faculty, and Director of the Institute of Philosophy, Dr. Marković took part in the Yugoslav war of liberation, 1941–1945, as a captain in the partisan army. He has lectured in many European countries, and was visiting professor at the University of Michigan, 1969–1970. His book include *Formalism in Contemporary Logic, The Dialectical Theory of Meaning, Revision of Marxism in the USSR,* and *Humanism and Dialectics.*

Gajo Petrović Professor of Philosophy at Zagreb (Yugoslavia), Dr. Petrović has focused his studies on man in society and the achievement of freedom. In addition to his schooling at Zagreb, he also studied philosophy in Leningrad and Moscow, as well as in Great Britain and the United States. His books include *English Empiricist Philosophy, Philosophical Views of G. V. Plekhanov, From Locke to Ayer, Logic,* and *Philosophy and Marxism.*

David Riesman Professor of Social Sciences at Harvard University, Dr. Riesman has also taught at the University of Chicago and at Yale. He initially took a law degree at Harvard and was once a deputy assistant district attorney in New York. His books include *The Lonely Crowd, Individualism Reconsidered, Constraint and Variety in American Education,* and *Thorstein Veblen—Critical Interpretation.*

Adam Schaff Born in Lvov, Poland, Professor Schaff studied there and in Paris before receiving his doctorate at the Institute of Philosophy of the Soviet Academy of Sciences. He has been a member of the Central Committee of the Polish United Workers' Party, and at present works in the Institute of Philosophy and Sociology in Warsaw. He is also president of the board of directors of the European Coordination Center for Social Sciences and visiting professor in philosophy at the University of Vienna. Among his books are *A Philosophy of Man, Introduction to Semantics, Language and Cognition,* and *The Objective Nature of the Laws of History.*

David E. Schecter Dr. Schecter was born in Montreal, Canada, and took his medical training at McGill University. He is currently studying early ego and family development at the Albert Einstein College of Medicine where he is an associate clinical professor. He is also director of training at the William Alanson White Institute of Psychiatry, Psychoanalysis and Psychology, and conducts a private practice.

Francis Otto Schmitt A prominent molecular biologist, Professor Schmitt founded (in 1962) the Neurosciences Research Program at the Massachusetts Institute of Technology, an interuniversity, international research organization with experts in many fields studying physiochemical, biophysical, and psychological aspects of mental processes such as memory and learning. He has published extensively and is coeditor of *Neurosciences Research Symposium Summaries* and *The Neurosciences: A Study Program.* Professor Schmitt has been elected to the American Academy of Arts and Sciences, to the National Academy of Sciences, to the American Philosophical Society, and to the Swedish Royal Academy of Sciences.

Harold F. Searles Dr. Searles is president of the Washington Psychoanalytic Society, a supervising and training analyst at the Washington Psychoanalytic Institute, and Clinical Professor of Psychiatry at Georgetown University School of Medicine. He is the author of *The Nonhuman Environment in Normal Development and in Schizophrenia* and *Collected Papers on Schizophrenia and Related Subjects.* In 1965 he received the Frieda Fromm-Reichmann Award for Research on Schizophrenia from the Academy of Psychoanalysis.

Erwin Singer Dr. Singer is Professor of Education (Psychology) at City College of the City University of New York and visiting professor of psychology at New York University (Postdoctoral Program). Born in Vienna, he received his Ph.D. from New York University. He is a training and supervising analyst for the William Alanson White Institute of Psychiatry, Psychoanalysis and Psychology. A new edition of his book *Key Concepts in Psychotherapy* has appeared recently.

George Wald Higgins Professor of Biology at Harvard, Dr. Wald is a corecipient of the Nobel Prize in Physiology and Medicine (1967). He has written extensively on the chemistry and physiology of vision and is coauthor of *General Education in a Free Society, Twenty Six Afternoons of Biology.* A Fellow of the National Academy of Science, the American Academy of Arts and Sciences, and the American Philosophical Society, he has received the Lasker Award of the Public Health Association, the Rumford Medal of the American Academy of Arts and Sciences, and the Paul Karrer medal in Chemistry, of the University of Zurich.

Otto Allen Will, Jr. Dr. Will is Medical Director of the Austen Riggs Center, an outstanding psychiatric care facility in Stockbridge, Massachusetts. In addition, he is Clinical Professor of Psychiatry at Cornell University Medical College and is on the faculty of the William Alanson White Institute of Psychiatry, Psychoanalysis and Psychology. His major research interests are in the areas of psychotherapy and schizophrenia and he has published widely on these topics. He obtained much of his experience in the treatment of schizophrenic persons at Chestnut Lodge in Maryland where he was Director of Psychotherapy from 1954–1967.

Ramon Xirau Professor Xirau is a philosopher who has studied in Spain, Mexico, Cambridge, and Paris. Among his present affiliations he is Professor of Philosophy at the National Autonomous University of Mexico, Professor of Philosophy at the Liceo Franco-Mexicano and director (and founder) of the journal *Díalogos.* A recipient of Rockefeller and Guggenheim fellowships, he has published literary criticism and poetry, as well as such philosophical works as *Método y Metafísica en la Filosofía de Descartes, Duración y Existencia* and *Palabra y Silencio.*